Asia-Pacific
Security

Less Uncertainty, New Opportunities?

Edited by
Gary
Klintworth

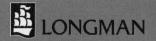 LONGMAN

ST. MARTIN'S PRESS
NEW YORK

Addison Wesley Longman Australia Pty Limited
95 Coventry Street
Melbourne 3205 Australia

Offices in Sydney, Brisbane and Perth, and associated companies throughout the world.

Copyright © Addison Wesley Longman Australia Pty Limited 1996
First published 1996

Designed by Rob Cowpe Design
Set in Palatino 10/12 pt
Printed in Singapore, through Longman Singapore

National Library of Australia
Cataloguing-in-Publication data

Klintworth Gary
Asia-Pacific security: less uncertainty, new opportunities?

    Includes index.
    ISBN 0 582 80321 7.

    1. National security – Asia, Southeastern. 2. National security – East Asia.
    I. Klintworth, Gary, 1945-

355.03305

ASIA-PACIFIC SECURITY: LESS UNCERTAINTY, NEW OPPORTUNITIES?

Copyright © 1996

St. Martin's Press, Scholarly and Reference Division.
175 Fifth Avenue, New York, N.Y. 10010
First published in the United States of America in 1996

Printed in Singapore through Longman Singapore
ISBN: 0-312-12107-5
Library of Congress Cataloging-in-Publication Data

Asia-Pacific security : less uncertainty, new opportunities? / edited by Gary Klintworth
    320 p. 15.6 × 23.4 cm.
    Includes bibliographical references and index.
    ISBN 0-312-12107-5 (cloth)
    1. National security--Asia. 2. National security--Pacific Area.
3. Arms transfers--Asia. 4. Arms transfers--Pacific Area.
I. Klintworth, Gary, 1945– .
UA830.A7668 1996
355' .03305--dc20

96-2597
CIP

The
publisher's
policy is to use
paper manufactured
from sustainable forests

Contents

Tables and Figures   v
Abbreviations   vii
Acknowledgements   x
Contributors   xi

Introduction   *Gary Klintworth*   1

Part I   Big Powers and the Region
1   The Asia-Pacific: Geopolitical Cauldron or Regional Community?   6
    James L. Richardson
2   The Future of American Policy in the Pacific   22
    Coral Bell
3   Greater China and Regional Security   35
    Gary Klintworth
4   Australia and Japan in the Post-Cold War World: The Special
    and the Uncertain   50
    Richard Leaver

Part II   Middle Powers
5   India and Asia-Pacific Security   65
    Sandy Gordon
6   Russia: A Terrier at the Feet of Asia's Great Powers   79
    Greg Austin and Tim Callan
7   Indonesia   94
    Bob Lowry

Part III   Regions

  8 Security and the Korean Peninsula   109
    Ian Wilson

  9 Post-Cold War Security in the ASEAN Region   120
    Leszek Buszynski

 10 Indochina   132
    Carlyle A. Thayer

 11 Australia and the Pacific Islands: The Limits of Influence   148
    Stephen Henningham

Part IV   New Opportunities

 12 APEC and Regional Stability: An Overview   160
    Andrew Elek

 13 Asia-Pacific Transport and Communications Networks and
    Regional Security   177
    Peter J. Rimmer

 14 Trends in Arms Spending and Conventional Arms Trade in
    the Asia-Pacific Region   198
    Graeme Cheeseman and Richard Leaver

 15 Disarmament, Arms Control and the Regional Security
    Dialogue   219
    Trevor Findlay

 16 Building Confidence and Security in the Asia-Pacific Region   245
    Desmond Ball

 17 International Peacekeeping: Issues for the Region   262
    Hugh Smith

Part V   Outlook

 18 The Regional Security Outlook   275
    Stuart Harris

 19 Conclusions   293
    Gary Klintworth

Index   300

Tables and Figures

Tables

3.1	China: A comparison	40
3.2	Trends in Chinese defence expenditure	41
3.3	Arms transfer agreements with the Third World	41
13.1	The world's 'top ten' container ports	180
13.2	Movements of international containers in China by road and water, 1991	183
13.3	Largest telecommunications routes of Japan, Hong Kong, Singapore, South Korea, Taiwan and China, 1992/1992–93	186
13.4	Ranking of airports having world's highest commercial traffic volume	191
14.1	Regional military expenditure	199
14.2	Regional military expenditure	200
14.3a	Regional military spending as per cent of GDP	201
14.3b	Military spending as per cent of GNP	202
14.4	Military expenditure as per cent of central government expenditure	202
14.5	Value of arms imported into the Asia-Pacific region, 1979–89	203
14.6a	Value of major conventional weapons imported into the Asia-Pacific region, 1983–92	204
14.6b	Value of major conventional weapons by sub-region, 1983–92	204
14.7	Leading Asia-Pacific arms importers, 1979–89	205

14.8	Leading Asia-Pacific importers of major conventional weapons, 1983–92	206
14.9	Suppliers' share of all arms imported into the Asia-Pacific region, 1965–89	207
15.1	Asia-Pacific parties to multilateral arms control/ disarmament agreements	220
17.1	Contributions by regional states to international peacekeeping	267
17.2	Contributions by Asia-Pacific states to UNTAC	268

Figures

13.1	Cosco's container shipping routes, 1993	181
13.2	China's international air services	189
14.1	Value of major weapons imported by Asia-Pacific countries, 1983–92	205
14.2a	Value of major weapons imported by ASEAN and Oceania, 1983–92	205
14.2b	Value of imports of major conventional weapons by sub-region, 1983–92	206
14.3	Asia-Pacific arms imports, 1979–89	206
14.4a	Sources of major conventional weapons imported into the Asia-Pacific region, 1987–91	208
14.4b	Sources of major conventional weapons imported into Northeast Asia, 1987–91	208
14.4c	Sources of major conventional weapons imported by ASEAN countries, 1987–91	208
14.4d	Sources of major conventional weapons imported by countries of Oceania, 1987–91	209

Abbreviations

ABM	Anti-Ballistic Missile
ABRI	Indonesian Armed Forces
ACDA	Arms Control and Disarmament Agency
AFTA	ASEAN Free Trade Agreement
ANKI	National Army of Independent Kampuchea
ANZUS	Australia, New Zealand and the United States
APEC	Asia Pacific Economic Cooperation
ARF	ASEAN Regional Forum
ASEAN	Association of Southeast Asian Nations
BJP	Bharatiya Janata Party
BWC	Biological Weapons Convention
CAAC	Civil Aviation Administration of China
CD	Conference on Disarmament
C&C	Computers and Communications
CIA	Central Intelligence Agency
CINCPAC	Commander-in-Chief Pacific
CITIC	China International Trust and Investment Corporation
CPAF	Cambodian People's Armed Forces
CPEs	Centrally Planned Economies
CPP	Cambodian People's Party
CSBMs	Confidence- and security-building measures
CSCAP	Council for Security Cooperation in the Asia-Pacific
CSCE	Conference on Security and Cooperation in Europe
CTB	Comprehensive Test Ban
CWC	Chemical Weapons Convention
CWRI	Chemical Weapons Regional Initiative

DPRK	Democratic People's Republic of Korea
DCP	Defence Cooperation Program
EAEC	East Asian Economic Caucus
EAEG	East Asian Economic Grouping
EDI	Electronic Data Interchange
EEZ	Exclusive Economic Zone
EU	European Union
FMS	Foreign Military Sales
FUNCINPEC	National United Front for an Independent, Neutral, Peaceful, and Cooperative Cambodia
G-7	Group of Seven Most Industrialised Nations
GDP	Gross Domestic Product
GATT	General Agreement on Tariffs and Trade
GNP	Gross National Product
HEU	Highly-enriched uranium
IAEA	International Atomic Energy Agency
IAME	International Association of Maritime Economists
ICBM	Intercontinental Ballistic Missile
ICO	Islamic Conference Organisation
IDC	International Digital Communications Inc
IGGI	International Governmental Group on Indonesia
IMF	International Monetary Fund
INCSEA	Incidents at Sea Agreements
IOZP	Indian Ocean Zone of Peace
IRBM	Intermediate Range Ballistic Missile
IRC	International Red Cross
ISIS	Institute of Strategic and International Studies
ITJ	International Telecom Japan
JIMs	Jakarta Informal Meetings
KDD	Kokusai Denwa Densha
KMI	Korea Maritime Institute
KPNLAF	Khmer People's National Liberation Armed Forces
LOSC	Law of the Sea Convention
LPA	Lao People's Army
LPDR	Lao People's Democratic Republic
LPRP	Lao People's Revolutionary Party
MFN	Most Favoured Nation
MITI	Ministry of International Trade and Industry
MOU	Memorandum of Understanding
MTCR	Missile Technology Control Regime
NAFTA	North American Free Trade Agreement
NAM	Non-Aligned Movement
NATO	North Atlantic Treaty Organisation
NGOs	Non-Governmental Organisations
NICs	Newly Industrialising Countries
NIEs	Newly Industrialising Economies

NPCSD	North Pacific Co-operative Security Dialogue
NPT	Nuclear Non-Proliferation Treaty
OAS	Organization of American States
OAU	Organization of African Unity
OPCW	Organisation for the Prohibition of Chemical Weapons
OPM	Organisasi Papua Merdeka (Free Papua Movement)
PAFTAD	Pacific Trade and Development
PBEC	Pacific Basin Economic Council
PECC	Pacific Economic Cooperation Conference, later Council
PKO	Peacekeeping Organisation
PLO	People's Liberation Army
PMC	Post-Ministerial Conference
PPP	Purchasing Power Parity
PTBT	Partial Test Ban Treaty
RAN	Royal Australian Navy
RCAF	Royal Cambodian Armed Forces
REMARSSAR	Regional Maritime Surveillance and Safety Regime
ROK	Republic of Korea
SCAP	Security Cooperation in the Asia Pacific
SDF	Self Defence Forces (Japan)
SEANWFZ	Southeast Asian Nuclear Weapons Free Zone
SEATO	South East Asia Treaty Organisation
SIPRI	Stockholm International Peace Research Institute
SOM	Senior Officials Meeting
SPNFZ	South Pacific Nuclear Free Zone
UN	United Nations
UNCITRAL	United Nations Commission on Trade Law
UNTAC	UN Transitional Authority in Cambodia
WPNS	Western Pacific Naval Symposium
ZOPFAN	Zone of Peace, Feedom and Neutrality

Acknowledgements

Thanks are due to David Sullivan, Lynne Payne and Robin Ward for their help in getting this manuscript ready for publication. The co-operation of the Northeast Asia Programme and the Department of International Relations, Research School of Pacific and Asian Studies, The Australian National University, is gratefully acknowledged.

Contributors

Greg Austin is a research fellow in the Northeast Asia Programme, Department of International Relations, Research School of Pacific and Asian Studies, The Australian National University.

Desmond Ball is a professor in the Strategic and Defence Studies Centre, Research School of Pacific and Asian Studies, The Australian National University.

Coral Bell is a visiting fellow in the Strategic and Defence Studies Centre, Research School of Pacific and Asian Studies, The Australian National University.

Leszek Buszynski is a senior lecturer in the International University of Japan, Tokyo.

Tim Callan is a graduate student, Department of International Relations, Research School of Pacific and Asian Studies, The Australian National University.

Graeme Cheeseman is a senior lecturer in the Department of Politics, Australian Defence Force Academy.

Andrew Elek was formerly a senior research fellow in the Department of Economics, Research School of Pacific and Asian Studies, The Australian National University.

Trevor Findlay is Project Leader, Peacekeeping and Regional Security, Stockholm International Peace Research Institute.

Sandy Gordon is a fellow in the Strategic and Defence Studies Centre, Research School of Pacific and Asian Studies, The Australian National University.

Stuart Harris is a professor in the Department of International Relations and Convenor of the Northeast Asia Programme, Research School of Pacific and Asian Studies, The Australian National University.

Stephen Henningham is a fellow in the Department of Pacific and Asian History, Research School of Pacific and Asian Studies, The Australian National University.

Gary Klintworth is a research associate in the Northeast Asia Programme, Department of International Relations, Research School of Pacific and Asian Studies, The Australian National University.

Richard Leaver is a lecturer in the Politics Department, Flinders University, South Australia.

Bob Lowry is a visiting fellow in the Strategic and Defence Studies Centre, Research School of Pacific and Asian Studies, The Australian National University.

James L. Richardson is a professor in the Department of International Relations, Research School of Pacific and Asian Studies, The Australian National University.

Peter Rimmer is a senior fellow in the Department of Human Geography, Research School of Pacific and Asian Studies, The Australian National University.

Hugh Smith is a senior lecturer in the Department of Politics, Australian Defence Force Academy.

Carlyle Thayer is an associate professor in the Department of Politics, Australian Defence Force Academy.

Ian Wilson is a senior lecturer in the Political Science Department, The Australian National University.

Introduction

Gary Klintworth

Security assessments about the Asia-Pacific region made by strategic studies institutes and intelligence agencies frequently posit the view that the post-Cold War world is undergoing fundamental change and that, by implication, such change is a cause for uncertainty and insecurity. Although 'change does not necessarily mean insecurity',[1] the particular changes often cited in this regard include the disappearance of Cold War constraints and hence the predictability of alliance relationships, the introspection of the United States, the emergence of new great powers vying to dominate in the Asia-Pacific region and the rapid spread of modern weapons systems. Despite the potential for conflict avoidance implicit in new structures like Asia Pacific Economic Cooperation (APEC) and the Association of Southeast Asian Nations Regional Forum (ARF), and in less formal transnational linkages, many security analysts remain pessimistic about the outlook for the Asia-Pacific region and the world in general. For them, peace is not likely in a realist world where daily life for states is a constant struggle for power and survival. Because states have little reason to trust each other, they are forced to engage in relentless security competition. In John Mearsheimer's view, co-operation is rare because the risks of being cheated are too high.[2]

In the realist view, economic imbalances will foster tension between mature economies like Japan and the United States, irrespective of economic interdependencies, while high rates of economic growth in developing economies mean that the latter will be able to spend more on defence, thereby contributing to the risk of misperception and the likelihood of a regional arms race. Second, the realists would argue that relationships between the major regional powers are shifting and that therefore the current relative peace in the Asia-Pacific region may not last. Indeed, Iraq's invasion of Kuwait illustrates the 'unpredictability of unrestrained middle powers' anywhere in the world, including the Asia-Pacific, and the need for continued military preparedness.[3] Similarly, conflict in the former Yugoslavia and the former Soviet Union might appear to support the view that ancient historical animosities, ethnic and national tensions, economic rivalry, disappointed aspirations for prosperity and religious or racial conflict could erupt and destabilise the Asia-Pacific region. Of course, instability as a consequence of any or all of these factors must always be a possibility, as too is social, economic and political unrest in complex, potentially fissiparous states like Indonesia or China. The latter, furthermore, is often portrayed as a prospective superpower that needs more living space and resources for a huge population that is growing every year by the equivalent of Australia's total population.

Many countries fear that any diminution of the United States commitment to peace and stability in the Asia-Pacific region might create a security vacuum that others would be tempted or compelled to fill.

Japan, China and India are invariably mentioned as the big three ambitious new players likely to assert a strong military role in the Asia-Pacific and their rivalry with each other, it is argued, could generate instability. Of these three great powers, China is often mentioned as the state most likely to be a source of regional instability.

For China, there is a concern about remaining intact as a state. For the region, on the other hand, China, whether as a rejuvenated powerful Middle Kingdom or a fragmenting society, is a cause of instinctive concern.

The Korean Workers Party in North Korea feels insecure because of the threat to its tenure posed by the forces of internal and external change, the challenge of South Korea's American-backed prosperity and the changing pro-South Korean priorities of China and Russia.

Japan remains concerned about Russian forces in Siberia. It worries over its relationship with the United States and, in the longer term, it fears the prospect of competition from a powerful, reunified China and perhaps a reunified Korea.

Some United States scholars regard the rift between Japan and the United States as the most destabilising threat to security in the Asia-Pacific.[4]

For their part, the Association of Southeast Asian Nations (ASEAN) states have a range of different security concerns, not all of which are shared by all ASEAN states. Apart from concerns about domestic political stability, a common list of external concerns would include the role of the Chinese navy and the activities of Chinese fishermen in the South China Sea and, in that context, uncertainty over the future United States involvement in the region in a way that effectively balances China.

Australia's security concerns focus in particular on the acquisition of sophisticated conventional military hardware by the ASEAN states.

For the United States, the possibility of a nuclear North Korea armed with missile delivery systems, the continued existence of communist regimes in East Asia, the spread of weapons of mass destruction, old conflicts and territorial disputes, and a Russia that retains a substantial military capability, are all matters of concern.[5]

As well as these security concerns, the concept of state sovereignty has come under assault following the end of the Cold War. The increased tendency of the international community to claim 'a right to intervene' in situations involving the systematic violation of human rights has opened up new possibilities for misunderstanding. Demands that Asian countries change their judicial, social and moral practices to meet Western standards are regarded by Asian states as an arrogant infringement of their state sovereignty.

Both China and Indonesia feel threatened by the Western focus on human rights. China fears a new Cold War led by a pro-democracy America intent on rolling back the last vestiges of communism. Ironically, China's very fears — and its sense of insult and insecurity because of the depredations it suffered at the hands of Western powers in the nineteenth century — are used to sustain the argument that China is a great power dissatisfied with the status quo, and therefore a threat to the region.

These enduring uncertainties, both real and imaginary, and the new ones perceived to be lurking around the corner, are often expressed in terms of the Asia-Pacific region being fluid, complex and, therefore, potentially more dangerous than hitherto. *Defence of Japan 1994*, for example, posits the view that 'the world's military situation is undergoing significant changes in containing fluid factors amid a continuing sense of opacity towards the future'.[6] Some analysts forecast an era of regional nervousness and soaring tensions.[7] Australia's Defence White Paper 1994 argues that security planners in the Asia-Pacific region must deal with a period of growing uncertainty and insecurity.[8]

On the other hand, there appears to be unanimity that one of the chief consequences of the end of great power rivalry for empire in Asia is that the region is more stable and more peaceful than at any time this century.[9] From the long historical perspective, it could be argued that there is a remarkable degree of peace and stability in the Asia-Pacific, with less insecurity and uncertainty than at any time since the pre-colonial period. This trend has allowed and has in turn been reinforced by a proliferation of transnational trade and investment linkages and complex networks of transportation and communications. One is hard-pressed to find sharply defined areas of great potential conflict or tension in the Asia-Pacific. North Korea's quest for nuclear weapons, rather than its rationale for a nuclear equaliser, is invariably mentioned as an illustration of the risks posed by nuclear proliferation. But even in the Korean peninsula, often referred to as the most dangerous 'flashpoint' remaining in the region, tension has dissipated: North Korea seems ready to join the mainsteam of the Asia-Pacific community following its 1994 framework agreement with the United States.

Economic interdependence, one could argue, has opened up new channels for regional co-operation, confidence-building and transparency in

security relations between Asia-Pacific states. This is evident in the proliferation of growth triangles, or transnational sub-regions that exploit natural economic complementarities — for example, between southern
China, Taiwan and Hong Kong; across the Yellow Sea between China's
northeastern provinces and South Korea; between China and Japan;
prospectively in the Tumen River development zone involving China,
Russia and the Koreas; and between Singapore, Johor in Malaysia, and
Indonesia's Riau island.[10] Most countries in the region are speaking in the
same language as far as trade, investment and economic co-operation are
concerned.[11] This circumstance has been matched by a habit of dialogue on
a broad range of regional diplomatic, humanitarian, political, environmental, cultural, security, nuclear, military, intelligence, trade, development and economic issues.[12] In the United Nations-sponsored peace
settlement in Cambodia, eleven regional states, including China, Japan
and Australia, worked together harmoniously to achieve the first instance
of co-operative peacekeeping in the Asia-Pacific region. The settlement on
the nuclear issue in the Korean peninsula is another example of successful co-operative security between the great powers in the Asia-Pacific
region. This evolving sense of regionalism — a sense of a Pacific community — and a common interest amongst Asia-Pacific states in co-operating
to preserve and enhance regional peace and stability has been accompanied by a proliferation of meetings on the need for some kind of regional
security framework.[13]

What is the security outlook for the Asia-Pacific region in the 1990s and
towards the year 2000? Is it one of unremitting gloom, with 'fluidity and
uncertainty' leading to growing insecurity, an arms race and unchecked
rivalry between the Asian great powers? Is the future for Asia-Pacific a
geopolitical cauldron, or a regional community, asks James Richardson.
What are the national interests of China, Japan, the United States and
India? What are the concerns of the smaller states? Is there a risk of a new
Cold War developing between China and the United States? Or is it reasonable to conclude that the majority of states in the Asia-Pacific have
never felt less threatened and that the region is more pacific and more
promising in terms of conflict resolution, security co-operation and economic development than it has been for most of this century? Are the conditions in the Asia-Pacific in the 1990s sufficient for co-operation to take
root as a preferred option to realist predictions of inevitable rivalry, anarchy and inter-state competition?[14]

These issues are discussed in the following chapters by contributors
from the Australian National University, the Australian Defence Force
Academy, the Stockholm International Peace Research Institute and the
University of Adelaide.

Notes

1 Department of Defence, *Australian Defence*, Australian Government Publishing Service, Canberra, 1976, p. 2.

2 See, for example, John J. Mearsheimer, 'The False Promise of International Institutions', *International Security*, vol. 19, no. 3, Winter 1994/95, p. 5.

3 Prime Minister Hawke, *Commonwealth Parliamentary Debates*, House of Representatives, Parliament House, Canberra, 21 August 1991, at p. 1119.

4 Alan D. Romberg, statement at hearings before the House Armed Services Committee Subcommittee for Defence Policy, Washington, 31 May 1992, in USIS (Canberra) Wireless File 063 of 1 April 1992.

5 Dick Cheney, speech to Australia-US Coral Sea Commemorative Council, Sydney, 1 May 1992, in USIS (Canberra) Wireless File 85 of 1 May 1992.

6 Japanese Defense Agency, *Defence of Japan 1994*, Japan Times, Tokyo, 1994, p. 6.

7 For example, Robert Karniol, 'Asian Build-up: Regional Powers Strengthen Their Hand', *International Defence Review*, June 1991, p. 611. Or headlines like 'Tensions Soar in East Asia as Superpowers Leave the Region', *Washington Times*, 8 August 1991, p. 8.

8 *Defending Australia, Defence White Paper 1994*, Australian Government Publishing Service, Canberra, 1994, p. 8.

9 US Department of Defense, *United States Security Strategy for the East Asia-Pacific Region*, Department of Defense, Washington, February 1995, p. 31.

10 See Myo Thant, Min Tang and Hiroshi Kakazu, *Growth Triangles in Asia — A New Approach to Regional Economic Cooperation*, Asian Development Bank, Oxford University Press, Hong Kong, 1994.

11 See Andrew Elek, 'The APEC Mechanism', Chapter 11, this volume; and Ross Garnaut and Peter Drysdale, *Asia Pacific Regionalism — Readings in International Economic Relations*, Harper Educational, Pymble, 1994.

12 See Paul Evans, 'Emerging Patterns in Asia-Pacific Security: The Search for a Regional Framework', paper for ISIS-Malaysia Roundtable, Kuala Lumpur, 31 August 1991.

13 Andrew Mack, 'CBMs in the Asia-Pacific Region', paper presented to Peace Research Centre ANU/ISIS Malaysia: Conference on 'Naval Confidence Building Regimes for the Asia-Pacific Region', Kuala Lumpur, 8–10 July 1991.

14 Charles L. Glaser, 'Realists as Optimists: Cooperation as Self-Help', *International Security*, vol. 19, no. 3, Winter 1994/95, p. 56ff, suggests that under certain conditions, co-operation should be a country's preferred option and that if several states reach the same conclusion, security co-operation becomes feasible and far preferable to arms racing, rivalry and the danger of a spiral of misperception, uncertainty and tension buildup.

1 The Asia-Pacific: Geopolitical Cauldron or Regional Community?

James L. Richardson

U ncertainties concerning the nature of the emerging international order are nowhere greater than in the vast region of the Asia-Pacific. Prognoses concerning the region's political future range from expectations that economic growth will bring democratisation, respect for human rights and peace to forebodings that latent historical animosities, cultural cleavages, demographic and ecological pressures, and the rivalries and arms races characteristic of changing power balances foreshadow a turbulent future — and quite possibly, in the context of over-crowding and nuclear proliferation, a disastrous one.

It would be more than foolhardy to claim to resolve these uncertainties, but the one-sidedness of most analyses justifies an attempt at a broad overview. The optimism of economists about the prospects for growth is at odds with the pessimism with which strategists contemplate potential security threats, but the tensions between these two approaches are for the most part addressed quite perfunctorily. What is needed is not only to link these dimensions, but to place them in a broader political setting. The more imaginative and challenging attempts to do this, like the 'clash of civilisations' thesis, with its alarming implications for the region, are marred by Western ethnocentrism. The same is true of a recent, broad-ranging survey, in many ways illuminating, by Barry Buzan and Gerald Segal in *Survival*, the journal of the International Institute for Strategic Studies.[1] Their assumptions and conclusions bear close examination, for they help to clarify the problems involved in contemplating the region's future.

The case for pessimism

Buzan and Segal offer a uniformly pessimistic reading of the legacies of history — unresolved rivalries, above all that between China and Japan, border disputes such as the Sino-Russian, Sino-Indian and Russo-Japanese, and potential flashpoints such as those over Taiwan and the South China Sea, and between the two Koreas. China, determined to reassert its traditional pre-eminence, claims the right to change the territorial status quo, Japan is politically enfeebled by hostility stemming from its occupation of most of the region during World War II, and the smaller states fear domination by either power. Tensions are heightened by the uneven pace of economic development and uneven coping with the pressures of modernisation. More generally, the historical legacies point to 'political fragmentation and hostility': as Cold War distortions unravel, suppressed historical patterns reappear. 'There is little that binds [the region's] states and societies together, but much that divides them.' (p. 7)

Most of their specific observations are correct in themselves — there are indeed many sources of tension and unresolved issues, and a few potential 'flashpoints' of great concern — but overall their analysis lacks balance. It neglects successful diplomatic efforts to resolve or defuse conflicts, by the Association of Southeast Asian Nations (ASEAN), for example, and by China and its neighbours, and extensive economic co-operation, such as that between Japan and China. It overlooks the new self-confidence in the successful societies of East Asia, the sense of release from centuries of Western domination, and the sense of new opportunities — indeed, the chance to out-perform the West. Why should these opportunities, these shared interests and aspirations, be forfeited in the pursuit of ancient conflicts where the stakes are relatively minor? Questions such as these point to the need for a more balanced account of the present historical conjuncture: making due allowance for special cases such as Korea and Taiwan, are the legacies of past conflicts so serious as to outweigh the common interests which have opened up in the present?

There is less to question in Buzan and Segal's account of the military balance. They draw attention to the arms buildup in the region, but note that it does not amount to an arms race. Except in Korea, 'there are as yet no highly focused competitive arms accumulations'. And few will disagree that the future military strength of China and Japan will be crucial for the regional balance, or the risk that, should North Korea acquire nuclear weapons, South Korea, Japan and even Taiwan may do the same, is 'particularly disturbing'.[2] They properly acknowledge some significant countervailing tendencies such as Japan's anti-militarist attitudes and the advantages of strategic insulation by water. However, their equation of the reduction in the American military presence with a power vacuum gives currency to alarmist imagery, and while they correctly point out that the region has limited historical experience of 'indigenous modern international relations', the suggestion that the situation might have a parallel in the relations 'emerging out of the wreckage of the Soviet Union, where a group of wholly new states have both to find their feet and work out their interrelationships' (p. 8), shows a readiness to write off the diplomatic experience of several decades. As in much current strategic analysis, where argument falters, imagery helps out.

Turning to the economic aspect of security, they offer several reasons why increasing economic interdependence may not make for regional cooperation or remove incentives for war. East Asia's involvement in the global economy is highly uneven, the most striking case of non-involvement being the interior regions of China, and most Asian states retain extensive forms of non-tariff protection. Where there is interdependence, it is more global than regional, and where it is regional, it tends to mask relations of dominance and dependence. The dependence implied in interdependence could leave East Asia highly vulnerable — indeed 'in the weakest position of all the major industrial centres' — in the event of a breakdown in the management of the global economy, a contingency which the authors consider should be taken seriously. And if it is the presence of democratic government rather than economic interdependence which renders war unlikely in the West, Asia's authoritarian political cultures render conflict and misunderstanding among them all the more likely.

Again, and allowing that these points in themselves have some substance, the argument reads more as an advocate's brief than a balanced analysis. It is rather facile, for example, to assume that Japan's extensive trade and investment links in the region amount to dominance, and the burgeoning investment in China from Taiwan and the overseas Chinese certainly cannot be seen in this light. Even if one shares the authors' scepticism concerning the 'governance' of the global economy, the political and financial influence of those engaged in global transactions appears sufficient to rule out a return to the 1930s levels of protectionism and, short of a breakdown of those dimensions, East Asia is the region best able to achieve unequivocal gains from interdependence. In the industrialised West, intensified interdependence may bring marginal gains, but the overall economic conjuncture brings far greater costs in the form of unemployment and social polarisation.[3] Elsewhere, there is the increasing deprivation of those unable to compete in the global marketplace. On the other hand, is not East Asia's combination of profiting from open markets while protecting its own key resources and vulnerabilities the classic approach of upwardly mobile economies? It goes without saying that the region's economic advance is fraught with tension, most visible at present in China, but the balance sheet needs to take account of its strengths, not only its vulnerabilities.

The same point applies to Buzan and Segal's discussion of the final dimension of security, 'international society'. No doubt security can be enhanced where it is underpinned by numerous multilateral networks and institutions, but is it appropriate to apply European yardsticks as confidently as the authors do — especially when the limitations of the European institutions have been so painfully exposed in the former Yugoslavia? It is true that, in contrast to Europe, there are few formal multilateral institutions in East Asia, but their assessment of those few is far too negative — a point which is taken up below. More importantly, they do not take account of informal networks which have existed for some time, or of the widely shared Asian preference for proceeding gradually, relying on informal understandings rather than formal rules and institutions. They go on to argue that the weakness of international society reflects the prevalence of weak states in the region — a generalisation that recalls the long-discarded domino theory. Allowing that there are some notable weak states, such as Cambodia, and that the political future of China is among the greatest uncertainties, the region is generally regarded as having more than its share of 'strong' states (the newly industrialising countries — NICs), and the states of Southeast Asia have consolidated to the point where their security policies are now seen as driven more by external than internal concerns.

Given Buzan and Segal's premises, their conclusion would indeed follow: East Asia's future would be determined by power politics much more than by interdependence. However, there is no reason to concede their premises. This does not mean that the alternative prognosis, peaceful interdependence, has been rendered plausible. The authors raise fundamental questions for that prognosis: it is their answers to those questions which fail to convince. Any prognosis, however tentative, requires more balanced answers to those questions.

Historical legacies

The lessons of history are open to contradictory readings, and an expectation that earlier patterns will recur can blind observers to the potential for innovation. What was there in the previous five centuries of European history, for example, dominated as it was by the rivalries and wars of the great powers, which pointed towards the integration of Western Europe since 1945? If East Asian history can be characterised in terms of 'fragmentation and hostility' — and which history cannot? — this does not imply that the end of the Cold War will restore that familiar pattern. Arguably, East Asia's traditional patterns have been more thoroughly disrupted than those elsewhere. A Sinocentric system gave way to fragmentation through Western dominance; the indigenous reaction, nationalism, was constrained by the Cold War in complex ways; and the region now finds itself propelled into the forefront of global economic growth. The crucial question, in Asia as in Europe, is how today's elites respond to their reading of the relevant history, in a present which is radically different from earlier historical settings.

Recent history has burdened the region with its share of conflicts, the most serious of which stem directly from the Cold War — the division of Korea, the weakness of the former Indochina and the uncertain status of Taiwan. These have the potential to generate major tensions — North Korea through its desperate attempts to ensure the survival of its regime, Indochina through its fragmentation, Taiwan should it seek formal sovereignty in a way which provokes a violent response from China. Longer historical memories underlie the Russo-Japanese dispute over the apparently secondary issue of the 'northern islands', but its perpetuation depends on changing circumstances. At the height of the Cold War, the United States discouraged compromise; more recently, on the Russian side, as the strategic significance of the islands has declined, the political sensitivity of territorial concessions has become more salient. If the use of force is ruled out, Japan cannot offer economic incentives sufficient to outweigh these political costs, and perhaps prefers not to, seeing no reason to assist Russia to become a more active power in Northeast Asia. But this has less to do with historical memories than with straightforward realpolitik.

In other instances of territorial conflict, stemming from the period of European expansion — most notably the disputes over China's borders which led to war with India and acute tensions with Russia at moments in the Cold War — the parties have proved willing and able to negotiate practical agreements. While these have not required a renouncing of historical claims, they have permitted agreements to demarcate the lines of actual territorial control, a reduction of military tensions and a normalisation of relations (including, in the Sino-Russian case, an upsurge in cross-border trade). Such claims could, no doubt, be revived in the future, but this would be a matter of political calculation in the context of redefined interests, not simply an expression of historical animosities. The important point is not the existence of historical grievances, but the manner in which they are addressed: especially since the waning of the Cold War, the governments of the region have done so pragmatically, or have set them aside in the interests of practical collaboration.

Generalisations about fragmentation and an absence of unifying factors in the region do scant justice to the experience of ASEAN, whose members have substantially enhanced their diplomatic influence through maintaining solidarity towards outsiders and through setting contentious issues aside if they cannot reach internal accommodations. In pre-colonial times, Southeast Asia had a degree of cultural unity but experienced frequent warfare among its empires and kingdoms. Neither this unpromising heritage nor the separateness imposed by colonial rule has prevented the original five (now seven) members from forming an exceptionally cohesive politico-diplomatic association, one which is planning to include additional members, and one whose annual ministerial meetings now provide the venue for whatever region-wide security dialogue may emerge at governmental level.

Economic perspectives

Even though a degree of scepticism is in order concerning the more euphoric projections that export-led growth in East Asia will lead to all good things politically — democracy, respect for human rights and peace — there are solid grounds for regarding the region's economic dynamism as the primary influence shaping its prospects, at least in the medium term, and as favouring peaceful external policies, if not necessarily the full range of political reforms anticipated in the West. The premise, of course, is that sustained economic growth in the region is likely to continue. Assuming that international markets remain reasonably open, the precedent of the NICs (South Korea, Taiwan, Hong Kong and Singapore) suggests that China, the members of ASEAN and possibly other neighbouring states may indeed be able to sustain export-led growth, while the original NICs continue to move up the ladder of technological sophistication. However, since there are now more countries seeking to export clothing, textiles and other light manufactures, and they are far more populous, it may be doubted that their rates of growth can remain as spectacular as previously — at least unless greater impetus can come from internal markets.

This points to even greater competitiveness among the next generation of NICs, especially if India is included as well as the East Asians, but this in turn is likely to enhance the incentives for restraint in foreign policy created by dependence on international markets and on foreign investment. In a competitive setting, a state which manifestly violates international norms is likely to incur serious penalties. The use of force to maintain internal order is another matter, and could be a source of international tension, but here international opinion is likely to be divided, and there are likely to be powerful voices for maintaining 'business as usual'. Moreover, although rapid growth can generate internal tensions, it offers a far more favourable setting than economic stagnation for averting major civil conflict.

Because the region ranks as the only clear 'winner' in the present competitive global economy, and can look to the prospect of joining the West, if not replacing it, at the apex of the system, its member states have every reason to avoid the kind of internecine conflict which, twice this century, accelerated Europe's loss of its pre-eminence in world affairs. Whereas the Europeans took their superiority for granted, the Asians know that theirs is still to be won. They are assisted by political geography: the distances between the major capitals are far greater than in Europe, and the powers do not jostle against one another in the same way. Nor do they have a tradition of fighting hegemonic wars, as did the Europeans over five centuries. Projections by European analysts which assume that this kind of Western pattern is likely to be repeated in East Asia may be unreflective or may amount to wishful thinking, but they show little regard for the interests of the states in question in a historical setting quite different from the former European one. Buzan and Segal, to their credit, acknowledge that the United States and Europe might indeed 'welcome a deterioration in security relations within Asia . . . the rise in tensions would prolong the West's view of itself as being more civilised than the rest of the world and would give it more leverage over Japan and China' (p. 13). There are indications that some Asians are aware of this potential Western interest, and of their own interest in circumventing it.

However, it must be conceded that states are not always rational actors pursuing their own best interests and, although there are substantial reasons for expecting East Asian governments to maintain the priorities which have brought unprecedented economic success, history seldom moves so smoothly over such an extended time-span. Moreover, the global economy might not prove so hospitable to expanding Asian exports. Even if a 1930s-style collapse or a retreat into autarky is unlikely, a general sluggishness and a disenchantment with globalisation and free trade are quite conceivable. If Western societies are unable to deal effectively with their mounting social problems, they are likely to become more inward-looking. And, if they do find ways of addressing the new social agenda, this may require not just a marginal shift in priorities, but a fundamental rethinking of the relationship between the economic and the political. The supremacy of the market, the ruling norm of Western policy for a generation, is unlikely to survive such rethinking, but if such icons lose their power, the expansion of international trade may well slow down quite sharply. This would not mean the end of interdependence, but markets for the second-generation NICs would be much less expansive than for the first generation.

Second, even if global markets remain open, one or more of the region's major economies may falter, for a variety of political and economic reasons. The most important of these, China, presents the most complex set of uncertainties. The Chinese themselves appear well aware that economic prosperity depends on political order. Beyond the immediate question of the political succession to Deng Xiaoping, there are the questions of legitimacy: can the Communist Party find new ways of legitimising one-party rule, or can there be an orderly transition to a new political system? How serious are the centrifugal forces which have led to the erosion of much of the effective power of the central authorities over the provinces, especially those experiencing the most rapid growth? And how serious are the tensions between the eastern seaboard, where the growth is concentrated, and the disadvantaged regions of the interior?[4] Even more fundamental are the ecological concerns. China's land, water and forest resources are already subject to severe stresses: can its ecosystem support the combination of further population growth and rapid development if, as some analysts suggest, its agriculture is vulnerable to the early effects of global warming?

If some observers fear that a weakened China could pose the greatest threat of regional instability, others fear the consequences of China's strength. Paul Dibb, for example, noting China's 'old-fashioned attitude to the use of force', points to a number of disturbing possibilities as its strength increases: 'unbridled competition between Asia's great powers', China's contending with the United States for leadership and 'major Asian wars two or three decades hence'.[5] Denny Roy suggests that a more powerful China is likely to be 'bolder, more demanding, and less inclined to cooperate with other powers in the region'.[6]

While such potentialities cannot be altogether discounted, the image of China depicted in these projections appears anachronistic. It is not just that interdependence and globalisation are assumed to be of no real consequence, but the role of regional hegemon (more bluntly, regional bully) is unlikely to satisfy the ambition of a China strong enough to challenge the United States itself for global 'leadership', whatever that may mean two or three decades hence. By then, according to the recently revised estimates of its GNP, China is likely to have the largest economy in the world, but would not such a power, aspiring to global leadership, seek to play a central role in global political and economic institutions? Such a China would inevitably be influential in its region, but that it should seek regional domination to the point of provoking major wars, at the expense of its global influence, appears an unlikely ordering of its priorities.

If a strong China would be a threat, should Western policy refrain from contributing to strengthen China? Should it limit trade and withhold investment? This may be the logical consequence of the preceding thesis, but Roy appears to be alone in recommending it. Fortunately, Western governments, and also the World Bank, appear to be acting on the assumption that interdependence — involving China deeply in the global economy — is the safer bet. To treat China as an enemy today because of fears for the day after tomorrow could very well be a self-fulfilling prophecy. The interdependence hypothesis is not, unfortunately, self-fulfilling, but to act on it improves its chances of realisation. More generally, the positive economic prognoses for the region are not simply predictions, but are also prescriptive. However, what they prescribe — a reasonably open international trade and financial regime — appears likely to enjoy sufficient political support to be maintained in its essentials, even if it is subject to more serious questioning than in the recent past.

Threats to security

Even if the long term offers no fundamental reason to expect major regional wars, the short term presents a number of perceived threats to security — longstanding disputes, 'flashpoints', an arms build-up, and fears of nuclear proliferation. An enumeration of potential threats, as in many strategic *tours d'horizon*, is well calculated to generate a sense of alarm, but gives little indication of their seriousness, either in absolute or in relative terms.

In North Korea, both the state and the regime are precarious, and the attempt to acquire nuclear weapons is best understood as a desperate attempt to shore up the security of both.[7] Neither diplomacy nor sanctions can ensure that a perception of North Korean nuclear weapons, however few in number, will not lead to further proliferation, especially in Northeast Asia. The United States, as the nuclear ally of both Japan and South Korea, is best placed to seek to dissuade both states from the momentous decision to acquire nuclear weapons, but if Japan, in particular, should do so, this need not be seen as undermining the nonproliferation regime. The world was able to live with China's acquiring nuclear weapons at a time when it was perceived as dangerously bellicose. Japan would present no such image, even though its 'going nuclear' would undoubtedly create alarm in the region.

The future status of Taiwan remains formally disputed, with China insisting on 'one China' while Taiwan flirts with the notion of 'one China, two governments'. But both sides have encouraged trade, travel and investment across the Taiwan Strait. The one circumstance which could provoke a crisis would be if Taiwan declared independence. This is unlikely at present.[8]

After Korea and Taiwan, the Spratly Islands are most widely referred to as a flashpoint, no doubt because of the prospect of major offshore oil resources in their vicinity.

The foregoing cases do not exhaust the list of potential security threats, but they are the most prominent at the present time. It can fairly be said that they are not the kind of issues which tend to generate great wars, and the overall geopolitical configuration is not such that specific issues of this kind constitute points of immediate friction between geopolitical adversaries contemplating a military confrontation. Perhaps the most adverse pattern that can be discerned in the shadows cast by these issues, should they be mishandled politically and diplomatically, is a general alignment of the states of the region against China — a new kind of 'cold war' which could indeed negate the positive economic prognoses sketched earlier. But this would presuppose rather gross and persistent diplomatic misjudgement on all sides.

For some analysts, the most alarming trend is the regional arms buildup. Contrary to developments in the rest of the world since the ending of the Cold War, arms expenditure is increasing, and the emphasis is no longer on internal security but on air and naval forces — 'power projection capabilities'. In particular, China, after reducing its arms spending in the early years of the economic reforms, has increased it since 1989, but only marginally in real terms.[9] There are concerns that if others respond in kind, the region will be closer to a competitive arms race, and this in turn could conceivably create pressures for pre-emptive strikes if, at some time in the future, political tensions were to increase.

However, dangers of this kind appear remote. The regional arms buildup needs to be seen in terms of sub-regions and special cases such as the two Koreas, for obvious reasons the most heavily armed states in the region, relative to GNP. Taiwan's heavy expenditure on advanced weaponry also has its obvious explanation in its need for a deterrent to invasion, and Japan, partly due to American prompting, has built up a formidable capacity to defend its immediate environment. The increase in China's military outlays since 1989 no doubt reflects the increased influence of the military, but also the high cost of modernising China's largely obsolescent forces, especially after the perceived lessons of the Gulf War on the advantages of high technology. In Southeast Asia, starting from a lower level, most states are similarly engaged in modernising and upgrading their armed forces and in acquiring more effective maritime capabilities, both in order to protect their exclusive economic zones and as a hedge against a further withdrawal of the American presence. This does not amount to a competitive arms race, but the members of ASEAN can be seen as countering the image of a 'power vacuum', at least in some measure, and to this extent enhancing overall regional stability. We may conclude, then, that with the possible exception of Korea, the various arms buildups in the region have limited rationales, and that their significance should not be over-dramatised.

Regional institutions

It is true that multilateral institutions at governmental level have been slow to emerge in the Asia-Pacific and that their significance will not be clear for some time, but this is not the whole story. Non-governmental economic institutions have existed since the late 1960s, and since the late 1980s there has been a proliferation of institutions engaging in a 'security dialogue'. 'Track two' diplomacy, bringing together officials 'in their private capacity' with non-governmental elites (business, military and/or academic), has become the characteristic format of the various dialogues, some involving a small number of parties, some the Asia-Pacific region as it is currently understood — East Asia, North America and Australasia — and a few extending more broadly to include states from South Asia or Latin America.

The first conference on Pacific Trade and Development (PAFTAD) and the first meeting of the Pacific Basin Economic Council (PBEC) both took place in 1968, the former a Japanese initiative, the latter an extension of the Australia–Japan Business Cooperation Committee. Japan and Australia also initiated the first Pacific Economic Cooperation Conference, later Council (PECC) meeting in 1980. These groupings have provided a basis for the formation of the intergovernmental body, the Asia Pacific Economic Cooperation (APEC) in 1989, a forum for high-level political discussions, not thus far an institution with specific functions and bureaucratic structures, but a forum which, importantly, includes both China and Taiwan.[10] The most contentious issue with respect to economic institutions has been Malaysia's proposal to establish an East Asian Economic Caucus, a grouping which would exclude APEC's North American and Australasian members, and is now expected to be a sub-grouping within APEC.

In the security field, the earliest and largest forum for multilateral discussions is the Asia-Pacific Roundtable, a 'track-two' initiative of the Institute of Strategic and International Studies (ISIS) Malaysia, now organised
by ASEAN ISIS, which brings together several hundred officials and non-
governmental experts for wide-ranging discussions. 1993 saw the establishment of the Council for Security Cooperation in the Asia-Pacific
(CSCAP), an association of non-governmental institutions ('think-tanks'),
whose primary function is to promote region-wide security co-operation
and to formulate proposals for consideration by governments. In mid-
1993 there were, according to a listing which did not claim to be exhaus-
tive, at least fifteen lesser 'dialogue channels', defined as ongoing
multi-country, trans-Pacific programs, as distinct from one-off meetings,
mainly organised by think-tanks and universities.[11] As in the economic
field, intergovernmental institutions came later, but after a shorter lead-
time: 1995 saw the second meeting of the ASEAN Regional Forum, associated with the ASEAN Post-Ministerial Conference (at which the ASEAN
governments traditionally meet with their principal trading partners and
certain other states from the region).

ASEAN has played a key role in these developments. Through acting
together in a cohesive diplomatic association, a group of smaller or less
developed states has ensured not merely the safeguarding of its members'
special interests but a major voice in institution-building. Although osten-
sibly not concerned with security issues, ASEAN can point to a record of
defusing internal disputes and effective diplomacy on regional security
issues, such as Cambodia, which amounts to a substantial contribution to
security in the broader sense. Its characteristic modus operandi has been
low-key diplomacy and the promotion of co-operation through informal
understandings, not formal institution-building.

This 'Asian' approach tends to be misunderstood by Western commentators, leading some to underestimate the significance of existing institutions such as ASEAN, or to impatience with the lack of institutional
developments in APEC. Both in the economic and security fields, a certain
tension can be observed between a Western preference for specific goals,
programs and proposals, sometimes ambitious in scope — a program for
trade liberalisation, an array of arms control proposals — and an Asian
preference for a process of political familiarisation and confidence-building.[12] In institutions overwhelmingly Asian in their membership, Western
impatience for concrete agreements at this early stage is misplaced.

There are, however, other grounds for concern over the manner in
which the process of regional institutional co-operation is developing. It is
not only that, to an even greater extent than in Europe, the process is elite-
driven, with little broader societal backing, but the elites themselves consist of two rather self-contained specialist professions — economists and
strategic analysts — each with well-defined but narrow agendas, the one
dominated by trade and market liberalisation, the other by what has been
termed 'Strategic Studies USA'. It may well be the case that the achieve-

ment of regional co-operation in an area so diverse as the Asia-Pacific may require the acceptance of certain orthodoxies, and that at the present time the natural source for these are expert policy networks, sometimes more grandly termed 'epistemic communities'. But are these the right orthodoxies, and are they sufficient?

The agendas of both groups are notable for their omissions: market liberalisation is 'in', but issues such as employment, the adequacy of infrastructure, or the social and environmental consequences of rapid economic change are left to themselves, or to individual states. Similarly, CSCAP is to address issues such as maritime co-operation, proposals for enhancing transparency and the mysterious concepts of co-operative and comprehensive security; but the larger political reasons for conflict and insecurity, or the tensions which brought United States relations with both China and Japan to near crisis point earlier in 1994, are not on the agenda.

More generally, what is lacking is any sense of the broader goals of policy, whether for the major bilateral relationships or for the 'Pacific community' as a whole. The driving force behind the European Community/Union was not just the freeing up of trade, and certainly not arms control, but passionately held ideas, a political vision, in the minds of Jean Monnet and his associates, later a rather different vision in the mind of Charles de Gaulle, and more recently a revival of the original vision by Jacques Delors. This dimension — and of course it would have to take quite a different form — has been lacking in the Asia-Pacific context. It may inform the thinking of a few exceptional individuals, but what is crucial is its absence at the institutional level.

A clash of civilisations?

This raises fundamental questions — not least the question whether the idea of an Asia-Pacific region corresponds to any kind of reality. Is the problem that, beneath the occasional rhetorical flourish, there is a sense of a yawning chasm? Could Huntington be right, that the future will see a clash between fundamentally incompatible cultures? Is this the basic reality underlying the tensions between the United States and Japan, or China? Despite the sound and fury of the accompanying polemic, there is much that speaks against this reading of the situation.

The polemic itself has been notable for the vigorous criticisms of 'the West', and more specifically the United States, by Singaporean leaders: the war of words over corporal punishment of an American youth convicted of vandalism, forthright criticisms of Western democracy by elder statesman Lee Kwan Yew, and critical articles by Singaporean scholar-diplomats in American policy journals.[13] Where the Chinese base their stand on human rights — for example on the defence of sovereignty — the Singaporeans have mounted a sophisticated case for Confucian authoritarianism. This can be read as an outright rejection of Western values, a confirmation of the pessimistic view that, as East Asia gains in strength and self-confidence, cultural incompatibilities will become clearer, and any notion of an Asia-Pacific community will be shown to be hollow.

Seen in the context of changes in East Asian societies, however, the polemic is open to a quite different reading. Western individualist values indeed have a strong appeal, but the timing and manner of their acceptance in societies governed by more communal values should be left to those societies to determine. Above all, the kind of pressure which the United States was threatening to impose on China through linking human rights with most-favoured nation status was inadmissible because, whether deliberately or not, it endangered political order in China — a threat not only to development but to the overall level of human rights in that country. It also evoked memories of Western claims of cultural superiority, and when these were backed by what was perceived as crude pressure, the sharpness of the regional reaction was not surprising.

Even at its most polemical, however, a debate about human rights and fundamental principles has a certain reassuring quality, given the infinitely more dangerous forms that international conflict can take. The disputants are, by and large, speaking the same language. The situation is thus very different from the ideological conflict in the more serious phase of the Cold War, when there was mutual incomprehension, when the same words meant quite different things to the two sides. Now the Singaporean authors acknowledge the positive side in Western values before proceeding to their denunciations of the negative.

A more clearly positive view of Western values is taken in *Towards a New Asia*, a report of the Commission for a New Asia, a group of influential policy advisers and elder statesmen from East and South Asia, convened by Noordin Sopiee, Director General of ISIS Malaysia.[14] This report sets out a vision of Asia in the year 2020, and is to be followed by further reports on strategies for their implementation. Viewed through Western eyes, the principles read as a synthesis of values which have come to be associated with recent Asian dynamism with selected Western values, enlivened by a rejection of perceived Western excesses and, albeit more discreetly, of some of the traditional values which used to be associated with Asian cultures. There is an emphatic rejection of extremism ('often the child of sincerity'), and an insistence on balance: constructive conflict, but societal harmony; pragmatism, 'a ferocious impatience with stagnation', but 'the wisdom of patience for the long haul'; development of the person but also devotion to the community, not 'the cult of selfish, self-centred individualism'.

The Report sets out 28 'most important fundamental human rights', the economic, social, cultural and religious rights preceding the civil and political. Only one of these is in any way contentious — 'the right to order and freedom from anarchy and chaos' — but, by implication, the West's insistence on civil and political rights while disregarding the economic and social shows lack of balance. The same general approach informs the discussion of political democracy: 'Man must not be made to serve democracy. Democracy must be made to serve man.' (p. 32) While democracy is endorsed as a goal, the tone of the discussion recalls E.M. Forster's *Two Cheers for Democracy*.

The Report recognises that 'peace and security such as Asia has not seen for generations is the *sine qua non*, the first precondition for the comprehensive advancement that Asia must have' (p. 11). It shows a refreshing readiness to confront awkward questions such as those concerning sovereignty and intervention. It acknowledges that 'even the principle of state sovereignty cannot be inviolable', but that under stringent conditions intervention may be justified: in extreme circumstances, as a last resort, for humanitarian objectives, and when 'not perceived to be opposed by the common people of the country concerned' (p. 15).

Three points here are noteworthy. First, and allowing as the authors do for all the limitations of a statement of aspirations, it is striking that, at a time when the lack of political vision is so evident in the West, here is a strong statement of a vision by respected figures from throughout the region. Second, if nations are 'imagined communities', how much more so is 'Asia', yet if the regional institutions noted earlier are to prosper, there needs to be an underlying sense of a wider community: the Report can be seen as part of the process of constructing such an identity. This incipient identity, however, is 'Asian', not 'Pacific': perhaps the idea of a Pacific community is destined to remain as tenuous as that of its Atlantic Community counterpart. And third, while it is distinguished quite sharply from the West, the 'New Asia' conceived by the authors is not defined in opposition to the West, nor is it distinctively Confucian or Islamic — nor, for that matter, Indian or Javanese. There is no predestined clash of civilisations: if anything, the authors look to cultural blending to defuse clashes among states.

Cultural differences in the Asia-Pacific are evident, but whether they should be aggregated into 'Asian' and 'Western' is problematic. Asian political cultures, it may be suggested, are more reflective, Western (or at least American) more activist; the Asian more inclined to look to the long term, the Western (or the American?) preoccupied with the immediate. But both political cultures are strongly characterised by pragmatism — although this may be less true of the United States today than in an era of greater self-confidence, and in any case there has always been a complex interplay between pragmatism and universalism in the American case.

Half empty or half full?

Surveying the developments under way in the region, Buzan and Segal's Hobbesian prognosis cannot be conclusively refuted, but its neglect of many of these developments detracts from its credibility. The buoyant confidence which one senses in the region stands in contrast to the malaise which is so evident in most other parts of the world. The task of constructing a regional security community might indeed appear formidable, but to allow the present favourable conjuncture to degenerate into major wars fought with the weapons of the twenty-first century would signify political and diplomatic mismanagement of a high order. The outcome will depend, in the final analysis, on the political and diplomatic skills of the region's decision-makers, and experience suggests that these are very considerable.

Rather more concern is in order, however, over the nature of the advice which they are likely to receive from the existing policy networks. Despite all the talk of a broader concept of security, it is not clear that the security dialogue is capable of addressing the most serious issues confronting the region. Military security in the narrow sense still claims disproportionate attention, whereas it is likely that the decisions of greatest consequence will be in the broader economic and political spheres, and quite possible that non-decisions concerning the environment will prove most consequential of all. Pessimists would do well to redirect their attention: in all probability, they are asking the wrong questions.

Notes

* This chapter was first published in *The National Interest*, no. 38, Winter 1994/95. It is reproduced, with minor revisions, with permission. An earlier version was presented in a paper to a panel on security in Asia, organised by Valerie Hudson of Brigham Young University, at the Convention of the International Studies Association in Washington, DC in March 1994.

1 Barry Buzan and Gerald Segal, 'Rethinking East Asian Security', *Survival*, vol. 36, no. 2, Summer 1994, pp. 3–21.

2 The argument of neorealist theorists that nuclear proliferation would be a stabilising factor meets with as little acceptance among strategic analysts as amongst the public at large.

3 The predicament of the West is discussed persuasively by Paul Krugman, 'Europe Jobless, America Penniless?', *Foreign Policy*, no. 95, Summer 1994, pp. 19–34.

4 These issues are discussed in Gerald Segal, *China Changes Shape. Regionalism and Foreign Policy*, Adelphi Paper No. 287, Brassey's for IISS, London, 1994.

5 Paul Dibb, 'Asia's Simmering Cauldron Could Soon Boil Over', *Australian*, 19 November 1993, p. 13.

6 Denny Roy, 'Consequences of China's Economic Growth for Asia-Pacific Security', *Security Dialogue*, vol. 24, no. 2, June 1993, pp. 181–91.

7 See Andrew Mack, 'The Nuclear Crisis on the Korean Peninsula', *Asian Survey*, vol. 23, no. 4, April 1993, pp. 339–59.

[8] Recent developments in Taiwan are discussed in Gary Klintworth (ed.), *Taiwan in the Asia-Pacific in the 1990s*, Allen & Unwin, St Leonards, Australia, 1994.

[9] It is often claimed that China's defence expenditure has increased by 60 per cent since 1989, but when inflation is taken into account, this may be only of the order of 3 per cent annually. Gary Klintworth and Desmond Ball, 'China's Arms Build Up and Regional Security', in Stuart Harris and Gary Klintworth (eds), *China as a Great Power: Myths, Realities and Challenges in the Asia-Pacific Region*, Longman Australia, Melbourne, 1995. However, it is generally acknowledged that the actual level of defence spending is much higher than the published budget figures suggest.

[10] Taiwan's membership is restricted to the extent that it does not participate at heads of government level.

[11] Paul Evans, 'The Council for Security Cooperation in the Asia-Pacific: Context and Prospects', Conference on Economic and Security Cooperation in the Asia-Pacific: Agendas for the 1990s, Australian National University and East-West Center, Canberra, July 1993. CSCAP initially includes institutions from ten countries: Australia, Canada, Indonesia, Japan, South Korea, Malaysia, Philippines, Singapore, Thailand and the United States. China, although involved in a number of the other dialogues, as yet has no participation in CSCAP.

[12] These tensions are discussed in Pauline Kerr, 'Security Dialogue in the Asia-Pacific', *Pacific Review*, vol. 7, no. 4, 1994 special issue, 'Ideas, Policy Networks and Policy Coordination in the Asia Pacific' pp. 397–410.

[13] An early statement of this approach was Kishore Mahbubani, 'The West and the Rest', *National Interest*, Summer 1992, pp. 3–12; see also, by the same author, 'The United States: "Go East, Young Man"', *Washington Quarterly*, Spring 1994, pp. 5–23. For critical discussion, see Eric Jones, 'Asia's Fate: A Response to the Singapore School', *National Interest*, Spring 1994, pp. 18–28; Denny Roy, 'Singapore, China and the "Soft Authoritarian" Challenge', *Asian Survey*, vol. 24, no. 3, March 1994, pp. 231–42.

[14] *Towards a New Asia*, A Report of the Commission for a New Asia, Kuala Lumpur, 1994.

2 The Future of American Policy in the Pacific

Coral Bell

Any discussion of the role of the United States in Pacific and Asian security for the rest of this century must start with the question of whether it will remain the dominant superpower of the region, or dwindle gradually to become merely one among a constellation of powers. *Primus inter pares* — or perhaps not even that for long? For the first year or so of President Clinton's term of office, the question seemed to be quite open.

That might be thought surprising, considering that the world was approaching at the time the 50th anniversary of the American triumph in the Pacific in World War II, and that the five subsequent decades of almost unchallenged American dominance had seen American economic interests in Asia and especially round the Pacific rim grow ever more important. If 'geo-economics' has succeeded 'geopolitics' as the dominant strand in world affairs, as some analysts have been arguing, Washington's commitment to the Asia-Pacific region ought theoretically to be vastly more secure than its commitment to Europe, since its economic interests are larger and growing faster across the Pacific than across the Atlantic.[1]

Yet, ever since the end of the Cold War in 1989, there has been a lingering air of anxiety among Pacific and Asian policy-makers and commentators that American commitment to the security of their region must inevitably wane in the alleged 'new world order'. In one respect that was logical enough. The relationship which has been most central to America's involvement with the whole area was universally agreed to be that enshrined in the US–Japan Security Treaty of 1951, and that treaty undoubtedly had been moulded, conditioned and made necessary by the Cold War tension between Moscow and Washington. America's first overseas military encounter after World War II (and a very serious and painful one, the scars and relics of which are still visible in American public life) was both Pacific and Asian: the war in Korea. That war might perhaps have been entered and endured for the sake of the United States commitment to South Korea alone, but its strategic justification at the time was largely in terms of the traditional view of Korea as 'a dagger pointed at Japan'. Moreover, it was the forward basing of United States troops and naval and air power in Japan that made early and effective military resistance possible. And that in turn, in President Truman's view, saved the United Nations, which he had feared would go the way of the League of Nations unless the United States could successfully block the North Korean push south.

So, though European anxieties about a possible Soviet push westward and southward towards the Channel coast and the Middle East might be considered the precipitating cause of the Cold War as a political and diplomatic engagement, and the reason for the creation of America's first peacetime military alliance, the North Atlantic Treaty Organisation (NATO) in 1949, it was *Pacific* anxieties which, in the saying of the time 'put teeth into NATO' — in other words, engendered the first American military buildup against the Soviet Union as the prime global adversary. The contrast in United States defence assumptions between 1949 and 1951 was very striking, and almost solely engendered by the Korean War.

Thus one might say that a conviction of the strategic importance of Japan was the pivot around which American policy in the Pacific revolved from the earliest years of the Cold War, and it remained enormously strong until the very last years of that encounter. For instance, when Mikhail Gorbachev, before his star began to wane in Moscow, made an optimistic speech in Vladivostok in 1986 taking a quite unrealistic view of the future of Soviet influence in Asia, it caused *frissons* of alarm in Washington, even though the process of economic and political failure in the Soviet Union was already by then beginning to be apparent.

Thus it was logical that the end of the Cold War, the dissolution of the Soviet Union and the marked reduction in Russian ability to project power in the Pacific should have vastly downgraded, at least for the time being, the strategic importance of the United States–Japan security link. If there is only one superpower in the Pacific, where can any serious challenge to it, or any serious threat to Japan for the foreseeable future, come from? The Japanese Self-Defence Forces should be more than enough to deter minor threats, and no new major ones seem likely to become visible for the rest of this decade, though next century may present quite a different picture. So, for the time being at least, Japan was seen as needing the United States alliance less, and conversely, the United States as needing Japan less. The great apparatus of naval and air forces, strategic maritime doctrines like those associated with the Commander-in-Chief Pacific (CINC-PAC), and forward United States deployments such as those in the Philippines began to look irrelevant as the once formidable global threat of Soviet power vanished like a mirage. No president (even assuming that Clinton is succeeded in 1996 by a Republican less oriented to domestic issues) could justify the kind of defence establishment that had been judged necessary ten years earlier without a new threat equivalent to that of the Soviet Union in its most dangerous-looking days. At the height of the Cold War (1953), defence had absorbed almost 15 per cent of America's enormous Gross National Product (GNP). By 1995, that allocation was in process of shrinking towards 3 per cent within the decade. That is the sort of level that had prevailed in the 1930s (in the days of United States isolationism) and that has been characteristic of middle powers like Australia.

Yet, until halfway through the Clinton first term, one could argue that it was Washington's excessive rhetorical engagement in Asian affairs, rather than the postulated reduction in commitment, that appeared to be the root of the problem. During the first six months of 1994, one could argue that the Clinton policy-makers had managed to tread heavily on the toes of all four major Asian powers (China, Japan, India and Indonesia), while simultaneously pushing a minor but very dangerous and unstable power (North Korea) towards crisis point, and also alienating useful and influential regional dignitaries of the Association of Southeast Asian Nations (ASEAN), like Lee Kwan Yew.

Even so convinced and longstanding an ally as Australia evidenced a new disenchantment with the United States. The 4 July (United States Independence Day) edition of the *Australian* (a paper whose editorial policy is thoroughly approving of the American alliance and which is, moreover, owned by an American citizen) used as the lead story of its special supplement for that American birthday celebration an article entitled 'The Lessons for Australia in the Crumbling of America'. That would not have happened even a few years ago. Though the overt public quarrels between Australian and United States policy-makers have recently been only about the trade frictions of the moment, it does indicate a fall in public confidence in the United States, related to its domestic social problems and the apparent inability of its political institutions to do much about those problems: crime, drugs, gun control, race relations, health care provision and the growth of an 'underclass' in the great cities. The advent of a Democratic administration in January 1993, after twelve years of Republican policy-makers, had earlier encouraged hopes of a more effective attack on the underlying issues, but by late 1994 those hopes had completely dimmed, especially in view of the Republican gains in the mid-term elections.

In foreign policy generally, Clinton's problems had their origin in the struggle for the White House in 1992. Because George Bush had been almost universally conceded to be a tough, 'savvy' foreign policy-maker, and Ronald Reagan had had the good fortune to be handed an enormous 'windfall gain' in central balance power relations by the collapse of the whole communist structure in Europe 'on his watch' (though its full extent was not revealed until George Bush's term), Clinton as an election campaigner in 1992 had to search hard for issues on which to challenge Republican prestige in dealing with the external world. He found those issues in the 'compassion' and 'human rights' field, promising, for instance, to reverse Bush's policy of turning back 'boat people' from Haiti, and accusing Bush of allegedly 'coddling tyrants in Beijing'. He also made much of Bush's disastrous trade efforts *vis-à-vis* Japan, promising to do better.

Thus, by the time he inherited office in 1993, Clinton had quite a lot of campaign promises to keep. As is usual in such cases, what looks easy to challenge in opposition proved difficult to resolve easily once in power. The promises regarding human rights in China, for instance, proved almost as much of an embarrassment as those concerning the refugees from Haiti.

The linkage between human rights issues and MFN (most favoured nation) status in the original Clinton policy line, though fought out chiefly in connection with China, had disturbing implications for many other Asian governments. Those governments are not long-established democracies able to accept a considerable measure of dissent with a shrug and a yawn and a tolerantly raised eyebrow. They are relative newcomers at best at the democracy game, quite liable to slide back into autocratic ways if the regime or the political establishment generally feels itself even under what might seem, to outsiders, to be very mild threats — critical comments in a few local magazines or newspapers, for instance. The Clinton policies did (perhaps unconsciously) make them feel under threat both directly (because of skeletons in their own closets) and indirectly via China and Japan. All the smaller countries had stakes in the political stability and economic prosperity of both of these two great engines for growth in the area. In the case of China, if that stability had to be autocratic stability, it did not worry them much, especially as Chinese labour conditions, for instance, were in some cases not markedly different from their own. Cynical observers around the Pacific rim therefore tended to depict the Clinton policies as trade-driven under a human rights banner. Thus when the new administration hinted, for instance, that unless the conditions and wages of Indonesian workers were improved, tariff privileges would be withdrawn from Indonesian goods, that could be interpreted (and not only in Indonesia) as an attempt to blunt the main competitive advantage of low-wage countries by imposing on them conditions that would make them uncompetitive in United States markets.

The Asian resistance to the Clinton linkage of trade and human rights issues had, moreover, some important allies in the United States camp. By 1994, China was an important market for United States goods, especially high-tech products like aircraft and telecommunications facilities, as well as commodities like wheat. All those products had powerful lobbies in Washington, as did the financial groups which saw China and the other fast-growing economies of the area as first-class investment opportunities. So when the crunch came in 1994 over whether China's MFN status should be renewed (despite the lack of much improvement in its human rights record), it was hardly surprising that the president opted to back down, and 'de-link' the two issues for the future.

That decision was undoubtedly welcome in the Asian region, save among those dissident groups which had pinned their hopes to the American crusade. It lost Clinton a few friends among the ranks of the liberal commentators in the United States media and on the left fringe of the Democratic Party, but on the whole it probably reassured more domestic 'influentials' than it disturbed. So there was not much real protest or resistance in Washington, and still less in Asia, of course. If China had lost its $30 billion of sales each year to the United States, and in return had taken action to restrict the $8.8 billion of United States sales to China, there would have been great 'collateral damage' to other economies. The entrepôt economy of Hong Kong would have been cast into deep shadow at a delicate moment of its transition from the British Raj to its future status as an autonomous Chinese region. The foundations of Taiwanese prosperity would have been shaken, and Asian investments in China would have been endangered. Australia, likewise, would have been economically damaged, since the prosperity of the region is the basis for its ability to buy our commodities.

One could argue that the reversal of policy on this point, by June 1994 in fact, signalled a conscious general change of direction in the Clinton policies round the Pacific rim. Two or three months earlier (April–May 1994), dissatisfaction with the new president's decisions was being clearly 'orchestrated' in a familiar Washington way, with well-leaked reports of a memorandum by Winston Lord (Assistant Secretary of State for East Asian Affairs) to the Secretary of State (Warren Christopher) presenting a litany of such complaints.[2] The occasional necessity for a high Washington official (ostensibly in charge of an area of policy) to 'go public' in this way with a denunciation of the direction being taken by the administration he serves arises from the almost infinite multiplicity of pressures from lobbyists and 'single interest groups' on Congressmen in Washington and through them on the State Department. It is a technique of redressing the balance by making it clear to influential media pundits and others that policy has been distorted by those pressures, and needs to be readjusted.

Those readjustments were clear by early June, in the 'de-linking' of trade issues from human rights issues, most importantly with regard to China. That change of stance had reassuring implications for other governments also. There seemed likewise to be a move away from tough-minded 'confrontational' tactics both concerning North Korea on nuclear issues, and vis-à-vis Japan on trade issues. The Korean signals will be examined in more detail later. The softening on Japan appeared to be linked to the rapid 'turnover' of Japanese prime ministers, and other indications of political and economic change in that complex society.

Undoubtedly, all the changes could in some degree be interpreted as a victory of sorts for assorted groups in Asia. American policies towards Japan on trade, as well as towards China on human rights, looked to a good many Asians like Westerners nagging and bullying them, telling them how to live, how to run their own societies, and what political and social values they had to adhere to. It tended to be called 'human rights imperialism' or 'trade imperialism'.

The resentments it engendered were increased by the generation change in American politics which Clinton's victory had embodied. The 'forty-somethings', ex-Vietnam protesters, ex-hippies, who had been the student generation of the 1960s and 1970s, and were now heavily represented in the new administration, were not a group which raised much enthusiasm among the mostly elderly decision-makers and opinion-formers of Asia. They had been more comfortable with George Bush's generation: Americans who remembered and had even fought in the Pacific War.

Feelings of that sort affected also the Hindu and Moslem decision-makers of the South Asian world, but they had some additional irritations of their own. This was particularly so for Indian policy-makers, because for them the Clinton advent had initially seemed to promise better things. Relations between Washington and Delhi had been predominantly stormy ever since the earliest days of Indian independence, partly because the original Indian mix of Fabian socialism and long-winded bureaucracy sat ill with the brisk impatience of American businessmen and policy-makers, and also because the blunt pursuit of power-politics by Washington policy-makers from the earliest years of the Cold War sat ill with the Nehru theory of non-alignment. But the relationship had one benign period, during the presidency of John F. Kennedy, who sent the eminent and sympathetic economist J.K. Galbraith to Delhi as his ambassador. Since Kennedy was Clinton's political hero, a return to that congenial relationship seemed to be promised by his advent. Moreover, Indian economic policy under the prime ministership of P.V. Narasimha Rao had moved much closer to the sort of structures American business felt easy with. And above all, in central balance diplomacy, India had lost its 'great and powerful friend' the Soviet Union, and Russia as the successor-state did not by any means exert the same sort of appeal — especially after Russian nationalists like Zhirinovsky began talking about the soldiers of some restored imperial Russia 'washing their boots in the waters of the Indian Ocean'.

Given all those factors, Washington at the beginning of the Clinton term seemed to have better cards in its hand than at any time since 1947. But it failed so abjectly to play them that by May 1994 a staff member of the House Foreign Affairs Committee could say that relations with Delhi were at their worst point since the Nixon administration twenty years earlier.[3] For the first eighteen months, the new policy-makers did not even manage the elementary task of finding and sending a suitable ambassador. So, in effect, Delhi was driven back on more or less re-launching the old relationship with Moscow, though in the collapsed state of the Russian economy it did not have much to offer, save the re-supply on favourable terms of the Russian weapon systems used by the Indian armed forces. Moscow now insists on payment in hard currency, but still provides high-performance aircraft, for instance, at bargain rates.

One has to say that the Clinton administration missed the original 'window of opportunity' through sheer diplomatic clumsiness, and added injury to insult, from India's point of view, by offering F16 fighter-bombers to Pakistan in pursuit of its policy of 'capping' the nuclear arms program, and by criticising (justifiably) India's stance on human rights in Kashmir and elsewhere.

Relations with Pakistan were also at a low point. Soviet retreat from the war in Afghanistan had ended Pakistan's one-time salience as a bulwark against an assumed Soviet push southward. The arming of the Afghan mujahadin had left some embarrassing legacies in the clan and factional fighting that continued to rack the country. In the complex new 'great game' for influence in Central Asia (the outcome of which is bound to affect the balance in South Asia) the United States seemed completely 'sidelined', the dominant players being Russia, China, Iran, Turkey and Pakistan. Only in oil exploration was the United States playing a role.

As mentioned earlier, the initial Clinton policy lapses began to be retrieved towards the middle of 1994. The Indian prime minister paid a reasonably successful visit to Washington, and an Ambassador to Delhi was finally appointed. That did not, however, altogether undo the original damage, or remove the impression of what was sometimes called 'foreign policy by CNN'.

The best example of that latter tendency was the brouhaha over an American teenager sentenced to (initially) six strokes of a cane in Singapore on a charge of vandalism. It was not an issue in which the United States president should ever have publicly involved himself, but in view of the publicity and his human rights stance, Clinton had to protest. (American teenagers would certainly regard freedom from caning as among their inherent human rights.)

The trivial incident crystallised all that Asian societies tended to dislike and distrust about American mores. Films and TV series and songs from the United States may be enormously popular with young people in Asia, but to the generation still in control of politics there they exemplify the dangers of 'the American way of life'. What they show are undisciplined and disrespectful children and adolescents: sons turning against fathers, daughters who become unwed mothers, wives who defy husbands, dysfunctional families. Most Asian households (Muslim, Hindu or neo-Confucian) are still heavily patriarchal. 'Cultural artefacts' of that sort are liable to alienate them rather than enhance the prestige of the United States.

Apparently minor matters of that sort were parts of a larger shift in the distribution of power and influence internationally, especially between Asia and the West. Economic power in particular has been redistributed from its earlier historical locations (mostly round the North Atlantic) to other places, especially round the Pacific rim. Military muscle tends in time to follow economic power.

Australian security was not necessarily enhanced by those changes in power distribution, but the policy-makers in Canberra did work hard at the task of adapting to them. That implied some reassessment or redefinition of the nature of the ties with the United States. As in the case of the Asian societies, generation change was a factor, though it worked quite differently in the Australian than in the Asian case. The American president and the Australian prime minister belong to roughly the same age-cohort, as mostly do the policy-makers around each of them. That is to say, they are predominantly to a greater or lesser extent those for whom Vietnam was a central experience of their younger lives and (as far as the Australians, though not the Americans, are concerned) an experience that they tend to connect with the ANZUS alliance. (That connection does not really apply on the American side because if Washington connects the military involvement in Vietnam with any defence of allies, those allies would be Japan and Thailand, not Australia.) For that particular age cohort in both countries, the alliance experience is of lives pointlessly lost because, in effect, of strategic misapprehensions in Washington and Canberra about the security importance to the United States and Australia of a civil war in Southeast Asia. For Bush and the Australian 'opposite numbers'in his generation, on the other hand, the predominant strategic memory was of final victory in a desperate struggle, and a long-term useful outcome, with a reconstituted Japan as the original engine of the vast economic growth around the Pacific rim in the decades since World War II.

There is a large difference between the memory of success and the memory of failure in estimating the usefulness and importance of an alliance. For George Bush's political colleagues and predecessors, Australia had been a vital base, an important supplier of goods and forces in the Pacific War, a friend and ally in Korea, the provider of suitable pieces of real estate for some of the most vital strategic and intelligence surveillance *vis-à-vis* the Soviet Union right through the Cold War.

For Clinton's generation and its successors, not much of that would remain relevant. Moreover, George Bush's foreign policy experience, as it impacted on his electoral fortunes, would have to be seen by Clinton as a warning rather than an example. Early in 1991, just after Bush's low-casualty victory in the Gulf War, and his successful coping with the Soviet Union's process of disintegration, a second term seemed as assured as any political victory ever can be. Yet he went down to defeat eighteen months later, his foreign policy successes almost being turned into a reproach against him, an apparent proof that he must have neglected domestic affairs. The moral seemed to be that even low-cost victories do not necessarily do you much good with the electors, even a relatively short time later. Clinton has often been charged by American journalists (and even more by 'outsiders') with devoting too little time to foreign policy, but judged by his predecessor's experience, he was showing political 'savvy' in that allocation of his time.

Quite apart from that general attitude shift, personal changes on both sides meant some loss of close familiar connections. Bob Hawke had been on easy terms with both Bush and Reagan, and an old friend of George

Schultz, Reagan's Secretary of State. Kim Beazley as Defence Minister had been close to his United States 'opposite number', Caspar Weinberger. The Clinton 'security team' — Warren Christopher, Anthony Lake, William Perry — remained by comparison relatively unknown quantities in Australia, even well into the Clinton term.

However, the questions that aroused conflict between Australian governments and United States administrations during the early 1990s were primarily about trade, not about security. Keating's external policies, like Clinton's, appeared essentially trade-driven. There is a certain symbolic quality in the fact that Keating deposed Bob Hawke as prime minister at precisely the time (December 1991) that the society of states moved into the yet-uncharted territory of the post-Soviet world. For quite a time, that great change generated a worldwide illusion that the end of the Cold War meant the end of international conflict: peaceful global competition in economic performance would therefore replace security concerns.

That illusion did not last long, of course. The post-Cold War world has proved to be a world of dispersed intractable turbulence. Yet the end of the Cold War did undoubtedly permit closer alignments in some aspects of Australian and United States security problems. It reduced almost to insignificance an issue that earlier prime ministers, especially those from the Labor Party, had found at times embarrassing: the allergy on the left of the party to what were usually called 'the US nuclear bases', that is, the installations at Pine Gap and Nurrungar (and at one time at Exmouth Gulf) which were strands in the vast American network of command, control, communications and intelligence ('C³I' in the jargon). Those installations did have to be interpreted as meaning that the patches of Australian real estate on which they stood would presumably be on Soviet targeting lists in various doomsday scenarios. So the end of the Soviet–American power contest did remove one cataclysmic (though improbable) risk to Australians from the alliance. Whereas 'Close the American nuclear bases' was at one time a regular demand from the Left to Labor prime ministers, it had by the Keating period become a plea from embattled wheat farmers (mostly from the right of the political spectrum) protesting at the American subsidies which reduced the price of wheat. Such cries were unlikely to be heeded, whichever party was in power: Pine Gap and Nurrungar remained strategically useful despite the end of the Cold War. They were, for instance, valuable to the coalition forces in the Gulf War. If some day there is a change in their control, it seems more likely to be because technical developments make them no longer necessary to the American surveillance system.

Similarly, the end of the Cold War brought arms control measures which, among other things, permitted the removal of nuclear weapons from surface ships, so the battle between the United States and New Zealand over the 'neither confirm nor deny' principle lost most of its saliency. Though the New Zealand government, and environmental protesters in Australia, continued to object to visits by nuclear-powered United States naval ships (on grounds of the possibility of accident or environmental damage), the whole issue of nuclear weapons as a factor in international politics had become focussed on the 'proliferation' question, and the question of French and Chinese nuclear testing.

On the larger question of Australia's American connection, Australia, as an intermediary middle power, could, as it were, 'diffuse' some of the benefits it received from that alliance around the neighbourhood. Indeed, the alliance operated as the main diplomatic signal that the United States remained concerned with the affairs of the South Pacific, that its small societies would not necessarily be 'easy morsels'. If a new predatory power should show an undue interest in their affairs, Australia, as a concerned regional middle power, would have an 'insider's' chance of putting their case in Washington.

Despite all these reasons for Washington's policies remaining of vital importance to Canberra, the United States alliance was by no means as much the central focus of Australian policy as it had been for the first four decades after World War II. The new central focus was Asian regionalism: Hawke and Keating advanced rival claims to the true paternity of that policy shift.[4] Primarily what had at first been sought from Asian regionalism was the economic betterment that might be found through partnership with the newly prospering economies of the Pacific rim. But by the mid-1990s, regionalism had a security component as well as the economic one, and that development was an entrance ticket to new complexities involving the United States.

Washington's policy in the Asia-Pacific region, as against its policy in Europe, had from the early 1950s tended towards bilateralism rather than multilateralism. The favoured State Department image was of Washington as the hub of the Asia-Pacific wheel, with separate spokes going out to Japan, South Korea, Taiwan, the Philippines, Australia and Thailand. The only time multilateralism was tried in those early days (SEATO in 1954, after the French collapse in Indochina), it was almost universally judged a failure.[5] Though State Department people were too diplomatic to put it that way, America in effect maintained a system of separate protectorates in the region. That bilateralism provided considerable advantages (at least during the Cold War years) for American policy-makers. It enabled them to control the separate agendas of each relationship without too many arguments. In Europe, by comparison, where multilateralism had been firmly secured by the Europeans (who knew a thing or two about diplomacy) from the earliest days of the formation of NATO (1948–49), there was scope for occasional 'ganging up' by the allies against Washington when they did not like a particular policy. Not surprisingly, Washington therefore tended to defend the bilateral approach quite toughly right up to the end of James Baker's time as President Bush's Secretary of State, pointing out that the system worked well enough, and citing the alleged old American maxim, 'if it ain't broke, don't fix it'.[6]

However, as a diplomatic system, it essentially reflected the context in which it had been created, a time when the societies of the area were economically undeveloped (save for Japan), militarily prostrate and had little diplomatic experience. By the mid-1990s, all that had changed profoundly. The societies concerned were riding a wave of economic prosperity, putting on military muscle with some speed, and had acquired considerable diplomatic 'clout' as well as a strongly nationalist determination, in some cases, to use that clout rather assertively.

So a reasonable case could be made by 1992 that the time had come for a reappraisal of the security structure of the region. And the Clinton policy-makers seemed to be signalling much more willingness than their predecessors to move from bilateralism towards multilateralism. The Seattle 'summit meeting' of November 1993, of which President Clinton was undoubtedly the star, seemed to augur the change. Thus, despite the immediate ambiguities of the Clinton foreign policies in the Asia-Pacific region, the administration could be said to be showing a hopeful movement towards what Australian policy-makers called 'co-operative security', as against the older system of bilateral connections.

Korea remained for some time a focus of uncertainties. American policy, in the original phase of zeal for 'anti-proliferation' measures, had appeared determined to prevent the regime from acquiring any nuclear weapons capacity. By mid-1994, that determination appeared to have softened into acceptance of the fact that, while Kim Il Sung was alive, his nuclear reactors had probably manufactured enough fissile material for one or two bombs, and that the best that could be hoped for from his heir, Kim Jong Il, was to prevent that number from growing much. The successor regime at the time of writing appeared to have accepted some reduction or slowing-down of its capacity to increase its nuclear weapon potential, by agreeing to the installation of light-water reactors (which do not produce much plutonium) in place of graphite-moderated reactors (which produce more). The agreement could probably be regarded as a success of sorts for the Clinton policy-makers, at least in the sense of reducing tensions and allowing the new regime, if it chose, to pursue more conciliatory policies. But no certain predictions could be made about its future.

Let us return finally to the question with which I began this paper. Will the United States remain the dominant superpower in the Asia-Pacific region, or will it decline into something less, something more like *primus inter pares*, first among equals?

The evidence of history, and the pressures of economics, indicate the limits of possible outcomes for United States policy this century. More radical and alarmist theses of some kind of United States 'withdrawal' or 'disinvolvement' are contradicted by the mere facts of geography and demography. The United States has a very long Pacific coastline, and a cherished constituent state, Hawaii, lies in the middle of that ocean. The American people are increasingly inclined to move towards their Pacific coastline, and their ethnic mix includes an increasing Asian component. Moreover, American history for almost the past 150 years has indicated that Americans are far less inclined to withdraw from the Pacific and Asia than from Europe. Isolationism is certainly a recurrent strand in American foreign policy reactions, but it has always tended to be from the entanglements and dangers of Europe that isolation has been sought. In the Pacific and East Asia, the central American tradition has been rather of a bold interventionism, ever since the nineteenth century days of the forcing open of Japan, the conquest of the Philippines and the 'open door' policies in China. Asia, in short, has been seen in the United States as a source of opportunities, and even as an extension of the area of 'manifest destiny', at times when Europe was seen as an area of potential danger.

That interpretation of Asia — as part of America's destiny — has cost many Americans their lives. All three of the most painful United States involvements in war of the past 50 years have sprung from Asian sources — the Pacific War, Korea and Vietnam. It seems logical to assume that those encounters may have induced a persistent wariness, to be seen already, for instance, in the cautious United States reserve concerning the conflicting claims for the Spratlys, and in the equally cautious avoidance of moves that might push the North Koreans into a corner from which they might see no way out save war. Even if that has meant that a few North Korean nuclear weapons (like a few in Pakistani and Indian hands) must be tolerated.

For the brief remainder of this century, no matter who occupies the White House or which party holds the majorities in Congress, there seems no doubt that the United States will play the dominant role in Pacific affairs, and those of many areas of Asia. Despite the clashes of culture and mores mentioned earlier, that will not be unwelcome in most Asian societies, nor of course in Australia. The ASEAN countries are growing richer and more self-confident, but they do not show much sign of wanting to be left alone with the great powers of the region, China, Japan and India. The United States remains a necessary 'balancer'. The Republican majorities in both House and Senate after the mid-term elections of November 1994 complicated President Clinton's task as policy-maker, but did not change that point. The world has learned to live equably enough with both Democrats and Republicans, and learned in the first two Clinton years that even when the president's party has a majority in both houses, it does not necessarily preclude gridlock. The victorious Republicans seemed at the time of writing to be intent more on domestic issues and their chances for the presidency in 1996 than on foreign policy. But if their most publicised foreign policy figures (Robert Dole as Majority Leader and Jesse Helms as Chairman of the Foreign Relations Committee) had any clear orientation in that field, it would seem to be towards unilateralism rather than isolationism. That tendency would show itself most clearly in impatience with the United Nations, and especially on foreign aid (including for instance the Mexican peso rescue of early 1995), but also possibly impatience with allies, and with ex-adversaries like Russia, China and Vietnam. It used to be said in Washington that the Atlantic was 'the Democratic ocean' and the Pacific 'the Republican ocean', meaning that the notion of 'manifest destiny' in Asia had been more readily accepted in the latter party. If the political tendency which emerged during the elections proves more than a short-term spasm of irritation on the part of the electorate, that might again be important.

On the other hand, the beginning of the new millennium loomed very close to the horizon of Asian and Pacific policy-makers' plans by the mid-1990s, and it seemed unlikely that any of them expected the United States still to be the dominant power of the region at the end of the new century, or even the end of its first 50 years. So, as they thought about their grandchildren's futures, the problem almost necessarily presented itself as devising a means of living at peace with those large local sovereignties without being submerged by them. The traditional mode of solving that problem for small and middle powers has been a system of co-operative or collective security, including alliance with a great power from outside the region. That has been the United States' role for the past 50 years in Europe. Perhaps it will repeat that role in Asia for the first few decades of the new millennium, now just over the horizon.

Notes

[1] Though the trans-Pacific trade and economic connections have been much less satisfactory to American policy-makers in recent years. While the trans-Atlantic trade is in rough balance, the United States has suffered very large deficits in its trade with Japan, and substantial ones also in trade with China. An influential statement of the 'geo-economics is supplanting geopolitics' line of argument may be found in Edward Luttwak, 'The Coming Global War for Economic Power', *International Economy*, September–October 1993.

[2] See *International Herald Tribune*, 6 May 1994.

[3] *Time*, 23 May 1994.

[4] ibid.

[5] See Leszek Buszynski, *SEATO: The Failure of an Alliance Strategy*, Singapore University Press, Singapore, 1983.

[6] Gareth Evans, for example, got a considerable snubbing when he raised the question of a regional security dialogue in Washington. See James Baker, 'America in Asia: Emerging Architecture for a Pacific Community', *Foreign Affairs*, vol. 70, no. 5, Winter 1991–92, for a statement of the Bush administration's position.

3 Greater China and Regional Security*

Gary Klintworth

There is something of a cottage industry predicated on forecasts about growing regional insecurity and, in particular, on China as a great power threat. The China threat proposition is easy to sell in the Asia-Pacific region and tends to fuel emotional regional responses. As Singapore's Senior Minister Lee Kuan Yew observed, when Western critics write about 'the China threat', they are 'mining a rich lode filled with apprehension and fears'.[1]

China, however, may never become a great power. Even if it manages to remain intact, it may be caught in a poverty trap formed out of the mismatch of its huge population and its very limited resources.[2]

Open door policies, meanwhile, have exposed Chinese society to enormously powerful political, technological, economic and religious influences.[3] These trends and the rise of entrepreneurial provinces have weakened Beijing's central authority. Unchecked, this could lead to tension between Beijing and assertive regions and even a struggle for power that might attract a new bout of interventionism by external powers.

In the past, a China beset by social disorder, inflation and civil war, attracted foreign intervention. The result was turbulence and instability inside China and on its borders.

On the other hand, if China does become as rich in per capita terms as Taiwan, it will be increasingly dependent on the region for its economic growth and prosperity. It may then follow the Taiwanese path to political reform and, ultimately, democratisation.[4] In that case, as Harry Harding suggests, economic modernisation could spill over into political reform and reinforce the diplomatic incentives and constraints that are shaping China's behaviour in world affairs today.[5] By 2010, a rich and powerful

China could well be a critical stabilising force and counterbalance in the strategic framework of Pacific Asia, for example, *vis-à-vis* Japan or a rejuvenated Russian empire.

Forecasts about China as a great power threat are not well supported by the trends in Chinese foreign policy that have emerged over the last few decades. In the 1970s, China joined the United Nations and began its shift towards diplomatic normalcy and market socialism. Today we see a relatively strong China that has joined, and has been largely accepted by, the community of nations. It is working more often with, rather than against, the interests of the rest of the world. It has become more willing to reciprocate with good neighbour policies. It has behaved responsibly in the United Nations Security Council, in the Pacific Economic Cooperation Council (PECC), the Asia Pacific Economic Cooperation (APEC) and the Association of Southeast Asian Nations Regional Forum (ARF). Its role in peacekeeping in Cambodia and in pressing North Korea to abide by its commitments on nuclear inspections by the International Atomic Energy Agency (IAEA) are examples of a good citizen China.

Indeed, much of the optimism about East Asia, at least amongst the economists, is based squarely on stability in an outwardly oriented China. That is why most countries near China prefer a China that has a strong central political authority, that remains intact, that makes steady economic progress and is increasingly a part of the global community. This China might then be expected to undertake a process of gradual political reform and begin to look more like its Asian counterparts. In their view, the door to China should be kept open and trade should not be used as a political weapon to bludgeon the government over human rights.

This is not to excuse China for past mistakes such as its support for insurgencies in Southeast Asia or its inclination 'to teach a lesson' to small neighbours. Nor is it to deny that China's behaviour in the South China Sea will always be beyond reproach. Few big powers have a perfect record when it comes to dealing with small neighbours, or when potentially rich energy resources in disputed territory are at stake. But over the last 40 years, China has peacefully delineated its borders with many of its neighbours. It has signed border agreements with Korea, Burma, Nepal, Mongolia, Pakistan and Afghanistan and has made significant progress in settling once disputed borders with India, Russia, Kazakhstan, Tajikistan and Kyrgyzstan. It has supported basic United Nations principles on the non-use of force, non-intervention in the domestic affairs of states and non-proliferation of weapons of mass destruction.

The relaxation of tension in bilateral relations between most countries in the region, especially between China, the United States, Russia and Japan, has been conducive to regional stability. The result, said Gareth Evans, was a 'tranquil environment and a mood of co-operation'. It contributed to a consensus that the time was ripe to formulate a Conference on Security Cooperation in the Asia-Pacific and develop other ideas designed to build confidence and transparency between once insecure and potentially hostile neighbours.[7] These favourable trends culminated in the

ASEAN Regional Forum in Bangkok in July 1994 where China participated alongside sixteen other Asia-Pacific countries and the European
Union to develop mechanisms designed to enhance trust, transparency
and co-operation in regional security.

Yet, with no easily identifiable enemy, some analysts are still casting
around for a new source of threat and instability to fit a Cold War-based
strategic framework that has little relevance to Pacific Asia in the 1990s.
For them, China is the logical candidate to fill a so-called power vacuum
left by the collapse of the Soviet Union and the reduction of forward-
deployed United States forces in the Pacific. China is seen to be the one
power with the potential to contend with the United States for regional
leadership in Asia in the twenty-first century.[8]

The rationale for this view of China is often expressed in the following
terms: China is a rising power and it is starting to stir. It is a large country,
and large countries, it is claimed, are inevitably ambitious, outward looking and intent on increasing their power and influence. Worse, China's
strategic circumstances have never been more favourable. It is unchallenged by any other major power: the Japanese were defeated in World
War II and renounced their claims to Taiwan. The French withdrew from
Indochina in 1954. The British and the Portugese are about to surrender
Hong Kong and Macao. The United States withdrew from Indochina in
1975, deferred to China over Taiwan after 1979 and later withdrew from
the Philippines. The Soviet Union effectively withdrew from Indochina in
the mid-1980s. China is thus more secure from external threats than at any
other time in perhaps two centuries.[9] In a word, China is uncontained. It
is continuing to modernise its nuclear and conventional forces, despite the
collapse of its former enemy, the Soviet Union. China, furthermore, has
what is claimed by some observers to be the fastest growing defence
budget in the region.[10] Further, China's defence doctrine has shifted away
from fighting a people's war to developing a mobile rapid reaction force.
It is expanding its naval capabilities with a new class of destroyers and
frigates. It is training marine and airborne forces in amphibious landings.
At the same time, China's acquisition of long-range Su-27 fighter aircraft
and Il-76 transport aircraft; its interest in inflight refuelling technology,
Kilo-class submarines, aircraft carriers and other military technologies are
seen as 'particularly menacing' because they give the PLA improved
mobility, greater lift and longer reach. These trends and what is perceived
to be a heavy handed approach to territorial issues in the South China Sea
are seen as evidence of a Chinese quest for regional dominance.[11] Confirmation might be found in China's construction of an airstrip and berthing
facilities on Woody Island in the Paracels and, further south, facilities for
'fishermen' on Mischief Reef in the Spratly Islands inside the Philippines'
exclusive economic zone. These facilities can be seen as stepping stones
that enable China to reach almost anywhere in the South China Sea.
Indeed, John Garver suggests that an overpopulated China is embarked
on a 'slow march south' into the South China Sea to satisfy its need for
energy resources.[12]

It is natural to cast China as an assertive and destabilising force in the Pacific Asia region. Its history, cultural spread, great size and central location give it a strategic overhang unmatched by other regional powers — if it remains intact and continues to grow at its present rate. India is too far away, Japan is too small, Russia is too weak and the United States seems to be increasingly a North American power. As Lee Kuan Yew observed, 'it's not possible to pretend that [China] is just another big player. This is the biggest player in the history of man.'[13] Such a greater China is seen to have unfulfilled, historically based ambitions to recover its ascendancy as the dominant power in the region.

What is greater China?

In a cultural sense, there is a greater China that includes the powerful overseas Chinese communities throughout Southeast Asia and Oceania. Economically, there is a greater China that includes Hong Kong, Macao and Taiwan. There is also a greater China that lays claim to Taiwan, the Senkakus in the East China Sea, most of the South China Sea and large chunks of land on the Sino-Indian border and the Russian Far East. Greater China is implicitly acknowledged by China's smaller neighbours, including South Korea, Taiwan, Thailand, Cambodia, Vietnam, Laos, Malaysia, Singapore, the Philippines, Burma and even Japan. While these states would like the United States to remain engaged in the affairs of the region as a counterbalance to China, they have chosen to treat China as it is perceived — the most important modernising phenomenon in East Asia.

China's quest to become a great China has its roots in poverty, insecurity and disunity. China took some time to find its way but in 1949, as Mao Zedong remarked in Tiananmen, China stood up. In 1964, China tested its first nuclear device. In 1971, it took up its position as a Permanent Member of the United Nations Security Council. More recent milestones were the economic reforms introduced by Deng Xiaoping in 1978[14] and his plans to quadruple Gross National Product (GNP) by the year 2000 and quadruple it again in the next twenty years, and the challenge of democracy that was suppressed in Beijing in June 1989.

Secure from external threats and preoccupied in satisfying the rising expectations of a relatively poor population, China's focus is on economic reform and development. In this area it has made impressive progress. According to the United Nations Development Program, China remains a very poor country in per capita terms, but it was one of the world's top ten performers over the period 1960–92 when measured in terms of human development indicators (longevity, literacy, knowledge and standard of living).[15]

China's rapid growth, raw materials, market potential, human capital and central location make it a natural hinterland and trading partner for Taiwan, South Korea, Japan, Singapore, the United States and other mem-

bers of the Asia-Pacific economic community. This in turn has helped provide new markets for the rest of the world. China is already the number
one export market for Hong Kong. China–Hong Kong is the number two
trading partner for Russia, number three for Singapore, Taiwan, Australia
and the United States, number six for South Korea, number five for
Canada and Russia, and number two for Japan.

But this greater China is the China that worries many European and
American security analysts. In looking at China, they tend to see a potential superpower poised to fill a so-called power vacuum. One could argue,
however, that there is no power vacuum in the Asia-Pacific for China to
fill.[16] Economically, the region is performing better than anywhere else in
the world. In the short term, there is an absence of immediate threats or
dangerous flashpoints.[17] Even the recent contretemps over Taiwan had its
uniquely Chinese limits. The ASEAN Regional Forum and the function of
APEC illustrate the progress that has been made towards a habit of co-
operation and dialogue even between China and Taiwan. Most countries
have relatively strong defence capabilities. Most (Japan, South Korea, Singapore, Malaysia, Indonesia, Thailand, the Philippines, Australia and,
arguably, Taiwan) retain ties of one form or another with the United States.
China, moreover, is very conscious that, for the forseeable future, the
United States will remain as the most powerful military force in the Asia-
Pacific region.

China is a central actor in the Asia-Pacific. But is it ruthless and expansionist? Is it determined to acquire control of all the islands in the South
China Sea? Has China's defence budget increased disproportionately in
the past few years and has it embarked on a major program of military
modernisation? Are nations in the region engaged in an arms buying spree
because they are worried about China's intentions?

China, whether greater or smaller, ought to be viewed in context. As
Paul Dibb suggested in looking at the insecurity of the former Soviet
Union, we should bear in mind China's history and geography when we
analyse its defence posture and defence expenditure.[18] China has long land
and sea borders and a long history. It has a deep sense of vulnerability to
attack from the north and from the sea to the east.

China also has many problems, not least the degradation of its environment, population pressure, rising expectations, infrastructural bottlenecks, political factionalism, the Deng succession, a crisis of legitimacy for
the Chinese Communist Party, the politics of corruption, regional disparities, a rising crime rate and the erosion of state authority.[19] Given these
considerations, it is by no means certain that the country will remain
intact. It may be premature, therefore, to talk about China as a great power
that can dominate the neighbouring region or project power and influence far from its physical borders.[20] The breakup of China, or at the very
least a weak government in Beijing, might unleash fissiparous tendencies
in China's outer regions, including Taiwan and Hong Kong. This could
trigger intervention by outside powers, such as Japan, the United States,

Britain and India and that in turn, would provoke a strong military response from the PLA. The possibilities are endless and that is why, of the two alternatives, a disintegrating China poses the greatest risk to regional and global security.

In other words, China's ability to provide for the welfare and security of a quarter of the world's population and its continued progress towards becoming a strong, well-governed state are vitally important for regional stability.

China's defence budget, size, income, population, weaponry and the like should also be placed in comparative context. Looking at Table 3.1, we can see that China's defence budget is less than that of ASEAN as a group. It is also less than that of Taiwan and is on a par with India's. It is a fraction of America's defence expenditure, whether you use the Chinese figures or inflate them several times using the PPP calculations.[21] As a percentage of GNP, China's military expenditure declined from 8.2 per cent in 1981 to 3.3 per cent in 1991, which is on a par with the ratio of most ASEAN states.[22] In renminbi terms, there were increases in Chinese defence expenditure (see Table 3.2) of 15 per cent in 1989–90, 12 per cent in 1990–91, 12.5 per cent in 1991–92/1992–93 and 20 per cent in 1994. By comparison, Thailand increased its defence budget by 50 per cent in the last four years, the Philippines by more than 43 per cent, Malaysia and Singapore by 100 per cent and Taiwan by 45 per cent.[23]

Table 3.1 China: A comparison

	China	Taiwan	India	Japan	Russia	USA	France	UK
Nuclear	Yes	?	?	No	Yes	Yes	Yes	Yes
Defence Budgetl ($US b)	7.5	9.2	8.0	34.0	133.7	289.2	34.9	41.2
Armed Forces (million)	3.0	0.360	1.26	0.25	2.7	1.9	0.43	0.29
Principal Surface Combatants	54	41	28	64	192	188	41	43
Carriers	nil	nil	2	nil	2	12	2	2
Submarines	46	4	15	17	250	110	17	21
SSBNs	1	nil	nil	nil	55	25	4	2
ICBMs	8	nil	nil	nil	1 400	1 000	nil	nil
IRBMs	Yes	?	Yes	nil	Yes	Yes	Yes	Yes
Combat Aircraft	4 970	486	674	440	3 700	3 485	808	466
Population (mil)	1 200	21.6	873	124	148	252	57	58
Land area 000 km2	9 597	36	3288	378	17 075	9 373	547	245
GDP $US b2	5 053	173	315	3362	na	5 674	1 212	1 018
GDP Growth 1980-90 Constant 1987 per cent)	9.81	8.32	5.67	4.11	n.a.	3.35	2.31	3.06
GDP/Capita 1990 Constant 1987 US$	328	6 003	371	22 821	n.a.	19 316	17 530	12 853

Notes:
1   Data for Russia and China are estimates. Data for all other countries are for 1992.
2   1991 for all countries except China, which is 1992.
3   The IMF's *World Economic Outlook*, May 1993, suggests China's GDP is closer to $1260 billion, using purchasing power parities. Greater China (China and Taiwan and Hong Kong) — US$674 billion.

Source: *World Bank Tables*, International Economic Data Base, the Australian National University, Canberra, for growth in GNP per capita. IISS, *Military Balance* , Brassey's for the Institute of International and Strategic Studies, London, various years for all other data.

Table 3.2 Trends in Chinese defence expenditure

	RMB mn constant 1990	US$ mn constant 1990	As a % of GDP
1981	27948	5845	3.5
1982	29392	6143	3.4
1983	29181	6100	3.1
1984	28328	5924	2.6
1985	27440	5738	2.2
1986	27722	5798	2.1
1987	26874	5617	1.9
1988	24684	5158	1.5
1989	26228	5485	1.6
1990	28970	6057	1.6
1991	30670	6353	1.6
1992	32918	6951	1.5
1993	42500	7378	1.4
1994	53000	8287	1.4

Sources: International Financial Statistics (Yearbook) 1992; PRC Government Finance Statistics (Yearbook) 1992, 1993, 1994.

Taking into account inflation rates in China of 10 per cent or more per annum, real growth in China's defence expenditure was less than 2 or 3 per cent per annum.[24] Indeed, according to the United States Arms Control and Disarmament Agency, in real terms there has been almost no increase in China's defence expenditure between 1981 and 1991.[25] Under-Secretary of Defense for Policy, Frank Wisner, said that China's defence spending had started from 'a relatively low base' and while it was being 'carefully watched', it was 'basically moderate' and the response among nations in Southeast Asia was also 'very moderate'.[26] Most of the increased expenditure in China has been spent on increased salaries and allowances and buying equipment for PLA units for an internal security role. The PLA, meanwhile, has often complained that it is being squeezed for funds.[27]

Table 3.3 Arms transfer agreements with the Third World, by supplier, 1984–92* (in millions of current US dollars)

	1984	1985	1986	1987	1988	1989	1990	1991	1992	Total 1984–91
United States	6 407	4 785	3 421	5 231	8 733	7 610	18 209	14 161	13 600	82 157
Soviet Union	21 300	17 100	24 800	20 400	12 500	11 500	11 200	5 000	1 300	125 100
France	6 500	1 500	1 300	3 200	1 300	3 800	3 100	400	3 800	24 900
United Kingdom	700	19 300	900	500	900	1 100	1 700	2 000	2 400	29 500
China	300	1 400	1 800	4 700	2 100	1 600	2 100	300	100	14 400
Germany	800	200	500	800	200	900	300	400	700	4 800
Italy	700	1 300	600	200	200	300	200	0	400	3 900

Source: US Government; and R.F. Grimmett, Trends in Government Arms Transfers to the Third World by Major Supplier 1984–1992, The Library of Congress, Washington, 1993.
* Based on US Department of Defense Price Deflator.

Reports that the PLA has access to large amounts of hard currency from foreign arms sales are exaggerated. The total amount earned by China in arms sales over the period 1984–91 was about $US14.4 billion (see Table 3.3).[28] Of this amount, 30 per cent of the proceeds would have been paid to the factories supplying the weapons and another 30–40 per cent would go to various State Council Ministries. Less than 30 per cent of the earnings from arms sales are returned to the PLA. However, assuming that all proceeds went to the PLA, it would mean an average addition to the PLA's defence budget over the period 1984–91 of US$1.8 billion per annum. This is a relatively modest sum, even if one added PLA earnings from extra-budgetary sources such as hotels, manufacturing enterprises, airline and shipping services and currency deals.

We might note from Table 3.1 that China has no aircraft carriers. It has a fraction of the number of ICBMs possessed by the United States and Russia. The number of operational, conventionally powered Chinese submarines has dropped by more than half, from over 100 in 1984 to around 47 in 1992, including one SSBN and five SSNs.[29] The number of China's principal surface combatants has increased marginally, from 52 in 1988 to 55 today. Of these, only the Luhu and the Jiangwei class are comparable to the modern warships in, for example, the Taiwanese navy. China has a limited air and sea lift capability and its marine force of about 10 000 is much less that Taiwan's 31 000 personnel.[30] Taiwan, in fact, has a greater amphibious lift capability and nearly as many surface combatants as China. While China's airforce may be the third largest in the world, it is 'essentially a defensive force equipped with obsolete aircraft'.[31] It does not yet have an operational air-to-air refuelling system.

In short, China's defence modernisation and its capabilities need to be kept in perspective. China has quantity but lacks quality, especially in submarines and aircraft. It is one of the weakest of the great powers and the least qualified to fill any so-called vacuum in Asia. United States defence officials believe China's PLA is bloated, unwieldy and ill-equipped for modern warfare. A Pentagon official said on 22 April 1993 that:

> China's 1950s vintage force of outmoded T-62 tanks, aging artillery and underpowered MiG-19 and MiG-21 fighters requires modernisation and this should not be misconstrued as hostile activity . . . Chinese purchases of Russia [equipment] . . . should not incite alarm . . . [because] it's a drop in the bucket compared to their aging force. So to say they've become a threatening military force is not true.[32]

China is improving its ability to project power beyond its immediate border areas and it is better able to defend itself than it was ten years ago. This does not, however, necessarily signal an intention to challenge the United States or destabilise the region. Furthermore, while China's capabilities are growing, we should not neglect to note, as the Chinese often do, that the defence capabilities of other countries are not standing still. The ASEAN countries, South Korea, Japan, Taiwan, Australia and Vietnam, are all modernising their air and naval forces. Vietnam, for example, is buying modern Su-27s from Russia and Malaysia is acquiring Russian

MiG-29s and US F-18s. In the South China Sea, China's limited ability to project air power and its weak shipborne air defences could leave it exposed and vulnerable in the event of a clash.[33]

To try to make up for its defence deficiencies, especially after seeing the methodical destruction of much of Iraq's Chinese-origin military equipment in the Gulf War, China bought 'fire sale' equipment from Russia, including 26 Su-27 long-range fighters. But even 126 Su-27s would seem relatively modest when compared to the 150 F-16s and the 60 Mirage 2000s being acquired by Taiwan, ASEAN's 100 or so F-16s, F-18s and MiG-29s and Japan's 160 F-15s.

As for the notion of an arms race, United States Under-Secretary of Defense for Policy, Frank Wisner, concluded that what was happening in the region was a modernisation process and there was 'no cause for alarm at this point'.[34] General Peter Gration, the former Australian CDF, dismissed alarmist claims about an arms race in the region.[35] He said that the expression 'arms race' to describe what was happening was misleading.[36] Australia should not, he said, feel threatened or alarmed by the greater military spending of nations in the region — Southeast Asia and the Western Pacific, after all, were amongst the most secure and stable areas in the world.[37]

There is, indeed, a fairly broad consensus within the region that the security environment of the Asia-Pacific is more stable and more secure than it has been for several decades, certainly compared to the 1950s, the 1960s and the 1970s. And if Asia is pacific, then China can claim some credit, not least for the contribution it has made in feeding a fifth of the world's population, improving their living standards and offering new markets to regional economies.

Elsewhere, relations between China and India, the two biggest powers in Asia, have made significant progress. They have reached agreement on measures to promote common security along their once tense border, including parity of border forces, transparency in troop movements and mutual force reductions.[38] China's relations with Russia have made even more progress, with agreement on the demarcation of most of the border, an enormous expansion of cross-border trade and economic co-operation and cuts to border force levels.[39] With Japan, the prospect is for a further strengthening of the relationship.[40]

Even China and Vietnam have improved their relations. The most recent talks on disputed land and sea borders between China and Vietnam produced positive results, according to Vietnamese and Chinese officials.[41] At the ASEAN Regional Forum in Bangkok in July 1995, China and Vietnam agreed to meet bilaterally to discuss their conflicting claims to islands in the South China Sea and to meanwhile exercise 'self-restraint'.[42]

Japan, India, Russia and Vietnam are watchful of China's progress, especially its defence modernisation, as China is of theirs. The smaller Asian countries also worry about an ambitious chauvinistic China. But all of them see a greater Chinese economy as presenting opportunities for trade and investment. In this more relaxed Asia-Pacific, there is a consensus amongst the countries in the region, including China, on the benefits to be obtained from establishing a multilateral regional security forum, and building on the habit of dialogue established in forums such as the ASEAN Regional Forum, APEC and Indonesia's South China Sea Workshops.

Most countries in the region are talking to each other; they have established informal channels for dialogue; they are increasingly interdependent with sub-regional economic zones in place or likely to be developed up and down the Western Pacific, particularly around China.

So why has China become a target of the West? Is it because China is simply large, communist and Chinese? Or is it that a greater China does not fit Western notions of world order?

One reason for our shivers of concern about a greater China is that the Soviet Union has collapsed. There is therefore little need for China in any form of strategic alliance. Yet at the same time we fear our lack of leverage over China. Meanwhile, China is making rapid economic progress. In our mind's eye, we have that Napoleonic image of China as an awakening Chinese dragon, a powerful, non-democratic, nuclear-armed, unified state with one of the largest economies in the world and what seems to be a huge defence budget. Too easily, we imagine over a billion Chinese, becoming more and more like the Chinese capitalist societies in Hong Kong, Taiwan and Singapore. This China we see as radiating power and influence throughout the Western Pacific, with an air base in the Paracels, aircraft carriers and shared interests with Taiwan in asserting Chinese sovereignty in the South China Sea.[43] This China is governed by a regime we see as one that disregards human rights, runs over students with tanks, exploits prison labour and won't consider independence for Tibet. It has a long-term perspective in nation building and often uses historical injustices as reference points in its foreign policy. It has extensive territorial claims. It is non-European, non-democratic and, avowedly, the last communist stronghold left in the world.

The West, stimulated by the Tiananmen affair, is demanding faster progress on political reform and human rights in China. The United States Congress has emphasised American ideological differences with China rather than the common strategic purpose that prevailed earlier. China has been described by some in the United States as 'a rogue elephant in the world community with no regard for international stability'.[44] It has been targeted by the United States Congress over its communism, its sales of missiles and chemicals to Arab countries, its allegedly unfair trade practices and its domestic human rights record. The futures of Hong Kong, Taiwan and Tibet are additional points of contention.[45]

There is no doubt that China has a public relations problem, especially in the United States, over human rights; and in Southeast Asia, over the way it has asserted claims to islands in the South China Sea.

China does not like negotiating over territory, such as Taiwan, that it regards as Chinese. Some in the PLA would argue that as the South China Sea islands are all Chinese, claimant states are simply using 'the China threat' argument as a way to negate China's sovereignty. So far, however, the Chinese Foreign Ministry retains the strongest voice in the conduct of Chinese foreign policy, whether on Taiwan or the South China Sea.[46]

In the meantime, we should not overlook the history of China's sovereignty in the South China Sea, where in the case of the Paracels, it has a relatively strong claim in international law.[47] China has, in fact, adopted a fairly pragmatic approach and has participated in all of the Indonesian-sponsored conferences on conflict management in the South China Sea with nine other Asian countries (Taiwan, Vietnam, the Philippines, Brunei, Malaysia, Indonesia, Singapore, Laos and Thailand). China's position on the South China Sea is that differences should be resolved through peaceful negotiations but if conditions for negotiations were not ripe, then the dispute should be shelved and joint development considered.[48]

On Taiwan, most countries acknowledge that island to be part of China and it is only when that principle is challenged, most recently by the US Congress, that tension and threats from Beijing arise. However, the last thing China wants to do is fan regional fears of a China threat. That sensitivity, and the reasons for it, should be borne in mind when we make forecasts about China and its neighbours. Equally, however, China may need to bear the same sensitivities in mind when it deals with issues that involve smaller neighbours or which challenge Western interests in human rights and the survival of Taiwan.

Notes

*   Adapted from an article reviously published in *Australian Journal of International Affairs*, vol. 48, no. 2, November 1994.

1   Lee Kuan Yew, quoted in 'A Sense of Insecurity', *Asiaweek*, 1 June 1994, pp. 24–26.

2   Paul Kennedy, *Preparing for the Twenty First Century*, Harper Collins, London, 1993, p. 190, suggests that, in the absence of technological breakthroughs, China may be stuck in a poverty trap indefinitely.

3   Discussed in Peter Van Ness 'The Paradox of Chinese State Security: The Transnational Challenge', unpublished paper, Australian National University, Canberra, September 1993.

4   Nicholas R. Lardy, 'China: Sustaining Development', in Gilbert Rozman et al. (eds), *Dismantling Communism: Common Causes and Regional Variations*, The Woodrow Wilson Center Press, Washington, 1992, pp. 205, 220.

5   Harry Harding, 'China at the Crossroads: Conservatism, Reform and Decay', *Adelphi Paper*, no. 275, 1992, pp. 36–48.

6   Australian Foreign Minister, Gareth Evans, speaking in Bangkok at the ASEAN Regional Forum, Australian Associated Press (AAP), 25 July 1994.

7   Desmond Ball, *The Council for Security Cooperation in the Asia Pacific*, Strategic and Defence Studies Centre, Australian National University,

Canberra, August 1993. William Tow, on the other hand, argues that without an effective mechanism for conflict resolution, regional turbulence is all too likely, mainly because of the contest for regional hegemony between China, Japan and other regional powers: William T. Tow, 'Reshaping Asian-Pacific Security', *Journal of East Asian Affairs*, vol. 8, no. 1, Winter/Spring 1994, p. 90.

[8] 'Excerpts from Pentagon's Plan: Prevent the Re-Emergence of a New Rival', *New York Times*, 8 March 1992, cited in Robert Jervis, 'International Primacy: Is the Game Worth the Candle?', *International Security*, vol. 17, no. 4, Spring 1993, pp. 52, 54.

[9] Yan Xuetong 'China's Security After the Cold War', *China Institute of Contemporary International Relations*, vol. 3, no. 5, May 1993, p. 1.

[10] See, for example, J.N. Mak, *ASEAN Defence Reorientation 1975–1992: The Dynamics of Modernisation and Structural Change*, Canberra Papers No. 103, Strategic and Defence Studies Centre, Research School of Pacific Studies, Australian National University, Canberra, 1993, pp. 45, 170.

[11] Michael T. Klare, 'The Next Great Arms Race' *Foreign Affairs*, vol. 72, no. 3, Summer 1993, pp. 136, 141.

[12] John Garver, 'China's Push Through the South China Sea: The Interaction of Bureaucratic and National Interests', *The China Quarterly*, no. 132, December 1992, p. 999.

[13] Lee Kuan Yew, quoted by Nicholas Kristof, 'China's Rise from Dinosaur to Dragon', *Australian*, 29 November 1993, p. 11. See also Nicholas D. Kristof, 'The Rise of China', *Foreign Affairs*, vol. 72, no. 5, November/December 1993, p. 59 and William H. Overholt, *China: The Next Economic Superpower*, Weidenfeld and Nicolson, London, 1993.

[14] When thinking about China as a threat, we should not overlook the fact that Deng Xiaoping's reforms released 800 million peasants from semiserf status and prevented what might otherwise have been a peasant revolt: Liu Binyan, 'The Long March from Mao: China's De-Communisation', *Current History*, September 1993, pp. 241, 242.

[15] *Human Development Report, 1994*, United Nations Development Program, Oxford University Press, London, 1994, pp. 94–96.

[16] See Gary Klintworth, 'Asia-Pacific: More Security, Less Uncertainty, New Opportunities', *Pacific Review*, vol. 5, no. 3, 1992, pp. 221–30.

[17] North Korea is often mentioned in the context of flashpoints but, arguably in that particular case, the problem — including North Korea's attempt to develop a nuclear equaliser — is one of an isolated state, with an obsolete ideology and a struggling economy, trying to come to grips with the reality of a rapidly changing neighbourhood. Indeed, the last thing that North Korea wants to do is provoke a confrontation with South Korea and the United States.

[18] Russia's strategic outlook is shaped by its history of successive invasions from the West and the East, the death of twenty million during the 'Great Patriotic War', a feeling of vulnerability that stems from the number of borders it has with other countries plus the fact that it has to defend the Far East as well as the European homelands: Paul Dibb, *The Soviet Union, the Incomplete Superpower*, Macmillan, London, 1986, pp. 7, 9, 21.

[19] See David Shambaugh, 'Losing Control: The Erosion of State Authority in China', *Current History*, September 1993, p. 253.

[20] See, for example, Robert Scalapino, 'China in the Late Leninist Era', *China Quarterly*, no. 136, 1993, pp. 949, 963; Gerald Segal, 'China Changes Shape', *Foreign Affairs*, vol. 73, no. 3, May/June 1994, pp. 43, 56; and Richard Hornik, 'Bursting China's Bubble', *Foreign Affairs*, vol. 73, no. 3, May/June 1994, p. 28.

[21] The World Bank questioned the accuracy of ppp calculations and concluded that currently there is no reliable ppp estimate of China's GDP: *China's GNP Per Capita*, Report No. 13580-CHA, World Bank, Washington, 15 December 1994, p. v.

[22] US Arms Control and Disarmament Agency, *World Military Expenditures and Arms Transfers 1991–1992*, US Government Printing Office, Washington, 1994, p. 58.

[23] Bilveer Singh, 'Arms Buildup in Southeast Asia not a Race', *Straits Times*, 20 March 1993 and IISS, *Military Balance*, 1988–89 and 1992–93 editions.

[24] Shunji Taoka, 'A Shrinking Tiger', *Bulletin/Newsweek*, 16 November 1993, p. 69.

[25] *World Military Expenditures and Arms Transfers 1991–1992*, p. 58.

[26] US Under Secretary of Defense for Policy, Frank Wisner, press conference, US Embassy, Tokyo, 2 August 1993, *USIS Wireless File*, 4 August 1993.

[27] Interview, Major General Pan Zhenqiang, National Defence University, Beijing, 21 July 1995.

[28] China's arms sales are fairly modest compared with the United States and the former Soviet Union. China's problem, however, is that it is alleged to have sold nuclear, missile and chemical weapons technology to countries in disfavour in the West such as Iraq, Iran, Pakistan, Algeria and Syria. For an analysis leading to the conclusion that Chinese arms sales 'threaten US interests' and indicate 'China's long term aspirations to become a more dominant and influential regional and continental power', see R. Bates Gill, *The Challenge of Chinese Arms Proliferation: US Policy for the 1990s*, Strategic Studies Institute, US Army War College, 1993.

[29] IISS, *Military Balance*, London, 1984–85 and 1992–93 editions; and *Jane's Fighting Ships*, Jane's Information Group, Surrey, 1993 edition.

[30] *Weyers Rotten Taschenbuch (Warships of the World, Warship Documentation)*, Bernard and Graefe, Federal Republic of Germany, 1990/91, pp. 81, 83; and IISS, *Military Balance*, London, 1993–94, p. 169.

[31] Harlan W. Jencks, *Some Political and Military Implications of Soviet Warplane Sales to the PRC*, SCPS Papers no. 6, National Sun Yat-Sen University, Kaohsiung, Taiwan, April 1991, p. 1.

[32] Barbara Opall, 'US, Allies Fear Chinese Buildup', *Defense News*, 26 April–2 May 1993, p. 1.

[33] Michael G. Gallagher, 'China's Illusory Threat to the South China Sea', *International Security*, vol. 19, no. 1, Summer 1994, pp. 169, 179.

[34] Wisner, press conference, USIS Wireless File, 4 August 1993.

[35] Chief of Defence Force, General Peter Gration, interview, *Australian*, 17–18 April 1993.

[36] ibid.

[37] ibid.

[38] See Gary Klintworth, *The Practice of Common Security: China's Borders with Russia and India*, Working Paper No. 1993/1, Department of International Relations, Research School of Pacific Studies, Australian National University, Canberra, January 1993.

[39] ibid.

[40] According to Michael Oksenberg, President of the East-West Centre, Honolulu, quoted in *USIS Wireless File*, 23 September 1993.

[41] BBC, Summary of World Broadcasts, FE/1780 G/2, 31 August 1993.

[42] *The Nation*, Bangkok, 23 July 1994.

[43] There is a possibility of joint mainland–Taiwanese exploration for offshore oil in the East and South China Sea, provided the mainland accepts Taiwan as an equal partner: *China Post*, 5 August 1993.

[44] United States Senator Joseph Biden, speech condemning China's arms sales to Middle East countries, reported in *South China Morning Post*, 16 May 1991.

[45] In September 1993, for example, the United States Senate Foreign Relations Committee proposed a draft bill that described Tibet as 'an occupied sovereign country and that its true representatives are the Dalai Lama and the Tibetan Government-in-Exile': Senate bill, Washington, *USIS Wireless File*, 20 September 1993.

[46] There have been indications of a growing PLA influence in the conduct of Chinese foreign policy, for example, in Sino-United States relations and on policy towards North Korea, the Spratly Islands, Burma and arms sales: Wo-Lap Lam, 'Senior Generals Involved in Foreign Affairs', *South China Morning Post*, 25 June 1994, pp. 40–41. A similar point is made by You Ji, 'Developments in Maritime Forces — China', in Dick

Sherwood (ed.), *Maritime Power in the China Seas: Capabilities and Rationale*, Australian Defence Studies Centre, Australian Defence Force Academy, Canberra, 1994, pp. 85, 103–4.

[47] Greg Austin, 'Island Claims of the PRC', unpublished Master's thesis, Australian National University, Canberra, 1985.

[48] Li Peng said China wanted a peaceful solution to the Spratlys issue by proposing joint development while shelving the sovereignty issues: *Far Eastern Economic Review*, 30 August 1990. Foreign Minister Qian Qichen said China would settle border disputes through 'the process of patient negotiations in a friendly atmosphere' and if 'an agreement cannot be reached in a short period of time, China was willing to put the contradiction aside for the time being' and, in the case of the Nanshas, China would consider 'joint exploitation under conditions of Chinese sovereignty': *Xinhua*, Beijing, 28 March 1991. In Bangkok on 21 July 1994, Qian reaffirmed that China was 'all along opposed to the use of force' and subscribed to the 1992 ASEAN declaration that urged countries with claims to the Spratlys to resolve the issue through peaceful negotiations: *AAP*, 22 July 1994

4 Australia and Japan in the Post-Cold War World: The Special and the Uncertain

Richard Leaver

Introduction

Since the study of strategy aims to illuminate the role of force in human affairs, most strategists slip all too easily and quickly into a preoccupation with the material processes and problems that bear immediately upon the evolution and disposition of military forces. My approach shies away from this normal predisposition in order to explore a cue that is implicit in the title of this volume. I am primarily concerned with questions of outlook — or, to be more specific, the categories through which middle powers like Australia construct their posture towards Japan and the region. I attempt no elaborate justification for this departure from convention other than to note that the policy changes of the last decade in Australia's relationship with 'Asia' are now so monotonously described by Canberra's official caste as 'a revolution' that a focus on the categories that constitute this upheaval seems unusually warranted.

My point of departure along this little-used fork is derived from a wide-ranging argument put down on the eve of that revolution by Gregory Clark.[1] His general concerns were with the bureaucratic debates that marked Australia's Vietnam experience, and in particular with the distinctive traits in the Australian theory and practice of anti-communism that were, as he wrote, entering their adumbral phase. As he saw it, Australian practice had consistently departed from the norm set by our great and powerful American ally in not being 'well-rounded' and 'ideological' so much as the product of an ethos of 'exaggerated particularism' — 'the propensity to judge the world exclusively on the basis of one's personal or particular situation'. The specific manifestation of particularism which caught Clark's eye was the long list of policy reversals — frequently unexplained, even long after the event — which marked the record of Australian regional policy: over China, over Taiwan and over Singapore. Particularism, Clark argued, generated a regional policy that was 'childish and inconsistent'.[2]

In this quite different context, there are two good reasons for remembering Clark's argument. First, in his closing paragraphs, he began to grapple with some hypotheses that might explain the dominance of particularism in Australian policy. He argued that the tyrannies of distance and small size that are the customary beasts of explanatory burden for Australian foreign policy lacked the necessary capacity, since New Zealand had more of these but less of the particularism in question. Looking more widely for useful analogies, the only parallel he found was Japan, where a particularist ethic produced the same combination of domestic pragmatism and international inconsistency — 'the ugly refusal to accept moral guilt or take responsibility for past mistakes'.

The second reason concerns the broader fields into which this analogy might be extended. In passing, Clark observed another form in which particularism commonly became manifest, and had his focus been on anything other than *regional* policy, he might have seen this as its dominant form of representation. The primacy of personalised knowledge dovetails neatly into the pride of place which the American alliance has hitherto enjoyed in Australian foreign policy — an argument, he would quickly have observed, that is equally true for postwar Japan. For both countries, elite images of and attitudes towards the world at large have traditionally been received through the lens of their bilateral relationship with Washington, and their domestic literatures on foreign policy both revolve around 'the special relationship' which governments in Canberra and Tokyo usually claim to enjoy with the United States.

If this simple extension of Clark's analogy is tenable, then it begs a pertinent supplementary question, namely, what long-run pattern might one expect to find in Australian–Japanese relations in a post-Cold War context?

Answers do not come as easily as first principles might suggest. One of the first working rules of *realpolitik* stipulates that 'the friend of a friend is also a friend'. If that were universally true, then the common status of Japan and Australia as America's Pacific allies should imbue their own bilateral relationship with a high degree of accord. But what is most notable about this principle of psychic consonance is that it simply does not capture the most revealing nuances that have always been present in the Australia–Japan relationship, even when the Cold War flourished. For while there is a long history — at least in Australia — of thinking about Japan as 'a special relationship', there is an equally extensive convention of acknowledging the excessive weight which trade issues bear within the overall matrix of their interaction[3] — an acknowledgment which, in turn, has underpinned a more or less constant search by Canberra for new means to produce a better semblance of overall balance.[4]

Australia's Japan has, therefore, undoubtedly been 'special', but this never-ending search for a broader foundation suggests a deep-seated fear that a one-dimensional commercial attachment may be unnatural and unhealthy in the long run. Given also that 'uncertainty' is now a common (if embarrassingly imprecise) cause for governmental concern throughout the Asia-Pacific region, it seems legitimate to wonder how confident Canberra can really claim to be about the future of its 'special relationship' with Tokyo when, even at the best of times, that relationship has seemed off-balance.

Couched in this way, the question now before us concerns whether the post-Cold War era will provide conditions conducive to the full matura-tion or the demise of this already very peculiar 'special relationship'.

Obsolescence and prescience

One might hope that documents like the Defence Department's *Australia's Strategic Planning in the 1990s* or *Strategic Review 1993*, since they are osten-sibly concerned with the forces that constitute the domain of strategic choice, would provide guidelines for thinking about these pertinent kinds of long-range issues. However, there are only a few short paragraphs covering Japan, and they exemplify the strategist's partiality for current issues so lamented by Buzan: 'an intense short-term policy orientation closely tied to the agenda of government decision-making on defence and military issues'.[5]

That failure provides good grounds for critical review of both docu-ments. But we are, in fact, given the cheap option, certainly in the case of *Australia's Strategic Planning in the 1990s*, of endorsing the minister's own criticism — that the end of the Cold War has made it prematurely obsolete. There are, however, a number of reasons for treating this 'official criticism' with scepticism. First, there are many older, even more obsolete Strategic Reviews that have yet to see the light of day; the fact that this one has been belatedly released suggests at least a minimal ability to live with what was put down some years ago. Second, it should not be forgotten that in the period of time when Australia's Strategic Planning in the 1990s was being formulated — in and around the collapse of the Berlin Wall — the Depart-ment of Foreign Affairs and Trade was able to promptly manufacture a Ministerial Statement on regional security policy which claimed immedi-ate relevance for the post-Cold War era that was just beginning to emerge.[6] It seems logical to presume that *Australia's Strategic Planning in the 1990s* signified a desire by Defence to realise some political value from it — a not insubstantial payoff, given Defence's ongoing battle with Foreign Affairs and Trade for the 'hearts and minds' of the body politic, and hence pri-macy over the content of 'external policy'.[7]

Third, and most importantly, there is little in the treatment of Japan that has proven sensationally wrong. It is noted that Japan, the world's third largest defence spender, is defensively and reactively oriented; that it is still activated by a perception of a Russian threat; that its foreign aid program has strategic value; that it desires to acquire legitimacy for its defence program by keeping the United States engaged in the East Asian region; and that it is likely to seek wider roles only under peacekeeping mandates from the United Nations. Rapid change in any direction is judged unlikely. Indeed, the last three years have seen Tokyo continue to drag the Western chain on the 'normalisation' of relations with the sequence of post-Soviet successor states; quantitative and qualitative trends in its pattern of defence spending have not shifted notably; and the Gulf War did indeed fortuitously clear a slender passage through the Diet for the Peacekeeping Organisation (PKO) Bill which, in turn, facilitated unprecedented (if highly circumscribed and qualified) contributions of Japanese human resources to United Nations peacekeeping. This, in turn, made possible the first-ever reciprocal visits by top Japanese and Australian defence officials, including relevant ministers — an exchange politically unthinkable earlier in the reign of Labor.

In addition, Japanese governments have strongly supported the institutional development of an open-ended Australian plan for a process of Asia Pacific Economic Cooperation (APEC) and some beginnings at the larger task of opening its internal agricultural markets were made in the final stages of the Uruguay Round. Hence, by staying on course while all about it has changed — which is precisely what the otherwise anodyne paragraphs of *Australia's Strategic Planning in the 1990s* and *Strategic Review 1993* hoped for — the general sense of satisfaction with Japanese external policies has been immeasurably boosted in Canberra.

At first sight, therefore, the obsolescence of these judgments about Japan is not at all easy to spot. But what has changed most — and dramatically so — is the overall sense of approval with which the current Australian government would now give to post-Cold War Japanese external policy. Since we can be extraordinarily confident that these public documents have been pruned of what are euphemistically known as 'frank assessments', it is all the more notable that they nonetheless found it unobjectionable to speak about the 'substantial sensitivities' which surround Australia's bilateral defence relationship with Japan, and of the need for 'careful handling' which builds, 'in a measured way', out of existing functional co-operation. Australians need 'to come to terms with the new strategic reality which Japan represents' — that is, one of the key determinants of the Asia-Pacific security environment in coming years. These admittedly veiled references about Japan avoid allusions to the 'domestic sensitivities' which have impinged upon past defence options, or such hopes that the level of public understanding about 'new realities' needs to be raised.

The novelty of these allusions about past sensitivities and hopes for a higher level of public understanding becomes apparent when we recall Defence's position on Japan less than a decade ago. For at the height of the 'second' Cold War, the then-current Strategic Basis is alleged to have said that:

Australia should not encourage the extension of Japanese defence activity into our region. There is a risk of displacement, rather than supplementation, of the US military presence there.[8]

These kinds of fears about displacement are totally absent from *Australia's Strategic Planning in the 1990s* and *Strategic Review 1993*. And since — as we will shortly see — even quiet reminders about past 'domestic sensitivities' are no longer given any prominence by Defence, the drift in Australian strategic thinking towards a more relaxed stance on Japan is plain. Indeed, in *Strategic Review 1993*, Defence notes that Japan is 'already interested in a more active regional security role' and recommends that Australia should 'expand the modest level of its defence contact with Japan'.

This new air of Defence relaxedness is well captured in the Department's submission to the 1993 inquiry by the Senate Standing Committee on Foreign Affairs, Defence and Trade into Japan's defence and security policies. On the one hand, Defence's submission[9] is in no way guilty of taking a starry-eyed gaze into post-Cold War 'deep peace'. It sees real potential for future dangers of a relatively unique kind that were unthinkable in the Northeast Asian region during the Cold War — questions about the future composition of governments in Russia, Korea and China are all admitted to pose difficult issues for regional security. But if the region as a whole appears unstable in novel ways, then what is most interesting is that the sources of this novelty — namely, the question marks that hang over the domestic basis for strategic policy — do not seem to apply to Japan, and consequently do not generate any new doubts about its future directions. In a region where Defence sees processes of domestic reorientation driving the strategic agenda, Japan stands as the great exception.

The final act of self-assurance comes with the submission's analysis of regional sensitivities to the projected real increases in Japanese defence spending which it foresees. For the most part, the submission speaks with a high degree of certainty about Japan's future strategic orientation as a continuation of the past, willingly basing its projections on declaratory positions that stretch back two decades or more, and finding much solace in the projected long life of the constitutional and political restraints upon revanchism. Hence, while almost all other governments within the East and Southeast region are said to be sensitive to this issue, any Australian reservations enter only in the concluding sentence, almost as an afterthought.

Two provisional conclusions are therefore prompted by this more recent submission. The first directly concerns the question of outlook. For, while Japan's strategic orientation and posture may not have changed much, there has clearly been a quiet but dramatic change in the official Australian attitude to it. What, then, can be said about the forces that have shifted our appreciation of Japan at a time when Tokyo has allegedly stood still?

The second interim conclusion concerns the groundswell of domestic changes which this most recent Defence argument rightly identifies as a major cause of strategic uncertainty in Northeast Asia. Since Japan has ultimately not proven immune to these forces — four decades of LDP rule came to an abrupt end soon after Defence's submission was made — the argument prompts unasked questions about *which* 'Japan' might tomorrow be at the centre of Australian and regional defence analyses.

A focus on these two issues guides the balance of this chapter. I attempt to arrive at some contingent answers by investigating the forces which have traditionally animated the long history of defence aversion between Canberra and Tokyo, and by displaying some circumspection about the economic affinities that have more recently led the bilateral relationship into a heady new era of comity.

The changing sources of strategic sensitivity

As is well known, the original foundation of the Australian sensitivity to questions of Japanese defence lay in the memories of Japan's Pacific War. During the immediate postwar years, the political power of the lived experiences of Australian ex-servicemen and women was such that Australian governments willingly became some of the last defenders of 'the Spartan peace' with Japan even as Cold War logic pushed America's Japan policy towards a 'reverse course'. The speed of that American *volte face*, coupled with an occupation style that was always heavily unilateral, left the American preference for a regional alliance system in the western Pacific stranded in the waters of political impossibility; neither the Japanese, nor Australian, nor any regional government supported an extra-national role for Japan's defence forces, and most were suspicious of the limited SDF structure that came into being.

But if historical memories were the only cause of aversion in the Australia–Japan defence relationship, then one might expect that the passage of time would quite naturally open the door on both sides to a more fully rounded relationship — and all the more so, given the spectacular growth of Australia–Japan trade from the early 1960s. But although Sissons claimed to detect a waning in the direct power of wartime memories by the late 1960s,[10] Australia and Japan nonetheless remained, as Hedley Bull once put it, 'allies at second remove'.[11] Even those who advocated the application of American pressure to forge Japan and the ANZUS framework into a more comprehensive alliance system were compelled to acknowledge the strength of 'the insularity' which kept these 'friends of friends' at a safe arm's length.[12] The long life of defence sensitivity therefore seems to require further explanation than arguments about direct wartime experience can alone provide.

One source of additional explanation lies in the slow drift of Australian policy towards active engagement with its immediate region. These diplomatic efforts — first targeted at the Association of Southeast Asian Nations (ASEAN) in the 1970s, but gradually expanded to 'Asia' as a whole through the next decade — brought Australian policy into contact with, and under the influence of, a more resilient strain of anti-Japanese animosity grounded in the experience of actual occupation rather than mere 'threat'. In addition, ASEAN's contemporary economic relationship with Japan was, in the early 1970s, subject to a level of political questioning not evident in Australia. Though the heady period of Tanaka riots soon abated, these generic tensions were displaced to a slowly smouldering resentment at the trade surpluses which Japan normally runs with the Southeast Asian region. Insofar as Australian governments did not share this commercial fate, they failed to appreciate the indignation it continues to generate amongst those with whom they mingle in regional forums.

What may be a more potent explanation for lingering defence sensitivities can be derived from the institutionalised pattern of behaviour associated with the international politics of the Pacific. In the aftermath of the initial postwar moves described above, America's Pacific alliance system — colloquially known as the 'hub and spokes' model — was made from a network of bilateral defence treaties. What little multilateral content there was in this order of things — most notably, in the South East Asia Treaty Organisation (SEATO) — was weak in coverage and frequently ignored in practice; substantive decision-making for the Vietnam War, for example, was routed around rather than through SEATO, with its more enthusiastic members reduced to the subsidiary role of political supporters.

The practice of containment in the Pacific was therefore expressed in a unique way, for it implied both the protection of Japan against communist expansion and the protection of the region from Japanese expansion.[13] Although the same double-sided problem also marked the postwar management of Germany's relations with its neighbours, the critical point is that it was solved in that theatre by binding American power to regional, rather than bilateral, practices. The most significant implication of this difference is that the 'hub and spokes' structure brought with it a pervasive conservative bias. It tended, on the one hand, to preserve American power *vis-à-vis* each and every one of its Pacific allies, but at the cost of ossifying the historical animosities that lay between them. And insofar as American power became committed, from the early 1970s onwards, to the task of pushing up the level of Japanese defence spending as an offset to their trade imbalance, it rekindled regional worries about the long-run purpose to which Japan's increased defence capability might ultimately be committed. In the final closing of the circle, the solution to that pervasive regional fear has seen those allies turn once more to the United States for protection of the regional order. Ruggie is therefore quite right to observe that it is precisely the recursive pattern of behaviour associated with the bilateral structure of Pacific politics which now constitutes the critical impediment to present-day hopes for a new regional multilateralism.[14]

All of these issues have a particular resonance in the history of Australia's Japan policy. When the ANZUS 'spoke' of the Pacific wheel was forged, protection from Japan was a widely understood, if implicit, Australian objective. More importantly, the 'special relationship' that both

Canberra and Tokyo developed with Washington was for each the privileged conduit for defence co-operation, albeit in radically different ways. For Canberra, the freedoms that Tokyo obtained through its special status in Washington — an explicit, non-reciprocal American commitment to the defence of Japan, and the consequent ability to concentrate domestic energies upon the singular goal of economic growth — were a source of envy precisely because they remained so much in doubt throughout the Cold War, and the lopsided character of their bilateral relationship with Japan was shaped by the primary fealties that both allies gave in different ways to Washington. Consequently, the dramatic expansion of Australia's commercial relationship with Japan through the 1960s did not function as the thin edge of a broader politico-strategic wedge, because that dimension was, by definition, off limits.[15] When consecutive Australian governments later sought to develop wider linkages to complement this primary economic relationship, they acknowledged this demarcation by committing their energies to other domains where priorities were more in conformity — the cultural and social, rather than the political and military.

Finally, and in the light of the above comments, it should be noted that the persistence (until recent times) of 'defence sensitivity' about Japan owes something to the process of Australian defence reform of which documents like *Australia's Strategic Planning in the 1990s* and *Strategic Review 1993* are a part, for a reaffirmation of the past has tended to become endemic to the domestic legitimation of that process. As I have explained elsewhere, the defence reform process which commenced with the Dibb Report had an initial focus upon the concept of 'strategic denial'.[16] Coming from a context where an 'expeditionary mentality' had traditionally been at the centre of defence, that objective was a quite radical disjuncture from past practice. Not surprisingly, it was therefore difficult to sell both within the military and the broader polity. In the White Paper that followed Dibb, the Labor government therefore sought to legitimate the changes in force structure recommended by Dibb in a different way — by reference to the more complex (and, by implication, more dangerous) regional order that was coming into being.

The origins of this alleged 'complexity' had nothing to do with the end of the Cold War, for all of this occurred well before the Berlin Wall came down. By the government's account, 'complexity' could be traced back to the Nixon Doctrine where a slackening in the sinews of superpower rule — and, by implication, greater room for manoeuvre by 'middle powers' — were implicitly acknowledged. Although the Australian government subsequently sought to develop the positive side of this room for manoeuvre with its doctrine of 'middle power internationalism' (conveniently summarised by Nossal),[17] the argument simultaneously countenanced a gloomy possibility: that middle powers might act as bulls in the proverbial China shop. In a nagging kind of way, the arguments which justified the Australian move to 'self-reliance within alliance' posed uncomfortable questions about the future trajectories of non-WASP middle powers.

Paradoxically, therefore, Labor's attempts to contract the geographical scope of its foreign and defence policies have concurrently enhanced the salience of arguments about the future possibility of regionally based middle power threats to its preferred order of things — a systemic threat which Canberra saw dramatically confirmed in the Kuwait crisis.[18] And, although Australian defence planners have eschewed the naming of threats, it has not been difficult to see the shadows of India, China and Japan lurking in their sub-texts around the edges of 'Australia's own region'. Hence, while it is now certain that Japan has moved down that threat register (just as it is equally clear that China has moved up it), the most important thing may well be that the lineage from which *Australia's Strategic Planning in the 1990s* came will continue to give pride of place to precisely those arguments about 'the more uncertain, more dangerous world' which, in turn, will tend to regenerate covert threat lists of this kind.

A new economic harmony?

As noted above, Australian governments have, over a period of decades, tried valiantly (if unsuccessfully) to build a broader political raft beneath their heady bilateral commercial relationship with Japan and the healthy trade surplus which it continues to generate in Australia's favour. That failure should not be entirely surprising to those who pursued the task, since many of them would agree that modern Japan is indeed the archetype of 'a new kind of world power'[19] that Rosecrance has dubbed 'the trading state':[20] if that is indeed so, then an old-fashioned search for 'balance' simply does not belong in the same historical time-frame. However, what Canberra manifestly failed to achieve by its own direct efforts, it now thinks it has accomplished indirectly by promoting the process of Asia Pacific Economic Co-operation — a success that, in its turn, reinforces Canberra's new-found optimism about Japan.

At its highest, APEC appears to offers a possibility for realising a vision of Pacific economic integration that was frustrated during the Cold War period. Though the preferred American design for the economic prosperity of postwar Japan sought its integration into the markets of Southeast Asia, progress along this 'southern' axis was slow in coming; what initially rescued Japan from the vicious circle of recession and balance of payments crisis was the expansion of its economic relationship with the United States — initially for military procurement, and then for access to the world's most developed and extensive market.[21] Consequently, for at least the next two decades, the rate at which Japan was economically drawn into the East Asian rimlands lagged behind its high level of dependence on the American market. When taken in conjunction with the political frustration of Japanese trade with the Chinese mainland, this postwar reorientation of commercial geography reminds us that Ruggie's theme of Pacific bilateralism applies with equal force to the economic domain.

Australia has always stood as a notable, but partial, exception to this rule. Being one of the first governments to respond to the American campaign to accord General Agreement on Tariffs and Trade (GATT) status to Japan,[22] and having the full range of industrial raw materials required for Japan's postwar reindustrialisation, the Australia–Japan commercial relationship developed at a much faster rate than the regional economy as a whole. Not surprisingly, nascent ideas about a political framework for the regional economy tended to find their first expressions in the two countries where the intensity of economic exchange was greatest.[23]

APEC conforms to this rule. Beginning in 1989, the initial moves towards APEC came at a time when the Bush administration had put in place the instruments for implementing trade sanctions against Japan, and these moves seemed to build a degree of political confidence in the desirability of multilateral trade outcomes that averted the full implementation of those sanctioning powers. Thereafter, the APEC process developed both by inheriting the quiet work schedule cultivated within the Pacific Economic Cooperation Council (PECC) through the previous decade, and by geographically expanding the scope of its membership across some tricky political cleavages. The Seattle summit of December 1993, which brought together Asia-Pacific heads of state on the eve of the conclusion of the Uruguay Round, seemed to vindicate Canberra's heavy investment in promoting and nurturing APEC.

In the aftermath of this summit and the eventual conclusion of the Uruguay Round, the Keating government appears to obtain a high degree of political comfort from two particular economic arguments. The first emphasises the high degree of commercial interdependence now in place across the Asia-Pacific region, pointing out that this at least matches the degree of economic integration inside the European Union. The second argument celebrates, *contra* Europe, the role of 'market forces' rather than inter-governmental agreements as the engine of this increasingly integrated regional economic environment. By extension, these two arguments collectively suggest that nineteenth century Cobdenite visions of 'peace through trade' might yet be realised within the Asia-Pacific community.[24]

Whether these twin pillars of the Australian understanding of Pacific economic dynamics will prove capable of bearing the political load placed upon them is another question. Arguments about the intensity of regional economic interdependence are, for instance, easily misconstrued. Asia-Pacific trade interdependence does indeed match the European benchmark if we define the region to include both the western and eastern rims, but the degree of trade interdependence along the western Pacific rim alone is well below that standard. While it is geographically tautological to define the Pacific in its broadest sense, the political difficulty with this inclusive definition is that much of the trade which flows between the two Pacific rims is not in the least politically benign, let alone productive of a higher kind of unity.

As the most recent American exercise in brinkmanship with trade sanctions as a tool for managing the Japanese trade surplus suggests, it is still too early to say with confidence that this kind of conflict is well behind us. Indeed, there are good reasons for suspecting that it may be the shape of the future. If the necessity for alliance management did indeed function as a strategic 'cap' on intra-allied trade disputes, then the end of the Cold War may provide both the conditions and the political will conducive to a less restrained exercise of American market power.

That problem, furthermore, may have begun historically with Japan, but it certainly does not end there, for one of the more important recent shifts in the American political landscape has been the increased willingness of the liberal establishment to live with precisely this kind of 'special treatment' of its Asian traders. Hence, over recent times, China and most East Asian Newly Industrialising Countries (NICs) have also been asked to satisfy similar American-made tests of 'fairness'. Evidently Canberra's beliefs in the political payoff from a sound regional and multilateral trading framework do not have the same political clout in Washington.

A focus on this shift in American opinion leads to a questioning of Canberra's second foundational belief in the virtues of 'market leadership'. As the belated development of APEC undoubtedly testifies, Asian-Pacific economic integration has unfolded well in advance of formal inter-governmental agreements of the European kind (as expressed in the Treaties of Rome and Maastricht). However, a political process much more insidious than guidance through formal treaties — to wit, the self-seeking market interventions of national governments — has had a profound impact on the form of Asia-Pacific economic integration that we now witness.

That proposition has always been true inside East Asia, where the morphology of state policy has historically been central in forging the chain of 'growth miracles'. Perhaps more importantly, it is now increasingly true for North America itself, where it is precisely the increased incidence of unbalanced trans-Pacific trade that bears primary responsibility for shifting the centre of gravity of American opinion in favour of greater 'management' of its commercial relations with East Asia.[25]

The risk for Canberra is that its high investment in the idea of market leadership will totally occlude its critical faculties. The dominant Australian fashion has for some time interpreted East Asia's economic miracles in terms of small government, high savings ratios and outward commercial orientation,with state guidance correctly predicting the choices which a free market would, in any case, have yielded. Although the government does not exactly turn a blind eye to the repeated American efforts to prise open the Japanese market, those tactics attract their most adverse comment when they are perceived as impinging upon Australia's current or prospective market share in Japan. About the stated American objective of a more open Japanese market there is little dispute.

The primary victim in this mix of predispositions and responses may be the government's own attachment to non-discriminatory principles as the proper foundation for the world economic order. One can make — as Ruggie has done[26] — a reasonably sophisticated argument that the objective of a more open Japanese market justifies virtually any means (up to and including the use of trade sanctions) intended to achieve it. However, as Winham has pointed out, the political danger lurking along this path will appear when American exporters feel confident that the threat of sanctions is the most effective way to expand their market opportunities, for then the domestic constituency for the process of multilateral trade negotiations tends, by default, to be captured by protectionist interests.[27] In that way, successive iterations of aggressive unilateralism are likely to corrode the political foundation for multilateralism at home as well as abroad.

With this consideration in mind, it should not be forgotten that, for 40 years, one of the basic working rules of the international economy has been that countries with trade deficits should shoulder the burden of economic adjustments necessary to correct for their own deficit. Now that the United States earns trade deficits, it conveniently forgets — at least for itself — a standard that it firmly triumphed when it once earned surpluses. Canberra's claim to be the local champion of multilateral righteousness would therefore be more convincing if it gave greater attention to this inversion of institutional principles occurring within these trans-Pacific trade disputes, and less to worrying about its self-interests in the Japanese market.

Conclusion

The thrust of the above argument is corrosive of specific predictions about the trajectory of individual relationships. We live for the foreseeable future in an epoch where long-repressed domestic agendas of 'systemic change' have come, somewhat unnervingly, to the fore. Unfortunately, there is very little in the dominant theoretical tradition that informs the study of International Relations — let alone the much narrower pursuits of Strategic Studies — that serves us well for dealing adequately with what Kratochwil has rightly called 'an embarrassment of changes'.[28] This admonition applies equally at the practical level, where many of the time-honoured alliance structures conceived for the prosecution of containment have been opened to question, and expectations of allied harmony — however good they might have been for the past — offer only diminishing returns for a more certain future. In conditions where it is hard to think of a polity that is not spellbound by some kind of 'identity crisis', the belief that a hard core of 'special relationships' can ride out this storm may ultimately reveal itself as the highest form of the failure to adapt.[29]

For all of that, there remain significant elements of continuity in the international politics of the Asia-Pacific region, precisely because the region was historically constituted by a bilateral structure of patronage — a structure whose fundamental characteristic is relative immunity to change. If the hesitant first moves of recent years towards a new economic and strategic multilateralism in the Pacific reveal anything about change, it is surely that the economic asking price for the continued American patronage which regional actors continue to demand has ratcheted upwards by several notches. Since the Australian–Japanese 'special relationship' has been primarily — if not quite exclusively — fashioned from economic rather than political or strategic exchanges, the impact of this higher asking price is likely to be particularly exaggerated, and the range of second-round choices correspondingly dramatic. If Clark was even halfway right about the hold of particularism over Australian policy, then even the conservative tenet — that things must change if they are to remain the same — will not come easily.

Notes

* *Editor's note:* This chapter does not traverse the familiar and predictable ground of Japan as an economic superpower with a peace constitution, a nuclear allergy, a security alliance with the United States, the burden of World War II and yet a developing interest in playing a more active role in international security, broadly defined. Instead, the chapter is presented from the perspective of Australia, a country that is, in many respects, Japan's primary partner in the Western Pacific.

1   G. Clark, 'Vietnam, China and the Foreign Affairs Debate in Australia: A Personal Account', in P. King (ed.), *Australia's Vietnam*, George Allen & Unwin, North Sydney, 1983.

2   ibid., pp. 31–35.

3   A. Rix, 'Australia and Japan: The Reality of the "Special Relationship"', in F.A. Mediansky & A.C. Palfreeman (eds), *In Pursuit of National Interests*, Pergamon Press, Sydney, 1988.

4   E. Clements, *Australia and Japan: A Defence Relationship?* Sub-thesis, Master of Arts (Strategic Studies), Strategic and Defence Studies Centre, Research School of Pacific Studies, Australian National University, Canberra, 1992.

5   B. Buzan, *An Introduction to Strategic Studies: Military Technology and International Relations*, Macmillan, Basingstoke, 1987.

6   G. Evans, *Australia's Regional Security*, Department of Foreign Affairs and Trade, Canberra, 1989.

7   In this regard, see Alan Thompson, *Australia's Strategic Defence Policy: A Drift Towards Neo-Forward Defence*, Working Paper no. 29, Australian Defence Studies Centre, Canberra, 1994.

8   *National Times*, 'The Strategic Basis Papers', 30 March–5 April 1984.

9   Department of Defence, 'Submission to the Senate Standing Committee of Foreign Affairs, Defence and Trade', Submission No. JD.11, 25 November 1992.

10 D.C.S. Sissons, 'Japan', in W.J. Hudson (ed.), *Australia in World Affairs 1971–75*, George Allen & Unwin, Sydney, 1980, pp. 260–65.

11 H. Bull, 'Australia and the Great Powers in Asia', in G. Greenwood and N. Harper (eds), *Australia in World Affairs 1966–1970*, Cheshire, Melbourne, 1974, p. 339.

12 W.T. Tow, 'Australia–Japanese Security Cooperation: Present Barriers and Future Prospects', *Australian Outlook*, vol. 38, no. 3, August 1984, p. 205.

13 M. Mochizuki, 'To Change or to Contain: Dilemmas of American Policy Toward Japan', in K.A. Oye, R.J. Lieber and D. Rothchild (eds), *Eagle in a New World: American Grand Strategy in the Post-Cold War Era*, Harper Collins, New York, 1992.

14 J.G. Ruggie, 'Multilateralism: The Anatomy of an Institution', *International Organization*, vol. 46, no. 3, Summer 1992, p. 563.

15 As Kent Calder expressed it, defence became 'the residual' in the matrix of postwar Japanese public policy — something that could hardly be said about the structure of Australian policy through the same period. K.E. Calder, *Crisis and Compensation: Public Policy and Political Stability in Japan, 1949–1986*, Princeton University Press, Princeton, 1988, Ch. 10.

16 R. Leaver, '"The Shock of the New" and the Habits of the Past', in G. Fry (ed.), *Australia's Regional Security*, Allen & Unwin, Sydney, 1991.

17 K.R. Nossal, 'Middle Power Diplomacy in a Changing Asia-Pacific Order: Australia and Canada Compared', in R. Leaver and J.L. Richardson (eds), *The Post-Cold War Order: Diagnoses and Prognoses*, Allen & Unwin, Sydney, 1993.

18 See, in particular, the prime minister's opening arguments about the meaning of the Kuwait crisis, *Commonwealth Parliamentary Debates* (House of Representatives), 21 August 1990, p. 1119

19 E.J. Lincoln, 'Japan in the 1990s: A New Kind of World Power', *The Brookings Review*, vol. 10, no. 2, 1992, pp. 12–17.

20 R. Rosecrance, *The Rise of the Trading State: Commerce and Conquest in the Modern World*, Basic Books, New York, 1986.

21 W. Borden, *The Pacific Alliance: United States Foreign Economic Policy and Japanese Trade Recovery 1947–1955*, The University of Wisconsin Press, Madison, 1984.

22 P. Drysdale, 'The Relationship with Japan: Despite the Vicissitudes', in L.T. Evans and J.D.B. Miller (eds), *Policy and Practice*, Australian National University Press, Sydney, 1987.

23 P. Drysdale, *International Economic Pluralism: Economic Policy in East Asia and the Pacific*, Allen & Unwin, Sydney, 1988, Ch. 8.

24 For an explicit affirmation of the relevance of Cobden, see S. Harris, 'The Economic Aspects of Pacific Security', *Adelphi Papers*, no. 275, 1993, pp. 14–35. For one important example of such reasoning, see R. Garnaut, 'Australia's Asia-Pacific Journey', *Australian Quarterly*, vol. 64, no. 4, 1993, p. 367: 'International commerce transmits political as well as

economic information and values, and over time contributes to elements of convergence in political values.'

25   D.P. Rapkin, 'Uncertain World Order Implications of Japan's Rapid Ascent', paper presented at the Seventh Biennial Conference of the Japanese Studies Association of Australia, Canberra, July 1991, pp. 29–32.

26   R.G. Ruggie, 'Unraveling Trade: Global Institutional Change and the Pacific Economy', in R. Higgott, R. Leaver and J. Ravenhill (eds), *Pacific Economic Relations in the 1990s: Cooperation or Conflict?*, Allen & Unwin, Sydney, 1993.

27   G. Winham, G., 'The GATT After the Uruguay Round', in Higgott, Leaver and Ravenhill (eds), *Pacific Economic Relations in the 1990s*, pp. 196–98.

28   F. Kratochwil, 'The Embarrassment of Changes: Neo-realism as the Science of Realpolitik Without Politics', *Review of International Studies*, vol. 19, no. 1, January 1993, pp. 63–80.

29   As Tarnoff has observed, new 'special relationships' are being forged, while old ones — including the Anglo-American prototype — struggle to survive. P. Tarnoff, 'America's New Special Relationships', *Foreign Affairs*, vol. 69, no. 3, Summer 1990, pp. 67–80. For reflections on the British attempt to halt their slide, see *Daily Telegraph*, 'Mr Major Makes his First Prime Ministerial Visit to a Curious but Welcoming America', 21 December 1990.

5 India and Asia-Pacific Security

Sandy Gordon

Introduction: India and global change

Over the last half-decade, the process of global change has administered two powerful shocks to India. First, the collapse of the Soviet Union and the ending of the Cold War effectively undermined New Delhi's strategy of 'non-alignment with a Soviet tilt' — a strategy that had provided access to cheap Soviet arms and underwritten India's rise as a significant Indian Ocean power.

Second, the tendency towards globalisation of economic activity and the intensification of competition that accompanied that process left India increasingly out in the cold. New Delhi's restrictive investment policies and autarkic management of the economy cut India off from access to international investment and state-of-the-art technology. India's share in world trade fell from 2.5 per cent at independence to 0.4 per cent in 1990. This diminishing share of world trade failed to accommodate growing demands for oil and an increasing hunger for borrowed money. By 1991 these processes together precipitated an economic crisis in India and a radical restructuring and liberalisation of the Indian economy.

But the political and social tensions that will likely be generated by liberalisation will make the next ten years a 'dangerous decade' for India as various political players seek to focus on the negative aspects of economic reform in order to weaken the Congress government.

The way in which India manages to handle economic liberalisation will be an important determinant of whether it has a potential role in the Asia-Pacific. Should it press forward vigorously with economic reform, then we are likely to witness the forging of closer relations between India and those parts of Asia lying to its east. Any such development would have implications not just for economic relations but also for security. A dynamic and rapidly growing Indian economy that is more closely linked into Asia will inevitably result in a leavening of Asian power relations.

Economic reform, globalisation and security

The politics of economic reform in India

In recent decades, India has suffered a prolonged crisis of governability. The unfolding of India's political crisis — or rather let us refer to it as malaise — is now closely tied in with the outcome of economic reform. Reform, when it came, was seen very much as an alternative means to alleviate poverty and improve general well-being. Reform will be judged by the electorate on whether or not it provides more effectively for the majority of the people than did the previous autarkic economic system.

Given the existence of this calculus, those developing the strategy of reform face a dilemma. Do they go for all-out growth on the model of the Asian 'tigers', in the hope that a very rapid rate of growth will cause sufficient 'trickle down' to ensure that the electorate continues to support the reforms, or do they try to temper the reform process to ensure that there is at least a perception that equity is being maintained? So far the Congress government has chosen to temper the process of reform.

The history of economic reform in India illustrates that a reform process in a fully fledged democracy such as India's is more delicate and uncertain than it is in the so-called 'guided democracies' of some of the Asian tigers, or in China. A further point that needs to be noted about the Indian reforms is that they are likely to exacerbate an existing trend according to which the advanced states of the Indian Union are pulling away from the more backward ones.

Economic reform in India has been further complicated by the fact that both major opposition groupings, the Hindu revivalist BJP and the parties broadly grouped on the left, such as the Janata party and various Marxist factions, are vehemently opposed to the reforms and are endeavouring to make political capital out of them.

But none of the above problems means that reform is likely to be reversed. The longer the process of reform continues, the more entrenched it will become. Although inflows of foreign capital are still modest by East Asian standards, they are likely to become quite substantial by Indian standards.

Given all the political factors outlined above, the reform process is likely to be uncertain, even 'lumpy', as respective governments continue to manoeuvre between political and international exigencies and expediencies. Nonetheless, economic growth may average a relatively strong 6 per cent for the decade of the 1990s as a whole.[1]

The economy and defence

Despite the sound economic recovery, over the short term, India is likely to have a continuing debt repayment and interest problem as the current concessional finance runs out and requires repayment. There will thus probably continue to be a squeeze on foreign exchange until well into the decade, and this will have repercussions in terms of the modernisation of the defence forces, especially now that India is denied Russian arms on a soft-currency, concessional basis.

Moreover, serious competition is emerging between the needs of the social sector and the burgeoning demands of infrastructure including power, water and sanitation, transport, telecommunications and urban development.

At the same time, in order to maintain macroeconomic stability, India must also restrain government spending. In these circumstances, there may not be a great deal of money available for defence, at least in the short term.

Eventually, however, higher rates of economic growth should allow military modernisation to resume. Furthermore, while India has experienced difficulties in producing more sophisticated weapons platforms, such as front-line fighters and main battle tanks, it is gradually overcoming its problems. The cessation of supplies of spare parts and the termination of the Soviet maintenance and retrofitting programs have had the effect of stimulating the domestic industry to carry out more of this work than ever before. Even so, Russia is now apparently more willing to enter into genuine joint production with India than was the Soviet Union. Developments such as the new joint venture with Russia — Indo-Russian Aviation Private Ltd — indicate a greater willingness on the part of the Russians to actually share production methodologies and skills with India.

A number of important civil-related technologies have offered synergies relevant to the defence industries. For example, the space and nuclear programs could eventually provide India not only with a strategic nuclear force, but also with the means of targeting and gathering 'real time' intelligence. India has now acquired near self-sufficiency in the nuclear sciences, and this makes it very difficult for the international community to limit its production of unsafeguarded fissionable material. India's expertise in computation and growing competency in electronics and the materials sciences also mean that it could achieve significant technologies that could assist it in the production of a strategic nuclear force, should it decide to go down that track. Indeed, India's determined thrust in the area of 'big science' seems to be designed with the defence industries in mind.

In time, the process of economic liberalisation will itself assist the defence industries. This is not so much because the private sector is likely to participate directly in the defence sector, but because other structural benefits to the economy will flow through to the defence sector. These include cheaper and more accessible high grade steel and other materials and compounds, significantly greater access to state-of-the-art manufacturing techniques such as CAD and CAM and, most important of all, better management techniques in the ordnance factories and defence public-sector undertakings.

Also, India has a number of relatively modern, but relatively under-equipped, platforms such as the Godavari frigate, the Kashin destroyer, the MiG-29 fighter, the Jaguar attack aircraft, and the T-72 tank that allow for considerable benefit to be derived from retrofitting and upgrading of weapons systems and sensors. Much more of this work can now be carried out locally than in the past. The absence of comprehensive systems of C^3I and aerial refuelling capabilities also means that these areas will likely be used as force multipliers in the future. The space program will prove particularly beneficial in providing a system of real-time intelligence.

But the greatest benefit that is likely to accrue from liberalisation as far as the defence industries and the process of military modernisation are concerned is that higher economic growth could eventually lead to increases in real defence spending. Over the last twenty years, India's impressive military growth has had more to do with economic growth than with higher allocations to defence as a percentage of Gross Domestic Product (GDP). In fact, defence spending as a percentage of GDP has tended to fluctuate within the narrow confines of between about 3 per cent and 4 per cent as real defence spending has closely tracked GDP growth. Already a rise in real spending is evident, although most of it would have been spent on making up for the backlog of cuts that took place over previous years rather than on military modernisation.[2]

Yet, in the final analysis, it must be said that India is unlikely now to emerge within the decade as an Indian Ocean power with all the military pretensions that it previously had. Its navy will be smaller in terms of major surface combatants than it is now, and its air force will possess an inventory of ageing aircraft (albeit substantially upgraded) such as the MiG-21. As for possessing three carrier battle groups, as envisaged in earlier strategic plans, India will be lucky still to have two aircraft carriers.

Looking somewhat further ahead — say to the year 2005 — it is useful to consider India's potential in terms of capabilities rather than what will actually be in the inventory. By that time it is likely that India will have the following capabilities:

- the capability to produce a state-of-the-art main battle tank, including at least some key assemblies, and to upgrade the existing very large inventory of tanks;
- a wide range of skills to enable the continuation of a flexible regime of missile production, including an Intermediate Range Ballistic Missile (IRBM), possibly an Intercontinental Ballistic Missile (ICBM) and a range of offensive and defensive tactical missiles;
- a comprehensive space program involving indigenously launched and built sensing and communications satellites, allowing for a reasonably sophisticated program for the military uses of space, including military communications and remote sensing;
- a developing capability in the production of military aircraft, but one that falls well short of the one possessed by leading nations in this area,

combining a wide range of associated technologies relating to the aero-space industry;

- near self-sufficiency in the nuclear sciences such that, should New Delhi decide to do so, India could produce a range of nuclear weapons, possibly including thermo-nuclear weapons and warheads capable of being delivered by ballistic missiles;
- an economy that is capable of meeting many of the needs of the defence industries and sustaining a significant defence industrial base, including in areas such as electronics, materials sciences, computation and engineering.

Instability and India's role as a global actor

The problems relating to political stability generated by the process of economic reform are only one of a number of ongoing difficulties faced by a government confronting the task of nation-building in a society confined within largely irrational and arbitrary post-colonial borders.

Perhaps the most severe problem faced by India is a consequence of its sheer size and associated diversity. While India is big, with a population approaching 900 million, it is a much more diverse nation in its ethnic, linguistic and religious constitution than China. India has fifteen major languages and literally hundreds of minor ones. It also has a major ethnic cleavage between the north and south, and many minor ones within those regions. Although 83 per cent of its population is Hindu, there are 120 million Muslims living within its borders, not to mention members of smaller minority religions such as Sikhs, Christians, Jains and Parsis. And Hindu society is itself highly fragmented, both in terms of regional tradition and caste.

The South Asian region within which India is located is equally diverse. Pakistan comprises at least five major ethno-linguistic groups. The cement that binds these people is Islam, a fact that itself tends to place Pakistan in opposition to India. Sri Lanka has two major ethnic groups that are locked into a debilitating civil war. Bangladesh is more homogeneous, but it confronts serious developmental challenges. Millions of its citizens have been forced by economic circumstances and security factors to migrate to India. These transmigrations have upset the ethnic and religious balance in India's northeastern region and damaged relations between the two nations. Like Pakistan, Bangladesh increasingly perceives itself to be an Islamic nation juxtaposed to Hindu India. These are not easy circumstances for a country required to carve out an Indian Ocean role, let alone one in the wider Asian region.

The instability evident in the South Asian region since independence has created in India a country that is essentially inward-looking and regionally focused. India's security posture thus exhibits many of the characteristics of a continental power, even though it is the only regional nation with potential strategic reach. This fact is reflected both in the capacity and deployment of the military forces and, closely related to this, the conduct of foreign relations.

The effect regional instability has on military capability is, however, paradoxical. At the level of aggregate force acquisition, the competition between India and Pakistan has produced a regional arms race.[3] But in terms of force structure, deployment and strategy, the effect of chronic regional instability has been to cause both India and Pakistan to focus on sub-continental defence systems, border defences and the maintenance of law and order at the expense of the acquisition of forces with significant strategic reach.

Nowhere is the emphasis on continental-type defence doctrine in South Asia more evident than in terms of the relationship between expenditure on the navy and expenditure on the other services. In the case of India, expenditure on the navy has never risen above 14 per cent of total defence expenditure, and for most of the nation's independent existence it has been well below that level. The army, on the other hand, has traditionally commanded the lion's share of the defence budget at about 62 per cent.[4] In Pakistan, the same generally holds true.

In both countries, force structures have closely reflected the requirements of short border wars. For example, the Indian air force relies heavily on tactical fighters. It has no true long-range strike aircraft and has not yet developed an aerial refuelling capability for the *Jaguar*. Only eight of India's 88 *Jaguars* are dedicated to the maritime attack role.[5] The Indian and Pakistani armies contain massive amounts of armour capable of fighting in the plains of Punjab or deserts of Rajasthan. India has over 3000 main battle tanks. By the same token, the training and strategy of the Indian army has until recently reflected the requirement of countering Pakistan in the plains and deserts, and dealing with China in the mountains.

The activities of smugglers, and the Tamil militants, have also caused a reassessment of the role and structure of the navy. Contrary to the wishes of the former Chief of Naval Staff, Admiral Ramdas, who wanted to reverse the trend away from small ships and move back to the concept of a blue water navy, the government has now directed the navy to build more smaller ships in order to patrol the inner, or 'brown' waters. This policy has now been endorsed by the new naval chief, Admiral Shekhawat, who has referred to a 'sudden unplanned commitment in internal security duties'.[6]

The increasing reliance on the army for the maintenance of internal security has meant that, despite earlier decisions to modernise equipment and reduce human resources, this has proved extremely difficult to accomplish, and the recommendation of the Arun Singh Committee that human resources be traded for modernisation has not been fully implemented. India has also been required to deploy the army in aid of the civil authority for the maintenance of law and order increasingly throughout the decade of the 1980s. There are reportedly now 320 000 army men deployed in Kashmir in addition to 35 000 paramilitary. According to some accounts,

50 per cent of army personnel are now deployed in aid of the civil author-ity.[7] In these circumstances, it will be difficult for India again to pursue in the 1990s the kind of Indian Ocean-wide regional role it envisaged for itself during the 1980s.·

Over the longer term, however, India is likely to benefit by progres-sively drawing ahead of Pakistan. India is more capable of filling the weapons gap through its own economic means — its economy being over five times larger than that of its rival. Pakistan is currently spending nearly 70 per cent of its budget in debt servicing and on the military — an unsus-tainable position given the enormous problems it confronts in the social sector, such as a population growth rate of 3.1 per cent and a situation in which only 14 per cent of couples accept any form of birth control. As India becomes militarily more capable than Pakistan, it will be able to break away from its South Asian shackles and exercise a wider role in the Indian Ocean region. India is not significantly constrained by any other regional power, and its path will be facilitated by the fact that it has drawn closer to the United States and the West generally, a development that gives it access to a larger range of dual-use technologies.

India in contemporary geopolitics

United States–Indian relations

Under the Cold War regime, it had been clear that the need to use Pakistan as a front-line state in the fight against communism outweighed any con-cern about proliferation or human rights. With the end of the Cold War, how-ever, Pakistan was no longer a front-line state in the war against communism. Nor is it an important state in global terms. On the other hand, Washing-ton's interests in relation to India are rapidly evolving in the context of India's economic liberalisation, its more outward-looking foreign policy, its closer engagement in Asia and its developing role in the Indian Ocean region.

The history of the Clinton administration's failure to bring India to heel on the nuclear issue and the Kashmir question indicates that, in the final analysis, the United States is not prepared to press its case on these issues at the expense of the broader United States relationship with India. Evi-dence suggests that, despite official pronouncements about the continuing salience of the nuclear 'roll-back' position, the United States has now moved to a policy of capping the Indian and Pakistani arsenals rather than demanding roll-back.[8] Nor have pronouncements about Kashmir being contested territory been repeated following the storm they engendered in India. On the contrary, the newly installed United States ambassador in New Delhi, Frank Wisner, seems to have backed away from that position.[9] These events indicate that an increasingly confident Rao government has been able to draw a 'line in the sand' which the United States administra-tion has not been prepared to cross.

Amongst the important factors which have shaped Washington's new attitude to India is a burgeoning trade and investment relationship that developed following India's program of economic liberalisation. United States investment comprises 42 per cent of the total direct foreign investment in India.[10] Trade has risen substantially, albeit from a fairly low base, and American companies are eyeing off what they see as the potential of India's rapidly growing middle class, now numbering 180 million.[16] During United States Commerce Secretary Brown's recent visit to India at the head of a delegation of business people, deals worth an estimated US$7 billion were signed.[12]

For its part, India has recently managed to become far more 'streetwise' in relation to Washington. It has hired its own lobbyist in the capital — a practice long adopted by Pakistan. In a move that Deputy Secretary of State Strobe Talbott described as a 'flood of good sense', it compromised on its dispute with the United States over textiles. It is now a fully fledged member of the World Trade Organisation; it is endeavouring to improve its record on human rights by allowing visits of Amnesty and the International Red Cross (IRC) (although not to Kashmir); and it has been generally more relaxed and compromising on a range of issues.[13]

Another, perhaps less tangible, factor in Washington's renewed interest in India relates to its broader strategic perceptions about the Indian Ocean. As the United States progressively draws down its forces and reduces its presence in the Indian Ocean in the aftermath of the Cold War, it is important to Washington to have a large, democratic and essentially status quo power such as India on side and positively engaged in regional security maintenance. In effect, India has subscribed to the larger role cast for it by the United States. Far from decrying the presence of extra-regional navies as it used to during Cold War days, India has conducted exercises with at least fifteen navies since 1991, many of them from outside the Indian Ocean.

Following signature of a comprehensive United States–India defence agreement during a recent visit by United States Defense Secretary Perry, the United States navy is now prepared to conduct far more comprehensive exercises with the Indian navy than hitherto, with the possibility of future joint operations. Perry described the agreement as a 'landmark' in Indo-United States relations.[14] Privately, officials in New Delhi recognise that the United States presence in the Indian Ocean is desirable in terms of oil security, with India becoming ever more dependent on Gulf oil to fuel its industrialisation.[15]

India and Southeast Asia

India initially felt isolated in the aftermath of the Cold War. Divested of its favoured treatment in the old Eastern bloc trading regime, it also felt shut out of evolving regional trading blocs such as the EC/EU and the North American Free Trade Agreement (NAFTA). It therefore adopted a 'look east' strategy of engagement with various regional forums such as Association of Southeast Asian Nations (ASEAN), the Asia-Pacific Economic

Cooperation forum (APEC) and various security arrangements such as the ASEAN Regional Forum (ARF).

For India, the key to its reception in APEC and other Asia-Pacific forums lay in its reception in ASEAN. The ASEAN states, however, grappling with the problems of achieving a measure of unity out of a widely contrasting region, were disinclined to make space for India. New Delhi's calling card was seen to be tarnished because of its previous relationship with Moscow and inept diplomacy.

New Delhi has, however, persisted. It has recognised that the way forward is to cultivate bilateral linkages and to be 'on good behaviour' in its dealings with ASEAN and to be more sensitive to regional diplomatic norms. Through these means, it is starting to have a little more success. India's trade with the Southeast Asia region is rising sharply, albeit from a low base. For example, Indian exports into the region rose by 300 per cent between 1992 and 1993.[16]

Of the ASEAN nations, India has had a reasonably close relationship with Malaysia since 1965, when each was opposed to Indonesia, albeit for different reasons. After a setback following India's recognition of the Vietnamese-backed regime in Cambodia in 1980, the Indo-Malaysian relationship again improved. India and Malaysia signed a broad-ranging defence Memorandum of Understanding (MOU) in 1993. India is also involved with pilot and ground crew training for the eighteen MiG-29 aircraft recently purchased by Malaysia. Maintenance and repairs on the aircraft are likely to be undertaken through the Indo-Russian joint venture mentioned above. Malaysia, in turn, supported India when it successfully applied for sectoral (trade) observer status with ASEAN.

India has close relations with Singapore, which is interested in India in the context of maintaining its competitive edge in technical areas, especially software development. Singaporean officials also see India as a userful 'hedge' against their concern about having too large a commitment in China.[17] Singapore has recently decided to invest substantially in high technology in India, with 42 joint ventures so far. Bilateral trade grew 20 per cent to S$3.1 billion in 1994.[18] Also in 1994, the two nations conducted a sophisticated four-day ASW naval exercise.[19] The Foreign Ministers of both Singapore and Malaysia have now stated that they would not rule out India participation in the ARF.[20]

Even those ASEAN nations not traditionally close to India have been more accommodating to New Delhi in recent years. Bangkok was once suspicious of India because of Thailand's closeness to China, which it saw as a counterweight to Vietnam. When Indian Prime Minister Rao visited Thailand in 1993, however, Rao was able to point to China's activities in Burma as an area of new regional concern. The two nations also undertook to raise bilateral trade from $400 million to $1 billion.[21] Recently, a Thai government study team suggested that India and Sri Lanka should be drawn into a wider Southeast Asian investment zone,[22] and a Thai military delegation visited India and expressed an interest in purchasing military equipment.[23]

There is also economic interest within the ASEAN nations in establishing stronger links with India. The emergence of a large middle-class market in India presents tempting prospects for these archetypical trading nations, just as India's large cohort of technically trained people is attractive to high-technology investors. Increasingly, Indians and other South Asians are filling technical and other positions in Southeast Asia, as evidenced by the fact that remittances from that region to India are now of the order of US$2.5 billion.[24]

On India's part, New Delhi would favour the emergence of a wider ASEAN grouping, one that might eventually include Burma. Such a grouping would provide a robust barrier to any greater assertiveness on the part of China in the Southeast Asian region. From India's point of view, a Burma that was tightly bound to an economically secure ASEAN, rather than a Burma that remained weak and dependent on China, would be an excellent outcome.

In short, despite the negative experience of recent history, there are common interests in closer relations between India and the East/Southeast Asian states. This is manifest in a hectic round of naval exercising, evolving defence-industrial arrangements (albeit at a low level), a buildup in the extent and level of bilateral visits and expanding trading and investment relationships. This slowly evolving pattern of more intense engagement will continue, whether or not India becomes part of larger regional groupings such as APEC.

Sino-Indian relations

There has been a marked change for the better in Sino-Indian relations since Rajiv Gandhi's visit to Beijing in December 1988. One of the factors pressing New Delhi to continue the process of rapprochement with China is the important 'peace dividend' derived by India from the new relationship *vis-à-vis* its competition with Pakistan.

The dividends of this strategy have already become apparent. China now assumes a position of 'careful neutrality' on Kashmir, claiming that the issue should be settled by bilateral negotiation as specified in the Simla agreement of 1972.[25] Furthermore, as a result of the improved climate on the Sino-Indian border, India has been able to remove as many as five of its eleven mountain divisions from the border. The ability to withdraw these troops has proved invaluable at a time when the Indian military confronts increasing problems maintaining the civil order. The troops are, moreover, potentially freed for engagement against Pakistan.

But, despite the undoubted progress in the relationship, India is still not entirely at ease with China. Commentators such as the noted journalist, Inder Malhotra, question whether India might be returning to the bad old days of *Hindi-Chini bhai-bhai* attitudes, according to which China could do no wrong and during which India 'let down its guard'.[26] Malhotra is not the only one who harbours such doubts. Sumit Ganguly notes that 'Over the longer haul, Chinese and Indian interests are bound to diverge' and that the Sino-Indian relationship is 'inherently competitive'.[27] Noted Indian economist, Prem Shankar Jha, sees this competition in economic terms. According to him, 'the dark side' of the East Asian success story is that there will inevitably be losers. India could be one of them, and this could have strategic implications.[28] In this context, anxiety about China has become an important factor in defining the pace at which India has pursued economic liberalisation. Such uncertainties are lent additional weight by China's alleged military involvement in Burma, a state with which India shares a long and porous border and, at times, a troubled relationship.

Given uncertainties surrounding China's attitudes and status in the post-Deng era, and given that New Delhi does not want to lose the benefits rapprochement has already brought, India has adopted a 'watch and wait' attitude towards China. It is willing to pick up on any advance offered in the relationship, but it will not let down its guard.

Conclusion: India as an Asia-Pacific player

India's role as an Asia-Pacific power will be shaped substantially by the success or failure of its program of economic reform. If the reforms succeed, India should achieve a comfortable level of growth of at least 6 per cent on average for the decade of the 1990s, which would give it an economy roughly of the order of China's today by the end of the century. Given these developments, it will be difficult for the nations of the Asia-Pacific to ignore India's market potential, with or without Indian membership of APEC and other regional forums. India is likely to be drawn gradually into a more intensive engagement in the wider Asia to its east. This does not mean that India will adopt a 'look east' strategy to the exclusion of other sets of relationships, especially those with the United States and Europe, which are likely to remain important venues for trade and investment. But in the evolving world of globalisation, the ties binding India to East Asia will become as important as those binding it elsewhere.

During the 1980s, some concern was expressed about India's naval buildup and about the development of its strategic resource in the Andaman and Nicobar Islands. That concern has now dissipated. In a climate of military cutbacks, the Indian navy has suffered more severe cuts than the other services. India has also become more 'transparent' in its dealings with its neighbours.

Moreover, India's engagement in Asia in the 1990s is quite different than it was in the past. India's current interests have far more to do with economics, technology, capital and trade than they have with security as such. But even in the area of security, India has tried hard in recent years to present itself as a power of 'internationalist' intent. It has contributed handsomely to United Nations peacekeeping efforts in Cambodia and Rwanda, with two naval vessels and 3500 troops to Somalia. It has exercised widely with regional navies, and it has evinced an interest in achieving association status in regional security organisations such as the ARF and the Council for Security Cooperation in the Asia-Pacific (CSCAP).

Although India is slowly developing its links with East and Southeast Asia, it does not wish at this stage to be juxtaposed as a 'balance' with China in the Asian region. Its own relationship with China is too important to allow that to happen.

The pattern of greater engagement by India in Southeast Asia is one that should be welcomed and encouraged by regional nations. An India more actively engaged in the region offers an important leavening of the Asian power equation. It potentially allows for the evolution of a more 'multipolar' equation, one in which smaller regional nations have greater manoeuvrability between the Asian giants.

As to India's emerging role in the wider Indian Ocean, it is unlikely that India will be in a position to act independently as a power in the Gulf, the Straits of Malacca or adjacent waters during the next fifteen years. India will, however, emerge as an increasingly important political and economic player in the Indian Ocean and even in the Asia-Pacific region.

In one area — the acquisition of nuclear weapons and delivery systems — developments could, however, have a significant, if indirect, effect on the region. Unless India's security concerns about China's nuclear force are resolved, the non-proliferation regime is unlikely to succeed in its aim of capping and eventually 'rolling back' the Indian and Pakistani nuclear programs. Although the de facto nuclearisation of South Asia is unlikely to have any direct bearing on Southeast Asia, it could have the indirect effect of making regional non-proliferation goals in the Asia-Pacific region much more difficult.

Notes

[1]   East Asia Analytical Unit, Department of Foreign Affairs and Trade, *India's Economy: At the Midnight Hour*, Commonwealth of Australia, Canberra, 1994, p. 1.

[2]   See *Defense News*, 10 June 1994. The rise between 1993 and 1994 was 20 per cent in nominal terms, or about 10 per cent in real terms. Some have argued that the rise was, in fact, much smaller than this. Such arguments depend on a Revised Estimate to Budget rise rather than a Budget to Budget rise, however.

[3]   See 'Swords Not Ploughshares', *Economist*, 23 March 1991, p. 52.

[4]   Government of India, *Defence Services Estimates 1991–92*, Government of India Press, 1991 (actuals for 1989–90). Note that these figures do not include items used in common between the services.

[5]   Institute for International and Strategic Studies, *The Military Balance 1991–92*, Brasseys for IISS, London, 1991, p. 163.

[6] See 'India Needs a Strong Navy: Shekhawat', *Times of India*, 2 December 1993.

[7] Rahul Bedi says that there are four army divisions posted in Kashmir. See 'Conflict in Kashmir Continues', *Jane's Defence Weekly*, 3 July 1993, p. 21. Other information comes from a non-disclosable source, New Delhi, December 1993. At least some of the troops located in Kashmir would still be deployed in the context of the Sino-Indian border dispute, however.

[8] See John F. Burns, 'India Rejects US Bid for Nuclear Pact with Pakistan', *New York Times*, 26 March 1994; Press Trust of India, as carried by Reuters, 'India: India's Envoy Says Reports on British Intelligence Pressure for US Talks "Bull"', 2 May 1994; and K.K. Katyal, 'More Nations in N-talks Net?', *The Hindu (International Edition)*, 2 April 1994.

[9] 'US Says No Warplanes Deal with Pakistan', Reuters News Service, Art No. 000499169847, 9 August 1994.

[10] 'India and America — Looking for Friends', Reuters News Service, Art. No. 000457179505, 21 May 1994; and 'Foreign Exchange Investment in India Seen Rising Rapidly', Reuters News Service, Art. No. 000510704347, 31 August 1994.

[11] These figures are based on latest National Survey data. They are based on a family income of $80 in the cities and $50 in rural areas. See Narayanan Madhavan, 'Indian Middle Class Market Estimated at 180 million', Reuters News Service, Art. No. 000501744791, 14 August 1994. A recent poll of United States chief executives revealed that almost half were considering entering the India market or were already entering it. See Aabha Dixit, 'US, India Face Crossroads', *Defense News*, 23–29 May 1994, p. 32.

[12] Nelson Graves, 'Brown Says India Trade Mission Exceeds Hopes', Reuters News Service, Art No. 000584119361, 18 January 1995.

[13] Thomas Abraham, 'US Official Hails Rethink', *The Hindu (International Edition)*, 23 April 1994; N Ravi, 'A New Phase in Indo-US Relations', *The Hindu (International Edition)*, 28 May 1994; Nelson Graves, 'India, With an Eye on Pakistan, Moves on Human Rights', Reuters News Service, 25 August 1994, Art. No. 000506503697; and Nelson Graves, 'India, US Burying Long-time Antagonisms', Reuters News Service, Art. No. 000505416985, 21 August 1994. Amnesty has not been allowed into Kashmir, however.

[14] 'USN Commander in Delhi to Discuss Joint Exercises', Reuters News Service, Art. No. 000568392619, 19 December 1994; Nelson Graves, India, US Begin New Era in Defence Cooperation', Reuters News Service, Art. No. 000581476609 of 13 January 1995.

[15] Interviews with senior officials, New Delhi, December 1993.

[16] 'India Seeks More Investment in Southeast Asia', Reuters News Service, Art. No. 000459326155, 25 May 1994.

[17] Conversation with senior Singaporean official, December 1993.

[18] 'Singapore Hails Results of Regional Trade Push', Reuters News Service, Art. No. 000584642077, 10 January 1995.

[19] See M. Satish, 'Military Ties with ASEAN Nations Improving', *The Economic Times*, 23 March 1994; Anon, 'India Takes to the Sea with Russia, Singapore', *Jane's Defence Weekly*, 19 March 1994, p. 16 for a description of the Indo-Singaporean exercise.

[20] Ajoy Sen, 'Indian PM to Discuss Business, Security in Singapore', Reuters News Service, Art. No. 000513819913, 6 September 1994; 'India May be Invited to Security Meet', *The Indian Express*, 23 March 1994.

[21] 'India, Thailand to Step Up Trade', *Hindustan Times*, 26 May 1989; 'India Club', *Far Eastern Economic Review*, 22 April 1993, p. 9.

[22] Alan Boyd, 'Thailand: A New Regional Grouping in the Works?', Reuters News Service, Art. No. 000500704957, 12 August 1994; and Richard Valladares, 'Rao Visit to Minimize "Threat" of PRC Presence in Burma', *Bangkok Post*, 10 April 1993. The Thai choices of India and Sri Lanka are perhaps interesting in the context of its relations with other Islamic ASEAN powers such as Malaysia and Indonesia.

[23] Satish, 'Military Ties With ASEAN Nations Improving'.

[24] Robin Abreu, 'Pick of the East', *India Today*, 31 July 1994, pp. 98–99.

[25] Selig S. Harrison and Geoffrey Kemp, *India and America After the Cold War*, The Carnegie Endowment, Washington DC, 1993, p. 10.

[26] Inder Malhotra, 'India, China and the Real World', *Times of India*, 28 May 1992.

[27] Ganguly, 'South Asia After the Cold War', p. 179.

[28] Prem Shankar Jha, 'Stagnation and Sovereignty', *The Hindu*, 15 July 1992.

6 Russia: A Terrier at the Feet of Asia's Great Powers

Greg Austin and Tim Callan

During the last century of Tsarist rule, Russia was a Pacific power, but this ended sharply in 1904–05 with defeat in the Russo-Japanese War. After the consolidation of the Bolsheviks in the Soviet Union in the early 1920s, the government in Moscow sought, fitfully, to regain Russia's lost status in the Pacific, winning some brilliant if short-lived successes, such as the formation of the Sino-Soviet bloc between 1950 and 1957. But the Soviet diplomatic record in the Pacific was poor, and after December 1991, the successor state of Russia found itself having to come from behind the play in its effort to win friends and influence people in the Asia-Pacific. Hence the inevitable conclusion: 'Russia is a power in Asia, not an Asian power'.[1]

In Russia itself, there is recognition of the new country's reduced role in world affairs compared with the former Soviet Union or the United States, and there is acceptance of the limits on its efforts to be a world power. Georgii Arbatov has summarised what is to Russians a bitter-sweet message: 'Russia is no more and will be no more a global power — it can claim a role no bigger than a regional power, albeit an important one.'[2]

Russia shares, seeks or is forced to assume many of the former Soviet Union's vital interests, but its capacity to realise these interests has been sharply reduced.[3] Russia has lost an empire, and is still searching for a role or an identity. It wants to acknowledge its Eastern interests, while Asian states continue to see it not only as Western,[4] but also as a power in decline — a country with shrinking international authority and prestige.

Russia recognises that it can play an important role in the transition to a new order in the Asia-Pacific, but the prospects of it becoming a valuable member of the Pacific Community depend on the Asia-Pacific community rendering political and economic assistance to the new Russian state.[5] It remains to be seen if Russia will be an Asian power, or an Asian outcast. The most worrisome outcome of the region's rejection of Russia would be its contribution to a resurgence of neo-authoritarianism and great power chauvinism that might grow on the fertile soil of economic, military and political decline. This is, however, an outcome which the region's great powers (Japan and China) can at least retard, if they act appropriately.

Security in the Asia-Pacific can be defined as the maintenance of regional stability, the 'even and predictable development of the economic, political, cultural and social progress' of regional states.[6] If there is no prospect for smooth development that includes Russia, then the prospects of a durable security regime for the Asia-Pacific region are accordingly weakened .

Thus, notwithstanding its current weak position, Russia can still have a powerful influence on security relations in the Asia-Pacific region — either as a spoiler or a supplicant. There is probably no better metaphor to capture the essence of this than that of a terrier at the feet of the Asian great powers.

Russia's historical burden in the Asia-Pacific

Russians by and large, like other Europeans, tended to consider Asian people as uncivilised and inferior. Tsar Nicholas II went so far as to refer to Japanese people as 'yellow monkeys'.[7] This Russian attitude has not totally disappeared and has been tinged over past decades with paranoia occasioned by the underdevelopment of Pacific Russia, its small population, and its isolation from European Russia. The paranoia has been fed by a very unhappy history of relations with Asia's two great powers, Japan and China.

Some notable events in relations with Japan include: its defeat of Russia in 1904–05;[8] Japan's intervention in the Russian Civil War in 1918; Japan's occupation of Manchuria in the late 1930s;[9] the Soviet attack on Japanese forces in 1945 in breach of its 1941 non-aggression pact with Japan; Soviet mistreatment of Japanese prisoners of war; and, in the Cold War, Japan's military alliance with the United States, one outcome of which was the inability of the two sides to resolve their dispute over disputed islands at the southern end of the Kurile Islands north of Hokkaido.

As for China, Soviet policy until the late 1940s had been to keep it weak and divided by supporting both the Nationalist and Communist forces. The Soviets did not consider the Chinese communists to be 'real' communists, but rather, as Stalin called them, 'margarine Communists'. Until it became clear the communists were going to win the Civil War, Soviet–Chinese communist relations were ambivalent.[10] Soviet–Chinese relations warmed during the Cold War, especially in the late 1940s, and through the 1950s, as the Chinese relied on the Soviets for aid. Both countries revelled in the new power they had acquired with the formation of the Sino-Soviet bloc. During the 1950s alone, the Soviet Union gave China US$1.35 billion[11] in military equipment, $430 million in economic aid and other financial support which, in real terms, was one of the largest transfers of aid and technology in the postwar period. But around 1957 and 1958, the two sides had a falling-out over differing domestic political agendas and China's claim that the Soviet Union had failed to support international communism with military power. Soviet attempts to exact greater control over China as a subordinate member of the Communist bloc aggravated the rift.[12] The dispute flared with progressively more violent border clashes between 1963 and 1969, with tens of Soviets and hundreds of Chinese military personnel killed in the most serious incident in 1969. A Soviet threat to attack China's nuclear facilities in 1969 and the Sino-United States rapprochement in the 1970s further widened the gulf between Moscow and Beijing. Relations with China remained cold and adversarial until the early 1980s.[13]

The Soviet Union's relations with the two Koreas suffered badly after 1950. While the North Korean regime was a Soviet puppet regime installed after the defeat of Japan in 1945, Stalin's failure to fully commit his forces to the defence of North Korea permanently damaged relations with Kim Il-sung, the ruler that he had installed. Yet Soviet backing for communist China and North Korea in the Korean War was sufficiently strong to alienate Japan and South Korea. Their hostility towards the Soviet Union intensified with the massive buildup of Soviet military forces in the region after the mid-1960s.

With Mikhail Gorbachev's ascent to power in 1985 came 'new thinking', a gradual subordination of ideology to the pragmatic pursuit of national interest and an avoidance of ideologically based confrontational policies which had hampered Soviet influence, including in the Asia-Pacific. Gorbachev sought to reduce the Soviet Union's military burden and to develop closer economic links with previously estranged countries. This led to a Soviet rediscovery of the economic powerhouses in Northeast Asia. In July 1986, at Vladivostok, Gorbachev launched a new policy of closer relations and integration with the Asia-Pacific, reminding his neighbours that 'the Soviet Union is also an Asian and Pacific country'.

Northeast Asia has not figured prominently in Soviet trade relations in the last three decades. Russia's attempts to reverse the trend of economic decay have dominated its Asia-Pacific foreign policy since the Gorbachev era. Russia has tried to stimulate trade with the Asia-Pacific, and to encourage investment in its under-developed but abundant natural resources in the region. These objectives have been stymied by legislative confusion and high taxes in Russia as a whole and lack of well developed infrastructure, human resources and diversified industry in the Far East.

There would have to be a fundamental change of circumstances for Russia to be able to rescue itself from this position of being a disdvantaged and weakened bystander in Northeast Asia. It is equally unlikely to be able to assert any strong claim to great power status in the region, except through the good will of its regional neighbours, or by force. The following sections sketch the complexion of the gradual changes that are underway in Russia's position in Northeast Asia, and the likely directions of its strategy.

Underpinnings of Russian power in Northeast Asia

In attempting to reshape the political, economic and security underpinnings of its claim to 'great power' status in the region, Russian political relations with South Korea stand out as something of a special case in the face of a still hesitant and hostile Japan, a problematic and unattractive North Korea, and a cool and correct, albeit not hostile China.

The Koreas

The establishment of diplomatic relations between the then-communist Soviet Union and South Korea in September 1990 was a major turning point in Russia's relations not only with South Korea, but with the region as a whole. Relations between Russia and South Korea have improved significantly since that time. In June 1994, President Kim Yong-sam held meetings in Moscow with President Yeltsin, discussing in particular South Korean investment in the Russian Far East, especially in the processing of raw materials and mining, the main sources of much-needed hard currency for Russia. Military ties have been established, with Pacific Fleet warships visiting South Korea in August 1993, and joint exercises tentatively planned for 1997.[14] South Korea, moreover, has expressed an interest in purchasing Russian MiG-29 fighter aircraft, anti-tank weapons, and anti-aircraft missiles.[15]

The Russian–South Korean relationship has taken on a special significance in the light of Japan's reluctance to forge closer relations and provide development aid and investment on the scale the Russian government thinks appropriate. For its part, South Korea values the close, positive relationship with Russia as a counterweight to any prospective regional balance of power that might unduly advantage its more powerful neighbours, Japan and China.

Russia was, for a brief period, the only state to have formal diplomatic relations with both Pyongyang and Seoul, and this gave it a little more prominence as a regional broker. But Russian influence has waned since China established ties with South Korea, and in late 1994, the United States and North Korea agreed to open liaison offices.

The most important feature of Russia's relations with the Korean peninsula has been the progressive deterioration of its relationship with North Korea, a country of no value to a struggling, impoverished state. Arms sales were discontinued several years ago due to North Korea's inability to pay for such purchases in hard currency. Oil exports were terminated for the same reason. Between 1990 and 1993, two-way trade fell sharply from $2.7 billion to $530 million, of which $80 million represented North Korean exports to Russia. The ability, as well as willingness, of the Russian government to subsidise its one-time ally has ended. A major problem is North Korea's long-standing debt of US$3.6 billion.[16]

In contrast to the poor prospects in Russian–North Korean relations, the Russian–South Korean economic relationship looks much more promising. Two-way trade has grown rapidly. In 1990 the South Korean government pledged the Soviet Union $3 billion in loans over three years, and in 1991, bilateral trade increased to $1.2 billion, helped and fostered by the South Korean loans. During a visit to Seoul in November 1992, Boris Yeltsin signed a 'Treaty on Basic Relations' pledging mutual cooperation in economic issues.[17] Russia also agreed to begin repaying interest to the South Korean government on $500 million in tied aid, and $36.8 million in overdue interest on a $1 billion commercial bank loan. In exchange, the South Korean government agreed to release $1.5 billion in trade credits that had been suspended pending a resolution of the recurrent Russian delinquency on its debts and loans.[18] In 1993, Russian–South Korean trade reached $1.49 billion, an increase of 70 per cent over 1992. Russian exports equalled $960 million, mostly raw materials and minerals, and South Korean exports totalled $530 million, mainly in consumer goods.[19] In 1993, South Korea's exports to Russia were 2.2 per cent of Russia's total imports, while Russia's exports to South Korea were 1 per cent of South Korea's total imports.[20] In the first half of 1994, bilateral trade grew 48 per cent, rising to $1.003 billion (Russian exports — $575 million, South Korean exports — $428 million).

In 1994, South Korean multinational corporations Daewoo and Samsung were ready to invest tens of millions of dollars in Russia. However, prospects for further investment appear to be fading due to unforgiving Russian tax laws, conflicting trade and fiscal laws, and the Russian government's refusal to grant tax concessions to attract foreign investment. Russia's debt to the South Korean government also remains a major hindrance to expanded commercial relations.[21]

Russia's economic and trading status with South Korea falls far short of the possibilities. Economic progress and development is clearly not matching Russia's success in political and security links with South Korea. As long as South Korean companies continue to refrain from investing in Russia, and Russia defaults on loan payments, the progress will not, and cannot, continue at the same rate.

China

Russia's relationship with China has normalised and both sides are keen to avoid any suggestion that the new relationship has any strategic consequences detrimental to the interests of other countries.[22]

The Russian Ambassador to Beijing, Igor Rogachev, has supported China's public position that relations between the two countries should not harm the interests of any third country.[23] This was reiterated during talks between Boris Yeltsin and the Secretary-General of the Chinese Communist Party, Jiang Zemin, in September 1994. Foreign Minister Qian Qichen told journalists that 'the two sides will not counteract each other, but they will not make a bilateral alliance either'.[24]

China's official view is that bilateral relations entered a new phase after President Yeltsin's visit in late 1992. They were characterised after that date as 'healthy and stable development of mutual cooperation'.[25] Russia and China signed a 'Joint Declaration on the Basis of Relations' during the Yeltsin visit that provided that neither party should join any military or political alliance against the other, nor harm the sovereignty or security interests of the other.[26] While China may not want to regard this document as a treaty, it has much the same effect. The Russian newspaper Izvestia described it as such,[27] and it has the same language as a treaty between China and Mongolia signed in April 1994.[28]

Apart from the normalisation of trade opportunities and issues that once set the two countries at loggerheads, especially the border demarcation, prospects for a thriving but non-alliance relationship are based on Russia's desire for Chinese investment and labour in return for transfer of high technology, most notably in energy development and military equipment.[29]

The joint communiqué issued at the end of the May 1994 visit to China by Russia's Prime Minister Chernomyrdin, in May 1994, demonstrates the quickening pace of a very productive and fruitful relationship, including co-operation in sensitive areas such as border delimitation, military and public security affairs.[30] During Jiang Zemin's visit in September 1994, several more agreements were signed, including a comprehensive document on principles for deepening bilateral relations.[31] China and Russia held their first consultations on consular affairs (since the collapse of the Soviet Union) in May 1994.[32]

In June 1994, the two countries agreed on the alignment of the western section of the border, after the fifth round of talks established specifically for this purpose.[33] By that time, China and a group of four former Soviet republics, including Russia, which border on China, had completed twelve rounds of talks on border delimitation and confidence-building measures.[34] The two countries have exchanged 'basic data' on border deployments.[35]

Trade between the two countries enjoyed spectacular growth between 1991 and 1993 with China becoming Russia's second biggest trading partner (after Germany) in 1993.[36] Russia ranked seventh on China's list of international trading partners in 1993.

Military trade and co-operation are of considerable importance. Whether or not the report of Russian approval of Chinese manufacture of SU-27 aircraft[37] proves to be accurate, China was determined as of mid-1994 to purchase large amounts of Russian military technology and equipment.[38] Other aspects of bilateral military co-operation were also improving. For example, in May 1994, China's Navy sent three ships to Vladivostok for a goodwill visit, reciprocating a similar visit in August 1993 by three ships from Russia's Pacific Fleet to Qingdao.[39]

Investment is also growing rapidly. For example, in the Khabarovsk region, by January 1994, 199 China-funded enterprises (144 joint ventures and 55 wholly Chinese owned) had been established on the Russian side of the border area, accounting for 45 per cent of the total number of foreign-funded enterprises, although total capital of $11 million represented only 10 per cent of the region's registered total assets.[46] In March 1994, the State Council developed a three-year plan on aid to Russia in the light industry, food and textiles sectors.[41]

Both sides looked to an intensification of the relationship, particularly in trade and economic co-operation,[42] exploiting as fully as possible the advantages of contiguity.[43] China asserted the need for good relations with Russia as arising not only from the fundamental interests of the two countries, but as important for global strategic reasons.[44]

By the time Jiang and Yeltsin signed the joint statement on deepening relations in September 1994, the two countries were ready to commit themselves to joint action on a number of fronts. These included co-operation in the reform processes in the two countries; solving residual border demarcation disputes; no first use of nuclear weapons; a commitment not to target strategic nuclear weapons against each other; a quicker pace in border disarmament and mutual confidence-building measures; carving out a new role for the United Nations; and mutual support in opposing 'expansionism' — that is, the United States policy of exerting pressure on foreign governments to advance what it sees as appropriately democratic and liberal values, particularly in the field of human rights.

The two governments committed themselves to work together as great powers in addressing security problems, both at the global level and in the Asia-Pacific region. Specific issues identified included proliferation of 'weapons of mass destruction and relevant delivery vehicles'.

Mutual suspicion has, however, been hard to overcome. Some 2.5 million people reportedly crossed the border in 1993,[45] and illegal immigration (Chinese citizens in Russia) is viewed with serious concern in Moscow. Also, China has yet to cut PLA forces assigned to its military regions (beyond 100 kilometres from the border where the main disparity in forces — in China's favour — lies).[46] These suspicions, nonetheless, reflect doubts about the possibility of an eventual return to the acrimony and confrontation of the past rather than any fear that this is either imminent or likely.[47]

Japan

In some respects, the impact of Russia on Japan has been remarkably slight despite the fact that Russia has always occupied a major place in public presentations of Japanese policy-making.[48] Throughout the Cold War, the Soviet Union attempted alternatively to coax or coerce Japan out of alliance with the United States and into an economic partnership with the Soviet Union in development of the Soviet Far East. However, Japanese suspicion of Russia was too strong, and this trend continues today. In fact, the Japanese government is using 'its growing relative power to extract the maximum possible concessions from a weakened Russian Federation'.[49] Mutual distrust and suspicion continue to be present in most facets of Russo-Japanese relations.

In 1986, Japan was the Soviet Union's biggest trade partner (in volume and value) in the Asia-Pacific. But, compared with Soviet trade levels with other states outside the region, its trade with Japan was very low. By 1989, the value of trade had increased slightly to $6 billion, but by 1991 fell below 1986 levels to $5.3 billion.[50]

With the collapse of communism in the Soviet Union, Japan at first linked any susbstantial economic assistance to Russia to the resolution of the Kurile Islands dispute, but relented after the August 1991 coup, with an emergency aid package of $2.5 billion. This was, in a style soon to become typical of Russo-Japanese relations, delayed until August 1992, when $700 million was given to assist the Russian oil industry. By 1992, Japan had invested only $299 million in Russia, and hesitated to provide more because of the continuing domestic problems and turmoil in Russia.[51] Bilateral trade, however, did rise 50 per cent in 1992, although from a low base. In 1993, Japan announced a $1.8 billion bilateral aid package for Russia, in addition to the $2.8 billion already 'committed' to Russia and other former Soviet republics.[52]

Such positive developments were followed by a Russian agreement to begin debt payments of $1.2 billion to Japanese businesses in exchange for the release of a Japanese Export-Import Bank loan of $200 million to finance the construction of a fibre optic communications link between Moscow and Khabarovsk.[53] This good start has been dampened by the emerging view that these Russian moves were motivated by a 'rather mis-guided belief in the willingness of the Japanese to grant Russia economic aid and financial assistance'.[54] Bilateral trade is also starting to fare poorly after initial success, with Russian exports to Japan decreasing.

Problems continue to plague the Russo-Japanese relationship in a way not seen in Russia's relations either with China or South Korea.

A regional picture

Despite over 1000 joint ventures with Japanese, American, Chinese and South Korean capital in the Russian Far East, foreign business still remains sceptical and cautious about investing in Russia, and in the Russian Far East in particular.[55] Military hardware offers Russian exporters some prospects but total value of sales in any one year will remain small in com-parison with Russian total trade figures.

The trends are not entirely negative. By 1992, Russia's trade with the Asia-Pacific accounted for 33 per cent of its total trade, a significant increase from the Cold War level of 8–9 per cent.[56] Other positive economic trends include Russia's admission to the Pacific Economic Cooperation Conference (PECC); its attendance as an observer at the Association of Southeast Asian Nations (ASEAN) Foreign Minister meetings; member-ship in the ASEAN Regional Forum; and guest status at ASEAN Post-Min-isterial Conferences.[57] Russia may become a member of the Asia-Pacific

Economic Cooperation grouping as soon as it becomes more economically engaged in the area. Yet most countries in the Asia-Pacific still feel that Russia has too little to offer, economically, and that Russia is too problematic at this point for serious political partnership.

Military underpinnings of Russian power

With the end of the Cold War, internal chaos and disorder has become the norm in a once-proud military establishment and Russia has thereby probably lost its main claim to great power status in the Asia-Pacific.

In the mid-1980s, Soviet armed forces in the Far East were enormous: 25 per cent of all Soviet ground and air forces; and the Pacific Fleet the largest of the four fleets in the navy.[58] Notwithstanding substantial cuts during Gorbachev's rule in the late 1980s, new domestic pressures in 1993 forced Russia to cut its ground forces in the region by 100 000 troops, and the number of fighter planes and warships by 40 per cent.[59] Major scaling back of exercises and training occurred and the Pacific Fleet experienced a 33 per cent reduction in ship-days at sea.[60] The Pacific Fleet has suffered a 'staggeringly rapid rundown' in the number of warships available and fit for service and is considered to be in the worst shape of all four Russian fleets — notwithstanding the dispute with Ukraine over ownership of the Black Sea Fleet.[61] The Pacific Fleet now concentrates its activities almost solely in Northern Pacific waters. In May 1994, the Commander of the Russian Pacific Fleet, Admiral Georgii Gurinov, was dismissed for causing a 'sharp drop in the fleet's combat capability' — part of which involved his presiding over malnutrition and ill-treatment of recruits at a training centre in Vladivostok.[62]

Despite the weakness of the Russian military, it is still a very powerful force in Northeast Asia, and a regional security concern to China and Japan.[63] The important new feature of the response of Asian states to Russian military power is their willingness to consider co-operative responses, though these can only be described as embryonic. Russian and China agreed in 1994 on military exchanges, joint training, intelligence-sharing and logistical support, while South Korea and Japan have agreed to information exchanges and talks on security issues.

So will Russia destabilise Asia-Pacific security?

In spite of vigorous Russian efforts for better economic and military relations with Asian states, particularly with a South Korea that in some respects shares Russia's sense of pressure from China and Japan, Russia's inability to engage Asia-Pacific states is still very obvious.

As Russia's internal economic system crumbles, it daily becomes less stable and predictable — a situation which gives concern to its Northeast

Asian neighbours. At the same time, the two states most able to contribute financially to stabilisation in Russia — Japan and South Korea — are acting with relative reserve in their economic relations given the enormous magnitude of Russia's problems. Prominent Russian politicians, including extreme nationalists, have observed this phenomenon, and are urging a return to a more strident or robust foreign policy in the region. And the supposedly 'democratic' Yeltsin has taken a much tougher stand on some issues to accomodate this domestic sentiment.

If Russia is left out of the Asia-Pacific's economic and social progress, the potential for conflict between Russia and regional states will increase. Vladimir Ivanov's comment that Russia, 'if helped politically and economically, has good prospects for becoming a valuable member of the Pacific Community', is perceptive and enlightening, but the implied corollary is equally true. If Russia's urgent strategic and economic needs of powerful states in the Asia-Pacific cannot be satisfied, Russia's legacy of conflict with Northeast Asian states will remain alive. Protracted international isolation would become an issue in Russian domestic political battles in a climate which will be progressively more conducive to a Russian foreign policy based on hostility rather than on co-operation.

Yet, even if Russia were to eventually adopt a more hostile foreign policy in the Asia-Pacific in the next few years, it is unlikely to have the military power or the internal cohesion to pose a major threat to countries in the region.

At the level of more remote possibility, there are two outcomes which would be of more serious concern. The first would be a formal alliance between Russia and China in circumstances where both have been pushed into a corner by United States, Japanese and European opposition to high levels of domestic political repression. But, even here, such an alliance would not in itself be a military threat in the absence of a military crisis in which either country was confronting the United States, Japan or an European Union (EU) member.

A second outcome which might pose serious concern would be an alliance between Russia and any major Persian Gulf state which had become hostile to the United States, Japan or the EU — such as Iraq. The stability of oil supply from the Persian Gulf still remains the most alarming strategic vulnerability of states allied with Japan and the EU. Yet even in this circumstance, it is unlikely that Russia would want to risk serious defeat at the hands of the United States by committing forces to any conflict. The limits of Rusian intervention in such a crisis would be the same as those that applied to the Soviet Union in the Cold War.

One can therefore conclude with considerable confidence that there is little prospect that Russia will be a serious destabilising influence on the security of the Asia-Pacific in the next decade.

Notes

1   Mette Skak, 'Post-Soviet Foreign Policy: The Emerging Relationship between Russia and Northeast Asia', *Journal of East Asian Affairs*, vol. 7, no. 1, Winter/Spring, 1993, p. 153.

2   Georgi Arbatov, 'The End of the Cold War: Russian–American Relations and Their Implications for Northeast Asia', *Asian Perspective 1993*, vol. 17, no. 1, Spring/Summer, p. 95.

3   Graeme Gill, 'The Agenda for Reform in Russia: Linkages Between Domestic and Foreign Policies', and Peter Shearman, 'Russia's Three Circles of Interests', in Ramesh Thakur and Carlyle Thayer (eds), *Reshaping Regional Relations: Asia-Pacific and the Former Soviet Union*, Westview Press, Boulder, Col., 1993, pp. 29, 46

4   Vladimir Ivanov, 'From the USSR to Russia on the Pacific', *Southeast Asian Affairs*, ISEAS, Singapore, 1992, p. 71.

5   ibid., p. 86.

6   Arbatov, 'The End of the Cold War', p. 98.

7   J.N. Westwood, *Endurance and Endeavour: Russian History, 1812–1971*, Oxford University Press, London, 1973, pp. 135, 145.

8   Geoffrey Jukes, *The Soviet Union in Asia*, Angus & Robertson, Sydney, 1973, p. 76.

9   Apart from the work by Jukes cited in note 8, other useful accounts referenced for this chapter include George Hensen, 'The Russian Impact on Japan', in Wayne Vucinich (ed.), *Russia and Asia: Essays on the Influence of Russia on the Asian Peoples*, Hoover Institution Press, Stanford Cal, 1972, pp. 342–43; Westwood, *Endurance and Endeavour*, Alvin Coox, *Nomonhan: Japan Against Russia, 1939*, Stanford University Press, Stanford Cal, 1985 (2 vols), pp. 8–9, 914–15, 918–19, 923.

10   Charles McLane, *Soviet Policy and the Chinese Communists: 1931–1946*, Columbia University Press, New York, 1958, pp. 1–2; Chi Su, 'The Strategic Triangle and China's Soviet Policy', in Robert Ross (ed.), *China, the United States, and the Soviet Union: Tripolarity and Policy Making in the Cold War*, M.E. Sharpe, Armonk, 1993, p . 41.

11   All dollar amounts in this chapter are US dollars, but will be referred to without the, 'US', prefix.

12   Jukes, *The Soviet Union in Asia*, pp. 218, 224; Robert Manning, *Asian Policy: The New Soviet Challenge in the Pacific*, Priority Press Publications, New York NY, 1988, p. 47.

13   Jukes, *The Soviet Union in Asia*, p. 72; Gerald Segal, *The Soviet Union and the Pacific*, Unwin Hyman, Boston Mass, 1990, pp. 87–88.

[14] Eugene Bazhanov and Natasha Bazhanov, 'Russia and Asia in 1993', *Asian Survey*, vol. 34, no. 1, January 1994, p. 93.

[15] Research Institute for Peace and Security, *Asian Security: 1993–94*, Brassey's, London UK, 1993, p. 76; Andrew Mack, 'Arms Proliferation in the Asia-Pacific: Causes and Prospects for Control', Working Paper 1992/10, Department of International Relations, Research School of Pacific Studies, Australian National University, Canberra, 1992, p. 6; Andrei Martov, 'Russia's Asian Sales Onslaught', *International Defense Review*, vol. 27, no. 5, 1994, p. 52.

[16] Reuters Newsbriefs, 'Russian Foreign Ministry — Russia Will Not Automatically Support North Korea', 25 April 1994; Charles Ziegler, 'Russia and the Emerging Asian-Pacific Economic Order', in Thakur and Thayer, *Reshaping Regional Relations*, p. 95; Charles Ziegler, 'Russia in the Asia-Pacific: A Major Power or Minor Participant?', *Asian Survey*, vol. 34, no. 6, June 1994, p. 531.

[17] Leszek Buszynski, 'Russia and the Asia-Pacific Region', Working Paper No. 258, Strategic and Defence Studies Centre, Research School of Pacific Studies, Australian National University, Canberra, 1992, p. 14.

[18] Research Institute for Peace and Security, *Asian Security: 1993–94*, p. 76.

[19] Reuters Newsbriefs, 'Russia — Trade Figures for 1993', 8 June 1994.

[20] ibid.

[21] Reuters Newsbriefs, 'Russian Trade with South Korea 852M Dollars in First Five Months', 4 August 1994.

[22] The Secretary General of the Chinese Communist Party, Jiang Zemin, described relations during the visit of the Russian Prime Minister, V.S. Chernomyrdin, in May 1994, as 'mutually beneficial cooperation in various fields'; 'Jiang Zemin Meets Russian Prime Minister', *Xinhua* in English from Beijing, 27 May 1994; *Foreign Broadcast Information Service Daily Report China*, FBIS-CHI-94-104, 31 May 1994, p. 10. Russia's President Boris Yeltsin proposed to Jiang in early 1994 that the two countries develop a 'constructive partnership', which is presented by Russian officials as 'a normal relationship of good neighbourliness', 'Xinhua Interviews Russia's Chernomyrdin on Upcoming Visit', *Xinhua* in English from Beijing, 25 May 1994, FBIS-CHI-94-102, 26 May 1994, p. 7.

[23] 'Renmin Ribao interviews Russian Ambassador', FBIS-CHI-94-111, 9 June 1994.

[24] ITAR-TASS news agency (World Service), Moscow, in English, 4 September 1994.

[25] 'Jiang Zemin Meets Russian Prime Minister', p. 10.

[26] Ya-chun Chang, 'Peking-Moscow Relations in the Post-Soviet Era', *Issues and Studies*, vol. 30, no. 1, January 1994, pp. 83–99.

[27] ibid.

28   'Text of Amity, Cooperation Treaty', *Xinhua*, 29 April 1994, in FBIS-CHI-94-084, 2 May 1994, p. 16.

29   'Renmin Ribao Interviews Russian Ambassador', FBIS-CHI-94-111, 9 June 1994.

30   'Xinhua Publishes Sino-Russian Communique', FBIS-CHI-94-104, 31 May 1994, pp. 11-12. One section reads:

'The two sides positively appraised the ongoing negotiations on borders and cutting the military presence in the border areas and enhancing mutual trust in the military field; and agreed to stick to the provisions in the agreement on the eastern section of the Sino-Russian border, be willing to continue talks on the left-over border issues, and speed up preparation for the agreement on the western section of the Sino-Russian border. The two sides believe that it is of great significance to reach an agreement as soon as possible on cutting the military presence by both sides in border areas and enhancing trust in the military field.' (p. 11).

The agreement on the eastern section of the border was reached in May 1991, with a settlement still to be made for two small areas (one near Khabarovsk, the other near the Ergun River).

31   The text was carried by Xinhua Domestic Service in Chinese on 3 September 1994. See BBC Summary of World Broadcasts.

32   'Beijing, Moscow Consult on Consular Affairs', *Xinhua*, 13 May 1994, in FBIS-CHI-94-094, 16 May 1994, p. 7.

33   'China, Four CIS States End Fifth Round of Border Talks', FBIS-CHI-94-115, 14 June 1994, p. 8.

34   'Border Disarmament Talks Held with Four CIS States', FBIS-CHI-94-114, 15 June 1994, p. 14. A thirteenth round has since been held.

35   'Border Troop Information Exchanged with Russia', from the Hong Kong newspaper Lien Ho Pao, 5 May 1994, p. 9, in FBIS-CHI-94-088, 6 May 1994, p. 8.

36   Bilateral trade in 1992 was US$5.862 billion, an increase of 50 per cent over the 1991 figures for China–Soviet Union trade. In 1993, the figure reached US$7.679 billion, an increase of 30.9 per cent over 1992. 'Russian Minister Davydov Views Sino-Russian Trade', FBIS-CHI-94-102, 26 May 1994, pp. 9–10, broadcast of Xinhua Domestic Service, 25 May 1994.

37   'Russia to Grant License to Manufacture SU-27 Fighters', FBIS-CHI-94-102, 26 May 1994, p. 10, citing Hong Kong newspaper article, Kuo Hung-chih, 'Russia to Authorise China to Manufacture Sukhoi-27 SU-27 Fighters', *Lien Ho Pao*, 26 May 1994, p. 9.

38   Purchase of large amounts of technology and equipment, even if it reached US$5 billion as one reports suggests, would not necessarily have a destabilising effect on the military balance between China and its neighbours.

[39] 'Naval Task Force Reportedly Enroute to Vladivostok', Broadcast of an article by Lin Kang, 'Chinese Naval Task Force to Visit Russia for First Time', *Lien Ho Pao*, 12 May 1994, p. 1, in FBIS-CHI-94-092, 12 May 1994, p. 12.

[40] '"Newsletter" Depicts Economic Cooperation with Khabarovsk', FBIS-CHI- 94-101, 25 May 1994, p. 10, Broadcast of *Xinhua* Domestic Service, 23 May 1994.

[41] Jen Hui-wen,'China's Strategic Considerations in Developing Sino-Russian Relations', *Hsin Pao* (Hong Kong), 27 May 1994, in FBIS-CAI-94-105, 1 June 1994, p. 11.

[42] See, for example, the account of Li Peng's views in 'Premiers Hold Talks', *Xinhua*, 27 May 1994, in FBIS-CHI-94-103, 27 May 1994, pp. 9-10; 'Jiang Zemin Holds Talks with Delegation', *Xinhua*, 16 May 1994, in FBIS-CHI-94-094, p. 6; and, 'Qiao Shi Meets Russian State Duma Delegation', *Xinhua*, 14 May 1994, in FBIS-CHI-94-094, 16 May 1994, p. 7.

[43] 'Renmin ribao Interviews Russian Prime Minister'. The Russian prime minister observed that the two countries had yet to exploit the advantages of contiguity.

[44] See, for example, the account of Li Peng's views in 'Premiers Hold Talks', *Xinhua*, 27 May 1994, in FBIS-CHI—94-103, 27 May 1994, pp. 9–10.

[45] 'Legislator says China, "Foreign Policy Priority" for Moscow', *Xinhua*, 13 May 1994, in FBIS-CHI-94-095, 17 May 1994, p. 11.

[46] 'Border Troop Information Exchanged with Russia', from the Hong Kong newspaper *Lien Ho Pao*, 5 May 1994, p. 9, in FBIS-CHI-94-088, 6 May 1994, p. 8

[47] For an account of these sorts of concerns, see Bonnie Glaser, 'China's Security Perceptions: Interests and Ambitions', *Asian Survey*, vol. 33, no. 3, March 1993, pp. 254–56; and Shulong Wu, 'The PRC Girds for Limited, High-Tech War', *Orbis*, vol. 38, no. 2, Spring 1994, pp. 177–91.

[48] George Hensen, 'The Russian Impact on Japan', in Vucinich (ed.), *Russia and Asia*, pp. 367–68.

[49] Robert Miller, 'Russia's Foreign Relations: Recent Developments and Future Prospects', Parliamentary Research Service, Research Paper No. 7, 1994, Commonwealth Parliament, Canberra, 1994, pp. 18–19.

[50] Charles Ziegler, 'Russia and the Emerging Asian-Pacific Economic Order', in Thakur and Thayer, *Reshaping Regional Relations*, p. 95.

[51] Buszynski, 'Russia and the Asia-Pacific Region', pp. 5, 7–8.

[52] Yoshio Okiwora, 'The Asia-Pacific Situation: A Japanese Perspective', *Asia-Pacific Review*, vol. 1, no. 1, January 1994, p. 173.

[53] Reuters Newsbriefs, 'Russia Set to Begin Debt Payments to Japanese Private Firms', 8 June 1994; 'Japan's Export-Import Bank Extends Loan to Russia's Bank for Foreign Economic Affairs', 22 July 1994.

[54] Buszynski, 'Russia and the Asia-Pacific Region', p. 5.

[55] Bazhanov and Bazhanov, 'Russia and Asia in 1993', p. 89. The majority of Russian non-military trade with the region to this point has entailed fish, timber, oil, gold, diamonds, gas, coal and non-ferrous metals, all of which are exported for hard currency.

[56] Gennadi Chufrin, 'Russia is Looking East with New Interest and a New Flexibility', *International Herald Tribune*, 15 June 1994, p. 4.

[57] Pauline Kerr, 'Maritime Security in the 1990s: Achievements and Prospects', in Andrew Mack (ed.), *A Peaceful Ocean? Maritime Security in the Post-Cold War Era*, Allen & Unwin, St Leonards, 1993, p. 195.

[58] Robert Scalapino, 'The United States and the Security of Asia', in Robert Scalapino, Seizaburo Sato and Jusuf Wanandi (eds), *Internal and External Security Issues in Asia*, University of California Press, Berkeley, Cal., 1986, p. 64.

[59] Bazhanov and Bazhanov, 'Russia and Asia in 1993', p. 88.

[60] Tai Ming Cheung, 'The Eastern Front: Russian Military Development in Asia Sparks Concern', *Far Eastern Economic Review*, 26 November 1993, p. 28. The July 1994 launching of a new nuclear submarine for the Pacific Fleet at the Amur shipbuilding works was positive, but the state owed the civilian facility 'billions of roubles', and the workers had not been paid for four months. See Reuters Newsbriefs, 'Nuclear Submarine Launched in Far East', 18 July 1994. Shortly afterwards, workers in the Pacific Fleet shipyards at Vladivostok went on strike in July–August 1994 to protest unpaid wages.

[61] Joshua Handler, 'Russia's Pacific Fleet-Submarine Bases and Facilities', *Jane's Intelligence Review*, vol. 6, no. 4, April 1994, p. 159. John Jordan, 'The Russian Navy in Transition', *Jane's Intelligence Review*, vol. 6, no. 4, April 1994, p. 155.

[62] 'Fleet Admiral Fired', *International Herald Tribune*, 18 May 1994, p. 6.

[63] Hongchan Chun, 'The Security Situation in Northeast Asia Under Transition: Current Trends and Future Agenda', *Asian Perspective*, vol. 17, no. 1, Spring/Summer, 1993, p. 41.

7 Indonesia

Bob Lowry

Introduction

Indonesia is the leading power in Southeast Asia, and is a middle power within the wider Asian region. But it has no significant power projection capabilities in the orthodox sense and is unlikely to acquire them in the next ten years. This is consistent with its national priorities and its non-aligned and consensual foreign policy outlook. Indonesia's strategic importance stems from its size and its location astride the sea routes between the Indian and Pacific Oceans.

The global community has an interest in unimpeded and safe passage of the Indonesian straits and Indonesia is concerned that its strategic location does not invite foreign interference by nations seeking to secure or obstruct passage. Indonesia, in the words of Lieutenant General Sayidiman, 'needs to become the regulator of the crossroads or risk suffering and subjugation if others try to dominate them'.[1] The scope for foreign interference and Indonesia's attitudes to terms of passage will largely be determined by its ability to manage regime transformation.

As with most developing societies, security is a much broader and more immediate problem for Indonesia than for more developed societies. The fragility of political structures; circumscribed political participation; racial, ethnic, religious and regional diversity; and the economic deprivation of a major part of the population is fertile ground for social unrest and radical political alternatives. In this environment, success in economic development is vital to the legitimacy of the incumbent regime. Security, therefore, encompasses both internal security and defence against external aggression in all its forms.[2]

This chapter will canvass Indonesia's security concerns into the next century and its significance for the region.

Internal security

The government has three imperatives: first, to maintain the sovereignty and unity of the country within its present borders; second, to provide political stability as the basis for economic development; and, third, to ensure the survival of the present regime. All three are seen to be interdependent and a threat to any one is considered a threat to the others.

Such pervasive threat perceptions justify what some observers regard as excessive suppression of political activity and control of the economy. Nevertheless, whatever the form of the regime, the challenge is enormous. Indonesia's Gross Domestic Product (GDP) in 1993 was US$143 billion, about one-third that of Australia but with ten times the population and only a fraction of the infrastructure needed to bring living standards to a reasonable level. Moreover, it also has to cope with an expected population of 250 million by 2020, an increase of 60 million.

The government has identified the growing gap between rich and poor, the lack of employment opportunities and the exposure of the population to increasing external influences as the main threats to the regime. These are compounded by continuing regional separatist tendencies and insurgencies which threaten the integrity of national boundaries. Pressure for political reform is mounting as a better educated, less dependent, more informed and tax-paying middle class swells as a result of economic and social development. The presidential succession, the social role of the Indonesian Armed Forces (ABRI), and reform of the political structures will continue to be the focus of many of these pressures.

Regional insurgencies continued to fester in East Timor, Aceh and Irian Jaya during the 1990s and may well remain a problem into the next century. Each insurgency has its own particular background, but their intractability indicates the ineffectiveness of the policies being followed to address the root causes of the conflicts.

East Timor has been a millstone around the neck of the Indonesian government. It has been a drain on the domestic economy and has damaged Indonesia's international reputation. Maintaining a garrison of around twelve battalions and supporting operations of varying intensity since 1975 has been a drain on the government budget and a distraction for ABRI.

Military operations have succeeded in containing the insurgency, but a considerable military presence will have to be maintained in East Timor for many years to come. Plans to reduce the garrison in East Timor to two indigenous infantry battalions by 1995 have more to do with seeking international recognition of Indonesia's sovereignty over East Timor than any belief that support for separatism has been overcome.[3] Such force reductions cannot be realised unless they are substituted by police and intelligence units of various sorts. Significant political concessions, such as decentralisation of political and economic decision-making powers, are unlikely under the present regime.

The problem in Irian Jaya will be equally intractable. Like the East Timorese, the Irianese are culturally distinct and inhabit a defined geographic estate. They also share a belief that they have been incorporated into Indonesia against their will. As developments around the world illustrate, time, education and ideological indoctrination are unlikely to dilute these ingrained perceptions. Perceived economic exploitation and cultural insensitivity only add to what is already fertile ground for maintaining or inspiring demands for political autonomy and insurgencies.

In Aceh, sometimes described as the verandah of Mecca, Islam has provided the inspiration and ideological foundation for resistance to the central government. The Acehnese have historically been fiercely independent. The economic disparities between Java and Aceh and the perception that most of the profits from its resources end up in Jakarta have helped mobilise many in the Acehnese community, especially in isolated rural areas. Unlike the Irianese and East Timorese, most Acehnese are probably not interested in independence. Their desire is for the creation of an Islamic republic of Indonesia or at least to achieve a degree of autonomy which would include the introduction of Islamic law in the province of Aceh.

A complicating factor in all three insurgencies is the presence of a border with neighbouring states, each of which has migrant populations and indigenous groups sympathetic to the aspirations of the insurgents and willing to render support in various forms. To date, this has not included significant material support. Nevertheless, containing the potential for interstate conflict stemming from these insurgencies is an important factor in relations between the states involved.

While neighbouring states are not suspected of providing official succour, it has been reported that occasional external support has been provided, for example, by Libya.[4] There is also some suspicion, though not publicly stated, that some support was provided to the Aceh insurgents from or through the Acehnese community or its sympathisers in Malaysia. Likewise, the Timorese community in Australia, though unable to provide material support, provides a base for mobilising international political support for Fretilin.

None of these insurgencies, either separately or collectively, poses a serious threat to the integrity of the Indonesian state, but they are a drain on state resources, engage ABRI in domestic politics and undermine the ability of the national defence forces to deal with an external threat.

Islam

The only potential radical threat to the regime comes from Islamic fundamentalism. About 83 per cent of Indonesians profess to be adherents to Islam, although for many it is a nominal profession. Islamic insurgencies and acts of regional violence have erupted periodically ever since Pancasila was enshrined in the preamble of the 1945 Constitution. Competition for political support from the adherents of Islam was contained in 1973 when the government forced the amalgamation of the previous plethora of political parties into three parties: one for Islam, one for nationalists and Christians and a state-based party. Moreover, in 1985, after a long campaign, the government compelled all political parties and mass organisations, including the Islamic party and Islamic organisations, to adopt the Pancasila as the sole ideology of the state.[5]

Latterly, the government has tried to diffuse the fundamentalist streams of Islam by adopting a range of measures to provide a structure and acceptable norms for religious expression. The existence of a Department of Religion demonstrates the state's commitment to promoting religion through mosque building, prayer reading competitions and organisation of the Haj so as to co-opt religious leaders. The education base of religious officials has been broadened and many have been sent to Western universities so that when they return they will balance the militancy of graduates returning from Middle East institutions.[6]

Nevertheless, tensions remain and are heightened by a concern that the signs of Islamic revival evident in the Middle East and south Asia may spread to Indonesia.

Domestically, President Suharto has manipulated Islam for several purposes. While not wanting to encourage the fundamentalists, a nationalist Islam has been mobilised to help diffuse racial and ethnic tensions. Various campaigns have been mounted to encourage the Chinese community to convert to Islam and the promotion of Islamic devotion and education is designed to bring the racially and ethnically diverse community together.

The president has also used his patronage of Islam to create political space between himself and ABRI. Apart from the vested economic interests involved, and the question of presidential succession, ABRI feels that this strategy could backfire by giving the fundamentalists the opportunity to propagate their version of the Koran. This would allow the fundamentalists to build organisational networks which could undermine the path of non-theocratic political development that ABRI has charted for Indonesia.

Even though all political parties and mass organisations have accepted the Pancasila as the sole basis of the state, there is still considerable suspicion that it has been accepted under duress and that the Islamic party and mass organisations are not deeply committed to it. Consequently, ABRI is determined not to loosen the controls on political participation until such time as it believes that adherence to the Pancasila has been ingrained.[7] Despite the differences between the president and leaders of ABRI, there is little doubt that he shares ABRI's assessment. He has never shown any inclination to create structures or mechanisms which have the potential to limit or balance the authority of the executive.

The problem with this approach is that it presumes that the president and ABRI can determine the outcome and pace of political development in Indonesia. The policy provides little scope for genuine political participation through the authorised political structures. Such restrictions could have the reverse effect by promoting the formation of alternate structures committed to fundamentalism, thereby undermining the legitimacy of the authorised structures, especially among Indonesia's youth.

The Iranian revolution of 1979 sparked a new period of Islamic revival in Indonesia. Small revival groups, mainly based on foreign charismatic movements, have sprung up in many towns and tertiary education institutions, mainly in Java and Sumatra.[8] Most of these groups are non-violent, but extreme manifestations of this phenomena were the Woyla aircraft hijack of 1981, the series of major fires and bombings that occurred, mainly in Jakarta and Borobudur, in the mid-1980s, and the revival of the Aceh insurgency in the late 1980s.

Given Indonesia's history, especially the syncretic character and nominal status of the majority of the adherents of Islam, only a major social revolution would see the emergence of a theocratic state. That outcome is unlikely, but there is potential for the exploitation of Islam to mobilise support for social and political movements of various hues.

It is in this context that Indonesia views the critical issue of Western demands for human rights. The implementation of individual human rights would require the unravelling of the current authoritarian political structures and norms. The parliament and judiciary would have be to freed from control by the executive. ABRI, including the police, would have to be subject to parliamentary and judicial scrutiny. A major program of law reform would be needed and freedom of association and expression would have to be guaranteed. The question from the Indonesian perspective is how this can be done without unleashing the religious, ethnic, racial and social forces that are seen, rightly or wrongly, to have been the cause of instability and economic chaos in the 1950s and 1960s.

From the perspective of those in power, authoritarian rule and the associated suppression of individual rights of some individuals are justified by the stability such rule provides for economic growth which, in turn, improves the welfare of the majority of the population. It is also probable that this view is shared by a majority of the middle class who have no desire to see their position threatened by 'primordial' political forces of the left or right. This is not to deny that some sections of the middle class have a political reform agenda of their own.

Domestic political development

Although Indonesia's middle class values social stability, pressures are building for reforms which would allow them impartial treatment before the law, equal access to health facilities, equal educational and employment opportunities, and a reasonable distribution of the benefits of development.

Central to this is the question of presidential succession and the division of powers between the executive and parliament and between ABRI and civil society. President Suharto was re-elected for a sixth term in 1993 and is likely to serve the full five-year term. Because power does not lie within the formal structures of the state, there is potential for unrest if the succession is not carefully managed.

President Suharto rose to power on the back of the army and over time has managed to establish his supremacy over all the organs of state, including the army. Nevertheless, in the final analysis, it is the army which underwrites his authority. As a consequence, unless the next president is acceptable to the army, some other mechanism has to be built to provide an independent base of political support. As discussed earlier, neither the president nor ABRI seems particularly keen to allow the development of organic, grassroots political parties.

The struggle between ABRI and its middle class supporters and the opposing section of the middle class, represented by Dr Habibie, Minister for Research and Technology, will dominate the political agenda for the remainder of the decade. It is a debate about the pace of political and economic change and who is best equipped to guide it, rather than a debate about fundamentally different philosophies.

Through his close links with the president and with the latter's encouragement, Habibie has tried to create a base of support through the advancement of colleagues to cabinet positions, the cultivation of Islam and by attempting to co-opt the ABRI leadership. These measures have gained him the undying enmity of many ABRI leaders, even though some are sympathetic to his economic strategies and aspirations for Indonesia.

The president, meanwhile, has played each side off against the other to provide the space he needs to maintain his commanding position at the centre of the Indonesian state. Given his past reluctance to empower the other political structures of the state, it is unlikely that there will be any significant shift in the structure of the state before Suharto relinquishes the presidency.

At present, political participation is heavily circumscribed. The ideology of the state is not negotiable. Only three political parties are authorised. Unions are under state supervision and the press is obliged to be 'responsible'. Religious organisations are embraced in a way that ensures their effective quiescence. And all these measures are underpinned by the propagation of a hierarchical view of society and by the power of ABRI.

Unless the political structures of the state are allowed to perform the role envisaged by the authors of the 1945 Constitution, there is no institutional brake on the power and authority of the executive or ABRI. There is, therefore, scope for political turbulence should the president try to promote a successor not acceptable to ABRI. Likewise, ABRI risks creating divisions in its own ranks if it misjudges the limits of tolerance of the middle classes for the suppression of political freedoms in exchange for stability and economic development.

The economy

Indonesia's Gross National Product (GNP) in 1993 was US$142.7 billion, with growth averaging 6.4 per cent over the last twenty years. If the economy were to grow continuously at 7 per cent per annum, Indonesia's GNP at the end of the century would be around US$200 billion.[9] That would equate to a GNP per capita of around US$950, based on a projected population of 214 million. However, according to official figures, 25 million live well below the poverty line with under-employment reported to be 39 per cent in 1992.[10] With a growth rate of 7 per cent per annum, relative poverty, therefore, will still be a fact of life for many Indonesians and a potential source of domestic unrest for many years to come.

As the legitimacy of the regime is built on its ability to deliver economic growth in its broadest sense, policies which have the effect of exacerbating unemployment, even if only in the short term, could cause political problems for the government. This is particularly so because the burden would fall mainly on the urban lower and middle classes who could be more easily mobilised than the rural community.

The global economic slowdown of the early 1990s and the threat of regional trade blocs gave new breath to the economic nationalists. This was reflected in a lessening of the pace of economic reform and the more nationalist bent of the cabinet appointed for the five-year term beginning in 1993. But further incremental deregulation packages and President Suharto's commitment to Asia Pacific Economic Cooperation (APEC) indicate an acceptance that Indonesia cannot opt out of the international market.

The central debate is about the policy options for economic growth. The economic rationalists, known as technocrats in Indonesia, argue for a continuation of current policy, taking advantage of Indonesia's comparative advantage, cheap labour and following a progressive development path to more elaborate manufacturing as the skills and capital base expands.

The economic nationalists, known as technologists, argue that this course is too slow and that Indonesia needs to take a technological jump. This will require continued and, perhaps, additional protection of selected industries with attendant costs for the remainder of the economy. The technocrats argue that the costs of such an approach could well be justified by the end result. However, the risks are high and failure could have considerable security risks should the strategy not produce the benefits supposed for the population at large.[11]

ABRI is caught on the horns of a dilemma in this debate. Individual ABRI officers would generally support the technologists from personal interest and the benefits derived by ABRI business enterprises from various protective mechanisms. ABRI is also inclined to the technologists' side by its interest in the establishment of indigenous defence industries, research and development, and repair and maintenance facilities. On the other hand, it is repelled by political animosity for Habibie and the cost and capability burden imposed on defence by protectionist policies. It is also conscious that domestic social and political stability depends on continued economic growth and it knows from its own experience with various business enterprises just how inefficient protected industries can be.

Assuming the global economy does not retreat into exclusive regional trading blocs, Indonesia will probably be forced to open its economy to global competition. One of the major forces in this direction will be competition for investment and trade from other regional and global economies. This external pressure will be strengthened by the anticipated loss of the oil surplus which has so far shielded Indonesia from the full rigours of international competition.[12] The loss of oil revenue by the end of the century will remove the funds which have so far been a major source of patronage and which have enabled the government to subsidise inefficiency.

From a security perspective, this will have a twofold effect. First, it will loosen the powers of patronage by forcing the reduction of monopolies, propel the privatisation of government enterprises and encourage measures to regularise the bureaucracy. Second, the loss of royalties on oil will force the government to rely more heavily on consumption and personal taxes. On the one hand, society will be less beholden to the government for its income and on the other the government will be more beholden to society for its income. While the link between these developments and the demand for democracy has yet to be defined, these changes are likely to contribute to increased demands on the government to account for its policies and expenditure.

Such developments will fuel the debate on political development generally and invite support from external — especially Western — sources for the implementation of political reforms. External support in this form is often viewed as a security threat because of its potential to undermine the regime and the state as currently conceived.

External defence policy

The Pancasila ideology is designed to neutralise these foreign influences by providing an indigenous Indonesian ideology or concept of social and political norms. The inculcation of these values, it is hoped, will create a state of 'national resilience' which will in turn provide a sound foundation for internal and external security.

As discussed above, security is said to be dependent on successful economic development which is seen to benefit the state and society generally and provide the resources for defence and security. Under the New Order, economic development has consistently been given priority over the development of conventional defence forces.

This is reflected in the modest budget allocations to defence. The defence budget during the period 1980–92 has remained stable in real terms and has decreased as a percentage of GNP to around 2 per cent.

This allocation will rise due to the acquisition of new naval and air capabilities and their associated operating costs. Nevertheless, barring radical changes in the external security environment, it is unlikely that defence allocations will even approach the 4.5 per cent of GNP considered a reasonable maximum by the International Monetary Fund.

Indonesian foreign policy seeks to ensure that the future of Southeast Asia is decided by regional countries and is not dictated by external powers. As a result, it has resisted the establishment of broader regional security structures or mechanisms which would be dominated by the major powers. Hence APEC is supported as a mechanism for tying United States security and economic interests to the region and to give weight to the General Agreement on Tariffs and Trade (GATT) process, but it does not support the creation of a security structure within APEC at this stage. On the other hand, Indonesia would not oppose some sort of exploratory dialogue, such as the Council for Security Cooperation in the Asia-Pacific (CSCAP), which sought to explore ways of resolving regional disputes.

This pragmatic approach is indicative of Indonesia's consensual approach to international relations encapsulated in the concept of 'discussion and consensus'. This is said to be the means by which traditional society reached decisions and resolved conflict: theoretically, there are no winners or losers. In practice, this concept requires all parties to understand the power relationships between the parties involved; the strong consult the weak to curry support and avoid unnecessary conflict, and the weak can state their case and, hopefully, get the best deal available while realising the limits of what is possible. Conflict arises when the strong abuse their power or the weak have a different understanding of the rules. This could be characterised as a kind of 'consensual realist' perspective rooted in the traditional court structures and practices of the Javanese kingdoms.

Such cultural values underlie much of the frustration in Indonesia's relations with its neighbours in and outside the Association of Southeast Asian Nations (ASEAN). Malaysia's unilateral initiation of the ZOPFAN concept, the East Asian Economic Caucus, and its intransigence over the Sabah–Kalimantan border dispute show a disregard for these implicit norms promoted by Indonesia. In similar vein, comments attributed to the former Indonesian foreign minister in 1986 indicate that other countries should not only consider current realities but also take into account potential relative strengths.[13]

Despite such frustrations, ASEAN remains the 'cornerstone' of Indonesia's regional security focus, even though ASEAN is unlikely to become a defence alliance or coalition. This is not simply a function of the differences between ASEAN nations, but also an awareness that any form of alliance or coalition implies an obvious and imminent threat. When the threat is neither obvious nor imminent, there is little sense in antagonising any country which may see itself as the object of the alliance or coalition. ASEAN provides a forum for discussing regional security issues and promoting the peaceful resolution of disputes between ASEAN members. It helps develop a habit of co-operative behaviour through its endeavours to promote regional economic development and co-operation, even if progress has been slow.

Within the wider Asia-Pacific region, ASEAN provides a useful sub-grouping that aggregates the opinions of Southeast Asian countries. The final form of any Asia-Pacific security forum will emerge slowly over the next decade and, provided a co-operative regime emerges, it will be a useful forum for ASEAN to promote its long-held objectives for a Zone of Peace, Freedom and Neutrality (ZOPFAN) and the more recent proposal for a Southeast Asian Nuclear Weapons Free Zone (SEANWFZ). Confidence- and security-building measures (CSBMs) are also acknowledged to be a useful tool for encouraging co-operative behaviour, but they will be resisted if they are seen to impinge on national or regional sovereignty.

Central to these concerns for Indonesia is maintaining the integrity of its archipelagic outlook and the related issue of the Law of the Sea Convention (LOSC) which came into effect in November 1994. Some sections of the LOSC leave the implementation of particular provisions to the parties involved and the International Maritime Organisation. For Indonesia, the main outstanding issue is the status of those of its straits that are used for international navigation and a determination of archipelagic sealanes.

For security purposes, Indonesia proposes to recognise only the Malacca Strait as a strait used for international navigation and it is proposing the establishment of archipelagic sealanes allowed for by the LOSC. In essence, this would restrict the transit passage rights of naval forces to the Malacca Strait. They could still transit the other straits, but under the more restrictive rules of innocent passage. The establishment of sealanes also has potential economic implications if no provision is made for east–west lanes as well as north–south lanes.

These issues affect all trading nations using the straits but are of particular concern to the United States, which wants to retain maximum freedom for the passage of naval forces. Japan would also be sensitive to measures which increased the cost of transporting oil supplies from the Middle East. This issue is likely to become more important and may be compounded by concerns for the safety of navigation and marine pollution. Resolution of the problems raised will be complicated by a wariness on the part of user nations that any measures adopted do not provide an avenue for the imposition of de facto taxes on passing traffic and by a very strong and emotional nationalism in Indonesia.

Security outlook

The Indonesian assessment is that there is no threat of major invasion in the next ten to fifteen years.[14] However, the prospect of limited conflict, especially in the border areas, is considered more probable, though even these threats are seen to be manageable.

In pre-colonial times, the Indonesian archipelago was intermittently the outer limit of Chinese suzerainty. Indonesia hopes to encourage a new modernising China to adhere to its often-stated intention of becoming a constructive member of the Asian community on the terms of the ASEAN Declaration.[15] While China has stated that it has no desire or design to become a regional hegemon, Indonesia will be looking for consistency between word and deed.

Indonesia is ambivalent over the prospect of a re-armed Japan. Although the period of the Japanese occupation was a time of deprivation and hardship, it left many Indonesians with respect for Japanese capabilities and methods. Many Indonesians remember that it was the Japanese invasion which broke the back of the Netherlands colonial regime and facilitated their war of independence. This is reinforced by the unstated but obvious thought that Japan could help balance China, if the United States withdraws from the region and if efforts to create a viable regional security community fail to emerge as an alternative to a 'realist' prescription.

India is occasionally of some concern to Indonesia, not so much because of any fear of expansionism as due to its preparations to secure its maritime environment against the presence of the Chinese navy. If there were another conflict between India and China involving maritime forces, Indonesia's location would mean it might become embroiled. Indonesia's susceptibility in this regard is illustrated by its concern about the security of the Natuna Islands in the South China Sea. Indonesia is not a party to the Spratly dispute, but the Natunas are in a key location at the southern end of the South China Sea and would provide a useful forward base for any of the disputing parties. Of more immediate concern is the fact that the production of LNG is about to start in the Natunas, the world's largest liquid natural gas field. This is of critical importance to Indonesia's future prosperity and security because, unless major new discoveries are made, Indonesia will be a net oil importer by the end of the century.

Indonesia, keen to achieve a peaceful outcome to the Spratly Islands dispute, has hosted a number of informal workshops on the South China Sea. These are aimed at defining the issues and finding a mutually acceptable way of resolving the dispute.

Indonesia also has ongoing, though relatively minor, disputes over seabed and border demarcation issues with Malaysia, Vietnam and the Philippines. Although the display of force has been used in negotiations in at least one of these disputes, Indonesia is not concerned that they will lead to serious conflict.[16]

To deal with the strategic uncertainties of the future, Indonesia has developed a consistent and generally pragmatic set of policies. At the international level, it is promoting the reform of international organisations with the objective of weakening the dominance of the major economic and military powers and increasing the participation and influence of the wider community of states, especially those of the South.

In this context, Indonesia has promoted suggestions for the reform of the United Nations, especially within the Security Council. Similarly, it has lobbied for membership of the Group of Seven Most Industrialised Nations (G-7) in its capacity as the current Chair of the Non-Aligned Movement (NAM) (1992–95), but with little success. At the same time, the fragility of Indonesia's political structure has made it cautious in case the role and functions of international bodies encroach on its internal affairs under the guise of human rights, environmental protection, global communications, protection of international navigation and the like.

Indonesia would like to see the United Nations play a more proactive role in resolving international disputes and pre-empting conflict between states. Indonesia has contributed to many United Nations peacekeeping contingents since 1957 and provided a substantial contingent to the United Nations force in Cambodia. It has also been an active participant in regional arms control limitation initiatives, such as those on chemical weapons.

Indonesia maintains affiliations with a number of other international organisations formed to promote the interests of the lesser developed countries. Notable among these are the NAM and the Islamic Conference Organisation (ICO). Indonesia has been a moderating influence in these organisations promoting practical programs for co-operation rather than empty rhetoric. Its successful chairmanship of the NAM, 1992–95 and the APEC heads of government meeting in Bogor in November 1994 have helped to ameliorate some of the bad press Indonesia has been getting over Timor and human rights.

Military strategy

For Indonesia, alliances with major global or regional powers and an alliance within ASEAN are not feasible or desirable in the absence of an imminent threat. Alone among Southeast Asian countries, Indonesia does not perceive itself facing major security threats from its immediate neighbours and it has benefited from the balance that the United States has provided against the other regional powers. But, with the perception that the United States is in relative decline and concern about China as an emerging superpower, Indonesia has adjusted its security arrangements accordingly.

Given that Indonesia is unlikely to be able to match China's military potential, it is looking to maximise the potential of regional defence arrangements. The expansion of ASEAN to embrace all of Southeast Asia, including Indochina, and to encourage those nations to create their own version of national resilience as a contribution to regional resilience, is part of Indonesia's strategy. The gradual building of defence co-operation with its immediate neighbours, notably Australia, is another part of Indonesia's policy of creating strategic depth in the longer term.[17]

At home, Indonesia's military strategy is built on self-reliance. Its primary strategy against invasion remains guerrilla warfare. At the same time, it is continuing gradual development of its conventional defence capabilities to police its sovereignty and raise the threshold of military force that any potential enemy would have to employ to invade the archipelago or any part of it. These two approaches are being melded into a Nusantara (archipelagic) Defence Strategy built on strategic compartments capable of standing alone if necessary.

At first glance the army (212 000) seems quite large, but it is primarily an infantry force, two-thirds of which is tied down in internal security. Most of the planned increase of 30 000 personnel over the next five years will be committed to this role. The strategic reserve and special forces provide a ready response to internal security crises and low-level external threats which may arise around the borders of the state, with the primary focus being the South China Sea.

The air force is being slowly but systematically upgraded to provide air defence of the archipelago and maritime strike out to the boundary of the exclusive economic zone. By the end of the century it will probably still be a modest force of no more than six squadrons of modern medium-technology combat aircraft plus combat and logistic support squadrons.

The navy has a modest complement of mostly secondhand destroyers, corvettes and patrol boats designed for anti-submarine and anti-surface roles. It will continue to give priority to sovereignty protection of Indonesia's vast maritime domain. By the end of the century, the navy will have developed a modest integrated surface and sub-surface warfare capability, including a small submarine force, but its area of operations will be restricted due to the type of vessels employed and its reliance on land-based air cover.

Current planning envisages that these forces will be further developed over the next 25 years with a potential to deal with three crisis points at once with an infantry division and supporting naval and air forces being allotted to each.[18] But, despite improvements in maritime and air capabilities, the army will continue to provide the backbone of the defence force because of budgetary constraints, its pre-eminence in the guerrilla strategy and the continuing need to underpin internal security and regime maintenance for some years to come.

Conclusions

Like other middle powers, Indonesia's security against major external threats is dependent on preventing the assertion of predatory hegemony by a global or regional great power. It hopes this can be achieved through the development of co-operative global and regional structures, such as ASEAN, ARF and APEC, rather than a new 'concert of powers'. Should a concert of powers emerge, Indonesia will probably remain formally non-aligned but incline to the side that tends to balance the power of China.

No major external threat is seen to be imminent but there is concern that latent disputes between regional states could spill over into Indonesian territory or involve it in third-party disputes. It can be expected to co-operate in efforts to resolve these disputes in a peaceful way.

Within this context, Indonesia will continue to foster defence relations with its immediate neighbours and develop the defence capabilities required to become the 'regulator' of its sea-lane crossroads. This will undoubtedly have implications for those nations concerned with freedom of navigation should the LOSC not be honoured, but there is every prospect that workable arrangements can be reached.

Internal security will continue to be Indonesia's constant concern. Regional insurgencies will be an ongoing irritant but the real threat, from a regime perspective, will be demands for political reform pushed by external support for the promotion of individual human rights and the implicit demand for liberal democratic structures and norms.

A social revolution, such as that which occurred in Iran, is unlikely. While President Suharto remains in power, it is also unlikely that there will be any significant change in the form of the regime. The outcome of economic development combined with intensifying tensions within the regime has the potential to create instability during and after the succession, especially if ABRI is uncertain about the measures needed or if it is riven by disunity. Nevertheless, ideological commitment to the preservation of the state within current borders and ingrained nationalism will probably see ABRI retain overall control of the process of succession but only an ideologue would not have doubts about the direction of change thereafter.

Notes

1   Lieutenant General Sayidiman, 'Posisi dan Asumsi Dasar Indonesia Sekarang', *Kompas*, 25 January 1992, p. 4.

2   This conceptual approach can be found in the primary national defence doctrine publication, *Doktin Pertahanan Keamanan Negara*, Department Pertahanan Keamanan, Jakarta, 5 October 1991.

3   Interview with Major General Theo Sjafie, 'Semau Kembali ke Jawa', *Tempo*, 10 April 1993, p. 28.

4   It was reported that Libya trained at least 40 of the Acehnese insurgents, 'Dor untuk Robert', *Tempo*, 17 April 1993, p. 75.

5   Under the Pancasila, the state recognises that there is a God and compels all citizens to profess one of the five authorised religions but the state does not lay claim to any particular religion.

6   'Agar Masyarakat Islam Tak Emosional', *Tempo*, 3 April 1993, p. 68.

[7]   On being appointed C-in-C ABRI in 1993, General Feisal Tanjung said that the greatest threats to Indonesia were ethnic, religious, racial and social divisions and that it would take a very long time to create a cohesive nation. The United States had been independent for 200 years and was still affected by such problems, he said, citing the 1993 Los Angeles riots as an example, 'Setelah Pelajaran yang Mahal Itu', *Tempo*, 29 May 1993, pp. 17–19.

[8]   These are known as Usroh and are kept small so as not to fit the definition of political parties or mass organisations. Some groups are open, others are closed to varying degrees, but all would be subject to surveillance in various forms by ABRI.

[9]   *Asia-Pacific Profiles 1994*, Asia-Pacific Economics Group, Australian National University, Canberra, p. 140.

[10] Adam Schwarz, 'The Toll of Low Wages', *Far Eastern Economic Review*, 2 April 1992, p. 50.

[11] Suhadi Mangkusuwondo, 'Tentang Keunggulan Komparatif', *Tempo*, 17 April 1993, p. 97. As Christianto Wibisono has pointed out, protected industries, like the aircraft manufacturer IPTN and Krakatau Steel, have failed to produce the mid-term results expected, 'Soehartonomics', *Tempo*, 1 May 1993, p. 44.

[12] Adam Schwarz, 'Pressure Controls', *Far Eastern Economic Review*, 2 April 1992, p. 36.

[13] Dr Budiono Kusumohamidjojo, 'The Indonesia–Australia Relationship: Problems Between Unfamiliar Neighbours', *Australian Outlook*, vol. 40, no. 3, December, 1986, p. 146.

[14] For a discussion of threat perceptions, see Bob Lowry, *Indonesian Defence Policy and the Indonesian Armed Forces*, Canberra Paper No. 99, Strategic and Defence Studies Centre, Research School of Pacific Studies, the Australian National University, Canberra, 1993, pp. 9–16.

[15] For example, when Indonesia's vice-president visited China in 1992, he was reassured by the Secretary General of the Chinese Communist Party that China would not force communism on other countries or interfere in their domestic affairs and that China wanted to live in peace and assist in resolving world conflicts peacefully, 'RRC tidak akan paksakan sistem komunismenya', *Angkatan Bersenjata*, 13 April 1992, p. 1.

[16] Lowry, *Indonesian Defence Policy and the Indonesian Armed Forces*, p. 45.

[17] Australia and Indonesia signed an Agreement on Maintaining Security on 18 December 1995. The Treaty's Article 3 commits both countries 'to consult each other in the case of adverse challenges to either party as to their common security interests, and if appropriate, consider measures which might be taken either individually or jointly and in accordance with the processes of each party'.

[18] *Rencana Pembangunan Lima Tahun Keenam 1994/95–1998/99*, Book IV, Republic of Indonesia, Jakarta, pp. 627–68.

8 Security and the Korean Peninsula

Ian Wilson

The Korean Peninsula has long been regarded as one of the world's flashpoints or 'hot spots'. It has been characterised by fierce international conflict from 1950 to 1953, high-level border tensions at the 38th Parallel ever since, heavy concentrations of armed forces on each side of the dividing line and the threat that border clashes could again erupt and escalate into another war, drawing in allies of the rival regimes of North and South Korea. To this threatening situation have been added concerns that the economically challenged North may be unstable due to leadership change and that it may either already have or be developing nuclear weapons. Events in 1994 brought all these factors into sharper focus, thus making timely a reconsideration of the Korean security situation.

The Democratic People's Republic of Korea is usually cited as posing the major threat to the peace of the peninsula, particularly in assessments from Washington and Seoul. From that standpoint, the North is depicted as an unpredictable state which is at once both a 'bandit' and a 'pariah', unwilling to conform with the rules of international society. It is seen to be bent on reunification through any means at its disposal. Bombing attacks abroad, airliner sabotage, terror and subversion are listed as means whereby the leadership of the Kim Il-sung regime has pursued its goals, foremost among which is the reunification of the Korean nation under the leadership of Pyongyang. The death of Kim Il-sung in early July 1994 was not from this standpoint thought to change matters much because his son, Kim Jong-il, was frequently alleged in South Korean publications to have been behind the violence and illegality of this international behaviour pattern.

The North Korean political system is particularly opaque and it has not been possible to verify some of these claims, which have become part of the 'conventional wisdom' about its nature. Who in the leadership was really behind the Rangoon bombing in 1981 and the airliner disaster in 1987 remains unclear and until these matters can be clarified they are poor foundations for policy responses. It might be just as useful also to take into account the proposition that a regime which has seen one major ally collapse and relations with the other grow cool, suffered the loss of its founding father and must contemplate continuing economic decline might also be concerned to develop a new and hopefully more successful pattern to its interactions with its neighbours and the outside world. Since it can be assumed that the ruling group seeks to maintain itself in power, a new set of means may serve this end just as well and possibly better than the older set have done thus far.[1] Any analysis of North Korean foreign policy therefore must be open to a range of interpretative and explanatory propositions.

Threats to the peace should not be discounted and have been very real in the past. North and South have both desired unification on their own terms and feared attack from the other. For Japan and the United States, the prospect of a communist Korea so close and 'pointing like a dagger' at the heart of Japan was equally unacceptable and so they steadfastly supported the Republic of Korea. China and the Soviet Union sought a buffer of their own against a United States-backed Republic of Korea (ROK) and supported the Democratic People's Republic of Korea (DPRK) for strategic as well as ideological reasons. The intense rivalry of the two Korean regimes and their constant attempts to destabilise each other made for an explosive situation that lasted for nearly five decades. The external patrons assisted in the process whereby the Korean peninsula became one of the most heavily armed regions in the world and their clients deployed the latest weaponry against each other. A military gap favouring the DPRK was perceived to exist, leading the United States to station some 40 000 troops with nuclear-capable missiles and aircraft in the South to redress the imbalance. To the north, Kim Il-sung was able to exploit Sino-Soviet rivalry to obtain ever higher levels of military and economic assistance. This enabled him to keep almost one million troops under arms, more than matching the 700 000 or so south of the demilitarised zone. Kim Il-sung was denied nuclear arms, but the proximity of Seoul to the 38th Parallel made his conventional forces, particularly the long-range artillery, very threatening.

As time passed, it became clear that neither Beijing nor Moscow exercised much control over Kim Il-sung, whereas the United States forces and missiles and the main force units of the ROK Army were under United States command. This was seen as leaving open the possibility of Pyongyang striking south at Seoul, whereas a pre-emptive attack initiated by Seoul against Pyongyang was ruled out, although such a possibility was entertained by some during the Park and Chun years. After North Korea's economy was overtaken and left behind by that of South Korea during the late 1970s and through the 1980s, it soon became clear that reunification on Kim Il-sung's terms was becoming less and less likely.

The temptation for him to make a move before all prospect of success had gone was at least plausible and consonant with the official interpretation of life in the South. Northern propaganda had it that the people of South Korea were suffering increasing economic hardship and would rise in support of Kim Il-sung at the appropriate signal, a line that retained credibility only as long as the North could be kept free of any alternative sources of news and information. Once North Korea opened its doors to the outside world, that propaganda would be shown to be false.

First of all, changes in other communist states, then the gradual democratisation of the ROK and finally the impossibility of keeping the people of the North permanently cut off from all outside news, all served to undermine the propaganda line and public stance of the DPRK on reunification. Instead of a unitary Korean state, Kim Il-sung in 1972 proposed a confederal republic, to be called Koryo, within which the northern part would retain limited sovereignty and preserve, however improbably, some aspects of *juche* socialism. Then events moved even more quickly than Kim perceived and by the mid-1970s his external support began to melt away. First China embarked on a program of economic reform and opening up to the international economic system, a course which required a stable and peaceful regional (and international) environment within which to trade and develop. Second, the Soviet Union began to show severe structural damage and sought to reduce tensions with both the Western alliance and China. This effectively prevented Kim Il-sung from continuing beyond the mid-1980s with the hitherto successful stratagem of playing one communist state off against the other in order to maximise returns, often in the form of arms and modern weapons technology. Both allies put pressure on Pyongyang to reach a settlement with the South and the United States while themselves striving to establish profitable economic relations with the now prosperous southern economy.

The tide was obviously not favouring the DPRK and, on economic grounds alone, collapse seemed inevitable. More successful economies in Hungary and East Germany had not been able to avert the overthrow of communist rule and Romania, with a proportion of ruling party members in the population almost as high as North Korea's, experienced the most dramatic regime change of all.[2] The Korean Workers' Party had become highly personalist and the foremost interpreter and enhancer of Kim Il-sung's self-reliance philosophy of *juche* was his son, Kim Jong-il. Contrary to the view of some observers, *juche* does not rule out importing and adopting foreign technology and goods. The DPRK has always imported technology and machinery, as any visit to a state factory will show. But the leadership did rule out adopting the Chinese practice of opening up the country to foreign aid, credit, trade and investment. Despite strong pressure from China to set up special economic zones, the North Korean administration was not so impressed by official tours to Shenzhen as to follow suit. The end result was that Pyongyang followed the Chinese critique of Gorbachev's venture in undertaking political reform before implementing economic reform. But it also developed its own critique of the Dengist reforms by drawing attention to growing income disparities, corruption and the neglect of education and social services as equally undesirable consequences of that program.[3] The doctrinal rectitude reflected in this position did not halt the DPRK's economic decline and it continues to hamper the Tumen River economic development zone on the Russian/North Korean/Chinese triborder and progress in joint ventures using foreign capital and expertise.

The sequence of political and economic reverses that North Korea experienced during the late 1980s and early 1990s threatened to relegate the state to a very minor role in international affairs and may have done so had it not been for the nuclear question upon which much of its significance now rests. From the outset, there were sound reasons for North Korea to look towards nuclear power for energy generation and the production of fissile material for nuclear weapons. Without any domestic oil and gas deposits and with limited opportunities for hydroelectric power, nuclear power was an obvious alternative for North Korea, as it was in Japan and South Korea. Nuclear power was seen to be cheap and less polluting, and the disposal of waste had not yet become a problem. Although there are some uranium deposits in Korea, to opt for nuclear power would make the DPRK dependent on outside sources for enriched fuel but in the longer haul, through the technological assistance available through the International Atomic Energy Agency, North Korea might eventually become self-sufficient.

At the weapons level, the nuclear option also had attractions. To have, or to be believed to have, a quantity of such weapons could make up for the lost leverage North Korea once enjoyed through its conventional military strength and its ability to play China off against the Soviet Union. A small arsenal of nuclear weapons would prove a powerful deterrent to an attack from the South as well as providing a threat in that direction. National prestige is another important aspect of Pyongyang's foreign policy, vast sums being spent to cultivate influence, friends and respect among the smaller nations of the Third World. In this context, a bomb or two would certainly enhance Pyongyang's international prestige.[4]

To be taken seriously and treated on the basis of equality is a sensitive matter for Pyongyang's diplomacy. To a considerable degree, the events and posturing conducted by North Korea throughout 1993 and 1994 were aimed at getting the United States to the negotiating table without South Korea and to achieve a strong bargaining position. This was so whether the high cards were North Korea's threats to leave the Nuclear Non-Proliferation Treaty (NPT), its refusal to accept inspections, its threat to respond to sanctions with war, its demands over the errant United States helicopter pilot and its dramatic agreement, finally, to suspend all nuclear activity. Any lasting security arrangement for the peninsula must take account of this image factor in the North's strategic calculus. National prestige has already been mentioned as a driving force behind foreign policy, but it is not simply an end in itself. It is the means whereby other objectives can be achieved and the regime can develop something approaching legitimacy among its people and hopefully survive in a post-Cold War world of relaxed political tension and normal commercial and cultural intercourse with the rest of the world. As was shown by the October 1994 Agreed Framework signed with the United States in Geneva, North Korea's nuclear bluff of not revealing whether there was any threatening nuclear program at all or whether there were one or two actual weapons successfully achieved the objectives sought by the DPRK. Quite apart from the provision of light water moderated reactors and the supply of fuel oil until the the new reactors are functioning, the DPRK now has a forum with the United States in which to press other objectives, including full recognition, an armistice agreement and access to United States markets and technology for restarting and remodelling the economy.

The key question is whether, in the light of the dramatic events of 1994, the security situation has changed. What are the perceived threats from the North now that more democratic procedures in the Republic of Korea seem to rule out an attack from there, initiated by right-wing and militarist elements? Firstly, the size of the conventional war machines on each side of the border leaves armed conflict as a distinct possibility, although the military balance is shifting towards the South. While any United States nuclear weapons in the ROK have been moved offshore, the South now has an army, well-trained reserves and modern equipment to match the Korean People's Army. This it is able to achieve for a modest outlay in terms of expenditure as a proportion of GNP, whereas for the North to maintain parity it is forced to spend between 20 per cent and 25 per cent of a GNP which is now about one-twelfth that of the ROK. Maintaining parity for the DPRK is becoming much more difficult, if not impossible. Between 1985 and 1992, South Korean defence expenditure rose by US$2970 million, or 63.5 per cent (at constant 1985 US$ prices). The North spent an extra US$931 million or a rise of 22.4 per cent, a figure which puts enormous strain on an already weak and inefficient command economy.[5] Second, Pyongyang is no longer convinced that southern immiserisation exists and with that myth goes the prospect of a sympathetic revolution.[6] Instead, the prospect of complete economic collapse to the North has been concentrating the minds of ROK leaders for several years. Neither Seoul nor Japan, China nor Russia relishes the prospect of some twenty million economic refugees suddenly arriving should this happen. This, at the very least, provides a hopeful climate for regional co-operation to avert an economic collapse.

Other threats to the peace exist and constitute the basis for domestic criticism of the Clinton administration, but most have been greatly diminished by the Agreed Framework. While comprehensive inspection of every suspected site will not take place before 2003, the International Atomic Energy Agency (IAEA) and United States authorities are satisfied that plutonium extraction from the Yongbyon site has now ceased as it and other declared sites are now open. While it is certainly feasible that small concealed quantities of fissile material might be sold on to other users, the prospect of North Korea becoming the supplier of devices to terrorist groups or governments classified as 'rogue' by Washington is now dismissed in almost all quarters. Training and technical assistance to groups and insurgent movements may well continue, along with the sale of conventional arms and missiles, like the SCUD and Rodong series. The spectre of such weapons being used for chemical and biological warfare cannot be ruled out either. As yet there is no international control regime to guarantee that North Korea, or any of its potential customers, will not proceed down that track, but the general picture is one of greatly reduced tension and threat on the Korean peninsula. In all areas except that of verbal abuse of the Kim Young Sam government, there have been improvements.

It has been argued here that insecurity in Pyongyang has been a major contributor to tension in the region. Feelings of isolation, desertion and betrayal as China and Russia turned to South Korea added to longer term concern about hostile encirclement and threat from the United States, Japan and the ROK. Under Article III(1) of the Agreed Framework, 'The US will provide formal assurances to the DPRK, against the threat or use of nuclear weapons by the US, which eases these concerns, particularly when tied to steps towards diplomatic recognition and a context within which talks about economic assistance, trade and technology transfer can take place. The additional threat of hardship due to energy shortages is met by the agreement to supply fuel oil until the reactors are operational in quantities equal to about one-third of total import requirements in 1992.'[7] At the centre of the deal is the commitment by the North to dismantle two small reactors feeding no more than 30MW into the power grid, in return receiving more modern light water reactors generating up to 2000MW, albeit without weapons-useable plutonium as a byproduct. The North will not proceed with two less modern dirty reactors some two years short of completion and has frozen all weapons-oriented research to the satisfaction of the IAEA. As United States Ambassador-at-large, Robert Galluci, put it after Geneva, 'They are giving up a nuclear program that posed an enormous risk to South Korea, to Japan, to Northeast Asia and to the international non-proliferation regime.' The benefits of so doing were not inconsiderable.

The South Korean government has been guarded in its expressions of relief, but is also a beneficiary. It has been saved the costs of developing a countering nuclear capacity and will profit from the work of installing the power reactors. The United States has specified models based on the South Korean Uljin 3 and 4, designed and manufactured by a subsidiary of the United States Combustion Engineering. The all up cost will be in the vicinity of over $4 billion, to be financed by an international consortium. Pyongyang prefers Russian design and technology, but finance for this would be very difficult to raise.

The costs to Seoul are less tangible. There is some resentment and injured pride that its powerful ally had not included it in the negotiating process and to that extent had served the ends of the North. Furthermore, the conventional military threat remains. But so, too, does the United States security umbrella. Nuclear retaliation would also be invoked in the event of a nuclear attack from the North, an action which would presumably abrogate the whole Agreed Framework system. As Pyongyang often complains, the United States nuclear force has simply been moved off-shore to submarines and attack aircraft operating from aircraft carriers and Japan. Nevertheless, the Framework does something to allay Pyongyang's feelings of insecurity. For its part, the United States has bound the DPRK in paragraphs (2) and (3) of Article III to implement the Denuclearisation Joint Declaration of 1991 and to engage in North–South dialogue. Already, in January 1995, Pyongyang's tardiness on this provision has been met by threats to hold back further oil shipments.

Overall, there has been a toughening in the ROK stance towards Washington and the fairly pro-American Han Seung-joo has been replaced as Foreign Minister by Gong Ro-myong, a career diplomat. There is the fear that the United States might further sacrifice South Korean interests in the course of its relations with the DPRK, and on a range of trade and foreign policy questions it is to be expected that the formerly close ties with the United States will gradually weaken. These were bound to change with time and in response to a more assertive nationalism among the Korean people for whom the United States military command of ROK forces was an insult once it became less of a necessity. Growing might as an international trader will push South Korea to pursue its own interests and any reduction of tension on the peninsula will only accelerate this trend. One future source of conflict is the point at which the United States has to choose between the DPRK formula for reunification under a confederal 'one nation, two systems' formula and the South Korean proposal for a unitary 'commonwealth' within which it would be the more powerful member.

Finally, although Seoul's defence expenditure continues to grow, the South is now not locked into the sort of costly deterrents a nuclear-armed North would impose on it if it were to survive in such a hostile environment. The October agreement has effectively removed the nuclear threat, enabling more funds to be directed towards economic development. In the longer term, South Korea is strongly committed to reunification but the lesson of East and West Germany is pertinent in this case.[8] To absorb the North now, leaving aside the military problems this could involve, would bankrupt even the relatively prosperous ROK. Moreover, the complete economic collapse of the North is not to be desired, for this would also place unacceptable strains on the South. Instead, it would be preferable that the northern economy move out of stagnation through increased economic interaction with the South and the operations of southern firms seeking to utilise the resources and cheap labour available. Hyundai sought to move in this direction ahead of government guidelines but the

Agreed Framework may well create a more sympathetic environment for such economic ventures while at the same time helping to keep total collapse at bay.

President Clinton has not fared well out of the North Korean breakthrough. During the early part of 1994 he expressed exasperation as the DPRK continually shifted its position, obstructed the inspection process and finally declared that its status under the NPT was one of 'suspension', which seemed to bind it not at all. Clinton seemed to be sliding towards those advocating first sanctions and then direct action, which would leave the North resembling a 'parking lot'. United States Senator John McCain went further, claiming, 'The only thing that convinces people like Kim Il-sung is the threat of force and extinction.'[9]

North Korea has long occupied a place close to Cuba, Vietnam and Libya in the demonology of United States foreign policy discourse. In an election year, the temptation was to employ excessive language, particularly after reverses in Bosnia, Somalia and Haiti. It was left to former President Jimmy Carter to take the initiative for change and, by exceeding his very vague and unenthusiastic mandate from President Clinton, extract the basis for an agreement from Kim Il-sung. The death of 'The Great Leader' very shortly afterwards delayed but did not derail the settlement process which culminated in the October signing in Geneva. The timing was unfortunate, for it was immediately claimed by hard-line Republicans and not a few nervous Democrats that Clinton has conceded far too much. As Robert Dole put the matter, it was a 'lousy deal'. Largely for other and unconnected reasons, the November mid-term poll went strongly against the Clinton administration and the Agreed Framework has subsequently come under attack from the newly confident Republicans in both the Senate and the House. Soon after the poll there were threats to hamstring the agreement by attaching amendments against its spirit and letter, a position that was not ameliorated when, at Christmas, a United States helicopter strayed across the 38th Parallel and was shot down by Korean People's Army troops. One pilot was killed but the return of his co-pilot was delayed while Pyongyang extracted every possible propaganda advantage. Deputy Assistant Secretary Tom Hubbard negotiated the release but, awkward though relations were during late December and early January, two Republican senators and one Democrat congressman visited North Korea, as did former ambassador James Lilley.[10] The relationship established in October in Geneva quickly produced results and, whatever impediments might be thrown in its way, the DPRK clearly saw the agreement as beneficial and worth preserving.

The United States has achieved some further advantages from the Agreed Framework which did not lend themselves to ready explanations on the hustings but are important for the longer term security of the region and the achievement of some wider global objectives. First, for the DPRK to have left the NPT with impunity and rejected the system of IAEA safeguards would have irreparably damaged the non-proliferation regime. Whether or not the DPRK reached the stage of producing numbers of weapons and assisted others to a similar level, any state moving in that direction would be encouraged to push ahead and ignore the NPT regime. Even more serious was the prospect of existing participants refusing to extend the regime when it comes up for renewal in 1996. Second, the United States aims to install controls on the spread of other weapons systems, particularly the chemical and biological. For the NPT to collapse would have a carry-over effect on attempts to impose other limitations on arms proliferation, the end result of which would be a much more dangerous world. The agreement at Geneva has preserved the IAEA and the NPT system and holds out hope for the Chemical Weapons Convention.

Other benefits from the Agreed Framework and the discussions taking place around it must include the lowering of tensions on the peninsula. This has undermined efforts by hawkish minorities in Japan and the ROK to advocate the development of locally based nuclear capacities as a deterrent. In the improved regional climate, the United States has agreed to suspend the Operation Team Spirit joint military exercises with the ROK Army which the North has found so provocative and threatening for many years. This is not an understanding written into the Agreed Framework so the exercises could be resumed should Pyongyang prove recalcitrant in implementing other provisions which are in writing, such as the requirement to conduct significant North–South talks.

The Clinton administration has now come very strongly behind the Agreed Framework. Thomas C. Hubbard, in an important address to the Heritage Foundation at the end of January 1995, described it as a 'watershed' and 'the beginning of a process of building a new and inclusive security framework in Northeast Asia'. He went on, 'the world can only benefit from the prospect of a North Korea comfortably integrated into the community of nations'. He noted positive signs during the negotiations from the North Koreans who 'repeatedly stressed that in resolving the nuclear issue, their country was taking a fundamental step away from its history of proud self-reliance. They seemed clearly to realise that they were opening the door to constructive interaction and engagement with the US and with other countries across a wide range of activities.' Pending the implementation of its provisions, Hubbard described the Framework as 'an historic shift that redefined the parameters of security in a region that has been the locus of struggles among the great powers for centuries'.[11]

This is the most positive trend on the Korean peninsula for many years. It is a direct consequence of a co-operative approach amongst the great powers in Northeast Asia and the development amongst them — on this issue at least — of a habit of close consultation. China, Japan, Russia, the United States and South Korea shared a common concern in reaching a peaceful solution to what might have become a festering source of intense regional insecurity. However, the promise of a lasting peace on the Korean peninsula still requires some astute regional diplomacy.

It also requires deft political footwork on Capitol Hill to create a consensus on current policy. Only when a degree of American bipartisanship has been established will the Korean agreement withstand the currents of opportunistic domestic politics. This requires a better undestanding of North Korean political processes than has been demonstrated thus far. A useful working hypothesis might be to see a conflict in Pyongyang between older hardline views of the world which were set in the Cold War and emerging support for interaction with the outside world on a range of economic and political matters, even if only in a different attempt to preserve the regime.[12] Hubbard drew attention to recent changes and it has been the experience of diplomats, United Nations assistance personnel and foreign traders that there is a reformist wing to the Korean Workers' Party.[13] If this hypothesis has some foundation, then we should expect and accept DPRK hyperbole, obstructionism and obduracy as a function of such a domestic political conflict. Frequent concessions to older ritual may be the price of change, and over-reaction rather than moderate but firm responses to these outbursts could prejudice progress towards a lasting settlement. It would be premature to forecast success for some time yet because complex political changes in Pyongyang, Seoul, Washington and even Tokyo could upset the present course. The trust, mutual commitment to peace and readiness to engage in real dialogue across the 38th Parallel, which Hubbard mentions as the next essential steps, will still take time. All countries in the Asia-Pacific have a close interest in encouraging these steps to be taken.

Notes

[1] Although drawing rather different conclusions, see Paul Bracken, 'The North Korean Nuclear Program as a Problem of State Survival', in Andrew Mack (ed.), *Asian Flashpoint: Security and the Korean Peninsula*, Allen & Unwin, Sydney, in conjunction with the Department of International Relations, Research School of Pacific and Asian Studies, Canberra, 1993.

[2] Leslie Holmes, *Politics in the Communist World*, Oxford University Press, London, 1986, Statistical Appendix, pp. 403–11.

[3] Discussions with mid- and high-level officials, Pyongyang, 1990 and 1992.

[4] A state is, of course, prohibited from engaging in major weapons research and development once it becomes party to the Non-Proliferation Treaty and IAEA assistance with peaceful use technology is conditional on membership of the treaty. A group of states had developed or come very close to developing a nuclear capacity without membership, notably India, Pakistan, Israel and South Africa. The Iraqi case is more relevant because, despite the setback of the Israeli attack on the development installation, Saddam Hussein appeared to have resumed

research, if not production, while a signatory to the NPT by keeping all evidence carefully concealed from the IAEA inspectors for several years. For North Korea, and possibly for Iraq also, to be thought to have or to be on the brink of having a few bombs was equally effective as a means of attracting attention.

5   Barry Buzan and Gerald Segal, 'Rethinking East Asian Security', *Survival*, vol. 36, no. 2, Summer 1994.

6   Some DPRK officials will admit this in conversation. The propaganda line is slower to change.

7   Andrew Mack, 'Nuclear Endgame on the Korean Peninsula', Working Paper 1994/9, Department of International Relations, Research School of Asian and Pacific Studies, Australian National University, Canberra, 1994, p. 18.

8   On the background, see: James C. Cotton, 'The Two Koreas and Rapprochement: Foundations for Progress?', in Andrew Mack (ed.), *Asian Flashpoint*, pp. 137–46.

9   Quoted, Robert Perkinson, 'Notes From the Field: The Korean Nuclear Crisis: Introduction', *Bulletin of Concerned Asian Scholars*, vol. 26, nos 1/2, 1994, p. 128.

10 See *Reuters Textline* over this period for a fuller account of these events.

11 USIS Wireless File, 31/1/95, pp. 8–11.

12 Professor Byung-joon Ahn takes a different view: 'Kim Jong Il's dilemma is this: the North's increasing isolation and impoverishment make political and economic reform imperative; but Kim may find reform impossible. His legitimacy rests almost solely with the mantle of extreme nationalism inherited from his revered father.' See 'The Man Who Would Be Kim', *Foreign Affairs*, vol. 73, no. 6, November/December 1994, p. 94.

13 Interviews with DPRK officials very occasionally lend support to this view, which is otherwise based on discussions in Pyongyang and elsewhere.

9 Post-Cold War Security in the ASEAN Region

Leszek Buszynski

It was Singapore's Foreign Minister Wong Kan Seng who at the Association of Southeast Asian Nations' (ASEAN) 25th annual ministerial meeting in July 1992 claimed that 'there has never been a more favourable security situation across the Asia-Pacific region since the end of World War Two'.[1] On the other hand, Indonesia's Foreign Minister, Ali Alatas, declared that the new global security environment which had emerged after the Cold War was 'less predictable' and was marked by 'fluidity and instability'.[2] Within the region, post-Cold War security assessments differ considerably depending upon the time factor. All are generally agreed that the long-term future is favourable in view of the development of multilateralism which, in its security or economic form, has come to dominate the agenda of Asia-Pacific conferences. All generally admit, however, that uncertainty, and in some areas instability, characterises the present security situation, though in varying degrees.

The danger of conventional military conflict has been reduced as a consequence of the ending of the Cold War and Wong Kan Sen's own assessment of the security situation was based largely on this factor. There is no doubt that the security of the region has improved greatly given the termination of superpower confrontation and the defusing of the Cambodian conflict. The fear of the spillover effect of superpower conflict, which motivated such regional initiatives as the Zone of Peace, Feedom and Neutrality (ZOPFAN) or the South East Asian Nuclear Weapons Free Zone (SEANWFZ) has been put to rest and replaced by a sense of relief. Nonetheless, regional security cannot be defined solely in terms of the absence of conventional military threat which is a prevalent Western understanding of security. There are other and more significant elements in the notion of security, as applied to the developing world context, which support Ali Alatas's view of fluidity and unpredictability.

In the developing world, notions of security reflect the overriding problem of establishing stable political structures and minimising potentially destructive communal or religious divisions. The term 'security' includes those political and economic factors which may undermine existing authority structures or contribute to the erosion of state legitimacy. In this sense, security is not just about relations between states upon the assumption that states are the major actors in international politics. It also embraces ethnic and religious communities, political organisations and other non-state actors whose actions may have similar consequences. States may not be at war with each other, and in a technical sense the region may be at 'peace', but divisive political and communal conflict stimulated by economic failure or misguided policies could still disrupt the region and have the same effect as war.

External security concerns: The role of external powers

External powers can be termed higher-level security concerns for ASEAN in view of their capacity to affect the security of the region as a whole. The impact of external powers upon Southeast Asia will become more pronounced in the post-Cold War era as the United States relinquishes its role as primary security guarantor. The Singaporeans have been the region's avid supporters of 'vacuum' theory, claiming that an American withdrawal would provoke greater insecurity as external powers such as China, Japan or India would fill the 'vacuum'. The Singaporeans highlight the danger of rivalry between the external powers — between China and Japan, between China and India — which would transform Southeast Asia into an arena of conflict. Government representatives from the other ASEAN countries have generally rejected the more crude variants of 'vacuum' theory and have associated Singapore's views with its vulnerable position as a small state. Nonetheless, all express some degree of concern in relation to the future actions of external powers.

The most salient of ASEAN's external security concerns is the future role of China. The concern with China relates first to the evolution of China's political system and the prospects for internal stability in a country undergoing dramatic economic change.

ASEAN leaders recall with some trepidation the Cultural Revolution, when revolutionary movements in Southeast Asia were given strong support and fears of Chinese interference into the region's domestic affairs were intensified. But now China has the fastest growing economy in the world in which growth rates reached 13 per cent in 1993 and similar figures are predicted for the rest of the decade. The issue arises of the political impact of economic change and whether the result will be instability and conflict, or a transition to a more pluralistic political system.

China's intentions over the South China Sea also continue to trouble the ASEAN countries, as this is perhaps the one area in the region where conflict may be possible. At the 4th Conference on the South China Sea which was held in Surabaya in August 1993, Ali Alatas described the situation as 'potentially explosive' and declared that action was required to avoid 'a regional flashpoint after Cambodia'.[3] At this conference, Indonesian attempts to promote the notion of joint development of the resources of the South China Sea met an *impasse*. Ali Alatas had hoped that the 1989 Timor Gap Treaty, which provided for Australian–Indonesian joint development of the disputed section of the Arafura Sea, could serve as a model for the South China Sea. China's representatives had previously raised the possibility of joint development as a solution to the issue but were also insistent on affirming China's sovereignty over the area. Chinese Foreign Minister Qian Qichen declared in favour of joint development when he was a guest at ASEAN's 25th Ministerial Meeting in July 1992, but added the qualification, 'when conditions are ripe'.[4] Observers were left puzzled by the import of these remarks and as to when exactly circumstances would be propitious.

One school of thought within ASEAN holds to a very optimistic interpretation of Chinese intentions, claiming that the issue at stake concerns resources and that the Chinese are simply playing for time to strengthen their position in regard to future negotiations over the area. By stalling, the Chinese demonstrate to the ASEAN countries that joint development depends upon their endorsement for which the ASEAN claimants should be prepared to pay in terms of concessions. The pessimists within the region view Chinese intentions primarily as an issue of sovereignty linked with the reunification of Hong Kong and Taiwan with the mainland. They argue that joint development is used by Chinese representatives to conceal another agenda which includes eventual possession of the entire area. A third explanation is a mixture of the above, which claims that there is no cohesive policy over the issue within China. Within the Chinese government there are those for whom the idea of joint development and economic integration with the Asia-Pacific region is a desired aim. Within the defence establishment, however, there are voices which insist upon Chinese sovereignty over the area and which call for its eventual inclusion within the borders of the motherland. While these two groups jockey for influence over policy, China simply stalls and postpones a resolution of the issue.

Of particular concern to the ASEAN countries is the development of China's navy. Included in the discussions about the Chinese navy is the often-expressed intention to acquire an aircraft carrier which would ensure air support for China's naval units in the South China Sea. There is no doubt that the present leadership has a sense of great power status which demands the development of a powerful navy. How a future Chinese leadership will use the navy is a matter of conjecture, but the incentive for Vietnam and ASEAN to make concessions to Chinese claims will probably increase as China's navy expands. The idea of joint development of the area's resources can be continually vetoed by China in the understanding that more favourable conditions can be obtained in the future. The pessimists in ASEAN would argue that the PLA will play a major role in Chinese domestic politics in the post-Deng Xiaoping era, in which case China would become less receptive to the idea of joint development. If the PLA entrenches itself in a key position as a consequence of a succession crisis, China may assert its 'sovereign right' over the South China Sea to claim possession of all the islands. In February 1995, China occupied the previously unoccupied Mischief Reef, in the Spratly Islands, near the Philippines. Future clashes with Vietnam or the Philippines cannot be excluded and might serve to intimidate other ASEAN countries into accepting China's claims.

Other troubling developments for ASEAN include China's support for the military regime in Myanmar. Ever since an arms deal was concluded with Rangoon in October 1989, China has been its major arms supplier and in 1992 provided a reported $1 billion of military equipment.[5] Myanmar's army was due to expand from 190 000 to 300 000 in 1993 with Chinese weapons and support.[6] In return for the supply of military equipment, China has allegedly been granted the use of facilities at Bassein in the Irrawaddy delta.[7] It is unclear exactly what, if anything, the Chinese intend to construct there, but their interest in countering the Indian Navy and in establishing a presence in the Indian Ocean has been openly declared. Naval rivalry between China and India would immediately engulf the ASEAN region.

China thus presents a critical security problem for the ASEAN region in a way not entirely appreciated by the West. Many predict that China will become the twenty-first century's next superpower and that its economy may become greater than that of Japan. Moreover, China's political stability is uncertain and there is the strong possibility of the PLA assuming a major role in politics as the dramatic effects of economic growth undermine the existing regime. The establishment of a military–authoritarian regime in China would present particular difficulties for ASEAN, not just in relation to the South China Sea, or the development of its navy, but in terms of its attitude towards a region considered an area of Chinese influence. These problems could be negotiated and resolved if political change in China took the path of democracy and pluralism, but there is no guarantee that a move towards democracy would be any less convulsive than it was in Russia. Either way, it seems, ASEAN security may be directly affected.

Japan also presents a security concern for ASEAN, though not in the way anticipated several decades ago. Then, fears were raised after the 1973 Middle East War that a rearmed Japan operating outside the context of the United States alliance would move to secure its own oil supplies and markets. Such fears were symptomatic of regional concerns about Japan that have their origins in the Pacific War and the conviction that Japan could not tolerate its continuing dependence upon unstable resource-producing regions. Since that time, the idea that Japan would re-establish some kind of hegemony over the region by force has been rarely voiced. To avoid the prospect of disruption and instability, Japan has attempted to promote multilateral security frameworks which would retain the United States in a stabilising role. The then prime minister, Kiichi Miyazawa, claimed in Bangkok in January 1993 that 'Japan will think and act together with ASEAN' in ensuring stability. Miyazawa emphasised the need for the United States to maintain a military presence in the Western Pacific and called for a two-track approach towards regional security. At one level, specific regional problems would be resolved through multilateral negotiations involving the countries concerned; at another level, a region-wide security system would be created which would include both China and Russia.[8] This espousal of multilateralism is in keeping with the idea of Japan as a 'global civilian power' acting through already established or evolving multilateral frameworks to ensure peace.[9]

Japan's major contribution to the security of the ASEAN region is through economics. The area has become more important to Japan since the 1985 Plaza Agreement resulted in revaluation of the Yen and an increase in Japanese investment in Asia. Japanese subsidiary companies producing textiles, electronic parts, semi-conductors, etc. were relocated in Asian Newly Industrialising Countries (NICs) to take advantage of cheap labour and favourable investment conditions. Japanese investment on this scale was one of the contributory factors to the impressive economic development experienced by Asia's NICs, including Singapore, Thailand, Malaysia and, belatedly, Indonesia. In recognition of the critical economic role assumed by Japan, ASEAN leaders have, at various times, called upon Japan to establish or institutionalise the economic links with the ASEAN region. Singapore's Prime Minister Goh Chok Tong proposed that Japan assume the leadership of a new group of Asian NICs and declare the equivalent of a Marshall Plan for Asia.[10] Such sentiment found expression in Mahathir's East Asian Economic Grouping (EAEG) proposed in 1990 (later, the East Asian Economic Caucus (EAEC), from which the United States, Australia and New Zealand were to be excluded). The idea of an exclusive East Asian grouping has support within Japan, as it reflects the growing significance of Asia in Japan's trade. In 1987, both North America and Asia accounted for 35 per cent of Japan's trade; by 1991, Asia's share of Japan's trade was 41 per cent while North America's share was 30 per cent. These trends gave a powerful argument to Japan's Ministry of International Trade and Industry (MITI) to focus attention upon Asia rather than the United States as a reaction to congressional protectionism and America's interest in the North American Free Trade Agreement (NAFTA). Japan's political leadership may have avoided formal endorsement of Mahathir's EAEC for fear of offending the United States, but the idea expresses aspirations not only within the Japanese business community but within ASEAN as well.

Of prime concern to the ASEAN countries is to ensure the continuation of Japanese investment and to facilitate technology transfers that would enable ASEAN to move to a new stage of its industrialisation. The ASEAN countries hope that formalised economic arrangements could link Japan and the ASEAN region to ensure continuity without, however, creating an exclusive trading bloc that would rebound to the detriment of ASEAN's economic ties with the United States or the European Union. For this reason, at the 26th Annual Ministerial Meeting held in Singapore in July 1993, ASEAN agreed that the EAEC was to be a grouping within the Asia Pacific Economic Cooperation (APEC) which would meet concerns raised by Indonesia in regard to the exclusion of the United States. Nonetheless, ASEAN concerns are also raised by the direction of Japanese investment within Asia and the rise of China as a competitor. Japanese investment in China increased by 66 per cent in 1991 and by 85 per cent in 1992 and fell in ASEAN by 27 per cent in 1992. China has become Japan's second biggest trading partner while investment in the United States fell 23 per cent in 1992.[11] It may be that, with further revaluation of the Yen, investment in ASEAN will again reach previous levels and Japanese representatives have been reassuring ASEAN in this vein. Nonetheless, ASEAN countries are aware that China holds a special significance for Japan and its sheer size may compensate Japan for loss of economic benefits in North America in a way that ASEAN cannot.

ASEAN concerns about Japan have shifted significantly from the days when fears were raised about Japanese rearmament in response to a crisis. The concern that unstable regional or global conditions may provoke Japanese unilateralism still exists, particularly in relation to the Korean peninsula or the South China Sea. A crisis in these areas, however, would stimulate a global response which would probably shield Japan from the need to react unilaterally. Of greater concern to ASEAN today is Japan's future economic role in the region. For the ASEAN countries, Japanese investment, technology transfers and access to Japan's markets are the expected benefits of an institutionalised arrangement centred on Japan. Indeed, a recognition that political stability within the ASEAN region has an economic basis pushes the ASEAN countries to propose the kind of economic arrangements that would link them more tightly to Japan.

External security concerns: Lower-level contingencies

Lower-level security issues irritate the ASEAN countries but do not have the capacity to affect regional security overall. Such lower-level contingencies may stimulate or intensify suspicions between ASEAN neighbours, making security co-operation more difficult to achieve and preventing the development of an ASEAN multilateralism that has so far eluded the organisation. Intensified suspicions can be reflected in arms purchases or in defence policies directed against neighbours which may contribute to a vicious circle. In the worst case scenario, minor issues affecting intra-

ASEAN relations or ASEAN relations with neighbours may escalate into conflict which may require regional or international attention.

Piracy was a problem involving Singapore, Malaysia and Indonesia because of the frequency of attacks on international shipping in Indonesia's Phillip's Channel in the Riau archipelago. The concern was that collusion existed between the pirates and Indonesian customs authorities who were on duty at the maritime surveillance radar unit on Batam Island.[12] Suspicions circulated that the pirates themselves were Indonesian customs officials which provoked the Indonesian government into vigorous denials. Malaysia and Singapore were reluctant to press for multilateral measures to curb piracy given the Indonesian government's initial objections. Nonetheless, pressure from the international community and shipping companies induced a change of attitude within Indonesia and a concern about its image. In July 1992 a Singapore–Indonesian agreement was reached which permitted co-ordinated anti-piracy patrols in the Singapore Straits. The agreement allowed for direct communication between the two navies and gave them a limited version of the right of 'hot pursuit' in each other's sea zones. A similar agreement was reached between Malaysia and Indonesia, which created a joint body to co-ordinate anti-piracy measures in the Malacca Straits. The International Maritime Bureau established a piracy centre in Kuala Lumpur on 1 October 1992, which was to receive signals from vessels in distress and alert the navies concerned. As a consequence of these measures, the incidence of piracy in ASEAN waters declined significantly.[13]

Bilateral tensions between ASEAN neighbours can also be a security concern and in this respect the Singapore–Malaysia relationship stands out. Singapore is a cultural and historical extension of the Malayan peninsula and has been separated from its natural hinterland as a consequence of communal politics. As Lee Kuan Yew once declared, Singapore cannot exist independently of Malaysia, which is 'our guarantor for the economic and political stability of Singapore'.[14] Singapore's dependence upon Malaysia, however, translates into an obsession with its sovereignty and a desire to demonstrate and even assert its independence in relation to Malaysia. Within Malaysia, there are those, such as the Sultan of Johore's family, who question Singapore's sovereignty and who expect the island-state to behave as though it was still part of Malaysia. Singapore's forward defence policy, which envisages the occupation of Johore in the event of a crisis, is intended to be a statement of Singapore's sovereignty in this respect and is seen as unnecessarily provocative by Malaysians. Trivial incidents can become major issues in this relationship which can inflame feeling over existing problem such as the status of the Horsburgh lighthouse or Batu Puteh, Singapore's use of Malaysian airspace and the detention of fishing vessels. Malaysian–Indonesian exercises in Johore around Singapore's national day in August 1991 stimulated suspicions in Singapore, whose authorities called up reserve units as a response. Despite Singaporean paranoia and fears of Islamic fundamentalism in Malaysia, both countries have too much at stake to allow the relationship to deteriorate as a consequence of the many small incidents that arise between them.

The Malaysian–Philippine relationship is another weak point within ASEAN where security co-operation could not be expected. Territorial disputes bedevil the Philippine–Malaysian relationship, which was severely strained when the Philippines first raised its claim to Sabah in 1962. Diplomatic relations between the countries were ruptured in 1968 for eighteen months over the Sabah issue and their navies almost clashed in the 1979–81 period over the sea boundary dispute in the South China Sea. In April 1988, 49 Filipino fishermen were detained by Malaysia where the sea boundary claims overlapped. The incident caused an outcry in the Philippines and demands for retaliation. Filipino resentments and existing tensions were aggravated by Malaysian defence purchases and the decision to construct a naval base in Sabah in addition to Labuan. Corazon Aquino attempted to drop the Sabah claim in 1987 in preparation for the Manila ASEAN summit, but was obstructed by her own Senate which demanded some *quid pro quo* from Malaysia. The Senate sought compensation from Malaysia for the heirs to the Sultan of Sulu, the original owners of Sabah, a treaty of friendship and economic co-operation with Malaysia and joint sea patrols to prevent arms smuggling between Malaysia and Muslim Mindanao. All these demands were naturally rejected by Malaysia. President Fidel Ramos visited Kuala Lumpur in January 1993 in an attempt to overcome the difficulties in the bilateral relationship as part of his effort to strengthen ties with ASEAN. The Philippine Senate, however, still prevents the president from removing the problem of the Sabah claim from the agenda. Malaysia did at least accept a visit by a Philippine leader after having previously insisted that the claim be dropped as a precondition. The problems of the Philippine–Malaysian relationship are unlikely to escalate to conflict, despite occasional hysteria from the Philippine press or from Filipino congressional representatives looking for an external enemy.

ASEAN as a regional organisation has provided a framework, if not for the resolution of bilateral disputes, then at least for their mitigation, and has given the leadership an incentive to contain tensions and to prevent their eruption into conflict. Other territorial disputes include the Malaysian–Indonesian claim to Sipadan and Ligitan, two islands off the coast of Kalimantan. Indonesians were troubled by Malaysia's announcement that it was to build a tourist resort on Sipadan and Malaysia was disturbed by what was regarded as a buildup of Indonesian naval vessels around the area. No one expects conflict over this issue, however.

Fishing disputes have occurred within the region which have contributed to existing bilateral tensions and which have provided a justification for naval expansion. Thai fishermen have regularly intruded into Malaysian waters and Malaysian fishermen have been accused of poaching in Thai waters; Malaysia and Thailand have faced land border problems in relation to smuggling operations and alleged Malaysian support for Muslim rebels in southern Thailand. A joint survey of fishing resources was initiated in May 1992 and the other problems were handled within the bilateral context by the Thai–Malaysian joint commission.

Similar problems beset Thai–Vietnamese relations as the Thai Navy regularly seizes and impounds Vietnamese fishing vessels and vice versa. The maritime border between Thailand and Vietnam has not been clearly defined and such incidents will continue and, should the bilateral relationship deteriorate over the Cambodian issue, could trigger an escalation of tensions. In September 1993, Thai fishing vessels apparently harassed Indonesian fishermen around Aceh, prompting the dispatch of two Indonesian naval vessels as protection. Conflict is unlikely to arise from fishing disputes alone, but tensions may be stimulated. President Ramos has declared that illegal fishing and smuggling in Philippine waters was depriving the country of an estimated $1.8 billion annually in lost resources.[15] The Philippine Navy, however, is the most under-equipped in ASEAN and is unable to police the country's EEZ or its fishing resources effectively. It did not, for example, discover the Chinese presence on Mischief Reef until several months after the Chinese had built various structures on the Reef. Under the current naval modernisation plan, the Philippines has purchased twelve used South Korean gunboats and intends to purchase eight patrol boats from the United States, fast attack craft from Australia and Spain as well as long-range maritime patrol aircraft.[16]

Internal security concerns

Internal security has assumed greater importance for the ASEAN countries and in the future may constitute a priority rivalling their concern with external powers. An important factor in this development has been the expectation that legitimacy could be based upon economic growth which could mitigate the divisive effect of communal or religious tensions. The period of unprecedented economic expansion that began for the ASEAN region in the 1980s was one of the factors in the elimination of communist insurgency movements in Thailand, Malaysia and Indonesia. The continuation of insurgency in the Philippines, whether Muslim or what is loosely called communist, testifies to the salience of the economic factor, as the Philippines has had the worst economic record of all the ASEAN countries. ASEAN leaders regard with alarm the prospect of a further downturn in the world economy or an outbreak of protectionist sentiment in the developed world. Similarly, ASEAN has been affected by the emergence of China as a competitor for investment and as a country following a similar export-led growth strategy producing similar products. China was one of the major factors behind ASEAN's decision, proclaimed at the 4th ASEAN Summit in Singapore in January 1992, to launch the ASEAN Free Trade Agreement (AFTA).

Acute sensitivity to economic trends and developments is one characteristic of the ASEAN approach to security. Equally important is the concern for political stability in a way which distinguishes ASEAN from its Western partners.

Why does Thailand defend its policy of 'constructive engagement' of the military regime in Myanmar, which has been condemned for human rights violations by the Western world? From the Thai or ASEAN perspective, a sudden collapse of the military regime in Myanmar or a premature transfer of power to an unprepared civilian coalition could result in the country's dismemberment.

The disintegration of Myanmar, as a consequence of an internal social and political explosion, would destabilise Thailand's border regions and could provoke internecine conflict that would spill over into neighbouring countries. Moreover, China would probably become the predominant power in a Myanmar that has collapsed from within, in which case the eastern border would become an area of Sino-Indian conflict. For this reason, the ASEAN countries regard the constitutional convention convened by the military regime in Yangon since January 1993 as a positive sign and an opportunity for eventual democratisation. The ASEAN hope is that a constitution and a democracy would emerge from this convention which would obviate the need for the imposition of sanctions upon the military regime.

Cambodia's security has been a regional concern since 1970, when the internal conflict in that country was exacerbated by a coup which overthrew Sihanouk. ASEAN's aim over Cambodia has always been to defuse the internal conflict and ensure that it would never again draw in outside powers — Vietnam, Thailand or China. Although the United Nations-sponsored Paris agreements of 1990 did not work according to plan, the Khmer Rouge have been generally marginalised. However, some Thais continue to support the Khmer Rouge in clandestine ways. Though Thailand officially observes the United Nations Security Council's embargo on logs and oil which took effect from 1 January 1993, its military has not given up the idea of using the Khmer Rouge as a way of maintaining influence in Cambodia. Any escalation of internal conflict in Cambodia may involve Thailand as well as Vietnam and may postpone the process of regional reconciliation between these two countries.

Indonesia cannot be compared with Myanmar or Cambodia and its inclusion here does not imply that it is considered unstable or liable to collapse. Nonetheless, Indonesia's immediate neighbours, Singapore, Brunei and Malaysia, are concerned about future trends in that country in the recognition that political instability in Indonesia could undermine their own security. These countries recall the Konfrontasi period of Southeast Asian history when Sukarno launched Indonesia into a direct challenge of Malaysia and demonstrated to the region how important Indonesian stability is to regional security.

The question is whether Indonesia can survive democratisation. Domestic and international pressure upon Indonesia's military rulers to hand over power to a civilian leadership has intensified over the past few years. Indeed, Indonesia's military rulers have been increasingly regarded as an anachronistic remnant of the past and have been subjected to a volley of criticism for human rights abuses in Aceh and Irian Jaya as well as in East Timor. Army commander and the president's son-in-law Major-General Wismoyo Arismunandar noted that international developments could have a negative effect upon a multi-ethnic state such as Indonesia in recognition of the centrifugal forces the country will face in the future.[17] There are those in Indonesia who argue that the army is the country's only unifying force and, without it, ethnic and regional separatist movements would prompt its disintegration. Others argue that a political framework has evolved which can unify the country and will permit the army to withdraw from politics. In any case, Suharto's apparent unwillingness either to designate a successor clearly or to establish a stable basis for the transfer of power to a new leader raises questions about Indonesia's future stability (see also Chapter 7).

Conclusion

It would be facile to conclude that post-Cold War security concerns in the ASEAN region have shifted from the external to the internal. For a start, security in the ASEAN region always had an internal dimension in view of the region's experience of communist insurgency. Moreover, ASEAN has certain external security concerns relating to the roles of external powers that, if anything, have been heightened by the termination of the Cold War. Nonetheless, despite this, the probability of a conventional conflict will decline and to that extent it may be claimed that a South China Sea crisis or a similar crisis over the region's sea lanes is unlikely. A realistic assessment of security in the ASEAN region would focus more upon internal conflict which may break out spontaneously within a state between ethnic or religious groups, political or communal factions. Such conflict may be provoked by the failure of economic policies or economic decline, by internal political conflict or by ethnic and religious separatist movements. It may be that the post-colonial boundaries, considered sacrosanct within the region, may have to be redrawn to accommodate the results of political change and democratisation. In Myanmar, and perhaps even in Indonesia, these changes may indeed have traumatic consequences for neighbours.

Notes

1   *Straits Times*, 30 July 1992.

2   'The Emerging Security Environment in East Asia and the Pacific: An ASEAN Perspective', address by H.E. Ali Alatas before the NUS Society, Singapore, 28 October 1992.

3   *Reuters*, 25 August 1993.

4   *Business Times*, 23 July 1992.

5   *Reuters*, 8 February 1993.

6   *Far Eastern Economic Review (FEER)*, 27 February 1992.

7   *Reuters*, 8 February 1993.

8   *FEER*, 28 January 1993.

9   Yoichi Funabashi, 'Japan and the New World Order', *Foreign Affairs*, vol. 70, no. 5, Winter 1991/92.

10   *Straits Times*, 14 June 1989.

11   *Financial Review*, 4 August 1993.

12   *FEER*, 2 July 1992.

13   *Lloyds List*, 30 July 1992 (*Reuters Textline*); *Reuters*, 2 February 1993; and *Lloyds List*, 7 September 1993 (*Reuters Textline*).

14   *Straits Times*, 5 July 1988.

15   *Reuters*, 23 June 1993.

16   *Straits Times*, 24 June 1993.

17   *Antara* 254/B, 1 September 1993.

10 Indochina

Carlyle A. Thayer

The security environment in Southeast Asia has undergone a complete transformation since the end of the Cold War and the conflict in Cambodia. No longer is the region divided into two antagonistic blocs, each backed by Cold War rivals, contesting control over Cambodia. The most remarkable change has been the dissolution of Indochina as a unified sub-region under Vietnamese hegemony and dependent on the Soviet Union. Indochina is now in transition from being a zone of contention to a zone of peace and economic development. The outcome of this process is by no means certain. Cambodia remains debilitated after a decade and more of internal war; and Thailand still retains suspicions about its traditional mainland rival, Vietnam.

The three states of Indochina are also in transition in other ways. Cambodia, Laos and Vietnam have abandoned central planning and have moved, in varying degrees, to develop market economies and open their doors to foreign investment. Each of the three states is now poised to become integrated into the larger region. Vietnam joined the Association of Southeast Asian Nations (ASEAN) as a full member in 1995; Laos and Cambodia are set to follow.

A process of political transition is also underway. It is most noticeable in the case of Cambodia, which has reverted to constitutional monarchy after a decade and a half of communist rule, first under the Khmer Rouge and then under protegés of Vietnam. The communist-ruled states, Laos and Vietnam, are both experiencing challenges to one-party rule. How these political systems will respond to demands for greater pluralism, if not democratic freedoms, remains uncertain.

The strategic basis for the national security policies of the Indochinese states has also changed fundamentally. The three states no longer share a common threat. Each now faces a different set of primarily internal security issues.

This chapter examines the new national security policies of Vietnam, Laos and Cambodia.

Dissolution of the 'Indochinese bloc'

Traditionally, Vietnamese strategists have argued that Indochina formed a 'single strategic battlefield'.[1] The Third Indochina War (1979–89) resulted in the emergence of a unified bloc of Indochinese states backed by and dependent on the Soviet Union. Military, political and, to a certain extent, economic policies were co-ordinated on an Indochina-wide basis.

But despite the appearance of unity, the 'Indochina bloc' never had a firm foundation. There were always underlying tensions among its members, the most potent of which was Khmer nationalism. In December 1981, for example, Cambodia's party chief, Pen Sovan, was reportedly removed from office because of his dislike of Vietnamese dominance.[2] Laos, meanwhile, never fully shared Vietnam's enmity towards China. It may be surmised that Vietnam's failure to create a trilateral economic co-ordinating body foundered on fear of Vietnamese domination by its smaller allies.

Gorbachev's 'new political thinking'

During the mid-1980s, the national security assumptions of the Indochinese states were challenged by a series of external and internal developments.[3] Foremost among the external factors was 'new political thinking' in Soviet foreign policy promoted by Mikhail Gorbachev. His initiatives in settling regional conflict by political means and normalising relations with China set in motion a major change in the strategic environment in the Asia-Pacific region, not least in Indochina.

Factors shaping national security policy

Indochina's strategic environment is shaped by a number of factors, foremost of which are geography and the military disposition of adjacent states. Indochina shares land borders with only three countries, China, Thailand and Burma. All the Indochinese states, of course, share borders with each other. When maritime boundaries are included, the circle of states with which Indochina interacts includes Indonesia, Malaysia and the Philippines.

Vietnam and Laos are single-party political systems that have been in power since 1954 and 1975, respectively. National security policy is virtually congruent with regime security. It has as its central objective the maintenance in power of single-party rule and socialist ideology in addition to guaranteeing the independence and sovereignty of the nation-state. National security threats — both internal and external — are viewed within this framework.

The national security perspectives of Vietnam and Laos contrast with the situation in Cambodia where the regime itself is an unstable coalition and in danger of collapse. The Cambodian state is also weak, poorly developed and unable to exert administrative control over large sections of the countryside.[4] In reality, the Cambodian People's Party (CPP) remains the dominant political actor.

In the mid-1980s, a variety of internal and external factors combined to produce a change in thinking about national security policy. These factors included the cumulative effects of a crisis in the domestic economy, the effects of an international trade and aid embargo, the costs of conflict in Cambodia, Chinese politico-military pressures, and Soviet insistence that the Indochinese states readjust to new political thinking. For example, as the Gorbachev reforms began to take hold in the Soviet Union, Laos and Vietnam were pressured to refashion their national security frameworks by giving greater emphasis to economic and technological factors.

In mid-1987, Vietnam's national security managers 'bit the bullet' and adopted a major new national security doctrine. This was embodied in Politburo resolution no. 2, 'On Strengthening National Defence in the New Revolutionary Stage'.[5] This doctrine completely overturned Vietnam's national security orientation of the previous decade. The past emphasis on forward deployment of forces in Laos and Cambodia was replaced with an inward-looking, more defensive posture.

Under the new policy, Vietnam withdrew its combat units and other support forces from Cambodia and Laos. Main forces stationed along the Sino-Vietnamese border were ordered to adopt a non-provocative stance, and as tensions declined, their numbers were reduced. At the same time, Vietnam undertook a massive demobilisation of its main forces. An estimated 600 000 regular soldiers, including 200 000 officers and civilian defence specialists, were released from service by the end of 1990.

National strategy policy

Vietnam

The basic tenets of Vietnam's national security policy were re-endorsed at Vietnam's seventh national party congress, which met in June 1991.[6] They were incorporated into the 'Guidelines and Tasks for the 1991–95 Five-Year Period' issued by the VCP Central Committee's Military Commission. Since then, Vietnam has attempted to integrate all aspects of Vietnamese society — military, internal security, economic, social, cultural, political and foreign relations — into a single national security policy. The new defence doctrine is termed simply 'people's war and all people's national defence'.

Vietnam's defence doctrine was designed to meet what it perceived as the most likely threats to its security in the 1990s. High on the list of likely contingencies were what it termed low-level or limited conflicts. These were likely to occur in disputed offshore territories in the Eastern Sea (South China Sea) or along Vietnam's land and sea borders. China is undoubtedly viewed as Vietnam's likely main protagonist. Vietnam is also concerned about possible border incidents with Cambodia and clashes at sea involving Thai vessels in disputed fishing waters.

In order to prepare for likely contingencies, special defence zones were designated in strategic areas. These were fortified and efforts made to link economic production and military defence. In the initial stages of limited conflict, the responsibility of meeting and countering an external attack will rest with the local militia and self-defence forces. At a later stage the main forces, supplemented with ready reserves, would be employed.

Vietnam's much reduced military establishment now places prime responsibility for meeting external threats to national security in the hands of a mobile regular standing army equipped with the best weapons that Vietnam possesses. The regular army is backed up with a large strategic reserve composed of newly demobilised soldiers. In local areas, defence is the responsibility of militia and self-defence forces. These forces are also assigned to work with the Ministry of the Interior in maintaining public order and internal security. Each military region, province, city, district, ward and village is given responsibility for fortifying strategic defence zones, such as land and sea borders, including offshore islands.

Laos

In recent years, Laos has perceived its security environment as benign. This was reflected in the Political Report of the Lao People's Revolutionary Party (LPRP) to the Fifth Party Congress in March 1991. This report contained comparatively little discussion of defence and security issues compared with previous political reports. The main emphasis on national defence was internal and focused on maintaining 'peace and order, national unity and solidarity and concord among tribes in the national community'. Only passing mention was made of possible external threats.

In line with similar developments in Vietnam, the Lao People's Army (LPA) was directed to involve itself in economic production tasks. As Secretary General Kaysone Phomvihan noted, 'The national defence and security forces must promote the factors for self-strengthening, produce their own logistics supplies, partly fulfill the internal demands of their units, and contribute to socioeconomic development.'[7]

Cambodia

The rapidity of changing national security perspectives and alignments in Indochina is best illustrated with reference to Cambodia. Between 1989 and 1993, the government in Phnom Penh underwent three name changes before becoming a constitutional monarchy.[8] Despite this, one element of continuity has remained. The Khmer Rouge has continued to be viewed as the main threat to Cambodia's national security.[9] As a result of the adoption of a state constitution and the formation of a coalition government in 1993, a national army — the Royal Cambodian Armed Forces (RCAF) — was formed by merging ANKI and KPNLAF (Khmer People's National Liberation Armed Forces) military units with those of the CPAF. According to a 1994 assessment, 'RCAF strength on paper is about 130 000 but a more realistic figure would be less than 100 000, the difference being accounted for by "ghost soldiers" who remain on the payroll to help boost the income of unit commanders.'[10]

The new commanders have been charged with overseeing the process of merger, reorganisation and demobilisation of surplus military units. Also, they have had to deal with a number of urgent matters including adoption of a common uniform, provision of housing and social welfare for soldiers, demobilised troops, war invalids and their families and the adoption of standardised procedures. The new national army has taken charge of the de-mining program, and the storage, maintenance and/or destruction of surplus equipment, weapons and ammunition.[11]

While the process of reorganisation and restructuring was underway, the new Cambodian armed forces were assigned the responsibility for maintaining internal security. From the outset, the newly established government and its armed forces were beset by endemic violence. The Khmer Rouge has continually refused to disarm or observe a ceasefire. Khmer Rouge-instigated violence continues to occur in a number of provinces, most notably Siem Reap, Banteay Meanchey, Preah Vihear and Kampot.

Continued Khmer Rouge-instigated violence in mid-1993 led the Phnom Penh government to declare that it had 'no other choice than to take firm measures to actively exercise the right to self-defence'. First Prime Minister Norodom Ranariddh called on the military to mop up Khmer Rouge forces. In August 1993, RCAF units, comprising forces of the newly merged factional armies, launched offensive operations in Preah Vihear, Siem Reap, Banteay Meanchey, Batambang, Kompong Chhnang, Kompong Cham and Kompong Thom provinces. These actions sparked a record number of defections from Khmer Rouge ranks, including senior officers.

In 1993–94 the RCAF unsuccessfully attempted to seize and hold two major Khmer Rouge base areas. RCAF forces mounted an initial thrust against Anlong Veng in October 1993 and succeeded in capturing it in early February. Almost immediately, a RCAF strike force of 7000 was directed to capture Pailin, an important Khmer Rouge gem mining centre. In response, the Khmer Rouge mounted widespread diversionary attacks before counter-attacking and driving out government forces. Anlong Veng was retaken by the Khmer Rouge on 24 February 1994. At least ten thousand civilians were displaced from their homes as a direct result of fighting. In May 1994, foreign observers estimated that the Khmer Rouge were in control of more territory in Battambang and Banthey Meanchey provinces than before the May 1993 elections.

The upsurge in fighting in late 1993–early 1994 led the Khmer Rouge to renew their calls for the formation of a quadripartite army and for their inclusion in the government in an advisory capacity. The Royal Government, under prodding by King Sihanouk, explored possibilities for a negotiated end to a looming civil war. Eventually round-table talks to discuss 'national reconciliation' were held in Pyongyang and Phnom Penh in May and June 1994. These talks proved inconclusive. In June, after the Ministry of the Interior stated it could no longer guarantee the safety of Khmer Rouge representatives in the capital, they departed for their jungle headquarters. The Cambodian government then proceeded to pass a law outlawing the Khmer Rouge and offering an amnesty for those who chose to defect. The Khmer Rouge responded by declaring the formation of a provisional government and stepping up their acts of harassment.

The Cambodian government suffered a great loss of prestige as a result of these military setbacks and morale in the armed services sunk to an all-time low. The ineptitude of the CPAF, with its top-heavy rank structure, was exposed for all to see. The government's position was made even worse later in the year when local Khmer Rouge forces seized Western hostages and demanded ransom for their release.[12] In the face of these debacles, Cambodian officials have called upon foreign countries, including Australia, to provide military assistance.

The failed government offensives of 1993–94 and the hostage incidents later that year served to expose weaknesses in the command structure and logistics organisation of the RCAF, as well as poor morale among the troops. The reputation of these forces has been further dented by a United Nations report which revealed that a specialised military intelligence group in Battambang was involved in torture and other violations of human rights. The General Staff of the Royal Cambodian Armed Forces have responded to these shortcomings by unveiling a major reform program which would pare down the size of the military and adopt more professional standards.[13]

The formulation and implementation of Cambodia's national security policy is hostage to domestic circumstances. One important factor which could have a decisive bearing on future developments is the health of King Sihanouk. His death could precipitate a period of political instability. Rivalries and suspicions between the CPP and FUNCINPEC have not entirely abated, particularly at provincial government level, where the CPP political structure remains in place. While there are signs that Norodom Ranariddh and Hun Sen have been able to forge a working relationship, a continuation of this partnership cannot be taken for granted.

Each leader presides over a party structure believed to be riven with cliques and factions.[14]

Continued instability in Cambodia raises the possibility that Cambodia's transition process may be delayed and the democratic gains of the United Nations Transitional Authority in Cambodia (UNTAC) period will be lost. Cambodia could revert to a single-party dictatorship, military rule or prolonged internal war. Any of these scenarios could invite foreign intervention. In short, the continued debilitation of Cambodia acts as a brake on the transition process and negatively affects the possibility of Cambodia's integration into regional affairs.

Threats and threat perceptions

Each of the Indochinese states perceives internal threats as the greatest challenge to national security. Both Laos and Vietnam stress the 'strategy of peaceful evolution' as one of their major concerns. This section examines the main contemporary threats to national security as identified by Vietnam, Laos and Cambodia.

Peaceful evolution

Vietnam and Laos both identify themselves as among the last bastions of socialism in the world. They allege that they are the targets of the so-called 'plot of peaceful evolution' and that 'imperialists and international reactionaries' are seeking to eliminate one-party rule by encouraging domestic groups to advocate political pluralism. This linkage is used to justify periodic crackdowns on domestic dissidents on the grounds of national security.

Vietnamese Politburo member and Minister of National Defence, Doan Khue, described the strategy of peaceful evolution as:

> the combined use of unarmed and armed measures against us to undermine in a total manner our politics, ideology, psychology, way of living, and so on, and encircling, isolating, and destroying us in the economic field, with the hope that they could achieve a so-called 'peaceful evolution' and make the revolution in our country deviate from its course. They have been trying to seek, build, and develop reactionary forces of all kinds within our country; at the same time to nurture and bring back groups of armed reactionaries within our country; and to combine armed activities with political activities, hoping to transform the socioeconomic crisis in our country into a political crisis and to incite rioting and uprisings when opportunities arise. They may also look for excuses to intervene, to carry out partial armed aggression, or to wage aggressive wars on various scales. Our people thus have the task of dealing with and being ready to

deal with any circumstances caused by enemy forces; peaceful evolution, riot and uprising, encirclement, blockade, surprise attacks by
[enemy] armed forces, aggressive wars on various scales. The
politico-ideological front is a hot one . . .[15]

Laos adheres to an identical threat assessment. On 5 October 1992, for
example, the LPRP issued a resolution declaring 'peaceful evolution' to be
the main security threat. But while the LPRP media continues to warn
against the threat of the 'strategy of peaceful evolution', internal political
dissidence has dropped off. Repressive action taken against party dissidents and returned students appears to have had its desired effect.

Other internal issues

The other main national security problems facing Laos in the 1990s are
border security and internal insurgency. In recent years, Laos has placed
priority on reaching frontier control and border delineation agreements
with all of its neighbours. Laos is primarily concerned about unauthorised
border crossings along the Mekong, smuggling from Thailand and unreg-
ulated settlement of Vietnamese in its southern provinces. To a lesser
extent, Laos is concerned to prevent disputes over undemarcated territory
from flaring up into armed conflict, as happened in the late 1980s. Finally,
Lao officials are also apprehensive about the negative impact that the
opening of the Friendship Bridge across the Mekong will have on Lao society. Specific concerns include smuggling, illegal narcotics, prostitution and
the spread of AIDS.

Officially, the Khmer Rouge has been identified as the main threat to
Cambodian national security. The draft reform plan of the RCAF General
Staff, for example, sets as its major priority the objective of defeating the
Khmer Rouge within two years. Cambodia's national leaders have also
identified increasing lawlessness and violent crime, border delineation and
the status of Vietnamese residents as additional national security concerns.

Vietnam no longer faces a serious security threat from armed domestic
insurgents, such as ethnic minorities or remnants of the former regime.
Political stability is not challenged by an organised political opposition,
although the potential for a clash with militant Buddhists belonging to
the Unified Buddhist Church is a current cause for concern. Nonetheless,
the possibility exists that political turmoil could arise as a by-product of
socio-economic change.

External threats

Vietnam perceives China as its main external military threat and the South
China Sea (see below) as the most likely 'hot spot'. To a lesser extent, Vietnam views the possibility of a spillover of domestic instability in Cambodia as another potential threat to its national security.

Since 1975, the main external threats to Lao national security have arisen from Thailand. Thailand has supported anti-LPDR resistance groups and the armies of both countries have clashed over disputed territory. Laos has been subject to several Thai-imposed blockades of strategic goods. Although Laos was also threatened by resistance forces which operated from southern China for a brief period in the late 1970s, Lao leaders have not publicly expressed concern about a possible threat from China in recent years.

In 1987–88, Thailand and Laos engaged in a brief but fierce border war. At that time, H'mong guerillas operating from Thailand used this as a diversion to step up their attacks in Laos. By 1992–93, the threat of internal insurgency, particularly by H'mong rebels, had diminished to an all-time low. Thai authorities are generally given credit for curtailing the activities of anti-LPDR groups based on Thai soil following agreements reached between Bangkok and Vientiane.

In July 1992, Thailand publicly expelled several H'mong activists. A year later, Major General A-Sang Laoli, the Lao Minister of the Interior, visited Thailand at the invitation of his counterpart to discuss the suppression of armed rebels. Later that year, Thai officials disbanded an anti-LPDR group in central Thailand with links to exiled H'mong leader General Vang Pao. In February 1994, Thailand signalled a tougher line against Lao insurgents by arresting three pro-Vang Pao H'mong military officials.

Cambodia officially downplays external threats to its national security. However, during the fighting in western Cambodia in late 1993 and early 1994, Cambodian officials charged that Thailand was continuing to support the Khmer Rouge. For example, when Prince Norodom Chakrapong and his partner, General Sin Song, attempted a *coup d'etat* in July 1994, Cambodian officials were quick to accuse Thai nationals of involvement.[16] Independent observers believe that Thai support for the Khmer Rouge continued after the formation of the coalition government in 1993 until about mid-1994, when a new policy was adopted.[17] It is generally accepted that official Thai support has all but ended. This may have contributed to the spate of Khmer Rouge defections during the first quarter of 1995.

Border issues

Cambodian national security concerns also focus on securing recognition of Cambodia's borders by neighbouring states and preventing Cambodian natural resources, including timber and maritime resources, from being exploited without the consent of the central government. Cambodian officials generally point to Thailand as the likely source of external interference in Cambodia's internal affairs. The actions of private Thai businessmen and supposedly rogue elements of the Thai military establishment are singled out in particular.[18]

Cambodia's new constitution makes reference to maps drawn up 'between 1933 and 1953 and recognised internationally between 1963 and

1969' as the basis for Cambodia's present borders.[19] This reference is seen by some observers as deliberately ambiguous. The status of Vietnam's land and maritime border agreements with the People's Republic of Kampuchea, signed in 1982 and 1985, is also unclear. From time to time, the Cambodian press alleges that Vietnam has moved border markers into Cambodian territory. In February 1995, during the course of an official visit to Vietnam by Norodom Ranariddh, the two sides agreed to set up a working group to study the border problem. Cambodian leaders have also stressed that the border with Thailand must be demarcated properly. While a similar situation prevails with Laos, this border does not appear to be a major concern.

The other main security issue is the status of ethnic Vietnamese living in Cambodia. This includes those who fled rural areas to escape Khmer Rouge violence during the pre-electoral period in 1993 and are now encamped along the border. In September 1994, the Cambodian National Assembly passed an immigration law which empowered the government to expel foreign residents who were without permanent residence documents. This law has provoked repeated diplomatic protests by Vietnam and criticism by the United Nations Secretary General.

The Khmer Rouge hopes to stir up racial emotions and capitalise on anti-Vietnamese sentiments. It deliberately plays up the ethnic Vietnamese issue in its propaganda broadcasts, and continues to attack Vietnamese villagers living in Cambodia.

Maritime issues

In the 1980s, the strategic basis of Vietnamese national security policy altered as maritime issues assumed greater importance. Under the Law of the Sea, littoral states may claim a 200 nautical mile exclusive economic zone (EEZ) and marine resources and mineral deposits within this area. Vietnam claims sovereignty not only over its territorial waters and continental shelf, but over the entire South China Sea, including the Paracel and Spratly archipelagoes, and other islands in the Gulf of Thailand. Vietnam has conflicting maritime territorial claims with China, Taiwan, the Philippines, Malaysia, Indonesia and Cambodia.

Both Vietnam and China have moved to assert sovereignty over islands in the South China Sea by physical occupation. This resulted in a clash of naval forces in March 1988. Since 1989, Vietnam has awarded 27 oil production-sharing contracts to foreign companies. This has resulted in the leasing of 38 concessions and the drilling of 42 exploratory wells.[20] Exports of crude oil rank among the most important sources of export income for the Vietnamese economy.

In 1992, China occupied two additional reefs in the South China Sea and awarded a oil exploration contract to an American company, Crestone Energy Corporation, in a concession area Vietnam claims lies on its continental shelf. As a result, Vietnam responded by occupying remaining territory in the South China Sea. Vietnam then began building civilian infra-structure as well as military fortifications.[21]

Both sides have since engaged in provocative actions at sea. In 1994, for example, Chinese ships blockaded a Vietnamese oil rig while Vietnamese naval vessels turned back Chinese ships. A number of incidents involving Vietnamese naval ships and Chinese fishermen in the Gulf of Tonkin also occurred. In February 1995, China set alarm bells ringing when its naval forces provided protection for a landing party which occupied Mischief Reef, an area claimed by the Philippines.

The military and the economy

The demise and collapse of the Soviet Union resulted in the Indochinese states being suddenly cut off from an assured supply of military equip-ment, spare parts and ammunition. None of the Indochinese states has a modern defence industry to manufacture these items, and none has the hard currency to purchase them.

In Cambodia, the CPAF witnessed a progressive deterioration of its equipment through combat and restrictions mandated by the 1991 peace agreements. The RCAF, like its predecessor the CPAF, earns extra budgetary income from its involvement in the export of timber. In 1993, after the deba-cles at Anlong Veng and Pailin, Cambodia unsuccessfully sought military equipment and weapons from a variety of countries, including Laos, Viet-nam, China, France, Australia and the United States. Press reports indicate, however, that Cambodia has been more successful in other quarters such as North Korea, India, Poland and the Czech Republic.

Laos' defence posture has been shaped by material backing it received from Moscow which, among other things, enabled Laos to form a modern air force. The collapse of the Soviet Union meant that the Lao armed forces were cut off from a major source of external support. Vietnam, whose mil-itary assistance program was always very modest, could not fill the vacuum. Laos approached China but was offered arms on a commercial basis only. These difficulties led Laos to reduce the size of its armed forces by 18 000 over the period 1987–92. The Lao Air Force has had to drastically curtail air operations due to shortages of spare parts and aviation fuel. In the absence of new sources of external assistance, there has been a deteri-oration in capability as equipment became worn out or damaged and could not be replaced. In order to acquire funds to meet operating costs, the Laos army has had to turn to commercial activities including logging and drug trafficking.[22]

Vietnam's adoption of a new defence doctrine also necessitated major changes on the home front, including a greater role by the military in eco-nomic activities. Regular forces were expected to become partly self-sufficient by growing food and raising animals. Other military units were specifically assigned to production tasks.

In March 1989, Directive 46 of the Council of Ministers decreed that army-owned enterprises were on the same financial and legal footing as state-owned enterprises. Nine major VPA-companies were converted immediately into either corporations or general corporations. The most notable such enterprise was the Truong Son General Construction Corporation. While its main concern was capital construction, it soon branched out into a variety of activities, such as exporting coal and marble, growing coffee, laying railway tracks and general support services. The corporation employs 7000 persons in nineteen enterprises. In 1991, it was assigned a major role on the North–South powerline, the largest construction project since the Ho Chi Minh Trail.

Vietnam's national defence industries were also expected to engage in production activities. In addition to military weapons and ammunition, they now manufacture a wide range of consumer items including electrical and mechanical goods, bicycle parts, oil cookers, electricity meters and fluorescent lamp bulbs. Other army enterprises assemble television sets and radio-cassette recorders, manufacture garments or process agricultural goods. By 1993, approximately 12 per cent of the standing army was employed full-time in over 300 commercial enterprises. A year later, the military had formed 26 corporations which were authorised to enter into joint ventures with foreign partners.

Power projection capabilities

Despite the massive reduction of main force regulars, Vietnam still maintains the largest ground army in Southeast Asia. Nonetheless, Vietnam's military establishment remains a 'poor man's army'. It is best suited to the continental defence of Vietnam and to meet low-level contingencies around its borders. The VPA has the capability to successfully intervene in Laos and Cambodia, but not elsewhere in the region. A weak industrial base and the lack of sufficient POL supplies would hinder its capacity to conduct or sustain large-scale operations on a continuing basis.

The Vietnamese navy is primarily a coastal-defence force which has been assigned the added roles of EEZ surveillance (in the South China Sea and Gulfs of Thailand and Tonkin) and protection of the Spratly Islands. It has little capacity or capability to project significant power into the South China Sea or farther afield. Vietnamese forces would probably be overwhelmed in any theatre conflict with Chinese naval forces or in any conflict involving ASEAN navies. Vietnam could probably inflict serious losses only against the Philippines.

As early as 1988, one review of Vietnam's air force concluded, '[it] suffers from ageing aircraft and a critical shortage of spare parts . . .'[23] This situation has worsened in recent years. The combat efficiency of the Vietnamese air force has been undoubtedly affected by the retirement of pilots with combat experience dating to the Vietnam War and by training restrictions imposed by fuel costs and the shortage of munitions. Pilot proficiency has dropped. Staff morale is low. When these factors are combined, it is reasonable to conclude that Vietnam has lost whatever qualitative personnel edge it may have had over regional rivals two decades ago.

Vietnam's air force is equipped for a self-defence role. It cannot mount strikes beyond the geographic region of Indochina, Thailand and southern China. It lacks in-flight refuelling and EWAC capabilities but several recently acquired Su-27 long-range fighters allow it to maintain some air cover over the Spratly Islands. In any conflict involving the use of air power, however, Vietnam would be hard pressed to make up for battlefield losses in equipment and trained manpower.

Over the last half-decade the Indochinese states have experienced a rundown in equipment caused by ordinary wear and tear and, more significantly, by their inability to provide proper maintenance. They also lack the funds to purchase spares and other major items. A net assessment of the military forces of the three Indochinese states would have to conclude that they represent no credible major conventional threat to their immediate neighbours.

Conclusion

This chapter has argued that the Vietnamese-dominated 'Indochina bloc' — which was always a shaky edifice — no longer exists. The security ties which bound Laos and Cambodia to Vietnam have been greatly weakened.

The issue of Cambodia's future regional role raises the question of whether Cambodia's current instability can be contained. ASEAN's ambivalent reaction to the Cambodian case is illustrative of the problems faced in coming to grips with the transition process as it unfolds. A question which needs to be asked is why the ASEAN states, which all had to overcome the challenges of domestic communist insurgencies, are so ambivalent about providing military aid to Cambodia which is beset by its own communist insurgency. ASEAN's hesitant and ambivalent attitude may be symptomatic of a lack of confidence in the outcome of the United Nations-initiated peace process. And it may also be due to differences among its members about Cambodia's place in a new regional order.

The Indochinese states no longer equate national security predominately with military strength. Their national security policies are now less ideological and much more multi-dimensional. Overwhelmingly, the focus of national security concerns is domestic. These internal concerns differ from country to country. While all of the Indochinese states have external security concerns, they no longer share the perception that they are threatened militarily by the same common enemy. This sea change in national security perspectives has made possible new forms of accommodation and co-operation between Indochina and ASEAN. It is in the region's self-interest to not only encourage this trend but to become actively involved in shaping its outcome.

Notes

1. A point first made by Gen. Vo Nguyen Giap, *Nhiem Vu Quan Su Truoc Mat Chuyen San Tong Phan Cong* (Uy Ban Khang Chien Hanh Chinh Ha Dong, 1950) and since reiterated, see Gen. Hoang Van Thai, 'Ve Quan He Hop Tac Dac Biet Giua Ba Dan Toc Dong Duong', *Tap Chi Cong San*, January 1982, pp. 17–24.

2. AFP (Takeo), 'Ex-leader Pen Sovan poised for comeback', *Bangkok Post*, 8 February 1992.

3. See Carlyle A. Thayer, 'Indochina', in Desmond Ball and Cathy Downes (eds), *Security and Defence: Pacific and Global Perspectives*, Allen & Unwin, Sydney, Wellington, Boston, and London, 1990.

4. In July 1994 it was estimated that the Khmer Rouge exercised control over 5–10 per cent of Cambodia and its area of control and influence was 10–20 per cent. Senator Gareth Evans, 'Cambodia: The Current Security Situation', Parliamentary Statement, Canberra, 29 November 1994, p. 4.

5. Resolution no. 2 was elaborated upon in a series of confidential directives issued by the VCP Central Committee's Military Commission, the Ministry of National Defence and the VPA General Staff's General Political Directorate.

6. See 'Political Report of the Central Committee (6th Term) at the 7th National Congress', in *Communist Party of Vietnam 7th National Congress Documents*, Vietnam Foreign Languages Publishing House, Hanoi, 1991, pp. 130–33.

7. Political Report of the Lao People's Revolutionary Party Central Committee read by Kaysone Phomvihan, General Secretary, at the Fifth Party Congress in Vientiane, 27 March 1991 in *Pasason*, 28 March 1991, pp. 3–9.

8. People's Republic of Kampuchea, State of Cambodia, Supreme National Council, Provisional National Government of Cambodia and finally Kingdom of Cambodia.

9. Author's interview with General Phuung Siphan, Deputy Chief of Staff of the CPAF, SOC Ministry of National Defence, Phnom Penh, 26 May 1993.

10. Evans, 'Cambodia: The Current Security Situation', p. 6. According to Western intelligence sources, at the time of merger, ANKI and KPNLF totalled 10 000 each while the CPAF stood at 90 000 (excluding a police field force of 40–45 000) for a grand total of 110 000. Each of these groups deliberately over-estimated their troop strength when reporting to UNTAC. ANKI and the KPNLF provided 'official' figures of 17 400 and 27 500 respectively. The CPAF reported a strength of 131 000 (excluding police), for a grand total of 175 900.

11. There are an estimated 450 000 weapons circulating in Cambodia. Estimates for the number of mines range from four to ten million.

12. On 31 March 1994, Melissa Hines, an American employee of the Swiss NGO Food for the Hungry International, and her Cambodian col-

leagues, were taken hostage and held for 41 days before being released on 11 May. Their ransom was paid in kind, a village well was dug and humanitarian supplies provided. On 12 April 1994, two British citizens and one Australian were kidnapped at Sre Ambel, Kampot province. Although ransom demands were made it appears the hostages were killed almost immediately. On 26 July three more Westerners — a Frenchman, an Australian and an Englishman — were taken hostage in Kampot province. They were later executed. This particular case was widely publicised by the foreign press as it unfolded.

13 John C. Brown, 'RCAP Outlines Reform Plan', *Phnom Penh Post*, vol. 3, no. 17, 26 August–8 September 1994, pp. 1, 5.

14 Cambodian specialists disagree about the extent of factionalism within the CPP. Some argue that the CPP is split into conservative and reformist factions led by Chea Sim and Hun Sen respectively. See David Chandler, *Cambodia*, Asia-Australia Briefing papers, vol. 2, no. 5, Asia-Australian Institute, University of New South Wales, Sydney, 1993, pp. 7–8; and Michael Vickery, *Cambodia: A Political Survey*, Regime Change and Regime Maintenance in Asia and the Pacific Discussion Paper Series no. 14, Department of Political and Social Change, Research School of Pacific Studies, The Australian National University, Canberra, 1994, pp. 35–38.

15 General Doan Khue, 'Understanding the Resolution of the Third Plenum of the VCP Central Committee: Some Basic Issues Regarding the Party's Military Line in the New Stage', *Tap Chi Quoc Phong Toan Dan*, August 1992, pp. 3–15, 45.

16 Ros Sokhet, 'More Thais to Face Coup Probe', *Phnom Penh Post*, vol. 3, no. 17, p. 6.

17 Morton Abramowitz, 'Pol Pot's Best Pal: Thailand', *Washington Post*, 29 May 1994. Abramowitz was the former United States Ambassador to Thailand. John Holloway, 'Cambodia: The Government and the Khmer Rouge', protected diplomatic cable dated 9 June 1994 reprinted in *Sydney Morning Herald*, 5 October 1994. At that time, Holloway was Australia's Ambassador to Cambodia. Thailand's new ten-point policy curbing support for the Khmer Rouge was outlined by a senior military spokesman to *Nation* (Bangkok), 4 June 1994; see also Chiraphon Chaisi, *Matichon*, 20 November 1994.

18 In late November 1994, Norodom Ranariddh charged that sixteen Thai companies were still engaged in gem mining in Pailin: *National Voice of Cambodia*, Phnom Penh, 1 December 1994.

19 Constitution of the Kingdom of Cambodia, chapter 1, article 2. At the opening of the first session of the Constituent Assembly, Norodom Sihanouk called for the restoration of 'full independence and complete neutrality along with the territorial integrity and land and maritime borders which existed up until 1969': *Voice of the People of Cambodia*, 14 June 1993.

20 Ho Si Thoang, 'State of the Oil and Gas Industry in Vietnam', paper presented to the Tenth Asia Pacific Petroleum Conference, Singapore, 20 September 1994. Thoang is chairman of PetroVietnam, the state oil company.

21 Tai Minh Cheung, 'Fangs of the dragon', *Far Eastern Economic Review*, 13 August 1992, p. 20.

22 Interview, Vientiane, 3 May 1993.

23 Murray Hiebert, 'Taking the Flak', *Far Eastern Economic Review*, 10 November 1988, p. 42.

11 Australia and the Pacific Islands: The Limits of Influence

Stephen Henningham

After World War II, developments in the Pacific Islands region received a relatively low priority, except for a brief period in the mid-1980s. But the region is inescapably relevant to Australia's security and political interests. Moreover, several countries, including the United States and Indonesia, look to Australia to maintain peace and stability in the islands region. This chapter considers some of the key issues and trends in regional affairs, and examines the limits of Australia's involvement.

Three sub-regions

The numerous and diverse Pacific Island countries and territories consist of three sub-groups: Melanesia and Fiji; Polynesia and British Commonwealth Micronesia; and American Micronesia.[1]

The Melanesia and Fiji group comprises Papua New Guinea, the Solomon Islands, Vanuatu, Fiji and the French overseas territory of New Caledonia. These entities are located to the south and west of the region, and are the largest in both land area and population. They have considerable strategic importance because of their location near to Australia and vital lines of communication between Australasia, Northeast Asia and the United States. While all are aid recipients, they have a broad range of resources which could permit them to attain economic self-reliance over the next few decades.

The entities of the Polynesian and British Commonwealth Micronesian group are located to the north and the east of the region and have greater political coherence, fewer economic resources and higher levels of aid-dependence than the Melanesian countries. They comprise the Polynesian countries of Western Samoa, Tonga, Niue and Tuvalu, the American territory of American Samoa, the French territories of French Polynesia and Wallis and Futuna, the New Zealand territory of Tokelau, and the Micronesian countries of Kiribati and Nauru. Some of them maintain reasonable living standards by means of remittances from migrants abroad. However, remoteness, small size and limited resources mean that most of these countries have little international significance apart from French Polynesia, the site of French nuclear tests. Nauru is also a special case because of its phosphate deposits, but they will be exhausted early next century. Although returns on invested wealth will help sustain the economy, the prospect is for an island with severe ecological damage, declining living standards and significant aid-dependence.

The American Micronesian sub-group is located in the northeast of the region and consists of three states in free association with the United States — the Federated States of Micronesia, the Republic of the Marshall Islands and Palau (Belau) — and two entities under the overall administration of the United States — Guam and the Commonwealth of the Northern Marianas. These countries and territories have strategic significance for the United States and its allies and partners because of their location close to key air and sea routes through North and Southeast Asia. In addition, the Marshall Islands host United States missile testing and development facilities, while bases and other military facilities are located in Guam and the Northern Marianas. While poor in natural resources, the Marshall Islands, the Federated States of Micronesia and Palau receive substantial American funding, under the Compact arrangements, and remain closely linked to the United States.

Australia as a regional player

Australia's main economic and trade relationships are focused elsewhere than the Pacific Islands countries. On an annual basis over the decade to 1994, Australian exports to the island countries amounted to less than 5 per cent of total exports, while annual imports comprised less than 1 per cent of total imports. Australia has, however, significant trade and investment interests in Papua New Guinea. This may increase as major oil and mineral projects come on stream, although this prospect is subject to resolution of sensitive land, compensation and environmental issues.

Australia has sought to encourage stability and peaceful change in the islands region. It is a major aid donor, both multilaterally and bilaterally, especially to PNG. It is the leading donor to the South Pacific Commission and contributes to other regional organisations. Australia has also assisted the island states with defence aid, including training, equipment and the supply and maintenance of patrol boats.[2]

Until the mid-1980s, Australian policy towards the South Pacific region was one of strategic denial to powers which were thought to be acting against Western interests.[3]

Australia and New Zealand

Despite converging interests and a tradition of co-operation, Australia's policy with respect to the region diverged somewhat from New Zealand's in the mid-1980s. The key issue concerned port visits by United States warships carrying nuclear weapons.[4] After conciliation efforts failed, the Australia–New Zealand–United States (ANZUS) treaty provisions relating to New Zealand lapsed, and New Zealand ceased to be an ally of the United States. While the return of New Zealand to full partnership in ANZUS seems unlikely, the bilateral United States/New Zealand relationship has in most other respects returned to normal.

The ANZUS rift created some tension between Australia and New Zealand, but both sides have worked hard to maintain the relationship. In late 1989, the New Zealand government decided to participate with Australia in a joint frigate-building program to increase its blue water naval capability, a decision that seemed to confirm that New Zealand intended to co-operate with Australia in pursuing shared security interests, especially in the Pacific Islands region.

Unlike New Zealand, however, Australia does not think of itself as a 'South Pacific' nation, even though Canberra frequently acknowledges Australia's close connection with the region. The cliché, rather, is that Australia is geographically part of Asia. Successive governments have also been conscious of Australia's vast land area and extensive maritime zone, its proximity to Southeast Asia, and the enormous difficulties in defending 'a coast too long'.[5] Against this background, Australian governments have therefore emphasised the central importance of Australia's close alliance with the United States in contrast to New Zealand's at times isolationist foreign policy.

Issues and trends in regional affairs

Compared with most other regions of the world since 1945, in the Pacific Islands region, the use or the threatened use of force to shape relations between states has been very infrequent. Apart from the land border between Papua New Guinea and Irian Jaya (discussed below), all the international boundaries in the region are maritime. The islands of the region are scattered over a wide area. There are great distances between the various island groups, compared with insular Southeast Asia or the Caribbean. The few differences and uncertainties over maritime jurisdictions have been mostly resolved through negotiation. In the few cases where they remain unresolved, they have not become a major cause of tension. There are, moreover, no foreseeable external military threats to the region, in part because it has been effectively part of the sphere of influence of the United States and the West since World War II, a condition that still prevails.

In the absence of maritime or land border disputes, and with the countries of the region enjoying good relations with one another, force has mainly been used within countries against internal dissidence or secessionist movements or, in Fiji's case, to reassert indigenous Fijian interests and authority.

Domestic developments in particular countries have on a few occasions created circumstances conducive to the use or potential use of force or to the provision of military assistance from another regional country. For example, at the time of the first Fiji coup in April 1987, elements of the Australian and New Zealand defence forces were put on notice to intervene to rescue nationals, or even, in certain scenarios, to affect the political process. More recently, Australia has provided materiel and training to Papua New Guinea in its efforts to cope with the Bougainville conflict.

Border tensions create some possibility for armed conflict between Indonesia and Papua New Guinea. The border is undisputed, but PNG–Indonesia relations are affected by anti-Indonesia resistance forces within Irian Jaya. Opponents of Indonesian rule have often been associated with the Organisasi Papua Merdeka (OPM — Free Papua Movement), a loose, factionalised nationalist movement which sets out to represent a variety of dissident individuals, groups and local communities. OPM militants and their supporters have sought sanctuary across the border in Papua New Guinea, prompting cross-border raids by Indonesian patrols. Although much sympathy exists within Papua New Guinea for the OPM, successive PNG governments have sought to resolve difficulties through negotiation. Reflecting PNG's priority in maintaining good relations with Indonesia, the Wingti government concluded a 'Treaty of Mutual Respect, Friendship and Co-operation' with Indonesia in 1987.

The present Indonesian regime does not have designs on Papua New Guinea. Barring the emergence of an expansionist Indonesian regime, low-level border tensions between Indonesia and PNG are unlikely to pose a wider threat to regional security and stability. Yet, should intermittent tensions escalate into a larger conflict, Australia would necessarily be implicated because of its close links with Papua New Guinea and its self-interest in promoting peace and stability in its northern approaches.

Tensions have arisen from time to time between Papua New Guinea and the Solomon Islands over the Bougainville conflict. Bougainville is part of the Solomons archipelago, and is only a few miles away from the closest island in the Solomon Islands jurisdiction. Around 1990, Papua New Guinea accused some Solomon islanders of breaking the Papua New Guinea blockade on Bougainville, and of assisting the insurgents in other ways. On several occasions, PNG troops launched raids into the Solomon

Islands. But, since late 1993, tension has been managed and both sides appear inclined to continue to contain the issue.

In the absence of military threats, and because of their economic weakness, the island states of the South Pacific have given the concept of security a broad definition emphasising the economic and non-military challenges to national sovereignty and well-being. They have spent relatively little on defence and tend to assume that Australia or New Zealand would come to their aid in a crisis. Only Papua New Guinea, Fiji and Tonga have armed forces but they lack any capability to mount substantial independent operations beyond their home territories.

Economic issues

The island countries are gravely handicapped by their distance from markets, by poor transport and communications links, by their limited range of exports, and by an over-supply on world markets of most of the commodities which they can produce. The island states have thus put special emphasis on the actual and potential resources of their exclusive economic zones (EEZs). But the vagaries of the migratory movements of tuna and similar species have blighted early hopes of high returns from fishing resources. Meanwhile, undersea mining faces huge technical, financial and environmental constraints and is unlikely to be viable before the early decades of the next century.[6]

The fisheries question has been a central issue. In the early 1980s, the refusal of the United States to accept the Law of the Sea Convention, combined with its cavalier approach to tuna fishing, sparked opposition to what the island countries regarded as its 'tuna piracy'. In the late 1980s, the island countries, supported by Australia and New Zealand, succeeded in banning the vacuum-cleaner practice of drift-net fishing by Japanese, Taiwanese and other trawlers.

This new assertiveness in island government attitudes was evident from the mid-1980s, when a new generation with fewer ties to the colonial past came into power. Institutions and arrangements set in place at the time of independence were questioned on the grounds that they were inappropriate to local traditions and customs and to changing circumstances.[7]

Island leaderships believe that donor states have an obligation to provide aid to redress historical wrongs and to correct present imbalances. Yet they also resent the dependence of their countries on aid. In part, the aim is to increase the level of assistance obtained and yet increase their freedom of manoeuvre and, hence, their political independence, by reducing reliance on any one trading partner or source of aid.

This effort to diversify external connections both encouraged, and was encouraged by, the increased interest and rivalry of external powers in the region in the mid- to late-1980s. Soviet interest in the region stimulated the United States to conclude that it could no longer take the region for granted. Since then, however, with the end of the Cold War, American interest has waned. For its part, France has responded to criticisms of its handling of New Caledonia and of its nuclear testing program in French Polynesia during the mid- and late-1980s by expanding aid and other links with the island countries. Other external countries and organisations that similarly established or consolidated a presence from the mid-1980s onwards, included China, Taiwan, the European Community and Israel.

Nuclear and environmental issues

The island countries have paid close attention to nuclear issues. The United States and Great Britain conducted atmospheric nuclear tests in the region until 1961. France tested in the atmosphere from 1966 to 1975, and continued with underground tests on Mururoa and Fangataufa in French Polynesia until 1992. Its resumption of testing on Mururoa in 1995 galvanised opposition to French testing of nuclear weapons in the South Pacific. Island governments have also opposed plans to dump nuclear and other toxic wastes in the region.

Opposition to testing and to the prospect of dumping was expressed in the Treaty of Rarotonga (also known as the South Pacific Nuclear Free Zone Treaty). This treaty was signed by most members of the South Pacific Forum — the regional organisation that comprises the heads of government of the island states and Australia and New Zealand — at its annual meeting in 1985 in Rarotonga, the Cook Islands. Since then, the treaty has been ratified by the signatories. Australia played an important part in helping to tailor the Treaty of Rarotonga to reflect a regional consensus which was not in conflict with what the Australian government regarded as essential Western interests in passage through the high seas and entry to friendly ports.

Opposition to nuclear testing forms part of a wider emphasis on environmental issues, which have come into sharp focus through the discussion of the 'Greenhouse Effect'. Should the predictions of rising sea levels prove well-founded, the very survival of some of the island countries will be under threat.[8]

Decolonisation issues

For the island states, determined to assert their political independence, decolonisation has also been an important issue. Coping with the challenges of independence has proved more difficult than expected, leading to frustration and disillusionment.[9] Island leaders are conscious that the French and American dependencies in the region receive substantial funding, and enjoy a higher average standard of living than their independent neighbours. But they are also conscious of the sharp inequalities in the distribution of wealth in the dependencies, especially since the indigenous communities therein are relatively disadvantaged. They are also concerned by the adverse social and cultural effects of continued dependence.

Support for decolonisation in the region in recent decades initially focused on the New Hebrides, which became the independent island state of Vanuatu in 1980, and New Caledonia. Despite the reservations of Fiji and some of the Polynesian countries, troops from PNG, with Australian logistics support, helped quell the French-encouraged secessionist movement on Espiritu Santo in July–August 1980.

In New Caledonia, conflict has developed between the indigenous Melanesians, known as Kanaks, who comprise 45 per cent of the population, and who mostly want independence, and the non-indigenous inhabitants, most of whom oppose independence.[10] The Forum cautiously welcomed the reforms implemented in the territory by the French Socialists after they won government in 1981, and delayed the tabling or 'reinscription' of New Caledonia by the United Nations Committee of Twenty-Four on Decolonisation. But in 1986, when the French conservative government reversed French policy on New Caledonia, the Forum decided to support reinscription. This led to the censure of France by a majority of United Nations members. However, the Forum responded positively to the Matignon Accords of mid-1988, whereby a new Socialist government, under Michel Rocard, established an interim peace settlement. New Caledonia has receded in importance on the Forum agenda, but if conflict breaks out again, it is bound to return as an issue at Forum meetings.

Island country leaderships strongly support the rights and interests of indigenous communities. This ties in with their emphasis on independence and their opposition to colonialism and its legacies. Most island governments perceived the 1987 Fiji coups as a proper reassertion of indigenous rights and interests that should take precedence over democratic principles and the rights of non-indigenous nationals.

Tension between 'locals' and 'immigrants' also exists between groups of islanders in other Pacific island societies, with conflict often focusing on rights to land. Examples include the conflict between the local people and the 'redskins' (immigrant workers from PNG) on Bougainville; tensions between Melanesians and Polynesian immigrants, mostly from Wallis and Futuna, in New Caledonia; and, adjacent to the islands region, tensions between the Maori of New Zealand and immigrants to that country from the Cook Islands, Western Samoa, Tonga, Tokelau and Nuie.

While essentially local, such conflicts can impinge on international relations within the region. The New Caledonian conflict, the Fiji coups, political tensions in Vanuatu and the conflict in Bougainville have all posed problems for regional diplomacy. In Vanuatu in May 1988, tension arising in part from conflict over land between the indigenous residents of the Port Vila area and internal immigrants to the capital from elsewhere in the country and helped create a political crisis. Prime Minister Lini requested, received, Australian help in the form of riot control equipment, and further Australian intervention was considered.[11]

Australia does not wish to assume the role of regional police officer, but as a last resort, assistance may again be given in comparable circumstances in the future. It could also be necessary to evacuate nationals. Responses to such contingencies will require political acumen and tactical flexibility.[12]

Limits and restraints: International, regional and domestic

Although there is no doubt that Australia exerts significant influence in the islands region, there are important limitations to this influence. These limits may be considered in three inter-related contexts: international, regional and domestic.

The context at the international level includes the norms and practices established by the international community in the era since the end of World War II. As Jackson points out, the transition of the island countries to full independence resulted more from changes in international law than from internal pressures.[13] Several newly established states in the Pacific Islands region consist 'of territorial jurisdictions supported from above by international law and material aid'.[14] They lack sufficient resources to provide essential social welfare. but survive because their sovereignty is upheld by current international norms.[15]

The regional context includes both institutions and changing circumstances. By acting as a supra-national body, the South Pacific Forum reinforces the legitimacy of even the smallest and weakest of island states. At the same time, the Forum provides a means within which Australia can pursue particular national interests, yet it also serves to restrain the way in which those interests are pursued.

Regional-level restraints on the influence of Australia have been increased by the 'internationalisation' of the region. The regional community has also become more diverse as new states have emerged. More recently, the Federated States of Micronesia and the Republic of the Marshall Islands have become members of the South Pacific Forum, while Palau is expected to join in 1995. These countries remain closely tied to the United States, their former administering power, and have only insubstantial links with Australia.

Recent developments in Papua New Guinea — the largest island country — have particular implications for Australia's standing. Because of its resources, Papua New Guinea is becoming self-reliant so aid from Australia could be phased out early next century. In addition, Papua New Guinea faces increasingly intractable domestic problems, including the secessionist revolt on Bougainville (see below) and uncertainties about the role of the police and the army. These problems are on a scale that is too great for Australia to resolve unilaterally. Accordingly, Australian influence on Papua New Guinea seems likely to diminish.

Furthermore, most Australians look towards Asia, Europe or the United States and not the Pacific Islands. There is a willingness to play an active part, via the Forum, in regional Pacific Islands affairs, but apart from PNG, the Pacific island countries are too small, and too poor compared with Australia's interests in North and Southeast Asia. Strategically, the island states and territories are insignificant.

Developments in Fiji and Bougainville in recent years illustrate the limits of Australian influence in the South Pacific.

Fiji

The initial response of Australia and New Zealand to the Fiji coups in 1987 was strongly critical. They began to moderate their position once it became apparent that Rabuka had broad support within the indigenous Fijian community and even amongst the Pacific island countries. Continuing pressure on the new Fijian republic was clearly counter-productive The enactment of a new constitution in Fiji in 1990 and the elections in April 1992 involved a return to constitutional rule. Yet the election results and Rabuka's appointment as prime minister also endorsed his assertion of indigenous rights. In effect, Australia and New Zealand have been obliged to accept the conditions established by the 1987 coups.

Bougainville

Antipathy to outsiders and a strong sense of local nationalism have been central to the Bougainville story since 1964. Simmering discontent resurfaced from 1988. Attacks on mining operations, forcing the closure of the mine, were combined with violence against both local people and outsiders. The politics of the dispute were complex, as May points out:

> in a pattern not unfamiliar to students of Melanesian politics, what appears at first to be a straightforward case of a landowner group seeking increased compensation from a mining company turns out to be a multi-layered mass of shifting elements whose motivations range from a broad Bougainville nationalism to internal family fighting.[16]

In early 1989, Francis Ona, the leader of the militants among the traditional landowners, announced that the 'Republic of Bougainville' had been established. Efforts by the Papua New Guinea government to contain the revolt failed, and the situation rapidly deteriorated. By late 1994, casualties from the conflict in Bougainville numbered in the hundreds while thousands more had died or suffered serious illness because of the absence of health and welfare services. There was also extensive damage to infrastructure and property. Several hundred Australians had been obliged to leave while the costs to Australian companies and investors has been substantial. The province, formerly one of the most prosperous and advanced parts of Papua New Guinea, is a disaster zone. In August 1994, then Minister for Finance, Masket Iangalio, estimated that the costs of the conflict included 'more than A$100 million annually in direct expenditure alone'.[17] The indirect costs, including revenue foregone and damage to plant, equipment and infrastructure, ran into billions of dollars. By this time, the Papua New Guinea defence force, in loose association with various local 'resistance' militias opposed to the Bougainville Revolutionary Army, had regained control over much of the island, paving the way for a renewal of negotiations.

Papua New Guinea is by far the largest and potentially the richest of the Pacific island countries. It has close links with Australia, reflecting its proximity and the colonial past. Yet, despite the gravity of the situation and the significant Australian interests involved, the Australian government has been forced to recognise the limits of its influence in a conflict that is both a source of concern and an embarrassment. The limits arise from the complexities of the conflict, from Papua New Guinea's determination to assert its sovereignty, and from Australia's lack of credibility to act as an independent arbiter. Although the Australian government has provided some equipment and training support to PNG, it has sought to minimise its involvement on the grounds that the problem is essentially a domestic matter for Papua New Guinea.

With respect to both Bougainville and Fiji, a case could have been made for a more substantial Australian intervention. Australia conceivably could have been more substantially involved in Bougainville, for example, by providing aerial surveillance and air and sea transport and by using naval vessels to support the Papua New Guinea blockade, with a minimal risk of casualties. Instead, it chose to stand back. In both cases, there was no support, in either the government or the electorate, for substantial intervention.

Conclusions

In the early 1980s, Australia exercised a largely unchallenged position of leadership among the island countries of the Pacific Islands region. A decade later, that status has come under question, even if Australian influence remains strong.[18] A new assertiveness is evident among island country leaders while intractable problems of social and economic development have emerged which are beyond Australia's means and ability to resolve unilaterally. These trends have encouraged the Pacific island countries to widen their range of external contacts beyond Australia and New Zealand. At the same time, external powers have initiated or further developed a presence in the region. Japan, for example, has begun to exercise increased influence through aid, trade, investment and diplomacy. Indonesia, Malaysia and Taiwan have also increased their profile. Australia, New Zealand and the United States are generally unconcerned about this development, reflecting the relaxation of tension in the Asia-Pacific region that followed the end of the Cold War and Australia's partnership approach towards Japan and the newly industrialising economies of East Asia and ASEAN.

At present, there is no power that is likely to use the Pacific Islands as 'stepping stones' to threaten Australia as in World War II. No military threat exists — or seems likely to develop in the foreseeable future — from or through the islands region. Papua New Guinea, for example, once regarded as 'Australia's first line of defence', is nowadays regarded as a 'strategic quicksand' in which Australia prefers not to be involved.

Notes

* This chapter draws in part on material from sections of my forthcoming book, *The Pacific Island States: Security and Sovereignty in the Post-Cold War World*, Macmillan, Basingstoke.

1   This categorisation follows on in some respects from that of Steve Hoadley, *Security Cooperation in the South Pacific*, Working Paper No. 41, Peace Research Centre, Research School of Pacific Studies, Australian National University, Canberra, 1988, pp. 15–16.

2   Commonwealth of Australia, *Australia's Regional Security*. Ministerial Statement by Senator the Hon. Gareth Evans QC, Department of Foreign Affairs and Trade, Canberra, 1989, p. 19; Stephen Merchant, 'Australia's Defence Cooperation Program and Regional Security', in David Hegarty and Peter Polomka (eds), *The Security of Oceania in the 1990s. Volume 1: Views From the Region*, Canberra Papers on Strategy and Defence no. 60, Strategic and Defence Centre, Research School of Pacific Studies, Australian National University, Canberra, 1989, pp. 71–77.

3   See Richard Herr, 'Regionalism, Strategic Denial and South Pacific Security', *Journal of Pacific History*, vol. 21, nos 3–4, 1986, pp. 170–82 and his 'Diplomacy and Security in the South Pacific. Coping with Sovereignty', *Current Affairs Bulletin*, vol. 63, no. 8, January 1987.

4   On New Zealand's stance and policies, see Helen Clark, 'New Zealand's Non-Nuclear Initiative', in Ranginui Walker and William Sutherland, *The Pacific. Peace, Security and the Nuclear Issue*, United Nations University, Tokyo, 1988, pp. 175–84 and Dennis McLean, 'Perspectives from New Zealand: Interests, Objectives, Means, and Prospects', in Henry S. Albinski, et al., *The South Pacific: Political, Economic, and Military Trends*, Brasseys, Washington, 1989, Ch. 5.

5   See Ross Babbage, *A Coast Too Long, Defending Australia Beyond the 1990s*, Allen & Unwin, Sydney, 1990.

6 Gerard Ward, 'Earth's Empty Quarter? The Pacific Islands in a Pacific Century', *Geographical Journal*, vol. 155, no. 2, July 1989, pp. 325–46.

7 See Peter Jennings, 'Political and Constitutional Change', in Peter Polomka (ed.), *The Security of Oceania in the 1990s. Volume 2: Managing Change*, Canberra Papers on Strategy and Defence no. 68, Strategic and Defence Studies Centre, Research School of Pacific Studies, Australian National University, Canberra, 1990.

8 The highest point on Kiribati is some 5 metres above sea level. Other low-lying countries include Tuvalu, the Marshall Islands, Nauru, Niue, Tokelau and the Commonwealth of the Northern Marianas. Meanwhile the other island countries include low-lying islands as well as high islands. And even on the high islands, good agricultural land and much of the infrastructure is often concentrated in low-lying coastal areas. See Harold Brookfield, 'Global Change and the Pacific: Problems for the Coming Half-Century', *Contemporary Pacific*, vol. 1, nos 1 and 2, 1989, pp. 1–19; and Muriel Brookfield and R. Gerard Ward, *New Directions in the South Pacific. A Message for Australia*, Academy of the Social Sciences in Australia, Research School of Pacific Studies, Australian National University, Canberra, 1988, p. 68.

9 See, for example, Albert Wendt, 'Western Samoa 25 Years After: Celebrating What?', *Pacific Islands' Monthly*, vol. 58, June 1987, pp. 14–15.

10 See Stephen Henningham, 'A Dialogue of the Deaf: Attitudes and Issues in New Caledonian Politics', *Pacific Affairs*, vol. 61, no. 4, Winter 1988/89, pp. 633–52.

11 See Stephen Henningham, 'Pluralism and Party Politics in a South Pacific State: Vanuatu's Ruling Vanua'aku Pati and Its Rivals', *Conflict*, vol. 9, 1989, pp. 171–95.

12 Stephen Henningham and Stewart Woodman, 'An Achilles Heel? Australian and New Zealand Capabilities for Pacific Islands Contingencies', *Pacific Review*, vol. 6, no. 2, pp. 127–43.

13 R.H. Jackson, *Quasi-States: Sovereignty, International Relations and the Third World*, Cambridge University Press, Cambridge, 1990, p. 85.

14 ibid., p. 5.

15 ibid., pp. 11, 21, 29.

16 R.J. May, 'Papua New Ginea's Bougainville Crisis', *Pacific Review*, vol. 3, no. 2, 1990, pp. 174–77.

17 Rowan Callick, 'Papua New Guinea: War That May Outlast WWII', *Australian Financial Review*, 25 August 1994, as quoted in *Reuters News Service*.

18 See Greg Fry, 'Australia and the South Pacific', in P. Boyce and J. Angel (eds), *Australia in World Affairs*, Longman Cheshire, South Melbourne, 1991.

12 APEC and Regional Stability: An Overview

Andrew Elek

Introduction

Since the end of World War II, there has been an unprecedented transformation in the prosperity and interdependence of the Asia-Pacific region. An economic community in East Asia is rapidly becoming a reality, driven by market forces that are increasingly transcending political boundaries.

The nature of international economic transactions has also been transformed in recent decades. When the General Agreement on Tariffs and Trade (GATT) was established, global commerce was dominated by trade in commodities or finished manufactures. This is no longer the case, as international flows of investment, intra-industry trade and intra-firm trade in intermediate products, as well as trade in services, have all grown in relative importance. Flows of finance, information and people are also essential complements to trade.

Bridging the Pacific: The emergence of APEC

As the economies of the Asia-Pacific region began to interact more intensively by the 1960s, statesmen and economists of foresight, including Dr Saburo Okita and Sir John Crawford, anticipated the need for more effective communications about international economic policies. A progressively more effective forum for co-operation was seen to be needed so as to seize the many new opportunities and to defuse the inevitable misunderstandings and tensions which, even now, threaten the cohesion of the region. Responding to the needs and characteristics of the region, a unique approach to policy-oriented consultation and co-operation emerged in the Asia-Pacific region in the 25 years since the establishment of the Association of South East Asian Nations (ASEAN) and the initial meeting of the Pacific Trade and Development Forum (PAFTAD).

Openness, evolution and equality

ASEAN and the Pacific Economic Cooperation Conference (PECC), which evolved from PAFTAD, identified shared economic interests and laid the foundations for a consensus-building approach to pragmatic regional co-operation. These early efforts suggested that successful co-operation in a diverse region had to be based on the acceptance of openness, equality and evolution:

- Openness emphasises the need to avoid creating needless new divisions and to avoid fixing exclusive boundaries around the Asia-Pacific region. The more economies that can be drawn into an open economic association, the more prosperous and secure all participants can become.
- Equality is an ideal as nation states or economies are seldom 'equal' at any point in time. But the key to a successful open economic association is to avoid the temptation to rely on current relative 'weights' to define the agenda of Asia-Pacific economic diplomacy.
- Evolution is a principle based on pragmatism. In a diverse region, it is important to respect the views of all participants and not have co-operation imposed from above.

APEC governments have demonstrated that they have the patience necessary to nurture regional consensus so as to gradually realise the regional potential for co-operation. When regional ministers met in Canberra in November 1989, they agreed on an outward-looking, evolutionary approach to co-operation, based on equal respect for the views of all participants. Many important decisions have been reached subsequently by careful consensus-building. The 1990 Singapore meeting endorsed a wide-ranging work program, which is now beginning to put substantive economic issues before APEC ministers for their consideration. The 1991 Seoul APEC Declaration reaffirmed the commitment to an outward-looking approach that set out the objectives of APEC as follows:

(a) To sustain the growth and development of the region for the common good of its peoples and, in this way, to contribute to the growth and development of the world economy.

(b) To enhance the positive gains, both for the region and the world economy, resulting from increasing economic interdependence, by encouraging the flow of goods, services, capital and technology.

(c) To develop and strengthen the open multilateral trading system in the interest of the Asia-Pacific and all other economies.

(d) To reduce barriers to trade in goods and services and investment among participants in a manner consistent with GATT principles, where applicable, and without detriment to other economies.

The Seoul APEC Declaration also set practical criteria for expanding participation. China, Hong Kong and Taiwan (as Chinese Taipei) were the first to join the original twelve participants.

The 1992 Bangkok meeting, APEC IV, cleared the way for establishing a modest secretariat for coordinating APEC activities. In Seattle in 1993, ministers endorsed an APEC Framework for Trade and Investment Co-operation, based on outward-looking, GATT-consistent principles. The first historic meeting of APEC leaders then set the scene for practical, sub-stantive decision-making to transform the concept of an Asia-Pacific eco-nomic community into a reality.

The Bogor Declaration by APEC leaders on 15 November 1994 marked an important milestone ineconomic co-operation in the Asia-Pacific region.[1] The commitment to dismantle all policy-based obstacles to trade and investment among APEC economies over the next 25 years is a valuable assurance for the region. We can now have greater confidence that the trend towards deregulation and 'opening to the outside world', which has been crucial for the growing prosperity and interdependence of the region, will be sustained. Fears of economic confrontation across the Pacific and the emergence of a three-bloc world economy have been reduced substantially.

It may be expected that, like all successful co-operative initiatives and concepts which have proved viable in the diverse Asia-Pacific region, the guiding principles of APEC will emerge on the basis of pragmatism, expe-rience and consensus, rather than from ideology.

The diversity of the region, however, means that decision-making will sometimes be hesitant. But APEC is gaining confidence and momentum as it starts to take substantive economic decisions, and as early decisions begin to generate shared benefits and a growing sense of trust among participants.

Market-driven integration

The fastest growing parts of the world economy are private-sector driven sub-regional economic associations within the Asia-Pacific. They are no longer defined by political or even geographical boundaries. The bur-geoning, intertwined economies of Hong Kong, Taiwan and more and more of mainland China are the most visible example. The remarkable interaction between China and Japan, China and South Korea, and prospectively, China, Russia and the Koreas in the Tumen River develop-ment zone and other 'growth triangles' linking various combinations of ASEAN members, notably the 'growth triangle' around Singapore and a 'Baht Zone' linking Thailand to Indochina, are further examples of inte-grated zones of efficient production.[2]

These initiatives are radically different from old-fashioned free trade areas. They are increasingly integrated zones of production, driven by

market realities and complementarities of adjacent areas in different political entities (especially in terms of space and other factor endowments).
Through these initiatives, governments are co-operating to provide sub-
regional public goods, ranging from better infrastructure for communications to more transparent and flexible policies on international investment.
Their aim is to compete globally, not merely in restricted local markets.
They certainly do not involve preferential trading arrangements, so they
are creating new trading opportunities for everyone, without any trade
diversion. They may involve some preferential treatment of investment
from economies involved in these special economic zones, but such pref-
erences are not fundamental to the success of the initiatives. Considerable
effort is being made to ensure that these sub-regional co-operative initiatives are transparent, since the essential motive is to attract investment
from all over the world.

These and other 'production networks' being created round the Asia-
Pacific region by investment from Northeast Asia are proving to be competitive and successful. The affluence of tens of millions of people is rising
as never before, creating a new expanding market.

The success of these cross-border economic regions does not depend in
any way on collusion between governments to deny the opportunities
being created by their success to any other economy. Because they do not
depend, to any significant extent, on formal intergovernmental treaties,
these sub-regional initiatives are increasingly overshadowing old political
divides. Meanwhile, government policies encouraging preference for particular sources of imports or investment are increasingly irrelevant.

To a substantial extent, forms of market-driven, sub-regional economic
integration, such as that taking place around Hong Kong, are prototypes
of open economic associations that are the building blocks facilitating
region-wide integration in the Asia-Pacific.

The constraints around these positive trends, however, include those
imposed by inadequate transport and communications infrastructure, by
inadequate understanding of the policy frameworks and intentions of different governments, and by remaining regulations which seek to distin-
guish between 'national' and 'foreign' firms.

This is where governments in the Asia-Pacific community can and are
becoming very usefully involved. The challenge for policy-makers is to
facilitate more trade and investment by reducing or removing these
impediments. Seizing the enormous opportunities created by East Asian
dynamism also requires a clear-headed assessment of the risks to prosperity and the development of co-operative strategies. Fortunately, there
have been many constructive regional economic initiatives which have
pioneered sensible understandings on many new issues, setting positive
precedents for future regional and global co-operation.

There are no intrinsic obstacles to productive interaction and links
between the several emerging 'growth triangles' — open economic associations are, by their nature, open to expansion and positive interaction
with their neighbours and with the global economy. By providing oppor-

tunities for closer region-wide communications and consultations among governments already involved in these creative initiatives, APEC can facilitate the expansion and coalescing of 'growth triangles' into an increasingly integrated, region-wide zone of efficient production.

The East Asian ascendancy

The remarkable growth in East Asian economies, their increasing share in world production, the associated growth of their export markets and the opportunities created by the massive growth of their markets is well known. In this chapter, it is most relevant to examine two important trends which can form the basis of a viable cohesive Asia-Pacific economic community.

The track record of relative economic performance, particularly since 1960, provides ample evidence that an open, outward-looking approach to trade delivers the goods. Those economies which have faced up to global competition and made clever use of comparative advantage to produce for world markets have prospered. They have spectacularly out-performed other economies which based their development strategies on protection, producing for local or narrow sub-regional markets while seeking to shelter their economies from global competition.

The most conclusive evidence that 'opening to the outside world' works is in East Asia — in Japan, South Korea, Hong Kong, Singapore, Taiwan and, more recently, in most of ASEAN and China. These countries have worked and saved hard to invest massively in human and physical capital. They have moved deftly to take advantage of changing international market opportunities as their own comparative advantage shifted when rising real wages rewarded rising productivity.

Most governments have a vested interest in a more open trade regime. They have taken significant steps towards more open trade policies, especially since 1980. In some well-publicised cases, steps were taken under pressure. But more and more of their market opening has been driven internally by economic logic, backed by evidence that the greatest benefits of liberalisation accrue to those who take these initiatives, as well as evidence that protectionism stifles sustained rapid growth. Successive market-opening steps in each economy have been encouraged by the benefits flowing from earlier steps as well as from similar steps in neighbouring economies. All these economies have prospered remarkably, led by the integrating forces of international trade and investment, with the most rapid growth in both taking place within the region itself.

There is an excellent opportunity to build on the willingness of most Asia-Pacific economies to undertake unilateral liberalisation, since the benefits of co-ordinated liberalisation would magnify the gains from the actions of each individual economy participating in such inititatives.

The success of outward-looking economic strategies in East Asia has seen Japan emerge as one of the world's three largest economies. The adjustment to Japan's emergence as a large modern economy, followed by the success of the four East Asian 'tigers', is still causing tensions in the rest of the world, but even larger adjustments are looming. China is about to resume its historical role as the world's biggest economy. Southeast Asia is booming. For example, with rates of growth in the order of 7–8 per cent per year, by 2050 the Indonesian economy will be comparable in size to that of Japan in 1994. On foreseeable trends, the big East Asian savers and investors of the last and the next generation will develop the economic clout to call the shots in international economic policy within the Asia-Pacific.

Although the share of trade within East Asia will expand most rapidly, East Asia's exports to North America and Europe will also have to continue to increase. An exclusively East Asian bloc would simply become an additional excuse for protectionism. As Lee Kuan Yew warned in 1990:

> A de facto emergence of [three] blocs will mean a world fraught with conflicts. Asians will feel that they have been quarantined into the Japanese Yen bloc so that they can be excluded from the markets of prosperous Europeans and Americans, that the whites have changed the rules just as Asians have learnt to compete and win under those rules.

> An economic division of the world on racial lines would add bitterness and animosity to the normal conflicts. If APEC can strengthen the open trade and investment environment which spans the Pacific, and make the Europeans and the Americans more aware of the dangers of racially biased blocs, it will do world peace a service.[3]

An economic caucus in East Asia

Recognition of such risks is likely to lead to continued resistance to any formal trading bloc in East Asia. But an East Asian economic caucus will certainly emerge, even though it may never develop a formal structure. Reflecting its growing economic strength and its ever-increasing, market-driven integration, East Asia will develop increasingly effective means of asserting its shared economic interests.

Fortunately, East Asia's long-term economic interests are essentially similar to the objectives adopted by APEC in its Seoul Declaration. Accordingly, such a caucus of East Asian governments will be able to work effectively within APEC, as decided by ASEAN. An effective caucus of Asian leaders can help reduce current tensions across the Pacific in several ways. First, they can adopt a joint strategy of insisting that disputes be settled by using multilateral mechanisms, while making it clear that they will no longer negotiate on trade issues bilaterally under threat.

An East Asian caucus in APEC can also remind the United States of the need to set sound priorities in deploying its limited capacity for trade reform. It should be possible to convince United States policy-makers to concentrate harder on developing synergy with East Asia, rather than to expend the bulk of their efforts on deals with other debtor nations, whose share in United States trade pales in comparison to trade with East Asia.

Asian leaders could also resolve to be more vigorous in proposing new initiatives for co-operation in the context of APEC in order to promote a new United States approach to the region. Perhaps, more importantly, a caucus of Asian economies can be helpful in developing a capacity for joint leadership of the global economic system with the United States, sharing the responsibility of defending and strengthening global economic rules.

For small economies, such as that of Australia, the preservation of a rules-based system to facilitate international trade and investment is vital. Australia, like all other relatively small economies, needs a global system which does not condone selective discrimination by the strong against the weak. It follows that Australia needs to work with other small economies to resist selective discrimination in trade, inconsistent with the fundamental objectives of the GATT. Japan and the other emerging economic giants of East Asia also need a global economic order, for different reasons. The European Union (EU) and the United States have both found it difficult to absorb the structural changes caused by the success of Japan and will need to adjust even further to competition from China, Indonesia and others.

The way forward for APEC is not a world of trade blocs. The imperative for APEC is to work co-operatively for a one-bloc global economy; sustaining the momentum of international consultations in the new WTO, defending sensible global rules where they already exist and to working together creatively to develop similar understandings for the ever-broadening range of international economic transactions.

Building on positive trends

A flexible, innovative approach has worked well in setting up the structure of APEC. There is reason to believe that, proceeding on the basis of openness, evolution and mutual respect, it will continue to serve the Asia-Pacific well in the next few decades.

Economic co-operation in the Asia-Pacific can build on two very powerful, positive trends in the region, which are particularly evident in East Asia, as described earlier. Most Asia-Pacific governments have taken substantial, unilateral steps in recent years to deregulate and open their economies in the interests of efficiency. There is already significant evidence of market-driven economic integration across political boundaries, including those radiating from centres such as Hong Kong and Singapore. These developments provide a natural base for deeper economic integration of the whole region.

Providing regional public goods

APEC's function of facilitating regional economic integration can be compared to the role of domestic governments in providing 'public goods', such as infrastructure, education and a legal framework (including property rights and rules to promote competition), to facilitate development through private-sector initiatives. In the regional context, public goods which can facilitate market-driven integration could include APEC decisions to promote the efficiency and compatibility of transport and communications infrastructure, harmonisation or mutual recognition of standards, regulations and administrative procedures. Competition can be promoted by doing away with any remaining tariffs or quantitative restrictions to trade. There is also considerable scope to reduce uncertainties by clarifying the rights and responsibilities of international investors and developing effective means to resolve any commercial or trade policy disputes.

In practice, actions to supply such regional public goods consist of co-ordinated decisions by governments to reduce or, if possible, to eliminate all impediments to international economic transactions among Asia-Pacific economies.

If all the governments of the Asia-Pacific can focus attention on problems due to inadequate transparency, consistency and predictability of policies influencing international economic transactions, then it will be possible to create an open economic association which could embrace all economies with a serious interest in participation. In turn, this will have a positive influence on the inclination of states to carry over habits of dialogue, transparency, consistency and trust into the sphere of regional security and co-operation. As a group of economies which already interact intensely, it should be possible for APEC participants to develop regional approaches to security-related issues, thereby setting positive precedents for subsequent consensus on many new issues. At the same time, however, it is important to avoid overloading the APEC agenda with non-economic regional issues, especially when other forums are available. The Asian Regional Forum (ARF), built on the foundations of ASEAN's Post-Ministerial Consultations, has already emerged as a successful forum for consultations on regional security. It makes sense for regional economic and security consultations to continue to proceed on parallel tracks, without making progress on one set of issues contingent on the other.

Open regionalism

APEC's primary objective is to advance the prosperity of the region as well as of its neighbours and to strengthen the international trading system. All these objectives can be pursued simultaneously if, and only if, Asia-Pacific economic co-operation is genuinely open.

Joint decisions by APEC governments should reduce impediments to international economic transactions within the region, without creating any new, artificial distinctions between APEC and other economies, and avoiding new forms of discrimination. This strategy will allow all Asia-Pacific producers to maximise their efficiency, and Asia-Pacific consumers to maximise their welfare, by allowing them to choose inputs or consumer products based on their competitiveness, irrespective of their origin. This is the logical strategy which is driving unilateral reforms in Australia and in the dynamic economies of East Asia.

Openness also means that APEC should evolve in a way which encourages broader participation in the process of deepening integration. Accordingly, APEC should avoid erecting difficult 'hurdles' for potential new entrants like Russia and Vietnam — for example, by requiring accession to complex treaties or requiring legislative approval of new entrants by all other participants.

Promoting broader participation without weakening the capacity for pragmatic co-operation also requires a strategy for careful selection of new participants. This can be achieved by ensuring that all APEC initiatives are non-discriminatory and transparent, and admitting those prospective participants who have adopted voluntarily many of the initiatives made by APEC — for example, by choosing to adopt some product standards supported by APEC economies, or by emulating any non-discriminatory trade liberalisation initiatives by APEC governments.

Voluntary association

The most pragmatic way for APEC to promote co-operation in the region is to evolve as a voluntary association of Asia-Pacific economies. There is no prospect of APEC governments being willing to cede sovereignty to any type of supra-national authority in the region. Nor, as discussed below, is there any need for a supra-national regional authority or for binding international treaties in order to achieve progress. The voluntary adoption of outward-looking guiding principles for economic co-operation on a gradually broader set of issues can help economic and trade policy formation in the Asia-Pacific become progressively more consistent, leading to greater mutual benefits.

Reducing impediments to international economic transactions

The objective of an open voluntary economic association is to supply regional public goods which will facilitate progressively deeper, market-driven integration of Asia-Pacific economies. This, in turn, requires a continuous, co-ordinated effort by APEC participants to reduce, or eliminate, all impediments to international economic transactions such as market access barriers, uncertainties, infrastructure shortages and divergent standards and regulations. This challenge can be met most efficiently by early agreement on the basic principles of an open economic association, namely:

- transparency;
- non-discrimination; and
- national treatment.

In a voluntary association, such criteria will be guiding principles, as there can be no binding formal rules. In the real world, no policy is fully transparent and there will never be a time when there is no discrimination among products or firms from different economies. The value of adopting such guiding principles is that they will allow APEC to focus on initiatives which will not prove divisive within the region and are consistent with the overriding objective of strengthening the global economic system as well as the region's own cohesion.

Learning from ASEAN

The consensus-based model pioneered in the region by ASEAN, a voluntary association of nations, is more appropriate for an open economic association in the Asia-Pacific than the European model. ASEAN has shown that a group of nations with quite distinct characteristics can evolve into a very cohesive alliance. There is a central, co-ordinating secretariat, but no supra-national authority or regulatory body. Co-ordination of policies is on a voluntary basis, achieved by consensus-building. It has taken some time to reach decisions on several important issues, but all of ASEAN's voluntary agreements reflect shared interests and have, therefore, proven to be flexible and durable. Consequently, ASEAN has emerged in recent years as a highly cohesive, influential and constructive coalition in shaping the agenda of Asia-Pacific security consultations as well as in determining the nature and agenda of APEC.

ASEAN and most other participants in APEC have made it clear that they will not allow APEC to develop into a negotiating forum. APEC decisions will need to be reached by consensus, convincing participants of mutual benefits, rather than by adversarial negotiations in which some participants accept decisions which they perceive to be against their interests in return for achieving gains at the expense of others in some other matter. This implies that patience will be required, but patience will prove a worthwhile investment, because evolution based on consensus has a number of overwhelming advantages.

Evolution based on shared interests

. . . economic competition is a plus-sum game potentially leading to higher standards of living on both sides, and contributing to the further development of the global economy.[4]

This important observation, by one of the founding fathers of economic co-operation in the Asia-Pacific, is the key to making substantive progress based on voluntary decisions by APEC governments. The basic premise is that, provided there are minimum safeguards to prevent predatory competition, then the progressive reduction of impediments to international economic transactions will yield net benefits to all participating economies.

Once any proposal to reduce some particular impediment to some economic transaction among Asia-Pacific economies is recognised as a positive sum game, then it will be possible to act on that proposal on the basis of consensus. For example, it has been recognised that all APEC economies would gain from adopting a compatible system for the recording and electronic exchange of customs documentation, without any adversarial negotiations. Extensive discussions will be needed to choose a technically efficient approach, but once that is adopted there will be no need for a binding, legalistic agreement to abide by the agreed procedures. All participants who implemented the common understandings would gain quickly in terms of lower transaction costs for firms located in their economies and a significant increase in the efficiency of their harbours and airports. There are very many such positive sum games to be played out by APEC. There is vast potential for mutually beneficial reductions of impediments to international economic transactions. In most cases, the potential gains will be realised by the creation of regional public goods, generated by agreements to co-ordinate policies, regulations or procedures.

Persuasion versus negotiation

The key to progress is to identify more and more positive sum games, then to convince potential participants that there are worthwhile all-round gains to be made. Once that is recognised, pragmatic Asia-Pacific leaders can be expected to act in order to realise these gains because in a positive sum game, it is in the self-interest of all participants to adhere to the 'rules of the game'. This means that once certain codes or understandings have been adopted voluntarily, the self-interest of each participant ensures there will be a genuine commitment to try to abide by these undertakings. For example, following the 1994 endorsement of a non-binding Asia-Pacific Investment Code, it is in the self-interest of all APEC participants to adhere to it. Given the vigorous competition for international investment, investors will vote with their funds in favour of those who do abide by the Asia-Pacific Investment Code. Once reached, voluntary agreements will prove durable on the powerful basis of mutually consistent self-interest.

The self-enforcing nature of voluntary undertakings to reap the benefits of positive sum games means that there is no need for time-consuming negotiations on the precise wording of legal texts. Nor is there need to wait for even more time-consuming ratification of legal texts or treaties by all the domestic legislatures involved. Perhaps even more importantly, there is no need for 'policing' adherence to undertakings, which would require APEC participants to cede sovereignty to some regional supranational monitoring and enforcement authority.

Yet another advantage of engaging only in positive sum games is that it will be possible to make progress on individual issues on their own separate merits. No one loses and everyone gains from acting on mutually beneficial proposals, one at a time.

Since each positive sum game — for example, moves to harmonise air-safety standards — yields benefit to every participant, there is no need to assemble complex 'package deals'. Accordingly, there is no need to negotiate the simultaneous implementation of several proposals in order to achieve some 'balancing' of potential gains. This is fortunate, since it would be very difficult to reach agreement about precise estimates of potential gains which would accrue to each economy. It is sufficient to establish consensus that there will be some net gains to each potential participant. To establish such a consensus, it will normally be sufficient to reach agreement that the proposal under consideration is transparent, non-discriminatory and avoids any new departure from the principle of national treatment.

APEC has already made significant progress without engaging in confrontational or adversarial negotiations. The creation of APEC was based on careful consultations.[5] Decisions on basic principles, criteria for participation, institutional structure and mode of operation (as reflected in the Seoul APEC Declaration) have all been based on voluntary agreements emerging from patient consensus-building. Perhaps most significantly, APEC leaders were able to achieve consensus in 1994 on an ambitious timetable to dismantle all obstacles to trade and investment in the region by 2020. Many other practical, voluntary APEC understandings will follow in order to implement that broad commitment.

The important corollary of basing decisions on consensus-building, rather than negotiations, is that there will be no APEC decisions until potential participants perceive each proposal to be a positive sum game. As perceived at the establishment of APEC, this implies the need for substantial policy-oriented analysis to identify new proposals and to provide evidence of the potential gains.

Sharing the gains

However, the reality of international politics suggests that there will be concerns about relative as well as absolute potential gains. There are also practical constraints on the number of proposals that can be evaluated or acted on in any period. Accordingly, consensus will be needed, not only on the merit of individual proposals, but also on the order in which they are considered. It may prove more difficult to agree on the ordering of APEC's agenda than on its implementation. For example, needless debate is likely to persist for some on whether liberalisation of traditional trade barriers such as tariffs is more urgent or important than other ways to facilitate international economic transactions.

A pragmatic way to select issues for early attention will be to give priority to those issues where the potential for all-round gains is evident to all APEC participants. In the early years, it will be sensible to concentrate only on issues where the benefits to all are quite obvious and reasonably evenly distributed. In the near future, APEC will need to steer well clear of options where there is no agreement about the reality of, or distribution of, potential benefits. Once a sense of trust is developed and objective analyses identify more opportunities for mutually beneficial co-operation, more options will start to open up and APEC will make worthwhile simultaneous progress on several fronts.

Promoting consistency

APEC is just over five years old. It is turning from an initial focus on procedural issues to making decisions on economic matters. It will not be an easy transition. Through APEC, however, individual governments will be increasingly aware of the effects of their actions on each other. They will develop a growing interest in policy consistency based on the principles of non-discrimination, national treatment and transparency.

In reality, most policy decisions influencing the Asia-Pacific economies will continue to be made by individual governments, acting unilaterally. APEC's existence can, nonetheless, lead to a gradually increasing consonance of the policies of individual participants with the economically logical and non-divisive principles of an open economic association. In this context, APEC will be radically different to the constraining, regulatory role of the European Union. The positive role of region-wide consensus-building by APEC will be more comparable to the role of the OECD in relation to its participants.

Moving at different speeds

As long as all joint initiatives by of APEC participants are consistent with the basic principles of non-discrimination, national treatment and transparency, they will not disadvantage other economies, but will set positive examples which they can follow at any time; any decision by any subgroup of APEC participants will not disadvantage any other participant.

During the early years of APEC, it will be important to foster broadly based confidence in the process by acting only on issues on which a genuine consensus has been established. Subsequently, once a progressively greater sense of trust has been fostered, it will be possible for some participants, or groups of participants such as ASEAN, to set positive examples to others in

APEC. There is no need for the majority to wait for the most reluctant to perceive the benefit of certain actions. Since adherence to the principles of non-discrimination, national treatment and transparency guarantees that no other economy will be disadvantaged, there is no need to provide for any explicit or implicit veto rights to individual APEC participants.

Correspondingly, there will be no need to pressure any participant to join in any particular initiative. The benefits from any positive sum game would be enhanced by the broadest possible participation, but there is no need to force the pace for those who do not see the advantage in doing so. Provided APEC adheres to the basic positive principles of an open economic association, there is no need for either 'uniform speed' of 'required majorities' for decisions to foster the mutually beneficial deeper integration of Asia-Pacific economies. As long as no new discrimination is created among Asia-Pacific economies, moving ahead at different speeds on different issues will set positive examples.

The 1990s

For the first five years or so, we will sit around the table looking at each other, deciding on objectives and gaining confidence in each other and in the process. Then we may actually decide to do something. We need to be patient . . .

These remarks, by a senior ASEAN Minister during the 1989 consultations leading up to the first meeting of APEC Ministers later that year, have proved to be not only helpful, but also prescient. After the important, careful work of laying strong foundations between 1989 and 1994, APEC governments have, in fact, taken their first important economic, as against procedural, decisions.

Reducing physical impediments to trade has proved to be a pragmatic starting point, since the potential for mutual benefit can be readily appreciated. Exchanging information about the pattern and trend of regional trade, investment and tourism can pinpoint the need for timely investments to avoid infrastructure bottlenecks. Such work has already commenced in APEC's sectoral working groups. For example, transport capacity will be boosted by achieving APEC's objective of electronic exchanges of trade documentation. There are many more ways to improve communications in addition to enhancing physical infrastructure. Uncertainties about interactions with the region can be reduced through the exchange of information and the movement of people. Ministerial-level consultations on macro-economic policies, which have already commenced, will help to reduce unnecessary tensions within the region — for example, by agreement on the extent to which trade imbalances are due to macro-economic imbalances in individual economies and the extent to which they are due to restrictive trade policies.

Reducing uncertainties

The increasing frequency and coverage of policy-oriented consultations among APEC officials in various working groups means that awareness of each other's concerns and motives will increase steadily. APEC consultations will also help ensure that the effects of domestic decisions on other participants will be better understood and increasingly taken into account. A greater coherence of decisions will lead to closer consistency of regional policy-making, with more and more decisions taken in co-ordination by several, perhaps all, APEC governments. Such a pattern of effective consultations, leading to more transparent and more consonant economic policies, will reduce uncertainties currently inherent in trade and investment in the region.

A good initial example of this pattern of gradually greater coherence in policy-making is likely to be the future evolution of the Asia-Pacific Investment Code after its adoption in 1994. The intense competition for international investment around the region will ensure close, voluntary adherence to the code. In future, it will become increasingly clear to participants that there would be advantage in further reforms of policies on investment to make them more transparent and less discriminatory. This could lead to supplementary undertakings about future reforms to the investment rules of each APEC government. For example, as mutual confidence increases, it will be recognised that increasing harmonisation of incentives provided to investors is also a positive sum policy game and voluntary agreements on some harmonisation of fiscal policies influencing international investment will be added to the Asia-Pacific Investment Code.

Resolving disputes

As Asia-Pacific economies interact ever more intensively, some disputes are inevitable. An urgent challenge to Asia-Pacific economic diplomacy is to develop a better approach to resolving trade disputes, in order to prevent the increasing risk of APEC being torn apart by unnecessary confrontations, while avoiding the need for any new cumbersome regional bureaucracy or supra-regional authority. A sensible first step would be to agree that all disputes about issues covered by the WTO will be referred for resolution under the new streamlined dispute-resolution processes which will be incorporated in the WTO's Articles. It is certainly in the interests of all APEC economies that any disputes be settled in a way that is transparent and does not lead to outcomes which result in some economies being given preference over others.

If all APEC participants agreed to try to make the WTO the first resort to resolve any trade disputes which could not be solved bilaterally, and to make a serious effort to making that process work quickly (as well as agreeing to abide by its outcomes), then a major present source of uncertainty in trans-Pacific trade would be eased.

Other areas where APEC can play a useful role include resolving issues concerning the non-membership of China and Taiwan in the WTO and the resumption of Chinese sovereignty over Hong Kong in 1997. There is also considerable scope for harmonising commercial legislation and regulations in order to reduce uncertainties and, hence, transaction costs of international trade and investment.

Conclusions

The next ten years, and the following decades, present opportunities as well as risks for economic co-operation in the Asia-Pacific. APEC can encourage increasingly co-operative policies to sustain and accelerate the remarkable trend of growth and market-driven integration in the region. APEC can also encourage substantive economic co-operation which can bridge the Pacific, sustain United States commitment to Asia and help the United States to find new ways to become engaged positively in Asia's dynamism.

Provided APEC can remain flexible and open, it should be able to cope with the ongoing changes in the relative size and strength of regional economies and to draw additional economies into the process. Above all, APEC can pursue an intra-regional economic agenda in ways which underpin the region's broader, overriding interest in an open, non-discriminatory trading system.

Having established a coherent membership, a sensible work program and a modest institutional base, including productive working links with other regional institutions such as ASEAN and PECC, the new APEC process is now ready to set ambitious objectives, then commence their realisation by means of carefully sequenced, politically digestible decisions.

The evolution of an Asia-Pacific Economic Community, based on the realities of a remarkably diverse and successful region, clearly has significant implications for the security outlook of the Asia-Pacific community. Many of the principles of APEC, first set out in the initial Canberra meeting of APEC ministers and reaffirmed by APEC leaders at Bogor in 1994, have indirect but nonetheless important consequences for regional security. For example, principles of economic co-operation, regional solidarity, mutual benefit, mutual respect and egalitarianism, pragmatism and decision-making on the basis of consensus and implementation on the basis of flexibility are relevant to the regional security outlook. Most of the regional leaders practising these principles in the economic sphere are the same prime ministers, presidents and foreign ministers who are equally concerned with matters of regional security. They are becoming to attuned and accustomed to pursuing goals of regional harmony, the peaceful settlement of disputes and progress by consensus. The APEC mechanism and the activities associated with its advancement, are also helping to develop habits of co-operation, consultation, regular dialogue, transparency and mutual confidence, as well as a vision of Pacific regionalism.

This is contributing to regional peace and stability. Maintaining a calm security environment can be helped immeasurably by sustaining the momentum of economic prosperity and ensuring the continued engagement of the United States. In this context, APEC is a timely and important contribution to regional security at a time of great opportunity.

Notes

[1] See Andew Elek, 'APEC Beyond Bogar', *Asia-Pacific Economic Literature*, vol. 8, no. 1, May 1995.

[2] See Myo Thant, Min Tang and Hiroshi Kakazu, *Growth Triangles in Asia — A New Approach to Regional Economic Cooperation*, Asian Development Bank, Oxford University Press, Hong Kong, 1994; and Ross Garnaut and Peter Drysdale (eds), *Asia Pacific Regionalism — Readings In International Economic Relations*, Harper Educational, Pymble, 1994.

[3] Lee Kuan Yew, Opening Address, Asia-Pacific Economic Cooperation Ministerial Meeting, Singapore, 1990.

[4] Saburo Okita, 'Approaching the 21st Century — Japan's Role', *Japan Times*, Tokyo, 1990.

[5] Gareth Evans and Bruce Grant, *Australia's Foreign Relations in the World of the 1990s*, Melbourne University Press, Melbourne, 1991, p. 124; H. Soesastro, 'The Institutional Framework for APEC: An Asian Perspective', paper presented at seminar on Australian, Indonesian and Japanese Approaches to APEC, the Australian National University, Canberra, September 1994.

13 Asia-Pacific Transport and Communications Networks and Regional Security

Peter J. Rimmer

Now the war is ended and the sole market of these war supplies has closed — let us hope forever, for the good of humanity. So from now on we are concerned with the problem of how a readjustment may be brought about.[1]

Dr Sun Yat-sen's (1928) 'rough sketch' for the International Development of China as a contribution to world peace gave prominence to the creation of transport and communications systems, comprising railways, highways, rivers, canals, telegraph lines, long-distance telephones and wireless services, and commercial harbours. Similar priorities underpinned Japan's design for a Greater East Asia Co-prosperity Sphere in the 1940s.[2] Today the critical importance of transport and communications in expanding intra-regional trade has been recognised in plans for a Pacific economic community. These have been mooted at regular Pacific Trade and Development (PAFTAD) conferences and Pacific Basin Economic Business Council (PBEC) meetings since the late 1960s, and in the inaugural Pacific Economic Cooperation Conference (PECC) in 1980. They crystallised in formal Asia Pacific Economic Cooperation (APEC) at an inter-ministerial level in 1989. As the transport and communications networks desired for APEC are still being elaborated and substantiated, they are worthy of more detailed consideration.

The end of the Cold War in the Asia-Pacific region left nation-states intact (though Korea is still divided and the status of Taiwan is still in doubt). Subsequent accelerated economic integration in the world's most dynamic region of trade and production has been less respectful of existing political boundaries. National barriers to trade have been weakened by opportunities for business enterprises to capitalise on the international specialisation in production associated with the intensification of global economic ties within the region. Unlike Europe and North America, nations and sub-national areas (e.g. growth triangles) have been incorporated into international trade and specialisation without formal inter-governmental institutional arrangements and trade discrimination.[3] The ultimate outcome of this much vaunted 'open regionalism' on a supranational scale would, in effect, be a 'borderless' community. This community would be driven by market processes, freed from official controls on international trade and payments and buoyed by the provision of public goods promoting regional trade expansion (e.g. special economic zones and open areas).

Several potentially important trading relationships in the Asia-Pacific region, however, were hindered by official controls on international trade and payments, and discrimination against movements of freight, information and passengers. Some of these Cold War legacies have been overcome by the United States' recognition of the People's Republic of China in 1979, the Sino-British agreement on Hong Kong in 1984, Taiwan's lifting of trade restrictions with the mainland in 1987, Sino-Korean mutual diplomatic recognition in 1992 and normalisation of United States relations with Vietnam in 1994.[4] Varying degrees of resistance still remain in China, Indochina and North Korea, where vested interests are endeavouring to perpetuate existing trading patterns.

Arguably, this resistance could be overcome and regional security enhanced by government support for extending existing international transport and communications networks to further develop the growing web of intense regional economic ties. This would be a significant step towards a common Asia-Pacific economy and culture. Once enmeshed in these networks, and subject to international conventions, most countries would, of necessity, adopt a more conciliatory policy as they have in ASEAN. Before examining this proposition, there needs to be an investigation of how changes in the structure and dynamics of transport and communications networks have developed in the Asia-Pacific region since the early 1980s. Then the repercussions of enmeshing areas of resistance into the structure and the dynamics of transport and communications networks can be explored.

The integrative role of transport and communications networks in the Asia-Pacific region is examined by studying international movements of freight, information and passengers. Reflecting differences in factor endowments, preferential trade agreements, variations in transport, communications and other transaction costs, each type of movement is discussed separately.[5] Particular attention is paid to the reduction of pockets of resistance in China, Indochina and North Korea.[6] Then the role of transport and communications as key forces for stability can be discussed.

Freight

Bulk cargoes — oil, coal and iron ore — dominate shipping movements in the Asia-Pacific region. Involving long and vulnerable sea lanes, the movement of bulk cargoes highlights the importance of 'choke points' in the Indonesian archipelago and the strategic importance of the Paracel and Spratly Islands. Interest here, however, is concentrated on containerised movements of general cargo.[7] Containerised cargoes are influenced by the policies and strategies of liner shipping companies offering fixed-day-of-the-week services, whereas bulk cargoes are predictable and handled by port authority facilities.[8] An examination of the structure and dynamics of container movements, therefore, offers a more sensitive guide to the state of regional sea–land transport networks. Particular attention is centred on the pattern of container ports, the established network of container shipping routes and land-based connections.

Ports

In 1991, the Asia-Pacific region (Far East/South Asia) accounted for two-fifths of world's container port traffic estimated at 93 million TEUs (twenty-foot equivalent units), with Europe accounting for more than one-fifth and the North American Free Trade Area less than one-fifth.[9] A prime feature of the top-ranking Asia-Pacific region is the concentration of container freight tonnage on a limited number of fast-growing hub ports in the sea corridor between Tokyo and Singapore. By 1992, six Asia-Pacific ports were in the world's 'top 10' container ports with Hong Kong (7.9 m TEUs) ranking first, Singapore (7.6 m TEUs) second, Kaohsiung (4.0 m TEUs) fourth and Pusan (2.8 m TEUs) fifth, Kobe (2.6 m TEUs) sixth and Keelung (1.9 m TEUs) tenth (see Table 12.1).[10] Over the past decade, trade in other Asia countries has outstripped that of Japan. With the movement of its low-productivity manufacturers offshore, the growth rates of Kobe, Yokohama and Tokyo had been lower than those of Hong Kong, Singapore and Kaohsiung.

Three sub-regional clusters of ports are identifiable in the Asia-Pacific region: (a) Northeast Asia featuring Pusan, Kobe, Yokohama, Tokyo and Nagoya; (b) Central Asia comprising Hong Kong, Kaohsiung, Keelung, Manila, Shanghai and a host of ports in the Pearl River Delta and adjacent areas of southern China; and (c) Southeast Asia focusing on Singapore, Bangkok, Tanjong Priok (Jakarta), Port Kelang and an emerging Ho Chi Minh (Saigon). Container throughput is closely linked to national economic development, but hub ports — Hong Kong, Singapore and Kaohsiung — have an additional advantage in attracting transhipment cargo.

China's ports have been incorporated into regional container networks (with 80 per cent of the country's container output going through Hong Kong).[11] Funds from the World Bank, Asia Development Bank and the Japanese Economic Cooperation Bank have been used to build 104 deep-

Table 13.1   The world's 'top ten' container ports

1982	'000 TEUs	1987	'000 TEUs	1992	'000 TEUs
1. Rotterdam	2 159	1. **Hong Kong**	**3 457**	1. **Hong Kong**	**7 972**
2. New York	1 909	2. Rotterdam	2 839	2. **Singapore**	**7 580**
3. **Hong Kong**	**1 660**	3. **Kaohsiung**	**2 779**	3. Rotterdam	4 122
4. **Kobe**	**1 504**	4. **Singapore**	**2 635**	4. **Kaohsiung**	**3 960**
5. **Kaohsiung**	**1 194**	5. New York/ New Jersey	2 089	5. **Pusan**	**2 751**
6. **Singapore**	**1 116**	6. **Kobe**	**1 997**	6. **Kobe**	**2 608**
7. San Juan	917	7. **Pusan**	**1 949**	7. Los Angeles	2 289
8. Hamburg	889	8. **Keelung**	**1 940**	8. Hamburg	2 268
9. Antwerp	846	9. Los Angeles	1 580	9. New York/ New Jersey	2 104
10. **Yokohama**	**843**	10. Long Beach	1 460	10. **Keelung**	**1 941**

Source: CI, 1984, 1989 and 1994.

water berths within China to reduce Hong Kong's port traffic.[12] Other investments from foreign consortia have been used, for example, to develop harbours in Shanghai, Tianjin, Dalian, Huangpu, Ningbo and Xiamen. In some instances, ports have entered into joint ventures and management arrangements with international terminal and shipping companies (e.g. Britain's P&O has management control of Shekou Container Terminal near Hong Kong).[13]

Shipping routes

These hub ports are linked into three major shipping routes and plugged directly into the world's most advanced economies in Europe, Japan and the United States.[14]

1 *Deep-sea mainline services* involving:
   a *Trans-Pacific services* with the West Coast of the United States hubbing on Japan, Hong Kong, Kaohsiung and, to a lesser extent, Singapore; and
   b *Europe–Far East services* hubbing on Singapore/Port Kelang, Hong Kong, Kaohsiung and Japan.
2 *Round-the-world (and semi-round) services* linking Europe–United States–Asia also use designated hubs and load centres.
3 *Intra-regional services* incorporating the feeder and regional traffic which ply to and from Kaohsiung, Hong Kong and Singapore hubs and between regional ports. Bangkok, for example, has feeder services to Kaohsiung, Hong Kong and Singapore, Manila to Kaohsiung and Hong Kong, and Port Kelang, Penang, Tanjong Priok and Surabaya to Singapore.

Direct mainline services by major shipping companies, typified by Sea–Land, Maersk and Nippon Yusen Kaisha, are operated either on their own or on a consortia/joint service basis. They use large mother ships (4000 TEUs-plus) for their trunk route mainline services with feeder services carrying containers to and from regional ports.[15] Round-the-world services by major shipping companies, exemplified by Evergreen and DSR-Senator, also use large mother ships and feeder services for regional cargoes. As intra-regional services now rival the deep-sea trades in volume and surpass them in growth they are considered in more detail.[16]

The stability of the existing intra-regional system focused on the hub ports of Hong Kong, Singapore and Kaohsiung is open to question. All three ports depend on relaying cargo originating and terminating in other countries. All three are expanding their container facilities to meet demands for economies of scale (e.g. larger ships) and improved service quality (e.g. shorter transit times). Hong Kong's land acquisition and terminal construction costs, however, have resulted in higher loading costs than its rivals. Its ability to respond to market forces after its return to the People's Republic of China in 1997 is also in question given the new government's likely interventionist nature. As China's ports — particularly those in the Pearl River Delta — are attracting an increasing number of direct shipping calls, their dependence on feeder services to Hong Kong may be reduced. As trade between China and Taiwan passes through Hong Kong, the port would be affected by the removal of restrictions on direct trade as both Kaohsiung and Keelung have a distinct locational advantage over Hong Kong for shipping to Central China. The availability of extensive terminals for lease in Kaohsiung gives the port the potential to capture large volumes of transhipment trade from Hong Kong involving both China and Vietnam.

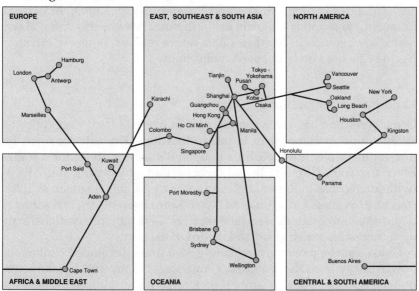

Figure 13.1   Cosco's container shipping routes, 1993
Sources: Various.

China's rapid economic growth has resulted in 36 maritime agreements being signed with other countries. Also, China has attracted the branch offices of foreign shipping lines — Sea–Land, American President Line and Maersk.[17] More than two-thirds of China's container trade, however, is controlled by the China Ocean Shipping Co. (Cosco), China's state-owned line.[18] Cosco has further developed its deep-sea container shipping network by taking delivery of new and larger ships as part of its ambitious expansion plans fuelled by the growth of China's export trade (see Figure 13.1). The company now ranks in the 'top 5' of the world's container ship operators. Between 1989 and 1994, Cosco's one-way nominal capacity on six major deep-sea trading routes had trebled from 312 200 TEUs to 938 800 TEUs.[19] Older tonnage has been redeployed on Cosco's extensive intra-regional services provided directly and in co-operation with other operators.

In May 1993, a container service was introduced by Cosco between China and Vietnam. Ho Chi Minh City, Vietnam's leading container centre, has attracted foreign operators, but its potential is handicapped by 'chronic infrastructure problems, incoherent management and the development of a deepwater port at the mouth of the Saigon River'.[20] The Intra-Asia Discussion Agreement comprising major containership operators has now set up an Indochina Local Committee and has introduced terminal handling charges.[21]

Prior to its Vietnam initiative, Cosco also set up a joint venture with South Korea's Heung-A in 1992 to operate a direct China–Korea service under the name CoHeung Shipping Co. This connection has led to the vision of a reunited Korea becoming the focal point of cargo distribution in Northeast Asia with its trans-Pacific seaport hubs serving both China and Russia — Inchon, Mokpo and Pusan in South Korea, and Haeju, Chongjin, Najin and Heungnam in North Korea.[22] Before this vision of economic co-operation in Northeast Asia can be realised, however, attention has to be focused on land-based connections.

Land-based connections

Containerisation has given coastal areas in the Asia-Pacific region better access to international than to inland locations. Key interior areas for development include the China mainland's border areas, the Yangtze River, the Trans-China railway line between Lianyungang and Alataw (with connections to Rotterdam), and southwest China. Inadequate infrastructure in China, Indochina and North Korea prevents the realisation of door-to-door multimodal sea–land services. Generally, international standard containers are stripped and stuffed at the port.

China, for the most part, remains a vast underdeveloped continental power. Away from the seaboard, China's geography and infrastructure militate against basing its growth on foreign trade. Although China has implemented and signed five railway transport agreements with other countries by 1992,[23] its outmoded and overburdened railways are ill-

Table 13.2 Movements of international containers in China by road and water, 1991

Province	Road TEUs		Water TEUs	
	Thousand	Per cent	Thousand	Per cent
Beijing	3.5	0.86	-	-
Tianjin	29.6	7.25	-	-
Hebei	5.7	1.40	10.8	3.23
Liaoning	54.1	13.26	11.3	3.38
Heliongjiang	0.1	0.02	-	-
Shanghai	142.7	34.97	-	-
Jiangsu	24.4	5.98	42.6	12.74
Zhejiang	24.0	5.88	28.2	8.43
Fujian	19.3	4.73	24.9	7.44
Shandong	36.4	8.92	33.3	9.96
Henan	8.3	2.03	-	-
Hunan	0.1	0.02	-	-
Guangdong	59.9	14.68	179.1	53.56
Guanxi	-	-	2.6	0.78
Hainan	-	-	1.6	0.48
Total	408.1	100.00	334.4	100.00

Source: ZJN, 1992, pp. 466, 468.

equipped to handle international standard containers. Ports at the mouth of the Yangtze and Pearl Rivers rely on water transport for inland movements (though there is a general shortage of roll on–roll off container vessels and barges). Other ports have to depend on an inadequate road transport system for moving containers (see Table 13.2) to participate in transnational growth triangles or economic zones.

The geopolitical implication of China's increasingly uncompetitive inland provinces is influencing infrastructural planning, particularly as rural roads have been left without an adequate system of financial support.[24] Priorities have been given to twelve trunk highways, the main water channel comprising the north–south coastal route, four rivers and a canal, nineteen distribution hubs and necessary support services such as telecommunications.[25] The accompanying reform and restructuring effort in transport includes a shift from policies of self-sufficiency and central planning towards outward-oriented policies. The latter include the introduction of user-pay principles, and experimentation with decentralisation, deregulation and privatisation. A market environment is being encouraged in which port and shipping firms work more closely with land transport companies to enable China to trade more effectively in global markets.

Indochina's state-owned railways also cannot accommodate international containers. The railways are beset with deteriorating infrastructure and financial problems — a condition attributed to their centralised administration and excessive government regulation. These difficulties are compounded by road quality ranging from poor to, at best, fair — a reflection of their rough formation, failing pavements, bridges in poor condition and inadequate maintenance. In a bid to enhance sub-regional economic co-operation, priority is being given by the Asia Development Bank[26] to road construction to knit the six countries — Cambodia, Laos, Myanmar, Thailand, Vietnam and Yunnan Province (China) — together (though railway and water projects have also been identified).[27] A master plan for roads is likely to be approved for upgrading or construction of highways between Ho Chi Minh–Phnom Penh–Bangkok, Bangkok–Kunming, Kunming–Lashio, Kunming–Haiphong, and three links between the Thai–Laos border and ports on Vietnam's coast (including Vinh). These roads are designed to facilitate cross-border movements of agricultural goods, forestry products, energy supplies, minerals, construction materials and manufactured goods, particularly from Thailand, Vietnam and Yunnan. When completed, these road networks will contribute to the proliferation of ties that are helping to pull the region together.

North Korea will also have to rely on road transport because of the parlous state of its two major railway lines — the Kyeongeuil and Peongra lines. The Kyongeuil line is inactive except in the vicinity of Pyongyang and it is doubtful if the short Peongra line from Kowon to Chongjin could move containerised cargo profitably. Clearly, a major priority of any National Plan for Comprehensive Development after reunification would be the creation of a major road network. The network has already been designed in the form of a lattice — seven north–south routes and nine east–west axes — to ensure all parts of the country can benefit from economic development. Associated developments in truck terminals and distribution centres will have to be built to capitalise on the new network. Coastal shipping between the south and north is likely to play a supportive role. Not only would jobs be created in road construction and related industries but a more efficient and systematic network would attract direct foreign investment to new industrial sites. As financial resources are unlikely to be available for such a mammoth project, it is likely private capital will be sought from South Korea and Japan.

Investments in infrastructure for facilitating freight movement need to be complemented by improvements in telecommunications so that China, Indochina and North Korea can trade more effectively in global markets. Whereas 'official' freight transport is controlled by governments that are confined by political boundaries, telecommunication networks are a global dynamic, the spread of which presages a shift in the axis of power in the world from geopolitics to telegeography.[28]

Information

The Asia-Pacific region has become increasingly enmeshed in the vast expansion of global telecommunications networks since the 1970s. Much of the new capacity has been largely invisible, involving the addition of cross-border terrestrial links, regional undersea cables and international switching facilities. On an intercontinental scale, there was the launch of INTELSAT V(1980) and V-A(1985) satellite series. The 1980s also saw the authorisation of two competing sets of trans-Pacific submarine cables: Trans-Pacific Cable No. 3 (TPC-3) owned by AT&T and national Post Telephone and Telegraph (PTT) authorities; and North Pacific Cable (NPC) owned privately through common carriers and PTTs share in the ownership. These new cables all used optic-fibre technologies and have added enormous capacity to the market. As international supply was no longer a problem business and regulatory concerns became demand-driven (e.g. the price of network access and competition for basic services).

During the 1980s and early 1990s, the rising demand for cross-border telecommunications in the Asia-Pacific region has reflected a variety of factors. Besides a larger installed telephone base and declining tariffs, the key factors have been rises in per capita income, growth in international tourism, and increased trade and investment flows associated with the internationalisation of production. Further economic growth and the addition of new access lines are expected to boost cross-border demand. Already, new information technologies — computers and communications (C&C) — have fostered the rise of the international network economy and favoured market forms of economic organisation at the expense of the hierarchical management of production and distribution. As C&C transaction and co-ordination costs have fallen, various kinds of markets (e.g. air travel reservations) and networks for Electronic Data Interchange (EDI) have proliferated. The Asia-Pacific region today has the world's highest growth rate in telephone lines, and in mobile and satellite communications.[29]

The unprecedented international telecommunications boom in the Asia-Pacific region has been stimulated by the new media. The facsimile has been most important (though Electronic Mail will become more significant). The fax accounts for the bulk of new cross-border traffic, particularly on trans-Pacific routes where differences in language and limited overlap of working hours give this medium a distinct advantage over conventional telephone services. Japan possesses more fax machines than both the European Union and the USA.[30] The fax accounts for between 50 and 60 per cent of Japan's international traffic. Similar experiences are reported in both Hong Kong and Singapore. Clearly, the fax is a step towards the future when cross-border traffic comprises networks of multimedia terminals.

At the centre of this growth in the Asia-Pacific region have been Japan and the four Newly Industrialising Economies (NIEs) — Hong Kong, Taiwan, Singapore and South Korea — where annual increases of 30–50 per cent have been common (see Table 13.3). Initially, Japan's international telecommunications providers — Kokusai Denwa Densha (KDD), International Digital Communications Inc. (IDC) and International Telecom Japan (ITJ) — have looked to the NIEs and then the United States for traffic. Other targets have been Asia's second generation of fast-growing economies and Europe, which has attracted both tourists and inward investment from Japan. Traditionally, KDD had exercised monopoly control over Japan's

Table 13.3. Largest telecommunications routes of Japan, Hong Kong, Singapore, South Korea, Taiwan and China, 1992/1992–93

Country	Rankings					MiTT
	1	2	3	4	5	
Japan	USA	Sth Korea	China	Philippines	Taiwan	1283.3
(1992–93)	(20.2%)	(10.4%)	(7.3%)	(7.0%)	(6.2%)	
Hong Kong	China	USA	Taiwan	Canada	Japan	1136.6
(1992–93)	(47.0%)	(7.0%)	(6.0%)	(5%)	(4%)	
Singapore	Malaysia	Indonesia	USA	Hong Kong	Japan	412.0
(1992–93)	(26.7%)	(9.7%)	(8.5%)	(8.3%)	(8.3.%)	
Sth Korea	USA	Japan	Hong Kong	Philippines	China	305.9
(1992)	(30.6%)	(26.2%)	(4.8%)	(4.1%)	(3.5%)	
Taiwan	USA	Hong Kong	Japan	China	Singapore	368.7
(1992–93)	(22.3%)	(17.3%)	(14.9%)	(14.3%)	(3.6%)	
China	Hong Kong	Japan	Taiwan	USA	Macao	635.1
(1992)	(64.9%)	(9.0%)	(7.4%)	(4.8%)	(3.9%)	

Note: MiTT refers to Minutes of Telecommunications Traffic.
Source: Based on Staple, 1993.

international telecommunications. Competition from IDC and ITJ have resulted in them capturing 30 per cent of the market by 1992. The emergence of a competitive Japanese market structure has had repercussions on other Asia-Pacific markets.

Cross-border traffic has seen Hong Kong Telecom among the world's 'top 20' international carriers (with a monopoly over international traffic until 2006). Although Beijing's official investment arm, China International Trust and Investment Corporation (CITIC), has a 20 per cent share in Hong Kong Telecom, Cable and Wireless (C&W) is its largest shareholder (C&W also has a share in Japan's IDC). In 1992, mainland China accounted for more than two-fifths of Hong Kong Telecom International's traffic (see Table 13.3). As Singapore's official statistics do not include cross-border traffic with Malaysia, the state-owned Singapore Telecom does not rank in the 'top 20' (though it has an absolute monopoly over domestic and international communications until the year 2007). Government carriers in Singapore (ranked 24th), Taiwan (25th) South Korea (32nd) and Malaysia (36th) are growing rapidly and are likely to dislodge smaller European states from the 'top 20'.[31]

A marked feature of telecommunications has been the rise of powerful, Chinese family-led conglomerates in both Malaysia and Thailand (e.g. Bina Riang, Shinawatra, Charoen Pokphand, Li and Kuok partnerships). Any foreign companies wishing to operate in Malaysia and Thailand would have to enter into partnerships with these conglomerates. This requirement has not been a deterrent for Australia's Telstra, the UK's Cable & Wireless and the US-based Nynex (a partner with Charoen Pokphand in Thailand's TelecomAsia). Their involvement has been prompted by the need to position themselves for entry into telecommunications markets within China's increasingly autonomous regions.

China's rapid and accelerating annual expansion in international communications between 1981 and 1991 (20.9 per cent) outstripped the growth rates of both GNP (8.8 per cent) and trade (12.2 per cent). China, in a sense, is being hooked up to the rest of the world. Nonetheless, some 50 per cent of rural villages have no telephones and the supply of telephones in large cities cannot meet demand.[32] In 1995, telephone penetration in large and open coastal cities was estimated at 20 per cent and 30–40 per cent was expected in the year 2000. Reflecting sharp differences with the rest of China, the national figure in 1995 was 2.5 per cent, with 5 per cent expected in the year 2000. These figures underline that 'China's telecommunications sector is still plagued by congestion and waiting lists'.[33] Only about 15 per cent of long-distance calls dialled in south and central China are successful and the waiting period for telephones in cities is usually eighteen months. To overcome these problems, China has laid out 22 optical fibre cables centred on Beijing connecting major cities.[34] Twenty interprovincial microwave trunk lines and nineteen satellite earth stations are linked to this network.[35] Also, the Chinese government intends to make use of the competitive mechanism in non-basic services (e.g. information services and other value-added telecommunications services).

Indochina has less than 0.3 main telephone lines per 100 people (compared with 42 per 100 for Japan).[36] Its high growth potential in telecommunications, however, is being targeted by international and regional groups. Myanmar and Cambodia have the greatest need for telecommunications services, though most rural areas lack effective services.[37] Public finances in Myanmar and Cambodia, as in Laos and Vietnam, preclude sufficient budgetary allocations being made available to redress the problem. Much reliance, therefore, will have to be placed on multiple private investors. A build, operate and transfer (BOT) arrangement has been used by Australia's Telstra to invest in satellite facilities in Cambodia. A similar arrangement is being used by Telstra to upgrade Vietnam's international telephone service. The Vietnamese government has also contracted Marconi of Italy to build an optic fibre cable between Hanoi and Ho Chi Minh. Siemens have been contracted to upgrade Myanmar's telephone system. As cable laying is difficult in Indochina's harsh terrain, there is a great opportunity for owners of satellites. Malaysia's Telecommunications Resource Industries has established a cellular system in Phnom Penh similar to that being operated by the military authorities in China's Beijing and Hebei provinces. Thailand's Shinawatra company hopes to use satellite technology for long-distance telephone services in Laos.

North Korea is a potential telecommunications market for Korea Telecom.[38] Ranked ninth in the world in terms of access lines, Korea Telecom still needs to import advanced technology and managerial skills. Yet it has the experience to assist infrastructure expansion in North Korea and neighbouring countries. In 1982, Korea Telecom lost its role as monopoly voice carrier with the introduction of 'competition' from Data Communications Corporation (though Korea Telecom retains a 34 per cent share).

Telecommunications has the potential to play an even greater international role in the Asia-Pacific region. Rising cross-border demand is still handicapped by inflexible regulatory and pricing arrangements. This penalty has focused attention on further liberalisation, tariff realignment and new services.

Passengers

The Asia-Pacific region is the world's fastest growing region in air passenger transport. The International Air Transport Association[39] anticipates a 7.5 per cent annual average growth in air travel between 1995 and 2000 and 7 per cent between 2000 and 2020. International scheduled passenger numbers are expected to increase from 132 million in 1995 through 189 million in 2000 to 375 million in 2010. The region's share of world traffic will increase from almost 36 per cent in 1995 to over 51 per cent in 2010. This anticipated growth underpins an expected surge in aeroplane purchases by Asia carriers (3000 new planes at a cost of US$245 billion between 1994 and 2013). As this represents 30 per cent of the world market, interest in developing an Asia-built jetliner has been triggered, particularly in Taiwan.[40] The next section focuses on Asia-Pacific airports and air routes, with particular attention paid to China, Indochina and North Korea. At present, they have low traffic bases but large travel potential for business travellers and leisure travellers (i.e. both vacationers and visiting friends and relatives).

Air routes

Flight activity in the Asia-Pacific region is concentrated in a corridor stretching from Tokyo to Jakarta.[41] Three main route areas dominate passenger traffic in the Asia-Pacific region:[42]
1 *Long-haul traffic* involving:
   a *Trans-Pacific traffic* (including Asia–Americas, Asia–Hawaii and Hawaii–Americas), accounting for 24 million passengers in 1990 (86 million by 2010), heavily concentrated on Japan, Korea and Hong Kong;
   b Europe–Far East traffic, amounting to 12 million in 1990 (over 48 million in 2010), focused on the United Kingdom, Germany and France; it stems largely from Japan, Thailand, Singapore and Hong Kong.
2 *Short and medium-haul, intra-regional traffic* totalling almost 58 million passengers in 1990 (262 million by 2010).
   Intra-regional traffic is the most important market and will grow at a faster rate than traffic between the Asia-Pacific region and the rest of the world. Consequently, Asia-Pacific carriers (e.g. Cathay Pacific and Taiwan's China Airlines) have been expanding their regional connections, whereas European and United States carriers have been focusing on their

transcontinental services. Already air space south of Japan is congested — a condition that will soon afflict air space over the South China Sea.

A large proportion of intra-regional traffic is focused on Northeast Asia, involving connections between Japan and Hong Kong, South Korea and Taiwan. Much of the increased growth on existing and new Asia-Pacific routes will stem from an increase in the number of flights rather than from using larger aircraft. These forecasts do not take account of potential growth from developments in China, Indochina and North Korea.

China's air transport industry has experienced phenomenal growth since the dismantling of the Civil Aviation Administration of China (CAAC) in 1988. The establishment of Air China International and six regional airlines allowed CAAC to concentrate on regulatory matters and provided the impetus to facilitate the boom in Chinese air traffic. By the end of 1992, China had signed and implemented 55 civil aviation agreements.[43] In 1994 China had twenty jet fleets and provided the largest order for new aeroplanes.[44] (China is now the third largest aerospace market after the United States and Japan.) All three major aeroplane manufacturers — Boeing, Airbus and McDonnell Douglas — are making strenuous efforts to capture a larger share of a China market that is buoyed by double-digit economic growth. Airbus Industries anticipate China's airlines will purchase 620 more aircraft by 2011.[45] Industry observers anticipate that the overriding importance of linkages to Japan within the Asia-Pacific region will be supplanted by China after the year 2000.[46] The China market is already an important part of the corporate strategy of Cathay Pacific, China Airlines, Japan Airlines, Korean Air, Malaysia Airlines, Singapore

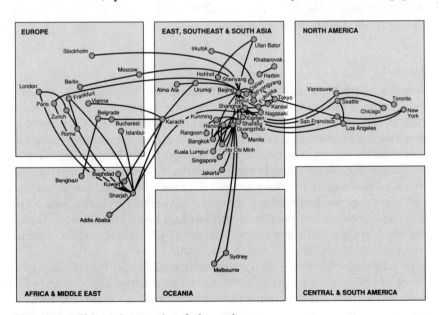

Figure 13.2 China's international air services
Source: CFERT, 1993.

Airlines and Thai Airways. (Singapore Airlines has a contract to manage China's Yunnan Airlines.) International travel by China's carriers, however, could eclipse services operated by Cathay Pacific and Singapore Airlines, the acknowledged market leaders (see Figure 13.2). Through its subsidiary, Dragonair, Cathay operates services to fourteen of China's major regional centres.[47] Apart from India and Australia, Cathay's expansion is concentrated on expanding its services to Indochina where the removal of sanctions imposed by the United States in January 1944 has enabled Vietnam to rejoin the international civil aviation arena.[48]

In Vietnam, eighteen scheduled international passenger airlines use Ho Chi Minh on a regular basis. Besides regional services connecting Asia capitals, wide-bodied services link the airport to destinations in France, Germany and the Netherlands. The influx of foreign airlines has prompted Vietnam Airlines to switch from the Russian-made Tupolev and Iluyshin passenger aircraft to European and United States models. Requiring US$1 billion for new aircraft, the government has been discussing co-operative agreements with Delta, United and Continental airlines of the United States.

North Korea's airline, Air Koryo (formerly Choson Minhang), with a fleet of Russian-made Tupolev, is expected to undergo an overhaul similar to its Vietnamese counterpart after reunification.[49] Besides knitting the two halves of Korea together, a major task of Korean airlines — Korean Air, Air Koryo and Asiana — will be to integrate the Korean peninsula's air network into the wider Asia-Pacific system. Through its links with China and Russia, Korea could become a major hub for Northeast Asia. Similar linkages between Taiwan and China will complement the regional proliferation of air transport networks.

Airports

New Tokyo International Airport (Tokyo) has been, and is likely to remain, the dominant hub in the Asia-Pacific region. As Japan is the dominant force in regional traffic generation, it ranks among the world's 'top 10' international airports (see Table 13.4). Narita is an important fuel stop for United States carriers with rights to fly beyond Japan. Hong Kong, Singapore and Bangkok have also become important intercontinental gateways offering breaks after ten-hour journeys. These nodes had developed as important regional financial and management centres and rank with New Tokyo International Airport. Forecasts suggest Seoul and possibly Taipei and the New Kansai International Airport at Osaka will be challenging for a position in the 'top 10' by the year 2010.[50]

These developments are associated with the development and strengthening of the hub concept. In 1990, over three-fifths of total seats on Europe–Far East flights stemmed from seven Asia-Pacific airports — Bangkok, Hong Kong, Osaka (Itami), Seoul, Singapore, Taipei, Tokyo (Narita). The figure for seats on trans-Pacific flights (excluding Hawaii)

Table 13.4. Ranking of airports having world's highest commercial traffic volume (international passengers embarked and disembarked), 1980, 1985 and 1990

1980	'000	1985	'000	1993	'000
London (Heathrow)	23 381	London (Heathrow)	25 867	London (Heathrow)	40 843
New York (JFK)	13 028	London (Gatwick)	16 376	Frankfurt	25 290
Frankfurt	11 773	Frankfurt	14 393	Hong Kong	24 420
Amsterdam	9 289	Paris (CDG)	13 663	Paris (CDG)	23 336
Paris (De Gaulle)	8 841	London (Gatwick)	13 130	Amsterdam	20 658
London (Gatwick)	8 665	Paris (Orly)	11 298	New Tokyo Int'l (Narita)	18 946
Paris (Orly)	8 594	Miami	9 856	Singapore	18 812
Miami	8 438	New Tokyo Int'l (Narita)	9 203	London (Gatwick)	18 660
New Tokyo Int'l (Narita)	8 200	Singapore	8 692	New York (JFK)	14 821
Zurich	7 235	Zurich	8 676	Bangkok	12 754

Source: International Civil Aviation Authority, *Airport Traffic*, Montreal, 1980, 1985 and 1994.

was 85 per cent. Only two of these major airports in the region — Singapore and Taipei — were thought capable of being able to cope with the forecast growth in demand. Both have been built on new sites since 1977 and planned expansion can accommodate new runways and terminals. Capacity was reached at Hong Kong's Kai Tak Airport in 1994, and at Seoul's Kimpo and Bangkok's Don Muang Airports in 1995. Apart from the addition of New Kansai International Airport in 1994 to relieve the congested Osaka (Itami) airport, new replacement international gateways include Hong Kong's Chep Lap Kok (1997), New Seoul International Airport on Yongjong Island (1998), and Bangkok's Nong Ngu Hau (2000). Already, Hong Kong is a major centre for intra-regional flights; Bangkok is a hub for Europe–Far East flights and is fast becoming a gateway to southwestern China and Indochina; and Seoul could become the hub for Korean peninsula and a gateway to northern China.

China has its own plans for 29 airports to meet the severe problems in infrastructure and safety brought about by rapid growth since 1987.[51] They include a new terminal designed by Lockheed Air Terminal Work for Beijing Capital International, the Nanjing Luko airport supported by a loan from the United States' Ex-Im Bank, the locally funded Three Gorges International (Yichang) and Cathay Pacific's joint venture at Xiamen Gaoqi. In Indochina, Cambodia will complete Pochentong International Airport in 1997 and has done feasibility studies for Siem Reap, but has deferred plans for a new international airport at Phnom Penh because of financial constraints.[52] Laos has targeted Luang Prabang and Pakse as being important for tourism and private investment. Vietnam is seeking to upgrade three major international airports — Hanoi (Noi Boi), Ho Chi Minh (Tan Son Nhat) and Da Nang, the former United States air base. In North Korea, no plans have been announced for a new airport but the New Seoul International Airport at Yangjong Island could become the hub for the Korean peninsula linking Beijing, Shanghai, Tokyo and Vladivostok.

Strategic implications

By the year 2020, the Asia-Pacific region should be free of impediments to international trade. Impositions by customs and government trading monopolies on freight movements should have been removed. Using the purchasing parity method for international comparison, China should be the largest economy in the world.[53] The 'Chinese Economic Area' — coastal China, Hong Kong, Macao and Taiwan — should be exporting manufactured goods and importing raw materials. China's interior, Indochina and even North Korea should be meeting the Economic Area's raw material demands.[54]

Recognition of China's emergence as an imminent 'economic superpower' has boosted its international status and prestige. This situation has enabled China's government to use its burgeoning economy as a powerful bargaining measure in international negotiations. Yet its new found economic capability has had negative implications. Its economic power has fuelled perceptions of China as an imminent 'threat' in an emerging multipolar international system — a view confirmed by increasing military expenditure, and territorial claims in the South China Sea.[55] Already there are meticulous studies of China's naval advance, exemplified by Hiramatsu,[56] detailing its objectives and capabilities. Less weight, however, is given to the obligations incurred through China's incorporation into a global trading web — a reflection of the development of transport and communications networks explored in this study.

Increased economic growth and global interdependence has boosted cross-border flows of freight, information and passengers. In turn, this has diminished the 'threat scenario' because states have achieved common objectives and moderated their behaviour and policy agendas. Conversely, the persistence of transport and communications bottlenecks in China, Indochina and North Korea has fostered greater separatist tendencies and increased concentration on national interests leading to territorial disputes and potential arms races. These contradictory global and national trends have both undermined national sovereignty.

As this study has shown, reconciliation could be encouraged by developing regional transport and communications networks bound together by accepted international rules and conventions. Improved relations between countries (and sub-regions) within the Asia-Pacific region offer China, Indochina and North Korea better prospects for practical progress than vague, general concepts at the global level of a 'balance of power' or a 'new world order'.[57] While regional tensions may be aggravated in the short term by trade disputes and leadership changes, further integration through trade, communications and travel is likely to promote greater confidence-building and security in the Asia-Pacific region in the long run.

Notes

[1] Sun Yat-sen, *The International Development of China*, 2nd edn. (1st edn, 1921), Hutchison, London, 1928.

[2] Tetsudo-sho, *Daitoa Kyoeiken no Kotsu Josei* [The Current Situation of Transportation Systems in the Greater East Asia Co-Prosperity Sphere], Unyu Kyokut, Tetsudo-sho [Transportation Bureau, Ministry of Railways], Tokyo, 1942; and Tetsudo-sho, *Nanpou Kotsu Chosa Shiryou* [References on Transport Systems in Southern Countries], Dai Ichi Bu, Sangyo-Hen, Dai Ichi Bunsatsu, Tetsudo-sho [Ministry of Railways], Tokyo, 1942.

[3] Ross Garnaut and Peter Drysdale, 'Asia Pacific Regionalism: The Issues', in R. Garnaut and P. Drysdale (eds), *Asia Pacific Regionalism: Readings in International Economic Relations*, Harper Educational, Sydney, 1994, pp. 1–8.

[4] ibid.

[5] T. Amelung, 'The Impact of Transaction Costs on Trade Flows in Pacific Asia', *Journal of Institutional and Theoretical Economics*, vol. 147, 1991, pp. 716–32; reprinted with deletions in Garnaut and Drysdale (eds), *Asia Pacific Regionalism*, pp. 62–74.

[6] In 1978, China had only 51 Category 1 trading ports (eighteen water transport, eight air ports, nine railway stations and sixteen highway trading posts). Tang Xiaoguang, 'Trading Ports in China', *Intertrade*, April 1991, pp. 7–12. In 1992, China had 161 Category I trading ports (91 water transport ports, 34 airports and 42 land transport ports).

[7] In 1993, the estimated tonnage of seaborne trade was 4221 million tonnes — containerised cargo was estimated at 300 million tonnes: N. Tanaka, 'Container Shipping and Container Ports of the World in Recent Times', unpublished paper, Research Division, NYK Line, Tokyo, 1993.

[8] Air cargo is not discussed in this paper. By 2010, however, Asia will account for 50 per cent of the world's total market: *Asia/Pacific Air Traffic: Growth and Constraints*, Air Transport Action Group, Geneva, 1992. About three-quarters of all cargo is carried in the bellies of passenger aircraft.

[9] N. Tanaka, 'Container Shipping and Container Ports'. This figure is inflated because transhipments mean that the same container is double or triple-counted.

[10] Comparable figures for 1993 are Hong Kong 9.2m TEUs, Singapore 9.0m TEUs, Kaohsiung (4.6m TEUs), Pusan (3.0m TEUs), Kobe (2.3m

TEUs), Yokohama (2.1m TEUs) and Keelung (1.9m TEUs). 'The Box League', *Lloyd's List Maritime Asia*, May 1994, pp. 24–29.

[11] The Japan–Vietnam trade was inaugurated in 1989 with Singapore and Hong Kong as transhipment points. 'Liner service analysis: Japan/Vietnam trade', *Box Carriers*, no. 2, April 1994, pp. 38–44. Sixteen carriers are now engaged in regular container services.

[12] J.F. Brooks, 'The People's Republic of China: The Context of Investment in the Port Sector', unpublished paper presented at Korea Maritime Institute (KMI) and International Association of Maritime Economists (IAME) Joint Conference on International Trade Relations and World Shipping, Seoul, 8–10 June 1994. Hu Xiaoyu, 'Status Quo Unsatisfactory, but Prospect Broad', *Economic Reporter*, vol. 2, 1994, pp. 11–13.

[13] K. Kishore, 'Foreign Lines' Increasing Presence in China Reflects Market Importance', *Box Carriers*, no. 3, April 1994, pp. 18–21.

[14] N. Tanaka, 'Container Shipping and Container Ports'; R. Robinson, 'Regional Container Shipping Networks: The Structure and Dynamics of Change', unpublished paper presented at Korea Maritime Institute (KMI) and International Association of Maritime Economists (IAME) Joint Conference on International Trade Relations and World Shipping, Seoul, 8–10 June 1994.

[15] In 1993 the worldwide movement of container units was estimated at 27.5 million twenty-foot equivalent units (TEUs). The three major trunk trades — the Trans-Pacific (5.9 million TEUs), the Europe–Far East Trade (5.1 million TEUs) and the Trans-Atlantic (2.3 million TEUs) — collectively accounted for 48 per cent of all movements. This figure is increased to 55 per cent if the triangular trade is augmented by Australia–New Zealand trade (1.57 million TEUs). In addition, there were two regional trades — Intra-Europe (4.6 million TEUs) and Intra-Asia excluding China, North Korea and Russia (3.9 million TEUs). Together the three major trades, Australia–New Zealand and the two intra-regional trades accounted for 23.4 million TEUs — over 85 per cent of the world volume.

[16] In 1992, six shipping lines based in the Asia-Pacific region ranked among the world's 'top 15' operators — China's Cosco, Japan's NYK and Mitsui O.S.K., Hong Kong's Overseas Orient Container Line (OOCL) and Taiwan's Evergreen and Yang Ming Lines. Collectively they accounted for 57 per cent of the 'top 10's' cargo-handling capacity.

[17] In 1992, American President Lines and Sea-Land were the first foreign shipping lines to be allowed to establish subsidiaries in China following intergovernmental talks with the United States: 'Japanese Shipping Firms Converge on China to Set up Operational Bases', *Box Carriers*, no. 3, May 1994, pp. 14–16. They were followed by Maersk of Denmark and Compagnies Maritime d'Affratement (CMA) of France. The Japanese lines, NYK, Mitsui O.S.K. and K-Line, have established subsidiaries in

Shanghai to redirect trans-Pacific cargo from Hong Kong to Japanese ports.

[18] China Ocean Shipping Co. opened its first container route from Shanghai to Australia in 1978.

[19] 'Cosco Joins the Major Containerline League', *Lloyd's Shipping Economist*, February 1995, pp. 19–21.

[20] J. Langdon, 'River City People', *Port Development International*, January 1995, pp. 30–31.

[21] 'Liner Service Analysis: Japan/Vietnam Trade', *Box Carriers*, no. 2, April 1994, pp. 38–44.

[22] Lee Sang-man, 'Economic Cooperation in Northeast Asia and Economic Exchanges Between South and North Koreas', in *Maritime Development of the Northeast Asian Pacific Rim*, Korea Maritime Institute, Seoul, 1992, pp. 49–58.

[23] Editorial Board, *Almanac of China's Foreign Economic Relations and Trade*, Beijing, 1993.

[24] V. Benziger, 'China's Rural Road System During the Reform Period', *China Economic Review*, vol. 4, no. 1, 1993, pp. 1–17.

[25] Between 1994 and 2000, China is expected to invest US$111 billion on transport infrastructure: P. MacArthur and J. Low, *Tapping into China's Transport Infrastructure Market*, East Asia Analytical Unit, Department of Foreign Affairs and Trade, Working Paper Series No. 4, Australian Government Publishing Service, Canberra, 1994.

[26] Asian Development Bank, *Subregional Economic Cooperation: Initial Possibilities Concerning Cambodia, Yunnan Province of the People's Republic of China, Lao PDR, Myanmar, Thailand, and Viet Nam*, Conference on Subregional Economic Cooperation, 21–22 October 1992, Manila, 1993.

[27] Cambodia's infrastructure is most serious, but Lao PDR, Myanmar and Vietnam have heavy requirements: Asian Development Bank, *Subregional Economic Cooperation: Initial Possibilities Concerning Cambodia, Yunnan Province of the People's Republic of China, Lao PDR, Myanmar, Thailand, and Viet Nam*, Conference on Subregional Economic Cooperation, 21–22 October 1992, Manila, 1993. Both Lao PDR and Yunnan are landlocked and need to be linked to seaports.

[28] G.C. Staple, *Telegeography 1993*, Institute of Communications, Washington, 1993.

[29] C. Gresser, 'Boom Times but Outsiders Beware', *Global Telecoms Business*, February/March 1994, p. 36.

[30] G.C. Staple, *The Global Telecommunications Traffic Boom: A Quantitative Brief on Cross-Border Markets and Regulation*, International Institute of Communications, London, 1990.

[31] Staple, *Telegeography 1993*.

[32] Liu You, 'China's Telecommunications Target by 2000', *Economic Reporter*, vol. 2, 1994, pp. 6–8.

[33] Zhao Di Ang and Junjia Liu, 'Telecommunications Development and Economic Growth in China', *Telecommunications Policy*, vol. 18, no. 3, 1994, pp. 211–25.

[34] China's variety of transmission media include three international satellite gateways in Beijing, Shanghai and Guangzhou, 40 000 kilometres of microwave links, 12 300 kilometres of coaxial cable covering metropolitan areas and provincial capitals, and an aerial 3000 kilometres of optical fibre system between Beijing and Guangzhou. Liu Shen, 'Satellite and Terrestrial Microwave Communications in China', *IEEE Communications Magazine*, July 1993, pp. 38–40; Qiu Shouhang, 'Present Status and Outlook of Line Transmission Systems in China', *IEEE Communications Magazine*, July 1993, pp. 46–47.

[35] Associated with this project are an economic information network, a customs network covering foreign trade and a project to promote electronic currency. Liu Shen, 'Satellite and Terrestrial Microwave Communications in China', *IEEE Communications Magazine*, July 1993, pp. 38–40; Xu Xin, 'China's "Information Expressway" on the Move', *China Today*, October 1994, pp. 62–63.

[36] C. Horwitz, 'Post-embargo Vietnam: Is the U.S. Too Late?', *Satellite Communications*, May 1994, p. 16.

[37] Asian Development Bank, *Subregional Economic Cooperation*.

[38] L. Fell, 'The Drive to Liberalise Asian Communications', *Australian Communications*, April 1992, pp. 51–60.

[39] International Association for Air Transport, *Asia/Pacific Air Traffic: Growth and Constraints*, Air Transport Action Group, Geneva, 1992.

[40] 'Ready for Take-off', *Asiaweek*, 28 January 1994, pp. 48–51.

[41] The Asia-Pacific region has six of the world's ten most heavily trafficked passenger routes. They are Hong Kong–Tokyo, Hong Kong–Taipei, Bangkok–Hong Kong, Honolulu–Tokyo, Seoul–Tokyo, Kuala Lumpur–Singapore.

[42] International Association for Air Transport, *Asia/Pacific Air Traffic*.

[43] The Editorial Board of the Almanac of China's Foreign Economic Relations and Trade, *Almanac of China's Foreign Relations and Trade*, Beijing, 1993.

[44] G. Endres, 'China Airlines: Phenomenal Growth, Stretched Resources and Safety Worries', *Avmark Aviation Economist*, vol. 11, no. 10, 1994, pp. 17–23.

[45] M. Stroud, 'Asia/Pacific Jet Capacity: No Sign of Overall Growth Slowing Yet', *Avmark Aviation Economist*, November 1993, pp. 12–15.

[46] M. Mecham, 'Asian Boom Continues but Profits under Pressure', *Aviation Week & Space Technology*, November 1993, pp. 77–80.

[47] Cathay Pacific has moved its accounting operations to China and has been joined by Singapore International Airlines and Japan Airlines to develop a new maintenance facility there: Mecham, 'Asian Boom Continues but Profits under Pressure', pp. 77–80.

[48] R. Douglas, 'Vietnam Reconnects', *Jane's Airport Review*, April 1994, p. 21.

[49] Stroud, 'Asia/Pacific Jet Capacity'.

[50] International Association for Air Transport, *Asia/Pacific Air Traffic*.

[51] 'World Development Survey: Asia-Pacific', *Airports International*, December 1994, pp. 2–5; G. Endres, 'China Airlines: Phenomenal Growth, Stretched Resources and Safety Worries', *The Avmark Aviation Economist*, vol. 11, no. 10, 1994, pp. 17–23.

[52] 'World Development Survey: Asia-Pacific', *Airports International*, December 1994, pp. 2–5.

[53] M. Kitano, 'The New China: Dynamism and Vulnerability', *Pacific Review*, vol. 7, no. 2, 1994, pp. 153–61.

[54] Cheng Chu-yuan, 'Concept and Practice of Greater China', *Chinese Economic Studies*, vol. 26, no. 6, 1993–94, pp. 5–12. Some versions of the Chinese Economic Area include Singapore and others in Southeast Asia's Chinese community.

[55] H.W. Jencks, 'China's Defense Buildup: A Threat to the Region?', in R.H. Yang (ed.), *China's Military: The PLA in 1992–93*, Chinese Council of Advanced Policy Studies, Taipei, 1993; S. Takagi, 'China as an "Economic Superpower": Its Foreign Relations in 1993', *Japan Review of International Affairs*, vol. 8, no. 2, 1994, pp. 93–117.

[56] S. Hiramatsu, 'China's Naval Advance: Objectives and Capabilities', *Japan Review of International Affairs*, vol. 8, no. 2, 1994, pp. 118–32.

[57] B. Harland, 'Wither East Asia?', *Pacific Review*, vol. 6, no. 1, 1993, pp. 9–16; W. Hu, 'China's Security in a Changing World', *Pacific Focus*, vol. 8, no. 1, 1993, pp. 113–34; Y. Miyamoto, 'Towards a New Northeast Asia', *Pacific Review*, vol. 6, no. 1, 1993, pp. 1–7; D. Armstrong, 'Chinese Perspectives on New World Order', *Journal of East Asian Affairs*, vol. 8, no. 2, 1994, pp. 454–81.

14 Trends in Arms Spending and Conventional Arms Trade in the Asia-Pacific Region

Graeme Cheeseman and Richard Leaver

This paper grapples with one of the major issues associated with the end of the Cold War — its implications for military spending and arms trade within the broadly defined Asia-Pacific region.[1]

Quantitative trends

One should first note the limitations of the sources used in this chapter: the US Arms Control and Disarmament Agency's (ACDA) World Military Expenditures and Arms Transfers, and the Stockholm International Peace Research Institute's (SIPRI) figures published annually in the *SIPRI Yearbook*.[2] They are constrained, in many cases, by what is available on the public record as numerous authors have made clear.[3] In the case of military expenditures in particular, the figures provided by some governments are quite incomplete.

A further cautionary note concerns the social indicators of an arms race. First, the issue of whether or not an arms race exists is not an either/or matter so much as a movement along a spectrum of escalation. One would initially expect an arms race to become manifest by a pattern of real increases in defence expenditure on a regional scale over a sustained period of time. If this trend to higher expenditure were funded by expansion of the military's share of the national budgets, it would indicate that the political perceptions and national priorities underlying these expenditure increases were also hardening. Therefore, a sustained rise in the share of national product devoted to the military offers the best confirmation of suspicions about hardening attitudes. Second, the political correlates of an arms race are every bit as important as the economic, though more elusive. Economically impressive military buildups do not necessarily lead to war, and wars

Table 14.1 Regional military expenditure (millions of 1988 US dollars)

	1980	1981	1982	1983	1984	1985	1986	1987	1988	1989	1990
Australia	4 827	5 070	5 309	5 524	5 934	6 272	5 334	6 116	5 910	5 916	5 951
Brunei	263	245	265	290	283	319	356	287	314	–	–
Burma	461	528	481	451	465	488	421	340	337	300	330
Fiji	5	4	4	4	4	4	4	7	7	7	6
Hong Kong	313	309	271	256	235	245	223	226	215	–	–
Indonesia	2 012	2 596	2 505	2 451	2 410	2 116	2 163	1 960	1 877	1 882	1 700
Japan	20 099	20 628	21 291	22 400	23 504	24 672	25 924	27 289	28 521	29 491	30 483
North Korea	1 279	1 349	1 454	1 583	1 713	1 765	1 783	1 781	1 743	1 821	2 003
South Korea	4 294	5 103	5 318	5 535	5 675	6 135	6 593	7 195	7 865	8 057	7 827
Malaysia	1 698	2 132	2 129	1 990	1 742	1 716	1 664	2 406	1 589	1 723	1 884
Mongolia	197	210	239	242	255	255	263	279	300	283	266
New Zealand	687	768	756	735	765	754	822	845	879	859	801
Philippines	797	815	854	851	550	422	463	478	520	705	676
Singapore	739	816	866	845	1 107	1 258	1 218	1 230	1 321	1 381	1 433
Taiwan	4 460	4 432	5 000	5 043	5 007	5 526	5 704	5 891	6 348	6 282	6 562
Thailand	1 886	1 808	1 895	2 013	2 174	2 240	2 182	2 181	2 161	2 146	2 392
Total[a]	42 541	45 254	46 944	48 389	49 855	52 167	53 071	56 451	57 864	59 278[b]	60 574[b]
Per cent increase		6.38	3.7	3.08	3.03	5.64	1.73	6.37	2.50	2.44[b]	2.19[b]
Regional share of global total	8.15	8.26	8.01	7.92	7.89	8.08	8.09	8.63	8.99		

Notes: Per cent increase for period 1980–88 — regional total, 36 per cent; global total, 23 per cent.
a Omitting North Korea and Mongolia.
b Includes estimates for Hong Kong and Brunei.
Source: SIPRI, 1990 and 1991.

Table 14.2   Regional military expenditure (millions of 1988 US dollars)

	1979	1980	1981	1982	1983	1984	1985	1986	1987	1988
Australia	4 073	4 253	4 538	4 777	5 154	5 349	5 678	5 898	5 918	6 170
Burma	284	299	326	310	311	312	332	341[a]	345[a]	350[a]
China[a]	25 500	23 160	22 700	22 680	22 200	21 370	21 740	21 270	21 180	21 270
Fiji	11	10	11	14	15	16	14	14	25	25
Indonesia	1 617	1 693	1 905	1 923	1 715	1 740	1 655	1 791	1 529	1 400
Japan	18 830	19 320	20 150	21 320	22 530	23 710	25 000	26 140	27 550	28 870
North Korea	6 452	6 197	5 860	5 700	5 698	5 696	5 750	5 796	5 826	5 840
South Korea	4 543	5 103	5 484	5 766	5 814	5 833	6 154	6 526	6 639	7 202
Laos	77					62[a]	60[a]			
Malaysia	807	1 002	1 472	1 530	1 363[a]	1 093[a]	1 062[a]	1 223[a]	1 350	980
Mongolia[a]	247	279	271	290	283	287	279	281	288	300
New Zealand	645	754	849	859	813	840	860	901	909	889
Papua New Guinea	40	45	45	44	44	51	48	50	49	49[a]
Philippines	806	715	695	644	635	440	446	673	675	680
Singapore	637	727	805	829	759	1 037	1 187	1 124	1 142	1 321
Taiwan	4 034	4 219	4 408	5 485	6 061	5 559	6 492[a]	6 724[a]	5 276[a]	6 156[a]
Thailand	1 355	1 420	1 413	1 574	1 578	1 712	1 969	1 830	1 774	1 718
Vietnam								2 557[a]		
Total[b]	37 682	39 560	42 101	45 075	46 792	47 692	50 897	53 235	53 181	55 738
Per cent increase		4.98	6.42	7.06	3.81	1.92	6.72	4.59	-0.10	4.81
Regional share of global total	4.38	4.40	4.54	4.62	4.67	4.66	4.83	5.05	4.98	5.40

Notes: Per cent increase for period 1979–88 — regional total, 47.9 per cent; global total, 19.9 per cent.
a Estimates.
b Omitting Vietnam, Mongolia, Laos, North Korea and China.
Source: ACDA, 1990.

are not always preceded by an economic escalation that signals the imminence of hostilities. A real expansion of military capabilities can be consistent with the maintenance of peaceful interstate relations if its rationale is fully explained in advance through regional consultative mechanisms.

Military expenditure

Bearing these limitations in mind, Tables 14.1 and 14.2 present SIPRI and ACDA figures on military expenditure and the regional share of global aggregates for the Asia-Pacific region through the last decade and into the early 1990s. These tables indicate that there has been a steady expansion of aggregate real military spending across the region through the last decade, sufficient to maintain the region's share of global military spending.

Table 14.3a Regional military spending as per cent of GDP

	1980	1981	1982	1983	1984	1985	1986	1987	1988	1989
Australia	2.6	2.6	2.7	2.8	2.8	2.8	2.8	2.6	2.2	1.9
Brunei	3.9	4.5	5.3	6.5	6.5	7.7				
Burma	3.9	4.1	3.6	3.3	3.3	3.6	3.2	3.0	3.1	
Fiji	0.4	0.3	0.4	0.4	0.4	0.3	0.3	0.6	0.7	
Hong Kong	1.0	0.9	0.8	0.7	0.6	0.6	0.5	0.5	0.4	
Indonesia	3.8	3.7	4.2	3.7	3.5	3.0	3.0	2.5	2.3	2.0
Japan	0.9	0.9	0.9	1.0	1.0	1.0	1.0	1.0	1.0	1.0
N.Korea	10.7	11.5	11.8	12.3	12.0			9.5	8.7	8.8
S.Korea	5.9	6.0	5.8	5.3	4.9	4.9	4.7	4.5	4.6	4.4
Malaysia	6.4	8.1	7.9	6.9	5.5	5.6	5.9	6.1	6.3	4.6
Mongolia						11.2	11.0	11.3	11.7	
New Zealand	1.9	2.1	2.1	2.0	1.9	1.9	2.0	2.0	2.1	1.9
Philippines	2.2	2.2	2.3	2.2	1.5	1.3	1.4	1.3	1.3	1.7
Singapore	5.0	5.1	5.1	4.5	5.5	6.5	6.3	5.8	5.5	5.1
Taiwan	6.6	6.7	7.3	6.8	6.1	6.4	5.9	6.3	6.0	6.0
Thailand	5.1	4.8	4.9	5.0	5.0	5.0	4.7	4.3	4.0	3.2

Source: SIPRI, 1990 and 1991.

Tables 14.3 and 14.4 present SIPRI and ACDA figures that highlight the domestic burdens entailed by this expansion — namely, trends in military spending in proportion to gross national product and central government expenditure. In a clear majority of the region, the indices of military spending as a proportion of Gross National Product (GNP) and Gross Domestic Product (GDP) have either declined or remained steady. This testifies to the even more rapid expansion of the national economic base around the region and the substantial margin of spare capacity which could, in the future, be harnessed for military purposes.

The most notable shifts within the region occur in the figures for the PRC and Taiwan. For the former, a decline of more than one-third across the period, taken in conjunction with the almost two-thirds secular decline in the ratio of military spending to GNP (Table 14.3) and the relatively heady performance of Chinese economic growth, suggests an official perception of a more benign regional environment over the medium term — at least prior to Tiananmen, after which some have detected increases of up to 100 per cent.[4] On the other hand, the estimated peaks reached in Taiwan are quite extraordinarily high — consistently within the range which ACDA reserves for 'garrison states'.

Table 14.3b   Military spending as per cent of GNP

	1979	1980	1981	1982	1983	1984	1985	1986	1987	1988
Australia	2.3	2.3	2.4	2.5	2.7	2.7	2.7	2.8	2.7	2.7
Burma	3.6	3.5	3.6	3.2	3.1	3.0	3.1	3.0	3.1	3.2
China[a]	10.8	9.1	8.5	7.9	7.0	6.0	5.3	4.8	4.3	3.9
Fiji	1.0	0.9	0.9	1.3	1.4	1.4	1.3	1.2	2.3	2.3
Indonesia	3.3	3.1	3.2	3.2	2.7	2.6	2.4	2.5	2.1	1.8
Japan	0.9	0.9	0.9	1.0	1.0	1.0	1.0	1.0	1.0	1.0
N. Korea[a]	20.0	20.0	20.0	20.0	20.0	20.0	20.0	20.0	20.0	20.0
S. Korea	5.2	6.1	6.2	6.1	5.5	5.1	5.1	4.8	4.4	4.3
Laos						10.5[a]				
Malaysia	3.8	4.4	6.0	6.0	5.1[a]	3.8[a]	3.8[a]	4.2[a]	4.5	2.8
New Zealand	1.8	2.1	2.3	2.3	2.1	2.1	2.1	2.1	2.2	2.2
Papua New Guinea	1.3	1.6	1.6	1.5	1.5	1.7	1.6	1.5	1.4	1.5
Philippines	2.3	1.9	1.8	1.7	1.6	1.2	1.3	1.9	1.8	1.7
Singapore	4.9	5.2	5.3	5.1	4.2	5.2	5.9	5.5	5.1	5.3
Taiwan	6.6	6.5	6.4	7.7	7.9	6.5	7.3[a]	6.7[a]	4.7a	5.2[a]
Thailand	4.2	4.1	3.9	4.2	3.9	3.9	4.4	3.9	3.5	3.1
Vietnam								19.4[a]		

Note: a Estimates.
Source: ACDA, 1990.

Table 14.4   Military expenditure as per cent of central government expenditure

	1979	1980	1981	1982	1983	1984	1985	1986	1987	1988
Australia	8.6	9.1	9.4	9.6	9.4	9.1	9.0	9.1	9.2	10.0
Burma	24.4	21.9	22.3	19.3	19.9	19.1	19.6	18.6	22.3	24.3
China[a]	32.8	32.4	35.2	34.3	30.4	26.1	23.8	19.3	19.5	20.0
Fiji	3.7	3.3	3.2	3.2	4.2	4.6	4.3	4.0	7.6	8.0
Indonesia	13.7	12.7	12.1	13.4	11.1	12.4	10.3	9.3	8.7	8.4
Japan	5.2	5.0	5.0	5.1	5.2	5.4	5.6	5.8	5.9	6.0
N. Korea								42.2	40.9	40.7
S. Korea	26.7	29.3	27.8	27.2	27.9	26.6	26.6	27.5	25.5	25.2
Laos						21.3				
Malaysia	14.4	13.1	13.7	13.3	13.2	11.1	9.3	10.4	13.8	8.8
New Zealand	4.3	4.8	5.0	5.0	4.7	4.5	4.5	4.7	5.0	5.8
Papua New Guinea	4.1	4.3	3.9	4.0	4.0	4.7	4.5	4.4	4.5	4.9
Philippines	16.8	13.5	11.5	10.6	11.5	9.5	9.5	10.5	10.5	10.2
Singapore	21.1	20.8	17.6	17.9	13.8	20.9	17.0	15.1	14.9	24.2
Taiwan	29.9	28.0		46.8	48.4	46.8	50.0	50.0	41.5	31.3
Thailand	23.6	20.9	20.4	19.3	19.2	19.8	19.7	18.6	18.3	18.2
Vietnam								40.7		

Note: a Estimates.
Source: ACDA, 1990

Table 14.5   Value of arms imported into the Asia-Pacific region, 1979–89 (millions of 1989 US dollars)

	1979	1980	1981	1982	1983	1984	1985	1986	1987	1988	1989
Australia	354	427	739	227	474	645	1 025	1 110	780	1 353	6 75
Burma	48	29	27	76	36	35	57	33	22	21	20
Cambodia	32	88	202	88	170	223	319	166	495	250	490
China	289	280	175	88	122	504	740	610	672	312	110
Fiji	8										
Indonesia	289	530	591	290	195	152	114	111	237	260	90
Japan	370	501	874	758	942	1 114	1 138	916	1076	1 249	1 400
N. Korea	338	133	269	429	231	141	433	466	452	1 041	525
S. Korea	844	707	524	543	474	445	490	610	672	703	370
Laos	113	192	81	114	170	152	114	111	151	156	100
Malaysia	289	236	121	126	328	481	535	67	75	42	70
New Zealand	16	15	13	25	61	70	91	55	43	94	50
PNG	16	44	27		24	35	11		11	31	40
Philippines	80	88	81	76	36	47	34	44	54	62	70
Singapore	145	59	121	63	255	211	137	311	280	333	120
Taiwan	322	921	739	884	584	469	655	433	1 398	1 249	430
Thailand	225	516	444	202	377	340	171	155	419	547	240
Vietnam	5 466	3 389	1 479	1 768	1 824	1 876	1 708	2 330	2 044	1 561	1 300
Total	9 244	8 155	6 507	5 757	6 303	6 940	7 772	7 528	8 881	9 264	6 100

Source: Figures extracted from ACDA, 1991, Table II.

Arms imports

Table 14.5 presents the ACDA (1991) estimates of the value of arms[5] that have been imported by countries in the Asia-Pacific region over the period 1979–89. According to ACDA, the annual value of arms imports initially dropped from a high of US$9.2 billion in 1979 (measured in constant 1989 prices) to US$5.8 billion in 1982, then steadily increased to reach US$9.3 billion in 1988 before again declining to US$6.1 billion the following year.

Similar movements can be detected in the more recent figures published by SIPRI (1993) for the value of major weapons imported into the Asia-Pacific region between 1983 and 1992 (Table 14.6a). As Figure 14.1 shows, the value of major weapons imports rose from US$5.8 billion (in constant 1991 prices) in 1983 to a high of US$7.7 billion in 1988 before declining to just over US$4.0 billion by 1992. In spite of this decline, the value of regional imports expressed as a proportion of the world trade in major weapons has increased from 13 per cent to around 20 per cent in the last decade, suggesting that the rate of decline in the Asia-Pacific area has not been as rapid as elsewhere. The values of the major weapons imported into the various sub-regions are shown in Table 14.6b. While the values for Northeast Asia and Oceania generally follow the trend for the region as a whole, the value of the Association of Southeast Asian Nations (ASEAN)'s major weapons imports actually increased between 1989 and 1991 before decreasing again in 1992 (Figures 14.2a and 14.2b).

Table 14.6a Value of major conventional weapons imported into the Asia-Pacific region, 1983–92 (millions of 1991 US dollars)

	1983	1984	1985	1986	1987	1988	1989	1990	1991	1992
Australia	825	498	390	888	568	692	827	437	250	398
Burma		3	1	9			20	107	256	126
Brunei	22	4	9		12	9	9	4		
Cambodia	4	84	69		68	2	193	76		
China	36	221	164	90	68	128	70	116	609	597
Fiji									5	3
Indonesia	210	110	259	551	370	359	265	198	256	97
Japan	1 826	1 587	1 838	1 741	1 784	2 544	2 673	1 915	998	1095
N. Korea	131	809	1 159	1 240	820	1 382	1 066	636	15	24
S. Korea	321	315	557	425	463	1 125	1 114	524	347	414
Laos	80	115	49		113	12	6	2		
Malaysia	282	696	126	400		15	38	17	32	29
New Zealand	12	166	12	6	3	50	27	2	58	58
Papua New Guinea		4	5		2	1	1	23		8
Philippines	247	62	130	12	19	17	35	22	25	28
Singapore	85	79	254	74	252	500	72	389	319	38
Taiwan	707	452	744	805	529	363	384	641	561	285
Thailand	426	401	383	100	745	518	536	419	929	869
Vietnam	554	247	556	432	6	6	6	6		
Total	5 768	5 853	6 705	6 773	5 822	7 723	7 342	5 534	4 660	4 069

Source: SIPRI Yearbook 1993, and SIPRI data base.

Turning to a country-by-country breakdown of the ACDA and SIPRI figures, Table 14.7 shows that Vietnam, Japan and Taiwan accounted for over half the value of all arms and military equipment entering the region between 1979 and 1989, with over 90 per cent of all imports going to just ten countries. Most of the principal importers have followed the general pattern for the region — relatively static arms imports through most of the decade followed by a decline towards the end — although there are some variations. The value of Japan's arms imports, for example, has continued to increase through this latter period (Figure 14.3). A similar pattern applies for the distribution of major weapon imports between 1983 and 1992, although the ranking of the key actors is somewhat different, with Japan, North Korea and Australia accounting for over 50 per cent of all imports (Table 14.8).

Table 14.6b Value of major conventional weapons by sub-region, 1983–92 (millions of 1991 US dollars)

	1983	1984	1985	1986	1987	1988	1989	1990	1991	1992
ASEAN	1 272	1 352	1 160	1 137	1 398	1 417	955	1 048	1 560	1 060
Oceania	837	667	407	895	574	754	856	467	338	467
NE Asia	3 659	3 834	5 138	4 741	3 850	5 552	5 531	4 019	2 762	2 542
Asia Pacific	5 768	5 853	6 705	6 773	5 822	7 723	7 342	5 534	4 660	4 069
World total	45 006	43 098	40 107	42 964	46 555	40 034	38 133	29 972	24 470	1 840
%	12.8	13.6	16.7	15.8	12.5	19.3	19.2	18.5	19.0	22.1

Source: SIPRI Yearbook 1993 and SIPRI data base.

Table 14.7 Leading Asia-Pacific arms importers, 1979–89

Recipient	Value ($USm)	Percentage of total	Accumulated percentage
Vietnam	24 745	30.0	30.0
Japan	10 338	12.6	42.6
Taiwan	8 084	9.8	52.4
Australia	7 809	9.5	61.9
South Korea	6 382	7.7	69.6
North Korea	4 456	5.4	75.0
China	3 902	4.7	79.7
Thailand	3 636	4.4	84.1
Indonesia	2 859	3.5	87.6
Cambodia	2 523	3.1	90.7
Malaysia	2 280	2.8	93.5

Source: Figures extracted from ACDA 1991.

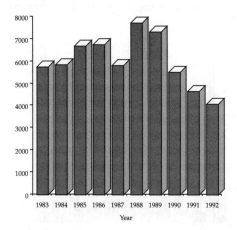

Figure 14.1 Value of major weapons imported by Asia-Pacific countries, 1983–92

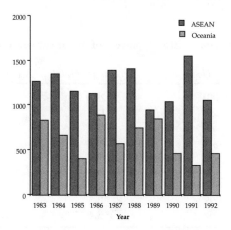

Figure 14.2a Value of major weapons imported by ASEAN and Oceania, 1983–92

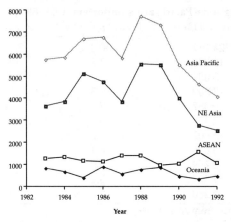

Figure 14.2b Value of imports of major conventional weapons by sub-region, 1983–92

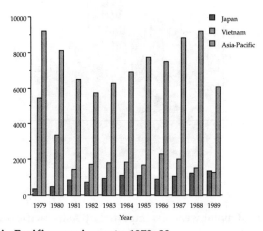

Figure 14.3 Asia-Pacific arms imports, 1979–89

Source: ACDA, 1990.

Table 14.8 Leading Asia-Pacific importers of major conventional weapons, 1983–92

Recipient	Value ($USm)	Percentage of total	Accumulated percentage
Japan	18 001	29.9	29.9
North Korea	7 282	12.1	42.0
Australia	5 773	9.6	51.6
South Korea	5 605	9.3	60.9
Taiwan	5 471	9.1	70.0
Thailand	5 326	8.8	78.8
Indonesia	2 675	4.4	83.2
China	2 099	3.5	86.7
Singapore	2 062	3.4	90.1

Source: SIPRI 1993 data base.

As Table 14.9 indicates, the vast majority of the arms and military equipment imported into the Asia-Pacific region through the Cold War came from the two superpowers. The United States was the principal supplier, although its share of transfers into the region gradually declined from around 75 per cent in 1965–74 to under 50 per cent in 1985–89. The Soviet Union, on the other hand, slowly increased its market share from 16.5 per cent to 36 per cent. A number of suppliers from Western Europe (principally the United Kingdom, France, the Federal Republic of Germany and Italy), as well as China and a number of Third World suppliers, made up the balance, although their shares remained comparatively small.

Table 14.9 Suppliers' share of all arms imported into the Asia-Pacific region, 1965–89 (% total imports)

Source	1965–74	1975–79	1980–84	1985–89
United States	73.3	56.3	44.7	49.0
Soviet Union	16.5	19.2	31.5	36.4
Sub-total	89.8	75.5	76.2	85.4
Western Europe	1.7	10.8	9.0	9.3
Eastern Europe	7.4	-	1.0	0.2
China	-	2.3	1.1	0.6
Others	0.9	11.2	12.7	4.5

Source: Extracted from ACDA, various volumes.

However, the latest SIPRI figures suggest that the United States may be reasserting some of its predominance as the regional supplier of (at least) major weapons in the wake of the Cold War; over 65 per cent of major weapons were sourced there between 1987 and 1991 (Figure 14.4a). The next largest supplier was the former Soviet Union (16 per cent), followed by western European manufacturers (9.6 per cent) and China (6.3 per cent). The distribution of sources of supply for Northeast Asia, ASEAN and Oceania are shown in Figures 14.4b, 14.4c and 14.4d. While the United States is the major supplier in each case, its predominance varies from a low of 51 per cent in the ASEAN market to almost 90 per cent for Oceania.

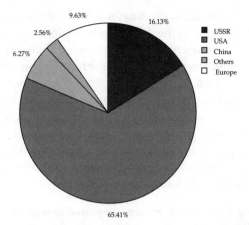

Figure 14.4a   Sources of major conventional weapons imported into the Asia-Pacific region, 1987–91
Source: SIPRI Yearbook 1992, Table 8B3.

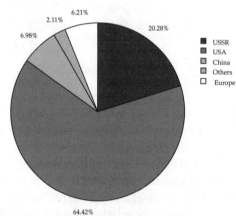

Figure 14.4b   Sources of major conventional weapons imported into Northeast Asia, 1987–91
Source: SIPRI Yearbook 1992, Table 8B3.

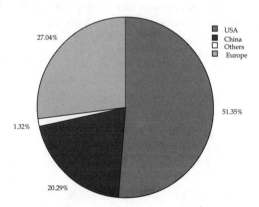

Figure 14.4c   Sources of major conventional weapons imported by ASEAN countries, 1987–91
Source: SIPRI Yearbook 1992, Table 8B3.

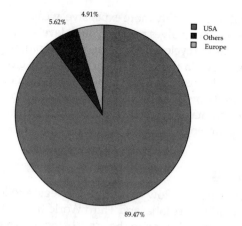

Figure 14.4d   Sources of major conventional weapons imported by countries of Oceania, 1987–91
Source: SIPRI Yearbook 1992, Table 8B3.

Contrary to liberal hopes, the expansionary pattern of regional arms expenditure has survived the end of the Cold War but, contrary to neo-realist fears, this expansionary pattern is not generally accelerating. In this regard, it is important to note that the increased Asia-Pacific military spending of the last decade is not as significant as the increases recorded during the 1970s. SIPRI tables indicate that aggregate regional military expenditure nearly doubled during the previous decade, while the region's share of the global total increased significantly rather than just holding ground.[6] Some of the national increases were quite spectacular: in most of the East Asia newly industrialising economies (NIEs), for instance, the level of military spending multiplied four to five times (see Table 14.2a); during the 1980s, only Singapore displayed absolute increases any-where near a single order of magnitude. While some of that acceleration might be explained by SIPRI's choice of a 1978 baseline — a low point for the US dollar — an error of more than 50 per cent would be necessary to bring regional aggregates for the 1970s back into line with the 1980s expe-rience. Bearing in mind the widespread regional decline in arms expendi-ture as a proportion of GNP through recent times, and the absence of significant — let alone uniform — movements in most national indices of military spending as a proportion of central government expenditure, this backdrop makes it hard to sustain an entirely pessimistic interpretation of recent experiences.

The data on arms imports also support this conclusion. The value of arms imported into the region began to decline towards the end of the 1980s. While the pattern of expenditure for sub-regions and individual countries is some-what more complex, exhibiting both increases and decreases, the magnitude of the increases and their rates of change are not sufficient to suggest a fully fledged regional arms race or even a series of mini-arms races. As we will argue shortly, the fluctuations probably reflect qualitative developments taking place in the region. Many Asia-Pacific states are in the process of mod-ernising their existing, and largely obsolete, military inventories with more modern, and considerably more expensive, weapons and support systems — a process which involves relatively high levels of initial expenditure which then decline as the cycle winds down. The upgrading process does not constitute an arms race in the generally accepted sense of the term, but it should not be entirely dismissed since the introduction of new, advanced technologies poses its own problems — not least an expanding economic burden, and the dilemma of whether (and how) to remain at or near the fore-front of military technology.

Qualitative trends

Qualitatively speaking, the flow of arms to the region follows some of the trends generally evident in global and Third World transactions. There is an increasing level of sophistication to the arms being transferred. During the 1950s and 1960s, major suppliers generally provided clients with second-hand equipment or less capable versions of front-line systems. But, from the mid-1970s, the gap between weapons for domestic use and export became largely restricted to specialist software contained in, and control-ling, the various items of hardware. Thus the military inventories of regional states are starting to, or will soon include, highly sophisticated weapons and support systems (such as the F-16, F/A-18 and MiG-29 combat aircraft), and both short- and medium-range precision-guided missiles (such as the United States Harpoon and the French Exocet anti-ship missiles).

This development reflects significant changes on both the supply and demand sides of the arms transfer equation. A continuing reduction in the demand for arms worldwide, combined with a steady increase in the number of arms suppliers looking overseas to take up their excess pro-duction capacity or to earn extra foreign currency, is creating a 'buyers' market' in which prospective customers are able to demand, and are increasingly getting, virtually whatever they want. The supply-side scram-ble to export arms and related technologies has increased notably with the dissolution of the former Soviet Union and its former Warsaw Pact allies.

On the demand side, many regional states are currently upgrading and modernising their armed forces. This process is influenced, in some cases, by the action of neighbouring states; in others, the initial moves reflect growing uncertainty about the credibility of superpower security guar-antees, or the emergence of new security challenges in the wake of the end of the Cold War.[7] Most ASEAN states, for example, now articulate less con-cern than previously with internal threats to security, and are beginning to reorient their defence postures towards protection against external threats that could arise in the future.

An additional demand for the development of maritime defence and projection capabilities flowed from the December 1984 introduction of the United Nations Convention of the Law of the Sea, which gave individual nations control over the resources contained within an exclusive economic zone extending outwards for 370 kilometres.[8] Since, by definition, the rim-lands of Asia are a maritime environment, this factor has enhanced salience.

As a result of these changes, regional air forces are showing an increasing preference for high-performance, fixed-wing combat aircraft (such as F-16s and Tornados) which offer air defence, maritime and ground attack roles, and are being augmented with advanced airborne early warning and aerial refuelling capabilities. Regional navies are being structured more for extended 'blue-water' operations than for coastal defence, and are beginning to acquire advanced missile-carrying destroyers, frigates and submarines. Likewise, regional armies are being provided with the latest armoured fighting vehicles and other weapons required for land warfare.[9]

A related qualitative trend concerns the increasing commercialisation of the market. During the 1950s and 1960s, most regional countries were supplied with weapons either free of charge or at very low cost through the superpowers' various foreign military assistance programs.[10] Since the 1970s, and in the context of persistent current account deficits, both superpowers have preferred to sell their products rather than give them away.[11]

This growing commercialisation of the market, combined with the increasing complexity and escalating unit cost of successive generations of weapons platforms,[12] has meant that the absolute number of weapons systems being purchased has tended to decline even where existing levels of military expenditures have at least been maintained; consequently, regional governments find it difficult to keep their military forces at current levels. In the case of small and medium-sized countries in particular, this difficulty is compounded by the increasing cost of operating and maintaining high-technology military forces.[13] Such resource/cost pressures are likely to increase in the future, compelling governments either to spend more on defence, or accept a reduction in their armed forces.

As Karp has argued, there are three possible exits from this dilemma.[14] The first is to take advantage of the availability of sufficient quantities of ex-Warsaw Pact (and post-CFE NATO) major weapons at 'bargain basement' prices.

Another option is for governments to rely on domestic arms production for the range of new weapons and equipments while simultaneously reducing the cost of domestic procurement by promoting export sales. As will be seen shortly, most countries in the region with significant industrial capability are, with varying degrees of success, already proceeding in this direction.

A third option is through regional arms control and disarmament measures, which reduce the need to re-arm and ensure that new weapons do not threaten regional security by provoking counter-armament. While there are recent and welcome signs of change — with the Conference on Security Cooperation in Asia and the Pacific (CSCAP), one can now at least point to 'talks about talks' at both government and non-government levels[15] — resistance and sensitivity to an overarching military-security framework remain imposing. Without significant and rapid progress in this arena, regional countries may have little choice other than to continue spending their way out of their security dilemma — with all the problems that will entail. As evidenced by the North Korean experience, one potential problem for the region is that states unable to meet that bill could turn to various weapons of mass destruction for cheaper means to offset the technological edge enjoyed by more affluent or determined neighbours.

A further significant qualitative change in the regional arms trade in recent years has been the shift in the nature of the transactions themselves from the simple transfer of discrete items of military hardware towards more extensive and complicated agreements involving various kinds of compensatory (or offset) arrangements.

If the arms market is increasingly made up of obscure transactions, possibly in dual-use technologies, then efforts to restrain its expansion from either the supply or demand side become even more complex. It is necessary, therefore, to investigate trends in the regional production of defence equipment.

Regional defence production and arms exports

Although an increasing number of regional states are producing arms, the value of production of at least major weapons systems continues to be dominated by the Northeast Asia states — China, Taiwan, North and South Korea. Definitive production figures for China are unavailable, but its expanding industrial capacity is evident from the fact that it was the fifth largest world exporter of major conventional arms during the period 1986–90, when it used the Iran–Iraq war to rise through the ranks.[16] Taiwan alone accounted for over 42 per cent of the major weapons produced by regional NIEs between 1965 and 1984. North and South Korea together accounted for a further 47 per cent, while the remaining producers of any note managed only 10 per cent between them.

In recent years, Japan has also begun to expand its arms and related industries. SIPRI (1992) listed six Japanese corporations — Mitsubishi Heavy Industries, Kawasaki Heavy Industries, Mitsubishi Electric, Toshiba, Ishikawajima-Harima and Nippon Electric — in its 100 largest private arms-producing companies in the OECD and developing countries for 1990.[17] The total value of arms sales by these five companies was estimated at US$6 billion. No other company from the region made the SIPRI list in 1992, although South Korea's Daewoo Corporation — whose arms sales were reported at US$600 million (in 1988 prices) — was included in the list for 1988.[18] Unlike many of their American and European counterparts, the defence sales of these major Japanese corporations constitute less than 20 per cent of overall sales. Their very large civilian sales enable these firms to absorb the relatively high costs of manufacturing a broad range of defence items locally as well as investing in specialised R&D. This latter investment has not only enabled Japan to expand its indigenous military technology base; it has also led it, through development of state-of-the-art, dual-use products, to participate in a number of joint projects with the United States, the latest and most controversial being the FS-X fighter aircraft.[19]

Of the arms producers in the Asia-Pacific region, the first group — China, Japan, Taiwan, North Korea and South Korea — all have in place a broad spectrum of defence and defence-related industries capable of producing virtually all categories of weapons from small arms to the more sophisticated systems such as fighter aircraft, armoured fighting vehicles, missile-carrying destroyers or frigates — and, lately, precision-guided missiles.

A second group of arms producers is made up of Australia, Thailand, Singapore, Indonesia, Malaysia, and the Philippines. Their defence industries are more limited in scope, being confined to the manufacture of small arms, munitions, the simpler categories of aircraft (trainers, helicopters and transport planes) and ships (patrol boats, landing craft and fast attack craft). This has sometimes been due, at least in part, to their limited industrial capabilities but also, for the ASEAN arms producers in particular, to the absence of any strong demand for sophisticated weapons platforms.[20] As already noted, this is beginning to change as ASEAN economies expand and their governments start to restructure and modernise their armed forces to meet the perceived challenges of the post-Cold War era. Taking full advantage of the changes in the international arms market since the end of the Cold War, a number of countries, including Australia, Malaysia, Singapore and Thailand, are now producing (or planning to produce) missile-carrying frigates for both local and overseas sales, and have reached agreements to assemble locally such items as ocean-going submarines, Tornado or F-16 fighter aircraft.[21]

The third group comprises those states who produce locally — mainly small arms and ammunition.

Both first- and second-group producers have relied heavily on foreign assistance to facilitate their respective defence industrialisation programs. While ready access to overseas technology and knowhow has enabled them to progress rapidly through the various stages of the industrialisation process, it has also meant that they have often substituted one form of dependence (on military hardware) for another (on military technology). This second form of dependence is serving, in a number of cases, to constrain their capacity to export arms which, ironically, could undermine the future viability of their newly established defence industries.

The case of South Korea is particularly instructive in this regard, although all regional producers are experiencing similar problems. As Nolan[22] and Baek and Moon[23] have detailed, much of South Korea's military hardware rests on services or technical data acquired from the United States. Under current United States arms export control laws, neither recipient governments nor private corporations can export any defence article produced with United States assistance, technical data or under a United States manufacturing licence to a third party without prior United States approval (so called third-country sales or 3CS approval). This effective American veto — governed as much by United States domestic political and commercial considerations as any other factor — can pose a severe impediment to any export-oriented strategy.

One option for countries in this position is simply to continue to invest more in local defence industries. For example, Japan, in light of its continuing disputes with the United States over trade and the transfer of dual-use technologies, appears certain to decrease its dependence on the United States as its principal supplier of military equipments and weapons systems. According to the 1991 Office of Technology Assessment report,

> [s]everal independent R&D projects have been launched [in Japan], aimed ultimately at self-sufficiency in complete systems and towards enhancing negotiating leverage vis-à-vis the United States and other potential foreign partners. These include a medium-range, surface-to-air missile to replace the US-designed Hawk and computers to replace IBM computers in the F-15 fire control system.[24]

Taiwan is also using its extensive foreign currency reserves and (primarily) United States technological assistance to establish an independent defence industry which would include the capacity to manufacture guided missiles, fighter aircraft and guided missile frigates.[25]

For its part, China, has sought to procure design and production technologies from Russia and various Western countries in order to ultimately reduce its reliance on overseas suppliers, and to modernise the PLA in the interim.[26]

However, even these countries are likely to find it difficult to become completely independent or to remain so over the longer term. This is because, as Brzoska has argued, 'state-of-the-art' of military technology in the main industrialised countries will continue to advance beyond that being imported by the Third World customer at any particular time.[27] Unless the importing nation can mount the kind of research and development efforts that their principal suppliers do, they will soon fall behind because, as the American and European experiences show all too clearly, research and development is an extremely expensive stage of the weapons production process.

Conclusion

This chapter shows that although real increases in regional military spending have been regularly recorded through the last decade, these are merely processions from a trend set in the previous decade when the rate of increase was even more rapid. There has been a general region-wide decline in the ratio of military spending to GNP through the 1980s, and where this ratio has increased, upward movements are neither large nor strong.

The pattern to these indices falls some way short of what a fully developed regional arms race would manifest; in the first instance, one would expect to see sharp and universal rises in the military share of government expenditure, leading over time to a rise in the proportions of military spending to gross national product. This has not happened. The current indicators are best explained as the process of force modernisation. A considerable distance remains to be travelled before one can speak about the existence of a mature arms race across or within the region.

Furthermore, in spite of an impressive list of recent military acquisitions by a number of individual states, the aggregate value of imported arms and major equipments has been declining from around the end of the decade. In spite of concerns being expressed about the post-Cold War order in Asia, there seems to be no concerted rush to buy in large quantities of weapons. Part of this overall decline is due to the continuing progress in regional defence manufacturing capabilities — most industrialised countries are now self-sufficient in basic military goods — and the associated shift in the nature of the arms trade towards the provision of military and related technologies.

As a first cut at overall explanation, the competing systemic expectations about the consequences of the ending of the Cold War provide little purchase over observed regional trends. There is neither evidence of a fall-off in military spending as superpower conflict winds back, nor of a general increase in military spending as regional states attempt to provide for themselves the degree of external security that allegedly once came from superpower rule. This primarily reflects the historical fact that the Asia Cold War was never simply a clone of the European genotype, but a pattern of conflict sui generis with respect to both the environment of inter-state relations and their domestic context. Since there remains substantial untapped potential for further militarisation and conflict within the region, those who seek to pre-empt such outcomes through arms control solutions would do well to base their prescriptions on an understanding of the features which are unique to the inter-state and domestic 'sociologies' of conflict within the region.

The real increases in military spending and continuing force modernisation are nonetheless cause for a different kind of concern. The economic potential of the region to sustain a more mature arms race has expanded considerably, and the mounting trend towards higher levels of indigenous defence production across the region could provide a strong domestic push in that unwelcome direction. Such a push, aided by opportunistic international arms manufacturers and their supporting governments, can easily reinforce the 'peace through strength' mentality that prevailed all too readily during the Cold War era and resulted in increasing resources being devoted to military security. With this potential in mind, the 1993 agreement to form CSCAP and the 1994 launch of the ASEAN Regional Forum assume great strategic importance for the Asia-Pacific region.

Notes

[1]   We have taken the Asia Pacific to encompass the states of Australia, Brunei, Burma, Cambodia, China, Fiji, Indonesia, Japan, North Korea, South Korea, Laos, Malaysia, Mongolia, New Zealand, Papua New Guinea, the Philippines, Samoa, Singapore, the Solomon Islands, Tahiti, Taiwan, Thailand, Tonga, Vanuatu and Vietnam.

[2]   Other important sources include the reviews of conventional arms transfers to the Third World published annually by the Congressional Research Service (CRS) of the US Library of Congress, and the 1991 *Global Arms Trade* published by the Office of Technology Assessment of the Congress of the United States, 1991.

[3]   E.T. Fei, 'Understanding Arms Transfers and Military Expenditures: Data Problems', in S.G. Neuman and R.E. Harkavy (eds), *Arms Transfers in the Modern World*, Praeger, New York, 1979, pp. 155–72; E.A. Kolodziej, 'Measuring French Arms Transfers: A Problem of Sources and Some Sources of Problems with ACDA Data', *Journal of Conflict Resolution*, vol. 23, no. 2, June 1979, pp. 195–227; J.T. Ostrich and W.C. Green, 'Methodological Problems Associated with the IISS Military Balance', *Comparative Strategy*, vol. 3, no. 2, 1981, pp. 151–71; J. Fontanel, 'A Note on the International Comparison of Military Expenditures', in C. Schmidt (ed.), *The Economics of Military Expenditures*, St Martins Press, New York, 1987, pp. 29–43; F. Blackaby and T. Ohlson, 'Military Expenditure and the Arms Trade: Problems of the Data', in D. Schmidt, *The Economics of Military Expenditures*, pp. 3–24; D.P. Hewitt, 'Military Expenditure: International Comparison of Trends', IMF Working Paper, WP/91/54, 1991, p. 2.

[4]   I. Wilson, 'China and the New World Order', in R. Leaver and J.L. Richardson (eds), *The Post-Cold War Order: Diagnoses and Prognoses*, Allen & Unwin, Sydney, 1993.

[5]   This covers military and support equipments, dual-use items where these were identified as military, and military services.

[6]   SIPRI Yearbook, *World Armaments and Disarmament*, Taylor & Francis, London, 1981, pp. 156–61.

[7]   A.R.A. Baginda, 'The Changing Strategic Environment of the Asia Pacific Region: A Malaysian Perspective', paper presented to the Conference on Security in the Asia-Pacific Region: The Challenge of a Changing Environment, Centre for the Study of Australia-Asia Relations, Griffith University, Brisbane, 15–16 July 1991; J.S. Djiwandono, 'The Security of Southeast Asia in a Changing Strategic Environment: A View from Indonesia', paper presented to the Conference on Security in the Asia-Pacific Region.

[8]   I. Anthony, *The Naval Arms Trade*, Oxford University Press, Oxford, 1990, p. 45.

[9]   A. Acharya, 'Arms Proliferation Issues in ASEAN; Towards a More "Conventional" Defence Posture', *Contemporary Southeast Asia*, vol. 10,

no. 3, 1988, pp. 242–68; C.A. Thayer, *Trends in Force Modernisation in Southeast Asia*, Working Paper No. 91, Peace Research Centre, Research School of Pacific Studies, The Australian National University, Canberra, September 1990; A. Mack, and D. Ball, *The Military Build-up in the Asia-Pacific Region: Scope, Cause and Implications for Security*, Working Paper, no. 264, Strategic and Defence Studies Centre, Research School of Pacific Studies, The Australian National University, Canberra, 1992.

[10] A.J. Pierre, *The Global Politics of Arms Sales*, Princeton University Press, Princeton, 1982; M.T. Klare, *American Arms Supermarket*, University of Texas Press, Austin, 1984; Pell, C., 'Problems in Security Assistance', *Journal of International Affairs*, vol. 40, no. 1, 1986, pp. 33–42.

[11] J.L. Husbands, 'How the United States Makes Foreign Military Sales', in S.G. Neuman and R.E. Harkavy (eds), *Arms Transfers in the Modern World*, Praeger, pp. 155–72; D.S. Louscher and M.D. Salome (eds), *Marketing Security Assistance: New Perspectives on Arms Sales*, Heath and Co., Lexington, DC, 1987.

[12] F.C. Spinney, *Defense Facts of Life*, Westview, Boulder, 1985.

[13] M. Binkin, *Military Technology and Defense Manpower*, Brookings Institution, Washington DC, 1986.

[14] A. Karp, 'Military Procurement and Regional Security in Southeast Asia', *Contemporary Southeast Asia*, vol. 11, no. 4, 1990, pp. 334–63.

[15] D. Ball, 'Tasks for Security Cooperation in Asia', in D. Ball, R.L. Grant and J. Wanandi, *Security Cooperation in the Asia-Pacific Region*, Center for Strategic and International Studies, Washington DC, 1993.

[16] For recent descriptions of China's emerging defence industries see J.W. Lewis, Hua Di and Xue Litai, 'Beijing's Defense Establishment: Solving the Arms-Export Enigma', *International Security*, vol. 15, no. 4, Spring 1991, pp. 87–109; J. Frankenstein, 'The People's Republic of China: Arms Production, Industrial Strategy and Problems of History', in H. Wulf (ed.), *Arms Industry Limited*, pp. 271–319; W. Frieman, 'China's Defence Industries', *The Pacific Review*, vol. 6, no. 1, 1993, pp. 51–62.

[17] SIPRI Yearbook, *World Armaments and Disarmament*, Oxford University Press, Oxford, 1992.

[18] ibid.

[19] S. Vogel, 'The Power Behind "Spin-Ons": The Military Implications of Japan's Commercial Technology', in W. Sandholtz, M. Borrus and J. Zysman, *The Highest Stakes: The Economic Foundations of the New Security*, Oxford University Press, Oxford, 1992, pp. 55–80.

[20] Y. Nishizaki, 'A Brief Survey of Arms Production in ASEAN', *Contemporary Southeast Asia*, vol. 10, no. 3, 1988, pp. 269–93.

[21] I. Anthony, 'The "Third Tier" Countries: Production of Major Weapons', in Wulf (ed.), *Arms Industry Limited*, pp. 362–83; G. Cheeseman, 'Australia: An Emerging Arms Supplier?', in Wulf (ed.), *Arms Industry Limited*, pp. 345–61.

[22] J.E. Nolan, *Military Industry in Taiwan and South Korea*, St Martin's Press, New York, 1986.

[23] K. Baek and C. Moon, 'Technological Dependence, Supplier Control and Strategies for Recipient Autonomy: The Case of South Korea', in K. Baek, R.D. McLaurin and C. Moon (eds), *The Dilemma of Third World Defense Industries*, pp. 153–84.

[24] United States, Office of Technology Assessment (OTA), *Global Arms Trade: Commerce in Advanced Military Technology and Weapons*, US Government Printing Office, Washington DC, 1991, pp. 109, 133–36.

[25] D. Van Vranken Hickey, 'American Technological Assistance, Technology Transfers and Taiwan's Drive for Defense Self-Sufficiency', *Journal of Northeast Asian Studies*, vol. 8, no.3, Fall 1989, pp. 44–61.

[26] D.L. Shambaugh, 'China's Defence Industries; Indigenous and Foreign Procurement', in P. Godwin (ed.), *The Chinese Defense Establishment; Continuity and Change in the 1980s*, Westview, Boulder, 1983, pp. 69–73.

[27] M. Brzoska, 'The Impact of Arms Production in the Third World', *Armed Forces and Society*, vol. 15, no. 4, Summer 1989, pp. 507–30.

15 Disarmament, Arms Control and the Regional Security Dialogue

Trevor Findlay

Introduction

For more than 30 years, the regional security environment of the Asia-Pacific has been shaped by arms control and disarmament agreements.[1] Ever since the 1963 Partial Test Ban Treaty (PTBT) drove nuclear tests underground, contributing to a dramatic decline in atmospheric nuclear fallout, the region has benefited from such measures. Most of them have, however, originated outside the Asia-Pacific region, either in multilateral negotiating forums like the Conference on Disarmament (CD) and its predecessor bodies in Geneva or in bilateral negotiations between the United States and the former Soviet Union. Disarmament and arms control has not historically been a preoccupation of the states of the Asia-Pacific region, whether directed at their own region or more broadly. Only the South Pacific Nuclear Free Zone and a small number of so-called confidence- and security-building measures (CSBMs) have originated from and been negotiated by states in the region. Moreover, a mere handful of Asia-Pacific states, including Australia, Indonesia and Japan, have traditionally participated actively in the multilateral arms control forums and/or followed closely the bilateral talks.[2]

However, the recent evolution of a regional security dialogue in the Asia-Pacific and the emergence of greater regional interest in CSBMs portend a larger role for regionally initiated co-operative security measures in enhancing Asia-Pacific security. While these may not be of the classic arms control/disarmament variety, they may lead to greater openness and transparency and pave the way for more substantial regional arms control measures. As for the future impact of global disarmament and arms con-

Table 15.1   Asia-Pacific parties to multilateral arms control/disarmament agreements

State	Geneva Protocol	Partial Test Test Ban Treaty	Outer Space Treaty	Non-Proliferation Treaty	Seabed Treaty	BW Convention	Enmod Convention	'Inhumane Weapons' Convention	Treaty of Rarotonga
Australia	1930	1963	1967	1973SA	1973	1977	1984	1983	1986
Bangladesh	1989	1985	1986	1979SA		1985	1979		
Bhutan	1979	1978		1985SA		1978			
Cambodia	1983			1972	S	1983			
Canada	1930	1964	1967	1969SA	1972	1972	1981	S	
China	1952		1983	1992	1991	1984		1982	P2: 1989 P3: 1989
Cook Islands									1985
Fiji	1973	1972	1972	1972SA		1973			1985
India	1930	1963	1982		1973	1974	1978	1984	
Indonesia	1971	1964	S	1979SA		1992			
Japan	1970	1964	1967	1976SA	1971	1982	1982	1982	
Kiribati				1985SA					1986
Korea, North	1989			1985SA		1987	1984		
Korea, South	1989	1964	1967	1975SA	1987	1987	1986		
Laos	1989	1965	1972	1970	1971	1973	1978	1983	
Malaysia	1970	1964	S	1970SA	1972	1991			
Mongolia	1968	1963	1967	1969SA	1971	1972	1978	1982	
Myanmar (Burma)		1963	1970	1992	S	S			
Nauru				1982SA					1987
Nepal	1969	1964	1967	1970SA	1971	S			
New Zealand	1930	1963	1968	1969SA	1972	1972	1984	1993	1986
Niue									1986
Pakistan	1960	1988	1968			1974	1986	1985	
Papua New Guinea	1980	1980	1980	1982SA		1980	1980		1989
Philippines	1973	1965	S	1972SA	1993	1973		S	
Russia	1928	1963	1967	1970SA	1972	1975	1978	1982	P2: 1988 P3: 1988
Samoa, Western		1965		1975SA					1986
Singapore		1968	1976	1976SA	1976	1975			
Solomon Islands	1981			1981SA	1981	1981	1981		1989
Sri Lanka	1954	1964	1986	1979SA		1986	1978		
Taiwan		1964	1970	1970	1972	1973			
Thailand	1931	1963	1968	1972SA		1975			
Tonga	1971	1971	1971	1971SA		1976			
Tuvalu				1979SA					1986
USA	1975	1963	1967	1970SA	1972	1975	1980	S	
Vietnam	1980		1980	1982SA	1980	1980	1980	S	

Abbreviations:
(S) Signature without further action
(P1, P2, P3) Protocols to the Treaty of Rarotonga
(SA) Nuclear safeguards agreement in force with the IAEA as required by the NPT or the Treaty of Tlatelolco, or concluded by a nuclear weapon state on a voluntary basis.
Source: R. Ferm, 'Major Multilateral Arms Control Agreements', SIPRI, *SIPRI Yearbook* 1994, Oxford University Press, Oxford, 1994, Annex A, pp. 761–91.

trol efforts, these are likely to be restricted to the effects of the implementation of the Chemical Weapons Convention (CWC) after 1995, the Comprehensive Test Ban (CTB) after 1996 and a fissionable materials cutoff sometime thereafter. Major new negotiated cuts in nuclear weapons by the existing nuclear weapon states are unlikely, although multilateral moves towards conventional arms control may produce greater transparency and some restrictions — for example, on the trade in land mines.

The impact of global arms control on the Asia-Pacific

To date, it has been global rather than regional arms control and disarmament developments which have most shaped the Asia-Pacific regional security environment.[3] The region has benefited in two ways. First, it has enjoyed the flow-on effects of such developments on global peace and security generally, such as the lowering of nuclear tensions between the former superpowers. Second, because of the strategic importance of the Asia-Pacific, especially the North Pacific, many global arms control treaties have had a disproportionate impact on the region compared with other regions. Most Asia-Pacific states, especially the medium-size and smaller powers, could indeed be said to have been 'free riders' on the arms control negotiating efforts of others. This is balanced by the fact that Asia-Pacific states are well represented among parties to the major international arms control and disarmament agreements currently in force.

The cumulative effect of such treaty coverage is to provide the Asia-Pacific region with prohibitions on the:
- first use of chemical weapons;
- acquisition of nuclear weapons by most states;
- acquisition and use of biological weapons by most states;
- testing of nuclear weapons in all environments except underground;
- deployment of nuclear weapons on the seabed;
- restrictions on some uses of some types of 'inhumane weapons'; and
- use of environmental modification techniques for warlike purposes.

Added to this, when the CWC enters into force, probably in 1995, it will be a ban on the acquisition of chemical weapons. If the current talks that the CD has initiated on a CTB reach fruition, a complete ban on nuclear tests in the region will be added.

Nuclear arms control

The region has benefited greatly from global nuclear arms limitation agreements between the United States and the former Soviet Union, now Russia. Sometimes the Asia-Pacific benefited more directly than other parts of the globe.

The first of the global nuclear arms control treaties, the 1963 Partial Test Ban Treaty, directly benefited the Asia-Pacific region by driving American nuclear tests in the South Pacific underground. Although France has not become a party to the treaty, Paris was sufficiently influenced by the PTBT's existence and by public opinion to eventually begin abiding by its strictures on atmospheric tests. China, the only other nuclear weapon state which regularly tested in the region, has done likewise.

The most important of the agreements that followed the PTBT were the 1968 Nuclear Non-proliferation Treaty (NPT) and the Strategic Arms Limitation Treaties (SALT I and II of 1972 and 1979 respectively), including the Anti-Ballistic Missile (ABM) Treaty. The latter agreements, by stabilising and regulating the nuclear arms race between the superpowers, helped avoid nuclear war and thereby improved the security of all states.

New United States–Soviet/Russian nuclear arms control agreements concluded since the late 1980s — INF and START I and II — have enhanced regional security and will continue to do so into the 1990s as they are fully implemented. Improvements to existing agreements, particularly in the area of verification and compliance, will also help.

The 1987 Intermediate Nuclear Forces Agreement

This agreement, which provided for the elimination of intermediate and shorter range ballistic and cruise nuclear missiles, had particular implications for the Asia-Pacific in view of the fact that Soviet intermediate-range SS20s were targeted against the Asia-Pacific as well as against Europe. Several Asia-Pacific countries, including Australia and Japan, pressed the parties to ensure that the agreement was global in coverage so that Soviet INF (Intermediate Nuclear Forces Agreement) missiles deployed in Europe were not transferred to Soviet Asia-Pacific. As of May 1991, all SS20s, along with all other United States and Soviet weapons on the INF category, were eliminated under the agreement. The Asia-Pacific can still, of course, be targeted by Russian and United States strategic nuclear weapons.

START I and II

As a result of a series of unilateral, reciprocal initiatives by Presidents Gorbachev, Reagan and Bush, and by the negotiation of START I and II which codified these and other cuts in nuclear forces, the trend in strategic nuclear weapons deployments by the two largest nuclear weapon states is dramatically down. The levels of the early 1990s are projected to be almost two-thirds lower by the turn of the century, though so far most progress towards that goal has been made by the United States, whereas Russia still lags well behind. There has, however, been a lowering of the state of readiness of the remaining nuclear forces and a de-emphasis of the role of nuclear weapons in United States and Russian, and more recently in French and British, military strategy.

There have been many benefits for the security of the Asia-Pacific region. It clearly gains from the further lowering of the already low threat of either deliberate or inadvertent global nuclear war and from the dissolution of tensions between the two former adversaries. As well as cuts in numbers, there has also been a geographical contraction of land-based nuclear weapons on the territory of the former Soviet Union. This resulted from the Lisbon protocol of May 1992 in which the three newly independent, non-Russian republics which inherited Soviet nuclear weapons — Belarus, the Ukraine and Kazakhstan — agreed to repatriate them to Russia within seven years, abide by START I and accede to the NPT as non-nuclear weapon states.[4] Of particular benefit to the Asia-Pacific region is the removal of nuclear weapons from Kazakhstan (which borders China, Russia and Mongolia) and its reversion to the status of a non-nuclear weapon state.

The withdrawal of Russian, British and United States tactical and short-range nuclear weapons from naval platforms and cuts in the number of Russian and American strategic submarine-launched nuclear weapons have been of more direct benefit to the Asia-Pacific. These developments have removed the danger of a surface nuclear weapons incident at sea, lessened the chance of an accidental launch of a sea-based nuclear weapon and decreased the possibility of nuclear contamination of the sea. However, strategic nuclear weapons continue to be deployed on submarines (although their numbers will decline) and all United States submarines remain nuclear-powered.

The Asia-Pacific's security environment might further improve through a reconciliation between New Zealand and the United States — since the United States neither-confirm-nor-deny policy should now be unnecessary. The report of the New Zealand committee of inquiry into the safety of nuclear-powered ships visiting New Zealand ports has contributed its part by recommending that such visits may be safely resumed. However it appears that the United States will not entirely drop its previous policy, even under the Clinton administration, despite the fact that the United States navy is never likely to deploy nuclear weapons again, even in a crisis.[5] Meanwhile, the New Zealand public strongly favours retaining the anti-nuclear legislation, making any change politically more costly than any New Zealand government could bear, at least for the present. It is likely that this issue will fade as nuclear weapons come to have decreasing relevance in the post-Cold War world, rather than being resolved through a negotiated compromise between Washington and Wellington.[6]

The Asia-Pacific region will benefit more directly from nuclear arms limitations if and when China, the region's only indigenous declared nuclear weapon state, and France, which continues to test nuclear weapons in the South Pacific, join the process. However, both France and China have undertaken to adhere to the CTB Treaty when it is signed in 1996.

A Comprehensive Test Ban Treaty (CTB)

First proposed as a discreet arms control measure by an Asian country — India — in the later 1950s, a comprehensive ban on nuclear tests is one of the oldest unrealised nuclear arms control goals. After several abortive attempts to negotiate such a treaty in the early 1960s and late 1970s, negotiations are currently proceeding at the CD.[7] The Clinton administration paved the way for such talks by transforming the Reagan/Bush policy from one of opposition to a CTB to one of active support. All the nuclear weapon states now profess to be in favour of a CTB Treaty being realised within a year or so.

For Australia, Indonesia, Japan, New Zealand and the small island states of the South Pacific, the achievement of a CTB Treaty, particularly if all the nuclear weapon states become party to it, will constitute a long sought-after improvement in regional security. In the South Pacific it will remove a continuing irritant in the relations of the sub-region with France and bolster the credibility of the South Pacific Nuclear Free Zone, especially if France, as a logical concomitant, accedes to the Treaty of Rarotonga's protocols. China's adherence to a CTB would help curb vertical proliferation in the Asia-Pacific region at a time when horizontal proliferation is placing strain on the nuclear non-proliferation regime. As a symbol of the nuclear weapon states' willingness to curb their nuclear options, the achievement of a CTB will satisfy longstanding demands from the Asia-Pacific non-nuclear weapon state parties to the NPT and the PTBT.

Cutoff of fissionable material

A verified, negotiated cutoff of the production of fissionable material, principally plutonium and highly enriched uranium (HEU), is another long-standing but so far unattained arms control goal. With the end of the Cold War, it is also now in prospect. The CD has just completed an examination of the feasibility of negotiating such a measure and preliminary talks may begin as early as 1995. Both Russia and the United States have indicated their support for a cutoff, which would supplement bilateral undertakings they have already made to each other. The importance of a cutoff agreement for the Asia-Pacific is to be found in its implications for China, which would be under strong pressure to sign a CD-negotiated agreement. This would further strengthen non-proliferation norms in the region, especially in relation to North Korea, India and Pakistan. The latter two states have been among the most vociferous in advocating real restraints on the nuclear production capabilities of the declared nuclear weapon states before they would consider restraint on their own nuclear ambitions.

The Nuclear Non-Proliferation Treaty

The Nuclear Non-Proliferation Treaty, which entered into force in 1970, is regarded as one of the most successful multilateral arms control treaties. It currently has 162 parties.[8] Since most Asia-Pacific states are party to the Nuclear Non-Proliferation Treaty (NPT), the treaty has played a major role in preventing the horizontal spread of nuclear weapons in this part of the world.

Yet two of the most troubling gaps in the NPT's global coverage are also to be found in the region — India (which has a demonstrated nuclear weapon capability) and Pakistan (which has an announced nuclear weapon capability).[9] The Indian and Pakistani nuclear capabilities and potential are one of the greatest challenges for arms control in the Asia-Pacific. Although neither country poses a direct nuclear threat to the wider region, the mere possibility of conflict between the two states escalating to the level of nuclear exchanges is destabilising.

Some limited progress has been made by India and Pakistan in the establishment of confidence-building measures between them, including an agreement not to attack each other's nuclear facilities, the setting up of a hotline between each other's military and political leaders, prior notification of military manoeuvres in border areas and measures to prevent air space violations. A similar set of CSBMs has been negotiated between India and China (with the exception of the nuclear facilities agreement).

But the chances of India and Pakistan reaching a nuclear *modus vivendi*, much less a subcontinental nuclear disarmament accord, are slim — at least until their historic enmities are attenuated, perhaps as a result of economic prosperity. One glimmer of hope lies in the possibility that multilateral CTB and cutoff treaties will be negotiated in the near future. The existence of a CTB would put pressure on both states, which have always declared such a treaty to be a precondition for curbing their own nuclear ambitions, to either accede to it or negotiate their own bilateral nuclear test ban, as Pakistan has advocated for some time. Asia-Pacific states can help influence this outcome by ensuring that India and Pakistan are involved closely in negotiating the multilateral CTB at the CD and by enjoining them to sign and ratify it. The CTB and cutoff verification systems are together likely to provide for an increase in transparency of the Indian and (especially) Pakistani nuclear programs.

North Korea, until recently, was the other major source of nuclear proliferation concern in the Asia-Pacific. North Korea, however, signed a Framework Agreement with the United States in November 1994. The International Atomic Energy Agency has verified that North Korea has frozen its nuclear capacity and sealed off the reprocessing facility that was the focus of much intense world attention over the past few years. Tension in the Korean peninsula, once described as the world's most dangerous flashpoint, has eased somewhat. According to Thomas Hubbard, United States Deputy Assistant Secretary of State, the agreement, if adhered to by North Korea, represents an historic watershed on the Korean peninsula and substantially reduces the risk of nuclear proliferation in the Korean peninsula and the region generally.[10]

The other potential nuclear proliferation danger in the Asia-Pacific region has evaporated with the decision of the only Asian nuclear successor state to the Soviet Union, the Republic of Kazakhstan, to divest itself of nuclear weapons and accede to the NPT as a non-nuclear weapon state. While Kazakhstan was unlikely to have threatened the region with nuclear weapons, their removal from Kazakh territory lessens the physical proximity of former Soviet weapons, eases potential tensions with Kazakhstan's neighbours, especially China, and removes an added incentive for India and Pakistan to pursue the nuclear option. The relatively recent accession of China and Myanmar to the NPT are similarly beneficial regional non-proliferation developments.

Other more distant developments in the area of nuclear non-proliferation, while less directly relevant to Asia-Pacific security, nonetheless strengthen a regime that has served global and Asia-Pacific security well. These include the accession to the NPT of France as a nuclear weapon state, the accession of Algeria, Belarus and South Africa as non-nuclear weapon states, the imposed nuclear disarmament of Iraq following the Gulf War and the bilateral nuclear non-proliferation accord between Argentina and Brazil. From the perspective of these developments, the nuclear non-proliferation regime has never been stronger. Even the revelation that Iraq's clandestine acquisition of nuclear weapon technology had not been detected by the International Atomic Energy Agency (IAEA) inspection system has had the positive effect of bolstering the Agency's commitment to greater accountability, improved safeguards and more intrusive inspections.

A critical juncture in the history of nuclear non-proliferation will come with the convening of the NPT Extension Conference, at which a decision will be made on extending the life of the treaty and the period of such an extension. With the end of the Cold War, the de-escalation of tensions between the two largest nuclear weapon states, the signing and implementation of START I and II, the denuclearisation of the non-strategic naval forces of the declared nuclear weapon states, the accession of France and China to the NPT and the likelihood of a CTB being negotiated, the auguries for an extension of the NPT are good. The only question at issue is likely to be the length of time the treaty is extended — whether indefinitely or by a specific period. Asia-Pacific's security interests would be best served by an indefinite extension.

Missile proliferation control

The existing arms control measure relating to ballistic missile proliferation is the Missile Technology Control Regime (MTCR), which is not a treaty but a mutual commitment by exporters of such technology to exercise restraint. The regime has been regularly tightened, by recruiting more adherents and by redefining the guidelines. Most recently, the controls have been broadened to include missiles capable of delivering a chemical or biological warhead, not just a nuclear device. The controversy over Russian assistance to the Indian space program and allegations of Chinese technology transfer to Pakistan illustrate that MTCR is struggling to control the problem in the Asia-Pacific. Ultimately the missile technology cat is out of the bag in certain parts of the region — India, Pakistan, Taiwan, the two Koreas and China. Regional solutions might be more appropriate in this situation. In any event the demand side of the proliferation equation will have to be addressed if regional solutions are to be found.

While the export of ballistic missiles to politically unstable regions is often portrayed as the ultimate proliferation disaster in terms of weapon delivery technology, cruise missiles and high-performance aircraft can be even more destabilising. Major aircraft suppliers, the United States, Russia, China, France and Sweden, have yet to grasp the nettle of export restrictions on such technology, given the lucrative financial rewards involved in sales and the domestic pressures to preserve jobs and technological capacity. Regional states would presumably have similar qualms about establishing a regime to control the spread of short-range missiles and high-performance aircraft. For example, as a major importer of high-performance aircraft like the F-111 and F-18, Australia would be reluctant to pursue such controls, despite the potential long-term gains in security as its northern neighbours become increasingly prosperous and able to match Australian spending on such aircraft. The potential security costs and benefits of restrictions on export of high-performance aircraft deserve greater study.

Chemical and biological disarmament

The 1992 Chemical Weapons Convention

The states of the Asia-Pacific have clear political and military interests in avoiding the introduction of chemical weapons into their region. Chemical weapons are relatively easy to produce, they can be used effectively against unprotected troops and civilian populations, principally as weapons of terror, and they have a greater effectiveness in hot climates.

Regional security has long benefited from the existence of the Geneva Protocol, negotiated in 1925, which bans the use of chemical weapons and which was respected by all sides during World War II campaigns in the Pacific.

Negotiations at the CD which produced a new Chemical Weapons Convention (CWC) in 1992 were one instance in which many states of the Asia-Pacific region were directly involved. Its outcome directly affects the security of the entire region. The fact that the treaty was completed was due in no small part to Australia, Indonesia, Japan and other Asia-Pacific states.[11] As a result of Australia's Chemical Weapons Regional Initiative (CWRI), for instance, the states of this region had already declared their non-possession of chemical weapons and were among the first to sign the new convention.

All Asia-Pacific states except North Korea are now signatories. Fiji and Australia were among the first signatories to ratify the treaty.

The effects of a CWC on the region are potentially substantial. Should all regional states ratify the treaty as expected, they will not be permitted to use chemical weapons or train for their use. Defensive measures, such as warning systems, protective gear and decontamination equipment, will be permitted, but states must reveal their defensive programs to the Organisation for the Prohibition of Chemical Weapons (OPCW) in The Hague. In addition, military bases and manufacturing plants will be subject to on-site challenge inspections if it is suspected that chemical weapons are manufactured or stored there. Allegations of the use of chemical weapons by armed forces in the region will be subject to on-site inspections of a much more vigorous and systematic kind than hitherto. All of this will be a unique experience for many Asia-Pacific states and, once the security benefits become clear, may lead to greater acceptance of disarmament and arms control in the region in future.

The 1970 Biological Weapons Convention

Biological weapons are not, as far as is known, prevalent in the Asia-Pacific region, although there are allegations that China and North Korea have at least conducted research into such weapons, as had Iraq prior to the Gulf War. A proper verification system comparable to that of the CWC would provide valuable reassurance to the treaty parties. The current provisions of the Biological Weapons Convention (BWC) and the helpful confidence-building measures adopted by successive review conferences are clearly inadequate to assuage fears of biological weapons proliferation. Efforts are underway, as mandated by the third BWC Review Conference in 1991, to examine the possibility of improved confidence-building measures and verification in the BW field. A fourth BWC Review Conference will be held in 1996.

Australia and other Asia-Pacific states have a security interest in pressing the United States, which has opposed improved verification measures on the grounds that it is not convinced they would be effective, to change its uncharacteristic policy. Small and medium Asia-Pacific states should also press the more powerful, such as China and India, to adopt greater transparency measures in relation to biological research in advance of any multilateral agreement to do so.

Confidence and security building measures

The Asia-Pacific region is already subject to a surprising number of so-called confidence and security building measures (CSBMs).[12] Most of them are the result of agreements between the United States and the former Soviet Union and they remain in force as a result of Russia's succession to

Soviet treaty obligations. Among the most important are several Incidents at Sea Agreements (INCSEA). The original Incidents At Sea Agreement, signed by the United States and the Soviet Union in 1972, was designed to prevent dangerous manoeuvres by ships, close air surveillance ('buzzing'), simulated attacks, use of live ammunition during exercises and other forms of harassment. Sean Lynn-Jones' seminal study of this 'quiet success for arms control' reveals that, since its signing, 'fewer serious naval confrontations have occurred, and those that take place have not generated dangers of escalation or political crisis'.[13]

This agreement was particularly relevant to the Asia-Pacific, where Russian and American naval vessels traditionally come into closer and more regular contact than anywhere else in the world and where there were more naval incidents than anywhere else. With the contraction of the Russian navy, however, this is less an issue than it used to be. Russia has inherited a number of other bilateral INCSEA from the Soviet Union, the most relevant to the Asia-Pacific being that with Canada. Russia and Japan have subsequently also negotiated an INCSEA. Other United States/Russian CSBM agreements that are particularly relevant to the Asia-Pacific include the 1988 Agreement on Notification of Ballistic Missile Tests, the 1989 Agreement on Advance Notification of Strategic Exercises and the 1989 Agreement on Dangerous Military Activities.

One interesting phenomenon that will increasingly affect Asia-Pacific security is the creep of European arms control agreements eastward. The 1992 Open Skies Agreement, for instance, negotiated by the Conference on Security and Cooperation in Europe (CSCE), establishes a regime of unarmed observation flights over the territory of all parties, from Vancouver to Vladivostok, including all of the territory of the United States, Canada and Russia. The new Central Asian republics — Kazakhstan, Krygystan, Tajikistan, Turkmenistan and Uzbekistan — which have all been admitted to membership of the CSCE, are eligible to join the regime, which would extend it further into Asia. It is hoped that other, non-European, states will also accede. The accession of major Asia-Pacific states such as Japan, China and India would be a revolutionary development in transparency and confidence building in the Asia-Pacific region.

The Central Asian states of the CSCE have already extended into Asia the general European confidence and security building regime, which formerly applied only from the Atlantic to the Ural mountains, by signing the 1992 Vienna Accord on CSBMs. Future agreements may emanate from the CSCE's new Forum for Security Cooperation, whose mandate it is to rationalise and extend existing CSBMs as well as negotiate new conventional arms control agreements. It is possible that in future such supposedly European agreements will apply to all of Russia, all the Central Asian republics and perhaps even to some Asia-Pacific states. Japan has already been granted observer status at the CSCE.

These developments are all likely to benefit Asia-Pacific security, not only by tying the potentially unstable Central Asian republics to a stable security regime like the CSCE, but also because of the possible exemplary effects on the Asia-Pacific region as it attempts to construct its own regional security dialogue and structures.

Conventional disarmament/arms control

Currently a ban on the use of particular types of conventional weapons in certain circumstances — detailed in the so-called Inhumane Weapons Convention — is the only multilateral arms control restraint on conventional armaments affecting the Asia-Pacific region. Moves towards actual reductions in conventional arms, restrictions on the import and export of conventional arms and further restrictions on their use are all currently stultified by the desire of most states — dependent as they are on conventional weapons for their national security — to preserve their options as far as possible. The only current move towards new conventional arms restrictions is in the area of land mines. The Asia-Pacific has provided two of the most horrific examples of the human misery that rampant use of land mines can bring: Afghanistan and Cambodia are two of the most heavily mined countries on earth and have among the greatest numbers of amputees as a consequence. Attempts are being made to extend the coverage of the Inhumane Weapons Convention to further restrict or ban anti-personnel mines or to negotiate a separate convention on the subject.

The only other likely area of movement in relation to conventional weaponry in the near future is in the area of transparency. There will be increasing pressure from some states to increase the coverage and effectiveness of the United Nations Conventional Arms Transfers Register inaugurated in 1993. So far there has been a reasonable response by Asia-Pacific states to providing the United Nations with information for the register.[14]

Regional arms control

While modern Asia-Pacific governments all claim to support the goals of arms control and disarmament, both concepts — either as political tools of statecraft or as alternative means by which national security might be enhanced — remain relatively alien to states in the region. Despite being part of the global diplomatic system for at least half a century and being increasingly exposed to the precepts of arms control and disarmament, the Asia-Pacific's ruling elites have had little first-hand experience with, or commitment to, such ideas. Nor do proposals for arms control initiatives in the Asia-Pacific have a long legacy, one of the earliest being Soviet General Secretary Brezhnev's much reviled 1969 proposal for an Asia-Pacific Security Conference. As Gerald Segal notes, 'Arms control is a "game" that Europeans have been playing for hundreds of years in various guises . . . In [the] Asia-Pacific, there is no such tradition.'[15] In the Asia-Pacific there exist both a different view of national security and an overriding concern with economic development and nation-building rather than with external military threats. Consequently, arms control has not been seen as a solution to the most pressing national security challenges.

Today, the only extant multilateral regional arms control agreement in the Asia-Pacific, and the only one initiated and negotiated by regional states, is the 1986 Treaty of Rarotonga which established the South Pacific Nuclear Free Zone (SPNFZ). Its geographical scope is however limited to the land and territorial waters of the parties located within a 'picture frame' centred on the South Pacific — a sub-region of the Asia-Pacific that is a relative strategic backwater compared with the North Pacific. Moreover, the treaty's achievements are modest, it being exhortative, exemplary and preventive rather than prohibitive of the presence of nuclear weapons. It does not and cannot ban transit by sea or air of nuclear weapons, nor does it prohibit port visits by ships carrying nuclear weapons. While three of the declared nuclear weapon states, the United States, France and the United Kingdom, are not parties, the issue has become academic since they have now removed non-strategic nuclear weapons from their naval fleets.

SPNFZ undoubtedly enhances the Asia-Pacific security environment by helping to meet some of the concerns of the South Pacific states, by reinforcing the commitment of Australia (the sub-region's only plausible potential nuclear power) to non-nuclear status and by promoting the idea of arms control in the region.

Other regional arms control initiatives, such as the Southeast Asian Zone of Peace, Freedom and Neutrality (ZOPFAN) declared by ASEAN in 1971 and the Indian Ocean Zone of Peace (IOZP), have remained purely declaratory and unimplemented and have done nothing to enhance Asia-Pacific security.

As for bilateral arms control agreements, it is only in the early 1990s that examples have appeared in the Asia-Pacific. Even then, they have mostly been of the confidence-building rather than arms limitation variety. They include the troop withdrawals and confidence-building measures (CBMs) negotiated between China and Russia and China and India for their common border areas and the CBMs agreed between Pakistan and India, including their undertaking not to attack each other's nuclear facilities.

The fact that arms control and disarmament are not prevalent activities in the Asia-Pacific region is perhaps surprising in view of the level of militarisation (such as on the Korean peninsula, in Indochina, the north Pacific Ocean and the Indian subcontinent), the presence in the region of major military powers (including all of the admitted nuclear weapon states plus India, Pakistan, Japan and the Koreas) and some medium-size powers (Australia and Canada) which favour and promote regional arms control and disarmament.

Several Asia-Pacific states, notably Australia, India, Indonesia, Japan, Pakistan, Sri Lanka and New Zealand, are active in pursuing new global arms control agreements. The Asia-Pacific members of the CD tend to be the most active proponents in the region of global arms control and disarmament, although, along with most other Asia-Pacific states, they do not necessarily favour arms control and disarmament for their own region or when their own interests are affected. They also vary markedly in the level of funding and personnel they devote to achieving arms control and disarmament, with Australia at the top of the list and Myanmar at the bottom.

The reasons why disarmament and arms control are not more common in the Asia-Pacific, particularly in contrast to Europe, have been canvassed widely elsewhere.[16] They include a lack of institutionalised regionalism (although sub-regional institutions like ASEAN and the South Pacific Forum have been very successful); the absence of two well defined negotiating blocs as in Europe; the lack of a common culture of diplomacy and a *lingua franca* of arms control negotiations; and the lack of an energetic neutral/non-aligned grouping, as in Europe. There has also been simply a lack of opportunity — outright armed conflict, including the Korean War, the various communist insurgencies and the Indochina wars have preoccupied the region since World War II. Other practical barriers to arms control include the persistence of territorial and state legitimacy disputes (the two Koreas, the two Chinas and, formerly, the Cambodian conflict), the complex regional balance of power, the existence of major force asymmetries (including the naval supremacy of the United States) and the lack of a convenient neutral negotiating venue. In contrast to Europe, there has traditionally been a lack of awareness of the concept of 'common security' and a tendency by all states in the region to acquire military forces and equipment in disregard of the effects such acquisitions might have on their neighbours' threat perceptions. The prevailing military doctrine in the region remains that of deterrence through strength rather than peace through co-operative security measures.

While some of these elements are immutable, others are in flux and may produce a changed attitude towards disarmament and arms control over time. Perhaps the greatest barrier to disarmament and arms control in the Asia-Pacific in the past has been the perception that there is no need for such measures because — with the possible exception of nuclear weapons — the problems of the region do not arise from the existence of excess numbers or types or particular deployments of weaponry. The region's problems have been seen, with some justification, as political and economic rather than military. With growing economic prosperity and national confidence in the region and a concomitant modernisation of military capabilities — by China, Japan and the ASEAN states particularly — this attitude may change. Surprisingly rapid change has already been seen in the attitude of Asia-Pacific states to the conduct of a regional security dialogue.

Regional security dialogue

The geographical spread and divergent definitions of the Asia-Pacific region in part explain why a regional security dialogue has been so slow to develop. Other factors include the great economic and cultural diversity of the region — compare Mongolia with Australia, for instance — and the weakness and self-absorption of many of the region's newly independent states after World War II. The naval superiority of the United States and the presence in the North Pacific of its Cold War antagonist, the Soviet Union, an Asia-Pacific power in its own right, also served to dampen regionalist sentiment. Furthermore, an array of wars, conflicts and disputes — the Korean War and the Vietnam War being the most destructive — prevented the emergence of region-wide co-operative arrangements.

Hence, unlike Europe, Latin America, Africa, South Asia and the Arab world, the Asia-Pacific has no regional organisation to approximate the CSCE, the Organization of American States (OAS), the Organization of African Unity (OAU) or the Arab League. Until now there has never been a region-wide multilateral security dialogue in the Asia-Pacific. Even at a sub-regional level, such dialogue has, until very recently, been rare. Regional security issues have been almost exclusively dealt with bilaterally or in global forums such as the United Nations.

The establishment of a multilateral security dialogue in the Asia-Pacific region has therefore been a painstaking process. General Secretary Mikhail Gorbachev first proposed such an idea as far back as 1986, in a speech in Vladivostok, subsequently in an interview with the Indonesian journal *Merdeka* in 1987 and in further speeches in Krasnoyarsk (1988) and Beijing (1989). Proposals were later made by Australia, Canada and Mongolia, the latter two only in respect of the North Pacific. Australian Foreign Minister Gareth Evans went so far as to coin a name — the Conference on Security and Co-operation in Asia (CSCA) — for his proposed forum.[17]

All of these proposals were met with widespread scepticism and suspicion — partly because they came from states located on the fringes of the region. Southeast Asians were especially wary of ideas that appeared to suggest the emulation of non-Asian models such as the CSCE. Asia was seen as strategically, politically, economically and culturally different from Europe. Post-colonial sensitivities were also a factor, particularly on the part of Indonesia and Malaysia. Additionally, most Asian states denied that there was a need for a regional security dialogue, arguing that they had other priorities, such as economic development and internal stability, and a different notion of security. Others, notably Japan, felt that regional security initiatives should not precede the settlement of outstanding issues, namely Japan's dispute with the Soviet Union over the Northern Territories. China was extremely wary and unresponsive.

Under the Reagan and early Bush administrations, the United States' attitude towards Asia-Pacific security was 'if it ain't broke, don't fix it'. The United States suggested that its bilateral connections, including alliances, with key states of the region were sufficient to ensure regional security. It also saw a regional security forum as a potential platform for the Soviet Union to exert greater influence over the region. Finally, as the pre-eminent naval power in Asia-Pacific, the United States feared that such a forum might be tempted to negotiate naval CBMs — seen as a 'slippery slope' towards naval arms control.

APEC paves the way

In the meantime, the economic dynamism of the Asia-Pacific was creating a growing economic regionalism which led to the establishment of several economically oriented regional organisations, which in turn paved the way for a regional security dialogue. In 1989 a governmental-level body, Asia-Pacific Economic Co-operation (APEC), was established at a meeting in Canberra, at the suggestion of Australia. An informal group of Asia-Pacific 'economies', APEC aims to promote trade and economic growth in the region. The designation 'economies' rather than states was designed to entice the three Chinese entities — China, Hong Kong and Taiwan — to join.

APEC has to date been a loosely structured forum for discussion of a broad range of essentially economic issues (see Chapter 12). Nonetheless, APEC is seen by some observers as a framework in which security issues might ultimately be considered. Both Australia and Japan have made such suggestions. Apart from Malaysian opposition, the China–Taiwan question will continue to be a barrier to such a development. It is one thing to induce China and Taiwan to discuss economic co-operation, in which they are increasingly heavily involved bilaterally, but quite another to expect them, under the polite fiction of being 'economies' rather than states, to discuss sensitive political issues such as missile proliferation or establishing an arms register.

While it is unlikely that APEC will ever evolve into a multi-faceted CSCE-type forum, its survival and growth in the face of widespread scepticism and opposition have proved that an Asia-Pacific dialogue in at least one field is feasible. Moreover, as Winston Lord, the Clinton administration's Assistant Secretary of State for East Asia, has admitted, APEC helps 'anchor' the United States in Asia, the implication being that this may have a spillover effect in the security field.[18]

One APEC-related venture into which some security issues have already intruded is the APEC heads of government meeting, the first of which was held in Seattle in November 1993. The summit meeting, the largest Asia-Pacific heads of government gathering since 1966,[19] was held in closed-door sessions, without advisers, on Blake Island near Seattle. In addition to the Taiwanese president, who bowed to Chinese sensibilities and stayed away, Malaysian Prime Minister Mahathir bin Mohamad was the only APEC leader not to attend. The only visible result of the meeting was an economic

'Vision Statement', directed mostly at the then deadlocked General Agreement on Tariffs and Trade (GATT) negotiations. Yet the gathering arguably ushered in the beginnings of an Asia-Pacific 'community' and launched a series of Asia-Pacific gatherings at the highest levels that can only be conducive to the growth of co-operative regionalism.

'Second track' diplomacy

In addition to the growth of economic regionalism, so-called 'second track' diplomacy seems to have been critical in stimulating the evolution of a government-level regional security dialogue in the Asia-Pacific.[20] Beginning in the late 1980s, this intensive series of informal consultations, research projects and conferences on Asia-Pacific security, involving a mix of academic and governmental representatives, appears to have been seminal in turning regional opinion around. Many of the members of ASEAN-ISIS (the ASEAN Institutes of Strategic and International Studies), an umbrella organisation which brings together the international and strategic studies institutes of the ASEAN states, have close links with government. Among the most important examples of 'second track' diplomacy were the annual Kuala Lumpur roundtables organised by the Institute of Strategic and International Studies Malaysia, the Kathmandu conferences organised by the United Nations Department for Disarmament Affairs, the North Pacific Co-operative Security Dialogue (NPCSD) program run by York University with Canadian government funding, and the early work of the Australian National University Peace Research Centre on CBMs and regional security in the North Pacific.[21]

Eventually, this second-track movement set an example to governments by establishing, in November 1992 in Seoul, a forum for conducting a non-governmental regional security dialogue, the Council for Security Co-operation in the Asia-Pacific (CSCAP).[22]

Key policy shifts

In 1992 and 1993, the prospects for an institutionalised regional security dialogue improved markedly as a result of changes in Japanese and United States policies and the evolution of ASEAN thinking.

By 1991 Japan was vocally supporting an institutionalised dialogue, its Foreign Ministry officials having carefully studied the ideas aired in the second-track diplomacy deliberations. Japan's search for a political role in the region commensurate with its economic might was also a factor in its policy change. In July 1991, Japan surprised the ASEAN-PMC in Kuala Lumpur by proposing that political and security issues be added to its agenda, an idea already recommended by ASEAN-ISIS and accepted by the Kuala Lumpur Ministerial Meeting which had preceded the PMC.[23]

In July 1992, Japanese Prime Minister Kiichi Miyazawa told the National Press Club in Washington that he favoured a 'two-track approach' involving a dialogue on specific sub-regional disputes (undoubtedly a reference to its Northern Territories dispute with Russia), presumably among the parties directly involved and an Asia-Pacific-wide dialogue on broader political/security issues. In the same month, Japan and ASEAN agreed to transform their Japan–ASEAN forum, established in 1977 to enhance co-operation in non-political fields, into a forum for discussion of political issues, including security.[24]

As for the United States, with the end of the Cold War, cuts in its overseas military deployments, the closure of its Philippine bases and the long-term prospect of a further pullback across the Pacific, it began slowly to appreciate the potential value of a regional security dialogue. It was goaded in this direction by Australia, Canada and, at a later stage, Japan. Towards the end of the Bush administration, the United States bureaucracy had swung around to restrained support. Winston Lord signalled the shift in United States policy in April 1993 by calling for the development of 'new mechanisms to manage or prevent' emerging regional problems.[25]

China eventually added its voice to those supporting a regional security dialogue, although seemingly more as a result of not wishing to be left out than from conviction. In his first major foreign policy address, in May 1993, South Korean President Kim Young Sam also called vaguely for 'the promotion of multilateral security dialogue in the Asia-Pacific region'.[26] Russia continued the support for a regional security dialogue that the Soviet Union under Gorbachev had so persistently given. Although its preoccupation with European security and with its own grave internal problems left scant political or diplomatic capacity to devote to the Asia-Pacific, Russia nonetheless continued to propose specific measures for enhancing security in the region, such as the establishment of regional conflict prevention and strategic research centres.[27]

ASEAN takes charge

It was ultimately ASEAN, however, which seized the initiative and brought the regional security dialogue concept to fruition. The dramatic shifts in United States and Japanese policy seemed to have coincided with a realisation by ASEAN that the United States would not be permanently engaged militarily in the region. A regional security dialogue could at least help retain United States political involvement in Southeast Asian security. The extensive 'dialogue about a dialogue', at both official and 'second-track' levels, had, moreover, convinced ASEAN policy-makers that they were not being asked to slavishly copy the European model and rush into arrangements that did not suit them. With greater exposure to the concept of common security, regional policy-makers seemed to see a genuine need for managing their security dilemmas — such as the Spratly Islands dispute — to avoid creating misperceptions of intention, instigating a regional arms race or, in the worst case, triggering armed conflict.

Perhaps the most important factor driving ASEAN to seize the initiative, however, was its realisation that if such a development was as inevitable as it now seemed, then it would be in ASEAN's interest to be in the vanguard. ASEAN could thereby protect its individual and collective interests, vet membership invitations, shape the content and form of the dialogue (and exclude contentious items such as East Timor and Malaysia's treatment of its Indian and Chinese minorities).

Moreover, the ASEAN states had come to realise that their organisation was beginning to enhance their influence and stature both individually and collectively. The proof lay in ASEAN's role in the Cambodia settlement (especially through the Jakarta Informal Meetings (JIMs)), the decision to locate the APEC Secretariat in Singapore, ASEAN's bloc influence on APEC decisions and the growing role of its individual members in wider Asia-Pacific diplomacy. Furthermore, ASEAN already had its PMC, in which most of the key regional players were already represented, on which to base a more thorough-going regional security dialogue.

At the fourth annual ASEAN summit meeting in Singapore in January 1992 there was agreement on an enhanced dialogue on security issues taking place at the ASEAN-PMC.[28] In February 1992, at a meeting in Tokyo, ASEAN agreed to Japan's proposal for a Senior Officials Meeting (SOM) prior to each ASEAN-PMC.[29] The first SOM was held in Singapore in May 1993, with an extensive agenda including preventive diplomacy and conflict management, non-proliferation, United Nations peacekeeping, the United Nations Conventional Arms Transfers Register, exchanges of information among defence planners, prior notification of military exercises and ZOPFAN and SEANWFZ.[30]

Within ASEAN itself, security discussions would also assume a more prominent place. At the annual ASEAN Ministerial Meeting in July 1993 it was agreed that the dialogue on security co-operation involving ASEAN foreign and defence ministers that had begun in Manila in June 1992 (notably on the Spratlys issue) should continue.[31] This goal was reaffirmed at the Fifth ASEAN Summit in Bangkok in December 1995.

The ASEAN Regional Forum (ARF)

In July 1993, the ASEAN Foreign Ministers Meeting surprised observers by agreeing to establish a Regional Forum for the wider Asia-Pacific region. The new Forum will include five new countries in addition to the ASEAN-PMC group: China, Laos, Papua New Guinea, Russia and Vietnam will join Australia, Canada, the EU, Japan, South Korea, New Zealand, the United States and the six ASEAN members. The eighteen-member group met for the first time in July 1994. Australian Foreign Minister Gareth Evans, whose own proposal for a CSCA had been rejected several years before, called the establishment of the Forum an 'historic milestone'.[32]

A pressing requirement in Asia-Pacific is transparency, a phenomenon still largely alien to the defence culture of the region. It should, however, be possible to begin with relatively basic transparency measures (such as military doctrine seminars) while working gradually towards more sophisticated measures (such as revealing the capabilities of newly acquired equipment) as confidence builds, as has occurred in Europe. A beginning was made in June 1993 when Malaysia hosted a 'defence dialogue', a forum for defence officials from ASEAN, Australia, the United States and other states to discuss such transparency issues as threat assessment, doctrine and acquisitions.[33] Even more significant would be the establishment of an Asian Arms Transfers Register as proposed by the Malaysian Defence Minister.[34]

Another agenda item would comprise more wide-ranging CSBMs, such as advance notification of military manoeuvres, so-called hotlines between political and military leaders and co-operation in avoiding airspace violations. Given the importance of sea traffic in the region, a multilateral incidents at sea agreement is one important possibility for Asia-Pacific. Quasi-military co-operation regimes have also been suggested, including a regional maritime surveillance and safety regime and a regional airspace surveillance and control regime.[35] A concern will be to match specific proposals to the strategic culture of the region.[36]

A third item, a favourite of the United States, is the implementation of regional measures to stem the proliferation of weapons of mass destruction and their delivery systems. The Forum could be used to support the NPT (especially in view of the 1995 Review and Extension Conference) and the CWC (especially in the early days of its implementation). Japan is currently leading moves to establish a uniform Asian dual-use technology control regime. Senior officials from ASEAN, Australia, Hong Kong, South Korea and the United States met in Tokyo in October 1993 for an initial seminar on export controls on such technology.[37]

Another role for a regional forum would be the discussion of regional disputes involving a wide range of states, such as the Spratlys issue. Bilateral conflicts (such as the Northern Territories dispute) are likely to be kept out of the Forum by the parties involved. In such cases, the Forum could, however, extend a 'good offices' function to the parties. In the longer term, a regional conflict prevention centre is a possibility.

A fifth role would be the integration of the states of Indochina — Cambodia, Laos and Vietnam — back into the Asia-Pacific security system after their long absence. Their admission to membership of APEC and ASEAN will assist this process. Their involvement in meaningful regional security discussions would — given Indo-China's history — be an extremely positive development. Cambodia should be admitted to the ARF as a matter of course.

Sixth, the Forum will have to deal with 'problem' states in the Asia-Pacific region — at present North Korea and Myanmar. Addressing the

North Korean issue will be problematic. As for Myanmar, in view of the sensitivity of the Southeast Asian states to Western concern about human rights violations in the region — a concern which they regard as interference in their internal affairs — the question of how to engender change in Myanmar and reintegrate it into the region will be a major challenge for the Forum and for ASEAN itself.

Finally, the Forum will provide an opportunity for states to exchange views on the concept of security itself. It is likely that vastly different and conflicting notions will be aired. Indeed, neither ASEAN nor any other participant seems at present to have any idea of what the basic conceptual assumptions of Forum discussions are likely to be, whether those of 'common security', 'co-operative security', 'collective security', 'comprehensive security' or some other formulation.[38] Nonetheless, such an exchange will be unprecedented and may lead to a greater mutual appreciation of the various countries' national perspectives.

Many obstacles to a productive regional security dialogue in Asia-Pacific remain, not least of which is the region's diversity. This includes a 'North–South' dimension, pitting developing (in many cases rapidly developing) states such as China, Indonesia and Malaysia against the region's developed states — Australia, Canada, New Zealand and the United States. Differences are especially acute over trade and human rights issues. Moreover, there are profound dissimilarities between the security situations of two of Asia-Pacific's sub-regions — Northeast Asia and Southeast Asia. These differences have been compounded by the location between them of Indochina — for decades war-torn and today economically backward although struggling towards economic takeoff like its ASEAN neighbours. Some observers fail to detect any region-wide security problems that might be tackled by an Asia-Pacific security dialogue and remain unconvinced that involving all states in the region will necessarily improve the prospects for resolving sub-regional conflicts.

What this new regional security dialogue will mean for the Asia-Pacific area's various components is not yet entirely clear. For ASEAN it will probably mean greater influence and a reinforcement of intra-ASEAN efforts to enhance its security environment through co-operative means. Indeed, there is a danger that ASEAN will have too much influence on the agenda and outcome of deliberations in its Regional Forum. For Indochina, its involvement in the regional dialogue could mean a new beginning in its tortured relationships with its neighbours and great powers further afield. For Australia, Canada, New Zealand and the United States, often regarded essentially as outsiders, the new dialogue will help consolidate their place in the security affairs of the region. For Papua New Guinea, the lone Melanesian member so far, it is an opportunity to inject South Pacific island concerns — for the first time — directly into the broader Asia-Pacific debate.

For Northeast Asia, however, the benefits are not so obvious. The Forum may have difficulty focusing on issues specific to Northeast Asia since

ASEAN's agenda is likely to be focused on its own sub-region. In addition, the Forum does not include two key players from Northeast Asia — Taiwan and North Korea — a situation which will take time to resolve. Nor are Hong Kong and Macao represented as separate 'entities', as they are in APEC. Mongolia is also missing from the current list of invitees. Until these membership gaps are resolved, crucial security-related problems such as those facing the Korean peninsula cannot be fully addressed. Even broader topics such as nuclear weapon proliferation and military transparency may meet with resistance if participants, such as China, sense that discussions are directed against them or are contrary to their national security interests.[39] Domestic preoccupations, particularly in China, South Korea and Russia, may preclude the active participation of some Northeast Asian powers. Finally, relationships between some of the sub-region's key members, such as those between Russia and Japan and Japan and China, are so sensitive that they may only be willing to engage in perfunctory talks in the context of a region-wide or even sub-regional security dialogue. Hence, while the ASEAN Regional Forum shows great promise in broadening the regional dialogue generally, its contribution to a multilateral security dialogue relevant to Northeast Asia is as yet unclear. It is in Northeast Asia that the implantation of habits of dialogue on security issues — and broader regional co-operation — will be most difficult to achieve.

Finally, the emerging regional dialogue has left South and Central Asia completely out, presumably on the grounds that its security problems, particularly the India–Pakistan standoff over Kashmir and other issues, would simply add further intractability to what will already be a difficult agenda. Given India's military and economic clout and the fact that the Indian subcontinent is irrefutably a part of Asia, ARF members will have to give serious consideration to admitting the sub-region's states as members. Similar considerations might eventually apply to Kazakhstan and other Central Asian republics. The admission of Mexico, Peru and Chile to APEC will strengthen the case of those who argue for India and its neighbours to be admitted to the Asia-Pacific security community. One of the underlying assumptions on which a regional security dialogue is predicated is the value of inclusiveness, in contrast to the exclusiveness of military alliances.[40]

Conclusions

Asia-Pacific security is entering a fascinating era when, for the first time, genuine attempts are being made to establish a co-operative security regime, beginning with a thorough-going dialogue and with the potential for at least modest arms control developments such as confidence and security building measures. There is also a growing recognition in the region that transparency in military matters can also enhance regional security, particularly among states which already have close political relationships.

Beyond this, the Asia-Pacific area is unlikely to see any move towards traditional arms control and disarmament measures on a regional basis. There may be continuing bilateral arrangements, such as between Russia and China on their border areas, or perhaps even sub-regional under-standings, most likely unwritten, such as between the ASEAN countries. However, the region currently lacks any political or military imperatives that would induce it to construct a conventional arms control regime along the lines of Europe's, replete with institutional arrangements and elaborate verification.

The impact of global disarmament and arms control on the Asia-Pacific could, meanwhile, be quite substantial in the short term, with the imple-mentation of the CWC providing many states with their first taste of intru-sive on-site verification and materials accountancy. A CTB and cutoff agreement would further intrude on the traditional Asian secrecy in mil-itary matters but would also bring with it security benefits that the region should welcome.

India, Pakistan and North Korea — and perhaps China, as it expands its military, especially naval, capability — will be the greatest challenges for Asia-Pacific arms control and disarmament in the near future. In the longer term, there is a chance that global moves towards conventional arms control will impinge on the Asia-Pacific region. But any resulting agreements are likely to be measured and, given the growing confidence and involvement of Asia-Pacific states in multilateral diplomacy — espe-cially on the part of China, Japan and the ASEAN states — adjusted to take Asia-Pacific perspectives into account.

Notes

[1] Disarmament refers to the complete abolition, by international agree-ment, of weaponry and armed forces under the control of nation-states — other than the minimum required for maintaining internal law and order. The term 'disarmament' can also mean the process of reaching complete disarmament through a series of partial steps or measures. Arms control refers to less ambitious limitations on the development, testing, production, deployment and/or use of weapons; on the size, capabilities and/or use of armed forces; or on the size of military bud-gets. Arms control does not necessarily have has its ultimate goal the grand vision of general and complete disarmament. A subset of arms control are so-called confidence-building measures (CBMs) and confi-dence and security building measures (CSBMs) of the type developed by the states of the Conference on Security and Cooperation in Europe (CSCE).

[2] Australia, China, India, Indonesia, Japan, Mongolia, Myanmar, Pak-istan and Sri Lanka are Asia-Pacific members of the CD. Others, such as New Zealand, Singapore, Thailand and Vietnam, are observers.

3   For a detailed analysis, see Trevor Findlay, *Arms Control in the Post-Cold War World: With Implications for Asia-Pacific*, Monograph No. 14, Peace Research Centre, Research School of Pacific Studies, The Australian National University, Canberra, 1993.

4   *Arms Control Today*, vol. 22, no. 5, June 1992, p. 18.

5   The United States does retain the right to redeploy nuclear weapons, including bombs and cruise missiles, to the region at short notice as part of a 'nuclear expeditionary force'.

6   See Pattrick Smellie, 'US–NZ security "quarantined"', *Australian*, 9 March 1994, p. 2.

7   For an assessment of the impact of a future CTB see Eric Arnett (ed.), *Nuclear Weapons After the CTB: Implications for Modernization and Proliferation*, Oxford University Press, for Stockholm International Peace Research Institute (SIPRI), Oxford, forthcoming.

8   As of 31 December 1993. See *Programme for Promoting Nuclear Non-Proliferation Newsbrief*, no. 24, 4th quarter, 1993, pp. 22–24.

9   Vanuatu, which poses no nuclear threat whatsoever, is the only other Asia-Pacific state which is not party to the NPT.

10 Deputy Assistant Secretary of State Thomas Hubbard, speech to the Heritage Foundation, Washington, 31 January 1995, in USIS Wireless File, Canberra, 31 January 1995.

11 For details of the treaty and its negotiation see Trevor Findlay, *Peace Through Chemistry: The New Chemical Weapons Convention*, Monograph No. 14, Peace Research Centre, Research School of Pacific Studies, The Australian National University, Canberra, 1993.

12 Examples of CBMs or CSBMs are the advance notification of military manoeuvres, 'hotlines' between military commands and the on-site observation of military exercises. These are designed to reduce or eliminate mutual misperceptions, suspicions and fears by making military intentions more explicit. By increasing transparency, openness and predictability in military matters, CSBMs aim to deflate worst-case scenarios, to avert pre-emption due to fear of surprise attack and to blunt any actual surprise attack — hence increasing mutual confidence and mutual security. By increasing contacts at the individual level, CSBMs can foster growing mutual confidence between military personnel at all ranks. Military CSBMs may also have the political function of paving the way for more far-reaching arms control measures and improving relations between states generally. Finally, CSBMs may facilitate the verification of arms control agreements.

13 Sean M. Lynn-Jones, 'A Quiet Success for Arms Control', *International Security*, vol. 9, no. 4, Spring 1985, p. 155.

14 E.J. Laurance, S.T. Wezeman and H. Wulf, SIPRI, *Arms Watch: SIPRI Report on the First Year of the UN Register of Conventional Arms*, SIPRI

Research Report No. 6, Oxford University Press, Oxford, 1993, p. 18. Those Asia-Pacific states which submitted returns in the first year (1993, with data for 1992) were Australia, Canada, China, Fiji, India, Japan, Kazakhstan, Malaysia, Mongolia, New Zealand, Papua New Guinea, Pakistan, the Philippines, Russia, Singapore, the Solomon Islands, Sri Lanka, South Korea and the United States.

[15] Gerald Segal (ed.), *Arms Control in Asia*, Macmillan Press, London, 1987, p. 6.

[16] See, for example, Trevor Findlay, 'Stockholm on the Mekong? CBMs for Asia-Pacific', *Pacific Review*, vol. 3, no. 1, 1990.

[17] See Gareth Evans and Bruce Grant, *Australia's Foreign Relations in the World of the 1990s*, Melbourne University Press, Carlton, 1991, pp. 110–12; and Gareth Evans, 'What Asia needs is a Europe-style CSCA', *International Herald Tribune*, 27 July 1990, p. 5. For analysis of the CSCA proposal, see Trevor Findlay, *Asia/Pacific CSBMs: A Prospectus*, Working Paper No. 90, Peace Research Centre, Research School of Pacific Studies, The Australian National University, Canberra, 1990, pp. 2–4.

[18] Interview with William Bodde, *Asian Wall Street Journal*, 20 May 1993.

[19] In that year President Johnson convened an Asia-Pacific summit meeting in Manila to enlist support for United States policy in Vietnam (*New York Times*, 21 November 1993, p. 14).

[20] A survey by Paul Evans discovered sixteen 'trans-Pacific' dialogue channels for multilateral discussions on Asia-Pacific security issues. See Paul M. Evans, 'The Council for Security Cooperation in Asia Pacific: Context and Prospects', paper presented at the conference on Economic and Security Cooperation in the Asia-Pacific: Agenda for the 1990s, Australian National University, Canberra, 28–30 July 1993, pp. 15–17.

[21] Andrew Mack, 'Dialogs for Defence', *Asia-Pacific Defence Reporter*, February/March 1993, p. 15.

[22] CSCAP was founded by a group of ten non-governmental research institutes from the region (Australia, Canada, Indonesia, Japan, South Korea, Malaysia, the Philippines, Singapore, Thailand and the United States), meeting under the auspices of the Pacific Forum/Center for Strategic and International Studies (CSIS). It was officially launched on 9 June 1993 at ISIS Malaysia's annual Asia-Pacific roundtable in Kuala Lumpur.

[23] ASEAN-ISIS, *A Time for Initiative: Proposals for the Consideration of the Fourth ASEAN Summit*, 4 June 1991.

[24] Y. Soeya, 'The Evolution of Japanese Thinking and Policies on Cooperative Security in the 1980s and 1990s', paper presented at the Conference on Economic and Security Cooperation in the Asia-Pacific, p. 8.

[25] Cited in Trevor Findlay, 'Regional Dialogue Hots Up', *Pacific Research*, vol. 6, no. 2, May 1993, pp. 19–20.

[26] 'Text of Pacific Era and Korea's New Diplomacy by President Kim Young Sam', *Korea Annual* 1993, Yonhap News Agency, Seoul, 1993, p. 394.

[27] S.L. Ryan, 'ASEAN's Regional Security Forum: Giving Southeast Asia a Voice in World Affairs', *Asian Defence Journal*, September 1993, p. 58.

[28] Quoted in A. Acharya, *A New Regional Order in South-East Asia: ASEAN in the Post-Cold War Era*, Adelphi Paper No. 279, Brassey's for International Institute for Strategic Studies (IISS), London, 1993, p. 3.

[29] Soeya, 'The Evolution of Japanese Thinking'.

[30] The SOM agreed to undertake further research in four areas: non-proliferation regimes and their application at the regional level; conflict prevention and management, including peacekeeping; security co-operation in Northeast Asia; and confidence-building measures applicable to the region. See Chairman's Statement, ASEAN Post-Ministerial Conferences, Senior Officials Meeting, Singapore, 20–21 May 1993.

[31] International Institute for Strategic Studies (IISS), *The Military Balance 1993–1994*, Brassey's for IISS, London, 1993, p. 146.

[32] See Ryan, 'ASEAN's Regional Security Forum', p. 60.

[33] See R.A. Manning, 'The Asian Paradox: Toward A New Architecture', *World Policy Journal*, vol. 10, no. 3, Fall, 1993, p. 59.

[34] Mohamed Najib bin Tun Abdul Razak, 'Towards Cooperative Security and Regional Stability: The Malaysian View' in David Horner (ed.), *The Army and the Future: Land Forces in Australia and South-East Asia*, Department of Defence, Army Office, Canberra, 1993, p. 137.

[35] See Desmond Ball, W.L. Grant and J. Wanandi, *Security Cooperation in the Asia-Pacific Region*, Significant Issues Series, vol. 15, no. 5, Center for Strategic and International Studies, Washington DC, 1993, pp. 20–21, for a list of proposed regional confidence and security building measures for the Asia-Pacific region.

[36] See ibid., pp. 23–24.

[37] L. Burgess and N. Usui, 'Japan Leads Quest for Asian Export Control', *Defense News*, 1–7 November 1993, pp. 1 and 36.

[38] For a useful discussion of various concepts of security in the Asia-Pacific context, see Andrew Mack, *Concepts of Security in the Post-Cold War*, Working Paper 1993/8, Department of International Relations, Research School of Pacific Studies, The Australian National University, Canberra, 1993.

[39] G. Ferguson, 'ASEAN Broadens Base for Regional Stability: Concern over China is Focus of New Forum', *Defense News*, 2–8 August 1993.

[40] David Unger, 'Asian Anxieties, Pacific Overtures', *World Policy Journal*, vol. 21, no. 2, Summer 1994, p. 42.

16 Building Confidence and Security in the Asia-Pacific Region

Desmond Ball

Adistinctive characteristic of our age is the rapidly accelerating pace of change. In the Asia-Pacific region, the pace and scope of change is more dynamic than in any other part of the world. This has profound implications for regional security, and not least the opportunities for the development of a regional security dialogue and trust building measures.[1]

A significant feature of the emerging security environment in the Asia-Pacific region is the widespread appreciation that new modalities and arrangements for multilateral dialogue, confidence-building and co-operation should be an essential and integral feature of the regional security architecture.

The institutionalisation of the regional confidence and security building measures (CSBM) process, albeit still in its formative phase, is itself a signal indicator of the rapidity and profundity of change in the security environment in the Asia-Pacific region. Only a few years ago, it was generally accepted that the prospects for regional CSBMs were very bleak. The United States — and indeed most of the Asia-Pacific countries — were firmly committed to bilateral approaches to security issues; multilateral endeavours were represented as being incompatible with fundamental aspects of Asia-Pacific strategic cultures, and even damaging to the architecture of bilateral arrangements which had arguably served the region well during the previous decades. The Asia-Pacific region, it was thought, was simply too large and diverse, in terms of the sizes, strengths, cultures, interests and threat perceptions of the constituent states, to support any meaningful region-wide security architecture. It has turned out, however, that these 'realities' were not immutable, at least insofar as they ruled out the institutionalisation of an active, purposeful and productive regional CSBM process.

Over the past few years, there has been an extraordinary proliferation of CSBM proposals for the Asia-Pacific region. Two aspects of this activity are especially noteworthy: first, it is not only remarkable in light of the regional indisposition towards multilateral modalities hitherto but also promises to surpass the experience with CSBMs in the European theatre in the 1980s;[2] and, second, there is the distinctly Asian fashion in which this new and remarkable CSBM activity is proceeding.

Proposals for confidence building and security co-operation in the Asia-Pacific Region

In the few years from the late 1980s through the early 1990s, as the nature of post-Cold War security concerns in the region became apparent, both government officials and non-governmental analysts proffered more than two dozen proposals for confidence and security building measures (CSBMs) for the region.[3] Some of these proposals (listed as Appendix 16A), such as the concept of a Conference on Security and Cooperation in Asia (CSCA), proposed by the Australian Foreign Minister, Gareth Evans, in July 1990, were very ambitious and over-arching;[4] others, such as mechanisms for enhancing transparency (including the establishment of a Regional Arms Register) and a Regional Maritime Surveillance and Safety Regime (REMARSSAR) were designed to address more particular concerns. Some of the proposals are much more practical than others; some are simply unrealistic in terms of official acceptance or meaningful implementation across the region.

It soon became apparent that the most fundamental building block for regional security co-operation and confidence-building is the institutionalisation of regional security dialogue. Such dialogue should lead to better appreciation of the concerns, interests and perceptions of the participating countries, enhancing mutual understanding and trust, and preventing misunderstandings and suspicions likely to cause tensions and even conflict. (Areas of residual conflict in the Asia-Pacific region are listed in Appendix 16B.) More generally, institutionalised dialogue would serve as a mechanism for managing some of the uncertainty which presently confounds regional security planners and analysts.

There have been some very significant developments in this area over the past few years. Mechanisms and arrangements have been established for the regular discussion by officials of particular security issues (such as the annual Workshops on Managing Potential Conflicts in the South China Sea, sponsored by the Indonesian government, which bring together representatives of the six countries with competing claims to the Spratly Islands),[5] or the regular meeting of officials from particular sectors of the respective national security communities. For example, the ASEAN (Association of Southeast Asian Nations) countries have instituted an annual meeting of senior officials of their various intelligence agencies to exchange intelligence assessments on regional security developments and discuss particular security issues.[6] In April 1992, at a meeting in Darwin involving senior defence officials from the region, the Malaysian Minister for Defence, Datuk Seri Mohammed Najib bin Tun Abdul Razak, proposed a regular series of meetings of defence officials, both military and civilian, for discussion of regional security matters;[7] these 'Najib talks', the first of which was held in Malaysia in June 1993, provide a forum for discussion of such matters as defence assessments, operational concepts, defence planning, exercises and weapons acquisitions which are important for regional transparency but which remain out of bounds for public disclosure.

Mechanisms have also been instituted for regular dialogue among regional navies. For example, the Western Pacific Naval Symposium (WPNS), a biennial conference initiated by the Royal Australian Navy (RAN) in 1988, brings together representatives of the navies of the ASEAN states, the United States, Japan, the Republic of Korea, the People's Republic of China, Papua New Guinea, Australia and New Zealand for a frank exchange of views on a wide range of issues, including the law of the sea and sea lanes of communications (SLOC) protection. It is a unique forum and a significant step towards better understanding between regional navies. Some of the important conclusions reached during the recent naval dialogues are that the focus of co-operative activities should be on operational matters, directed to very particular concerns (perhaps mostly nonmilitary in nature), and beginning with basic modes and procedures for information exchange rather than the erection of new structures for multilateral maritime surveillance efforts. For example, it was agreed at a Western Pacific Naval Symposium Workshop in Sydney in July 1992 to jointly develop a 'Maritime Information Exchange Directory', whereby information on certain maritime activities would be shared by the participating navies.[8] A suggested list of activities which require 'time-critical' reporting includes 'maritime pollution/environmental concerns' high seas robbery/piracy; fisheries infringements; search and rescue; suspicious activity indicating possible narcotics trafficking; [and] humanitarian concerns'.[9] The Directory will include formatting styles, addresses for reporting information, and the agreed means of communication (e.g. specific radio frequencies). The development of common procedures for communication between regional navies and vessels provides a capability with a significance for regional confidence-building that obviously far transcends the particular purposes of the Directory itself. Similarly, the process of reaching agreement between naval staffs on the priority areas for information reporting will enhance regional appreciation of particular national concerns and interests as well as increase the 'understanding of navies at the working level'.[10]

However, by far the most significant and comprehensive arrangements for institutionalised regional security dialogue are those which involve the ASEAN Post-Ministerial Conference (PMC) process. In 1990, the notion of using the PMCs of the meetings of the ASEAN Foreign Ministers as a forum for regional security dialogue was informally raised within the ASEAN Institutes of Strategic and International Studies. The essence of the notion was that the ASEAN PMC was already a well-established mechanism for bringing together the six nations of ASEAN and their 'dialogue partners', and that it was practicable to extend it in membership to include other Asia-Pacific countries and in agenda to include regional political-security issues. In June 1991, the ASEAN Institutes recommended to their governments that they move to effect this proposal.[11] The proposal was discussed by the ASEAN Ministers at the Twenty-fourth ASEAN Ministerial Meeting in Kuala Lumpur on 19–20 July 1991. They stated in a Joint Communiqué issued on 20 July that the ASEAN PMC was an 'appropriate base' for addressing regional peace and security issues.[12] This was endorsed at the Fourth ASEAN Summit in Singapore in January 1992. The first discussions on regional security took place at the Twenty-fifth ASEAN Ministerial Meeting in Manila in July 1992. This meeting produced (for example) 'a Declaration on the South China Sea that helped define some of the principles for a peaceful resolution to complex territorial issues like the Spratlys'.[13]

Several attendant developments have worked to transform the ASEAN PMC process into an institutionalised regional security dialogue mechanism. To begin with, the PMC arrangements have become much more multilateralised — in membership, to include the so-called 'non-like-minded' (China, Russia, Vietnam and Laos); and in agenda preparation, to broaden the purview beyond essentially ASEAN concerns. It was agreed at the Twenty-sixth ASEAN Ministerial Meeting in Singapore on 23–24 July 1993 that henceforth the security component of the PMC dialogue would be known as the ASEAN Regional Forum (ARF), with eighteen members — the six ASEAN countries (Malaysia, Indonesia, Thailand, Singapore, the Philippines and Brunei), their seven major trading partners (the United States, Japan, Canada, South Korea, Australia, New Zealand and the European Community), and the five 'guests' and 'observers' at the ASEAN meeting (Russia, China, Vietnam, Laos and Papua New Guinea).[14]

The first ARF meeting was held in Bangkok in July 1994. To begin with, the ARF agenda is quite modest — though, as Singapore's Defence Minister, Dr Yeo Ning Hong, has noted, the fact that eighteen countries 'at different levels of development and with different views on how to achieve regional stability and resolve security issues' can meet to discuss sensitive security matters 'is by itself *a significant achievement*'.[15] The first meeting was exploratory in nature and concerned as much with getting the mechanics and the process of dialogue right as with substantive issues. Confidence building measures, including transparency in arms acquisition programs, are expected to be the core of the substantive discussions over the next couple of years.[16]

In addition, it has been recognised that the PMC/ARF process must be supported by the development of some institutionalised infrastructure at both the official and the non-governmental levels. This development is also now underway at the official level. In June 1991, the ASEAN Institutes of Strategic and International Studies proposed that there be instituted a 'senior officials meeting (SOM) made up of senior officials of the ASEAN states and the dialogue partners' to support the ASEAN PMC process (e.g. with respect to the preparation of agenda and meeting arrangements).[17] The first of the SOMs was held in Singapore in May 1993, and involved extensive discussion of multilateral approaches to regional peace and security, including such subjects as preventive diplomacy and conflict management, non-proliferation (both nuclear and non-nuclear), United Nations peacekeeping activities, the United Nations Conventional Arms Transfer Register, the extension of the Non-Proliferation Treaty (NPT), exchanges of information among defence planners, prior notification of military exercises, and the concepts of the Zone of Peace, Freedom and Neutrality (ZOPFAN) and the Southeast Asia Nuclear Weapon Free Zone (SEANWFZ). The SOMs agreed to undertake further research of four particular measures: (i) non-proliferation regimes and their application at the regional level; (ii) conflict prevention and management, including peacekeeping; (iii) possibilities for security co-operation in Northeast Asia; and (iv) confidence-building measures applicable to the region.[18]

The first ARF SOMs was held in Bangkok in May 1994, preparatory to the ARF meeting in July. Various proposals for CSBMs were tabled at the SOMs,[19] but these received only perfunctory consideration, as most of the meeting was taken up with the protocol and organisational aspects of the first ARF. The second ARF SOMs were held in Brunei in May 1995, two months prior to the second ARF. In the meantime, however, a process of 'inter-sessional SOMs' has been initiated, which is likely to become the most important mechanism for the development and implementation of regional CSBMs. Already, for example, substantial progress has been made with the definition and prioritisation of three 'baskets' of CSBMs for implementation in the immediate, short term (the next one to two years) and longer term time frames.

The 'second track' process

At the same time as the ASEAN PMC process developed into a more fully multilateralised and institutionalised Regional Security Forum, there has been a burgeoning of non-governmental activities and institutional linkages, now generally referred to as the 'second track' process (see also Chapter 15). According to a recent compilation, these second track meetings now exceed one per week.[20] Some of these are small workshops, sometimes involving less than two dozen participants, and designed to address specific issues (such as security of the sea lanes through the region or territorial disputes in the South China Sea). The largest and most inclusive is the annual Asia-Pacific Roundtable, now organised by the ASEAN Institutes of Strategic and International Studies (ASEAN ISIS), which involves several hundred participants from some two dozen countries — that is, in addition to the eighteen members of the Regional Forum of the ASEAN PMC, Cambodia, Taiwan (Chinese Taipeh), North Korea, Mongolia, Myanmar and Fiji. As would be noted from the previous section, the ASEAN ISIS association is central to much of the networking and discourse with respect to security co-operation in the region.

In 1991, four institutions in the region, namely the ASEAN ISIS, the Pacific Forum in Honolulu, the Seoul Forum for International Affairs and the Japan Institute of International Affairs (JIIA) in Tokyo, together with representatives of other research institutes from the region, began a two-year project on Security Co-operation in the Asia Pacific (SCAP). One of the first products of this project was PACNET, which is a fax network organised by Pacific Forum in Honolulu, linking more than a score of research institutes in Japan, South Korea, China, the Philippines, Malaysia, Singapore, Thailand, Indonesia, Australia and the United States. PACNET is designed to enhance and institutionalise dialogue and exchange of information within the network of strategic studies institutes in the region.

In 1991–92, the core institutions of this group organised a series of conferences on Security Cooperation in the Asia Pacific. Participants from seventeen countries, including scholars as well as officials acting in their private capacities, took part in these meetings. The discussions at these meetings clearly showed the need for more structured processes for regional confidence building and security co-operation.

The Council for Security Cooperation in the Asia Pacific

The concept of a Council for Security Cooperation in the Asia Pacific (CSCAP) was first articulated at a meeting in Seoul on 1–3 November 1992. The critical achievement of the Seoul meeting was the agreement to establish the Council in order to provide 'a more structured regional process of a non-governmental nature to contribute to the efforts towards regional confidence-building and enhancing regional security through dialogues, consultation and cooperation'.[21]

Three essential themes permeated the discussions that attended the establishment of CSCAP.[22] The first was that the Council should be a non-governmental institution but that it should involve government officials, albeit in their private capacities. It was considered essential that the institution be independent from official control in order to take full advantage of the extraordinary vitality and fecundity of non-governmental organisations (NGOs) engaged in the second track process, as well as to allow relatively free discussion of diplomatically sensitive issues that could not be brought up in official fora. It was also recognised that official involvement was necessary in order to attract government resources and to ensure that the value and practicability of the NGO efforts secured official appreciation. In other words, the prospects for implementation should count for as much as the intrinsic worth of any ideas generated in the second track process. It was considered important that the official involvement include senior military personnel as well as defence civilians and foreign affairs officers.

The second theme derived from the experience of NGOs such as the Pacific Trade and Development Conference (PAFTAD) and the Pacific Economic Cooperation Conference (PECC) in the promotion of Asia-Pacific economic co-operation through the 1970s and 1980s.[23] These NGOs have contributed to the regional economic co-operation process in several important ways. They have, to begin with, developed and disseminated the ideas and stimulated the discussion that engendered the process. They have conducted the technical economic studies and analyses which showed the benefits of liberalisation of trade in the region, either through formal free trade arrangements or, more recently, the concept of 'open regionalism'. They have demonstrated to government officials that meaningful and productive dialogue on complex and important policy matters is possible notwithstanding the extraordinary disparity in the size and interests of the numerous parties involved. Indeed, some of them — and most especially the PECC — have explicitly been structured to involve officials themselves in this dialogue — albeit in their 'unofficial' capacities. PECC has even engaged in negotiation with respect to the resolution of differences between states which have arisen during the dialogue process.[24] By providing forums for official but 'unofficial' dialogue, the NGOs have contributed to greater official interaction and enhanced mutual confidence, as well as providing a sound 'building block' for supporting co-operative arrangements at the governmental level itself.

Many of the participants in the foundation of CSCAP were also actively involved in the PAFTAD and PECC processes. Indeed, several of the institutions represented in Seoul were also the co-ordinators of their national PECC committees. In a sense, CSCAP was loosely modelled on the PECC experience and practice. It was intended that CSCAP should support official forums concerned with regional security dialogue and co-operation, such as the ASEAN PMC and the SOMs, in much the same way that PECC supports the Asia Pacific Economic Cooperation (APEC) process. More particularly, the establishment of CSCAP national committees and working groups closely reflects those established in the PECC program in terms of their general rationales and operational activities.

The third theme in the foundation of CSCAP was the acceptance of the need to build on extant arrangements in the region wherever possible, rather than construct new structures and processes. In practice, this meant building upon the arrangements and processes developed by the ASEAN ISIS association, and particularly ISIS Malaysia, which are the most advanced in the region in terms of both their infrastructure and their co-operative arrangements and practices.

CSCAP activities over the near term

The agenda for those engaged in the CSCAP process over the next year or so includes three principal tasks. The first concerns membership. The CSCAP is open to all countries and territories in the region, but several countries have yet to become involved in the process. In most cases, inclusion should present no problems. For example, New Zealand, Russia and North Korea became members during 1994. On the other hand, the inclusion of Mongolia, Myanmar (Burma), Vietnam, Cambodia and Laos may take some time to effect, primarily because of their lack of institutions familiar with the second track process. The most difficult membership issue will involve mainland China and Taiwan. It is imperative that both be included, and the terminology of 'countries and territories' in the CSCAP founding statement is intended to soften the issue; however, the process will undoubtedly not be easy.

The second task involves the establishment of the initial CSCAP Working Groups, which have been be given 'the tasks of undertaking policy-oriented studies on specific regional political-security problems'.[25] Membership of these Working Groups, which are envisaged to be the primary mechanism for CSCAP activity, is open to those countries, institutions or individuals who wish to participate and are willing to make a contribution to their operation. Four Working Groups have now been established: the first is concerned with maritime co-operation in the Asia-Pacific region; the second is concerned with the enhancement of security co-operation in the North Pacific; the third is addressing the field of proposed CSBMs, and particularly proposals for enhancing transparency; and the fourth is studying the concepts of co-operative and comprehensive security (a subject suggested by the Malaysian Minister of Foreign Affairs, Datuk Abdullah Ahmad Badawi, in his opening address at the Seventh Asia-Pacific Roundtable in Kuala Lumpur on 7 June 1993).[26]

The third task, which is perhaps the most complex, involves consideration of the relationship between the CSCAP and official fora such as the ASEAN PMC Regional Forum. In the case of regional economic co-operation processes, 'a critical development has been the strong links that have emerged between the PECC and the Asia Pacific Economic Cooperation (APEC) process'.[27] In November 1989, APEC invited PECC to co-operate with its policy-making process, and 'PECC is now providing essential input into many of APEC's work projects'.[28]

The ASEAN ISIS, which comprises half of the initial members of CSCAP, is registered with ASEAN, and since 1991 has provided support to the ASEAN Ministerial Meetings, the ASEAN PMC and the ASEAN senior officials' meetings in terms of both the generation of ideas and the provision of research and studies on regional security matters.[29] Jusuf Wanandi, who is foundation co-chairperson of CSCAP and who was one of the principal proponents of both the establishment of the ASEAN PMC SOMs and the notion of using the PMC as a regional security forum, has said that the CSCAP 'would support the work' of the ASEAN PMC SOMs.[30] To begin with, the CSCAP Steering Committee prepared a comprehensive memorandum on security issues and CSBMs in the Asia-Pacific region for submission to the ARF SOMs in April 1994 for consideration prior to the first ARF meeting in Bangkok in July 1994.[31] Three of the four initial CSCAP Working Groups are to work on subjects identified as being of direct interest to the ARF SOMs. Further mechanisms and arrangements whereby CSCAP will support the ARF process are under consideration but must await the institutional development of the ARF process itself.

The establishment of CSCAP is one of the most important milestones in the development of institutionalised dialogue, consultation and co-operation concerning security matters in the Asia-Pacific region since the end of the Cold War. It is designed not only to link and focus the research activities of non-governmental organisations devoted to work on security matters across the whole of the Asia-Pacific region, but also to provide a mechanism for linkage and mutual support between the second track and official regional security co-operation processes. It represents a major achievement in the development of multilateralism in the region.

Expectations concerning the prospects for CSCAP must be modest. It has taken some four years of discussion of regional security co-operation to get this far, and some difficult issues are still to be faced — such as the incorporation of China (and Taiwan) into the CSCAP process. On the other hand, the second-track process has now acquired considerable momentum, and the security concerns that have conduced the interest in regional security co-operation are likely to intensify rather than enervate. In the end, the success of CSCAP will be determined by the extent to which the dialogue, consultation and co-operation which it engenders are able to address in some practical fashion the emergent security concerns in this region.

Conclusions

A new era in confidence building has begun in the Asia-Pacific region. In the past few years, there has been a burgeoning of CSBM activity, at both the official and non-governmental levels. The process is still in its formative stages, but has already led to the creation of new arrangements for dialogue and counsultation on security issues; a growing practice of transparency through multinational exchanges of intelligence assessments, policy information papers and defence planning documents; the enhancement of defence co-operation through joint exercises, training programs and personnel exchanges; and co-operation with respect to certain maritime issues, such as piracy, marine pollution, refugee movements and safety of SLOCs. A plethora of particular CSBMs is in the process of implementation or under serious consideration. The momentum cannot be ignored and should not be underestimated.

The burgeoning of CSBM activity in the Asia-Pacific region was really quite unexpected, not least to area specialists immersed in the extraordinary diversity of the region. The cultures, capabilities, interests and threat preceptions of the countries in the region seemed to be manifestly too diverse to support meaningful dialogue and co-operation. There was little experience with multilateral mechanisms in regional relations, and an avowed disinclination to adopt European modalities — including with respect to CSBMs.

However, this new CSBM activity is distinctly Asian. It is a response to concerns which regional security analysts and policy-makers have about certain aspects of the emerging regional security environment. It is as integral a part of the new regional security architecture as the developments that have conduced those concerns — a more complex and apparently uncertain regional security environment, high levels of economic interdependence and concomitant levels of vulnerability to potentially destabilising economic forces and economically inspired political conflict, the vigorous arms acquisition programs underway in the region, the prospect of proliferation of weapons of mass destruction (at least in South and Northeast Asia), a variety of maritime issues, the existence of numerous territorial and sovereignty disputes, and the possibility that one or more of these could erupt into war. The classic Asian reponse was proclaimed by Sun Tzu around 400 BC: 'To rely on rustics and not prepare is the greatest of crimes; to be prepared beforehand for any contingency is the greatest of virtues.'[32] Prudence requires a careful admixture of policies of greater self-reliance and enhanced regional dialogue and co-operation — or, more generally, in Indonesian terms, 'each country's Ketahanan Nasional (National Resilience) is the precondition of achieving Ketahanan Regional (Regional Resilience)'.[33]

The new CSBM activity is not only focused on Asia-Pacific security concerns, but is also proceeding in Asian fashion. Western predilections for creating organisations and formal structures, deciding modalities and delineating responsibilities are disdained. The Asian way stresses patience, informality, pragmatism, consensus and evolution.[34] Institutionalised mechanisms and arrangements for dialogue are an essential building block. The task for the near term, as Mahathir bin Mohamad stated more than a decade ago with respect to regional dialogue on economic co-operation, is 'the tedious one of getting to know each other'.[35] Rather than the establishment of new organisations, the path of progress has been through the strengthening, expansion and gradual multilateralisation of the myriad of bilateral arrangements, and the adaptation and augmentation of existing processes of regional dialogue to include security matters. The ARF and the various SOMs have developed as an integral element of the ASEAN PMC process. CSCAP was founded on the strong institutional links forged between the established strategic studies centres throughout the Asia-Pacific region.

The importance of the 'second track' process to the new CSBM activity is distinctively Asian. Much of the current activity is directly attributable to the efforts of non-governmental organisations (NGOs), and much is modelled on experience with Asia-Pacific economic co-operation. NGOs, and especially the ASEAN ISIS group, can claim major credit for conception of some 'first track' developments, such as the SOMs and the ARF, as well as 'second track' dialogues on the security of SLOCs and conflict resolution in the South China Sea. Other NGOs have stimulated CSBM activity with respect to security dialogue in Northeast Asia, the proliferation of weapons of mass destruction, maritime issues, and the concepts of cooperative and comprehensive security. The second track process provides an important buttress for official activities, as evinced in the relationship between the ASEAN ISIS group and the ASEAN SOMs and as expected of CSCAP in connection with the ARF SOMs. And it provides a venue for officials to meet and discuss, albeit in their 'private capacities', issues which involve sovereignty claims or which are otherwise too sensitive for direct negotiation. In Northeast Asia, independent though nonetheless government-affiliated defence institutes in China (such as the Academy of Military Sciences and the China Institute of International Strategic Studies), South Korea (the Korean Institute of Defence Studies), Japan (the National Institute of Defence Studies) and Russia (Institute of World Economy and International Relations) are developing a habit of dialogue and are getting to know each other through regular bilateral exchanges to discuss regional security issues. A multilateral forum that develops a Canadian initiative and American interest for such a forum in Northeast Asia is a likely prospect.

On the other hand, the virtues of patience, pragmatism, consensus and evolution necessarily mean that the process of building trust and institutionalising greater regional co-operation will be long and painstaking. Many of the emerging regional security concerns are really very complex and not amenable to simple solutions. And while the contextual constraints (such as the regional diversity, differences in security perceptions and the lack of practice with multilateralism) are clearly not immutable, they are nonetheless quite daunting. Moreover, the process is really just beginning. It could well take more than a decade for the developing dialogue processes to provide sufficient mutual understanding, confidence and trust for resolving or managing substantive regional security issues. It will be some time before any mechanisms for arms control or conflict resolution are acceptable, let alone constructed and operating effectively. The fact that much of the current and prospective CSBM activity is proceeding indirectly through the second track process is itself a manifestation of the hesitancy of officials in directly addressing security concerns.

The critical question that remains is whether the arrangements for enhanced regional co-operation can be instituted to the point where they enable the effective management of the extraordinary changes and the increasing complexities which characterise the emerging regional security environment — or whether the security concerns and challenges that have conduced the new CSBM activity will be too powerful for that fledgling activity to handle.

Notes

1   For more comprehensive discussion of the emerging security architecture in the Asia-Pacific region, including the emergent regional security concerns and the institutionalisation of regional confidence and security building measures (CSBMs), see Desmond Ball, *Building Blocks for Regional Security: An Australian Perspective on Confidence and Security Building Measures (CSBMs) in the Asia/Pacific Region*, Canberra Papers on Strategy and Defence No. 83, Strategic and Defence Studies Centre, Research School of Pacific Studies, The Australian National University, Canberra, 1991; Desmond Ball, 'Arms and Affluence: Military Acquisitions in the Asia-Pacific Region', *International Security*, vol. 18, no. 3, Winter 1993/94, pp. 78–112; Desmond Ball, 'A New Era in Confidence Building: The Second-track Process in the Asia-Pacific Region', *Security Dialogue*, vol. 25, no. 2, June 1994, pp. 157–65; and 'CSCAP: Its Future Place in the Regional Security Architecture', paper prepared for the Eighth Asia Pacific Roundtable, organised by the ASEAN Institutes of Strategic and International Studies (ASEAN ISIS), Kuala Lumpur, 6–8 June 1994.

2   For discussion of the European experience, see Johan Jorgen Holst and Karen Alette Melander, 'European Security and Confidence-Building Measures', *Survival*, vol. 19, no. 4, July/August 1977, pp. 146–54; Jonathon Alford, *Confidence-Building Measures in Europe: The Military Aspects*, Adelphi Paper no. 149, International Institute for Strategic Studies, London, 1979; Stephen Larrabee and Dietrich Stobbe (eds), *Confidence-Building Measures in Europe*, Institute for East-West Security Studies, New York, 1983; Rolf Berg and Adam-Daniel Rotfeld, *Building Security in Europe: Confidence-Building Measures and the CSCE*, Institute for East-West Security Studies, New York, 1986; and Cathleen S. Fisher, 'The Preconditions of Confidence-building: Lessons from the European Experience', in Michael Krepon, Dominique M. McCoy and Matthew C.J. Rudolph (eds), *A Handbook of Confidence-Building Measures for Regional Security*, The Henry L. Stimson Center, Washington DC, September 1993, pp. 31–41.

3   See Desmond Ball, 'Tasks For Security Cooperation in Asia', in Desmond Ball, Richard L. Grant and Jusuf Wanandi, *Security Cooperation in the Asia-Pacific Region*, The Center for Strategic and International Studies, Washington DC, 1993, pp. 20–21.

4   Gareth Evans, 'What Asia Needs is A Europe-Style CSCA', *International Herald Tribune*, 27 July 1990, p. 6.

5   See Desmond Ball, *Building Blocks for Regional, Security: An Australian Perspective on Confidence and Security Building Measures (CSBMs) in the Asia/Pacific Region*, Canberra Papers on Strategy and Defence No. 83, Strategic and Defence Studies Centre, Research School of Pacific Studies, The Australian National University, Canberra, 1991, pp. 83–85.

6   Jawhar Hassan, 'Managing Security in Southeast Asia: Existing Mechanisms and Processes to Address Regional Conflicts', paper prepared for a Conference on Enhancing Security in Southeast Asia, Canberra, 5–6 April 1993, p. 4.

7   The Hon. Datuk Seri Mohammed Najib bin Tun Abdul Razak, 'Towards Cooperative Security and Regional Stability: The Malaysian View', in David Horner (ed.), *The Army and the Future: Land Forces in Australia and South-East Asia*, Directorate of Departmental Publications, Department of Defence, Canberra, 1993, p. 137.

8   See Vice Admiral I.D.G. MacDougall, Chief of Naval Staff (CNJS), 'CNS presentation to WPNS III on the Inaugural Western Pacific Naval Symposium Workshop', Sydney, 9–10 July 1992, p. 8.

9   ibid., pp. 8–9.

10   ibid., p. 9. See also Captain Russ Swinnerton RAN and Desmond Ball, *A Regional Regime for Maritime Surveillance, Safety and Information Exchanges*, Working Paper No. 278, Strategic and Defence Studies Centre, Research School of Pacific Studies, The Australian National University, Canberra, December 1993.

11   ASEAN Institutes of Strategic and International Studies, *A Time For Initiative: Proposals for the Consideration of the Fourth ASEAN Summit*, 4 June 1991, pp. 4–5.

12   Joint Communiqué of the Twenty Fourth ASEAN Ministerial Meeting, Kuala Lumpur, 19–20 July 1991, p. 5.

13   Goh Chok Tong, Prime Minister of Singapore, 'ASEAN Cooperation in the 1990s', Opening Address at the 26th ASEAN Ministerial Meeting, Singapore, 23 July 1993, paras 25, 26.

14   Joint Communiqué of the Twenty-sixth ASEAN Ministerial Meeting, Singapore, 23–24 July 1993, Press Release, 26th ASEAN Ministerial Meeting/Post Ministerial Conferences, Singapore, 23–28 July 1993, para. 8. See also 'Ministers Endorse Security Forum', *Canberra Times*, 24 July 1993, p. 7; and Michael Vatikiotis, 'Uncharted Waters', *Far Eastern Economic Review*, 5 August 1993, pp. 10–11.

15   'The Jane's Interview', *Jane's Defence Weekly*, 19 February 1994, p. 52.

16   ibid.

17   ASEAN Institutes of Strategic and International Studies, *A Time For Initiative: Proposals for the Consideration of the Fourth ASEAN Summit*, 4 June 1991, p. 5. For further discussion of the role of SOMs, see His Excellency Dr Taro Nakayama, Minister for Foreign Affairs of Japan, 'Statement to

the General Session of the ASEAN Post-Ministerial Conference', Kuala Lumpur, Malaysia, 22 July 1991, pp. 12–13; and Jusuf Wanandi, 'Developments in the Asia-Pacific Region', paper prepared for a symposium on The Changing Asia-Pacific Scene in the 1990s: Security, Cooperation and Development, China Center for International Studies, Beijing, 10–12 August 1991, p. 27.

[18]   *Chairman's Statement*, ASEAN Post-Ministerial Conferences, Senior Officials Meeting, Singapore, 20–21 May 1993, paras 8, 10.

[19]   See CSCAP Pro-term Committee, The Security of the Asia Pacific Region, Memorandum no. 1, Council for Security Cooperation in the Asia Pacific, April 1994; and the Australian Department of Foreign Affairs and Trade, 'Australian Paper on Practical Proposals for Security Cooperation in the Asia Pacific Region', paper commissioned by the 1993 ASEAN PMC SOM and submitted to the ARF SOM, Bangkok, April 1994.

[20]   See *Regional Security Dialogue: A Calendar of Asia Pacific Events,* January 1994–December 1994, prepared jointly by the Regional Security Section, Department of Foreign Affairs and Trade, Canberra, and the Strategic and Defence Studies Centre, Research School of Pacific Studies, The Australian National University, Canberra, 2nd edn, January 1994.

[21]   Ball, Grant and Wanandi, 'Tasks for Security Cooperation in Asia,' p. 37.

[22]   For a more comprehensive discussion of CSCAP, see Desmond Ball, 'The Council for Security Cooperation in the Asia Pacific (CSCAP)', *Indonesian Quarterly*, vol. 21, no. 4, Fourth Quarter, 1993, pp. 495–505; and Desmond Ball, 'CSCAP: Its Future Role in the Regional Security Architecture', paper prepared for the Eighth Asia Pacific Roundtable, organised by the ASEAN Institutes of Strategic and International Studies (ASEAN ISIS), Kuala Lumpur, 6–8 June 1994.

[23]   For a comprehensive analysis and background to these organisations, see Ross Garnaut and Peter Drysdale (eds), *Asia Pacific Regionalism: Readings in International Economic Relations*, Harper Educational, Pymble, 1994.

[24]   See Lawrence T. Woods, 'Non-governmental Organizations and Pacific Cooperation: Back to the Future?', *Pacific Review*, vol. 4, no. 4, 1991, pp. 312–21; and Lawrence T. Woods, *Asia-Pacific Diplomacy: Nongovernmental Organizations and International Relations*, University of British Columbia Press, Vancouver, 1993, Ch. 8.

[25]   Ball, Grant and Wanandi, 'Tasks for Security Cooperation in Asia,' p. 37.

[26]   Datuk Abdullah Ahmad Badawi, 'Opening Address', Seventh Asia-Pacific Roundtable on Confidence Building and Conflict Reduction in the Pacific, Kuala Lumpur, 7 June 1993, p. 7.

[27]   Australian Pacific Economic Cooperation Committee, *5th Report to the Australian Government*, 1991, p. i.

28 ibid., pp. i, 10–12.

29 ASEAN Institutes of Strategic and International Studies, *A Time For Initiative: Proposals for the Consideration of the Fourth ASEAN Summit*, 4 June 1991.

30 Cited in Michael Richardson, 'Old Asia Adversaries Build Bridges', *International Herald Tribune*, 10 June 1993, p. 2.

31 See CSCAP Pro-tem Committee, *The Security of the Asia Pacific Region*, Memorandum no. 1, Council for Security Cooperation in the Asia Pacific, April 1994

32 Samuel B. Griffith, (ed. and trans), *Sun Tzu: The Art of War*, Oxford University Press, London, 1971, p. 83.

33 See Hasnan Habib, 'Technology for National Resilience: The Indonesian Perspective', in Desmond Ball and Helen Wilson (eds), *New Technology: Implications for Regional and Australian Security*, Canberra Papers on Strategy and Defence No. 76, Strategic and Defence Studies Centre, Research School of Pacific Studies, The Australian National University, Canberra, 1991, pp. 60–65, 76.

34 Desmond Ball, 'Strategic Culture in the Asia-Pacific Region', *Security Studies*, vol. 3, no. 1, Autumn 1993, p. 18.

35 Mahathir bin Mohamad, 'Tak Kenal Maka Tak Cinta', in *Asia-Pacific in the 1980s: Toward Greater Symmetry in Economic Independence*, Center for Strategic and International Studies, Jakarta, May 1980, p. 18.

Appendix 16A: Proposals for confidence building and security co-operation in the Asia-Pacific region

(i)   Mechanisms for enhancing transparency, e.g. publication of White Papers, Capability reviews, Doctrine Manuals, etc.

(ii)   Establishment of a Regional Arms Register.

(iii)   Intelligence exchanges.

(iv)   Strengthening and expanding existing bilateral co-operative arrangements.

(v)   Sharing concepts and methodologies for defence planning and force structure developments.

(vi)   Building on the ASEAN PMC and ARF process.

(vii) Establishing a forum for regional defence dialogue, as also proposed by the Malaysian Defence Minister in April 1992.

(viii) A forum for security dialogue in Northeast Asia.

(ix)   The establishment of Zones of Co-operation, e.g. a South China Sea Zone of Co-operation.

(x)   A Regional Maritime Surveillance of Safety Regime (REMARSSAR).

(xi)   Regional Avoidance of Incidents at Sea Regimes.

(xii) A Regional Airspace Surveillance and Control Regime.

(xiii) A Southwest Pacific Sovereignty Surveillance Regime, and the recently announced Regional Maritime Surveillance Communications Network.

(xiv) Proposals for a Regional Security Assessment Centre in the Southwest Pacific.

(xv) CSBM proposals concerning the Korean Peninsula.

(xvi) Proposals for naval arms control in the Pacific.

(xvii) A Regional Technology Monitoring Regime.

(xviii) The Australian chemical weapons initiative.

(xix) Proposals concerning economic security.

(xx) An Environmental Security Regime.

(xxi) Strengthening the networks of non-governmental organisations (NGOs) and the so-called 'second track' process.

(xxii) Bilateral security talks between Japan and Russia, Japan and South Korea, and Japan and China; and similarly, between China and the ASEAN states, individually and as an organisation process.

(xxii) Bilateral security talks between Japan and Russia, Japan and South Korea, and Japan and China; and similarly, between China and the ASEAN states, individually and as an organisation process.

Appendix 16B: Sovereignty, legitimacy and territorial conflicts in the Asia-Pacific region

- Competing Soviet-Russian and Japanese claims to the southern Kurile Islands — referred to by the Japanese as 'the Northern Territories, namely, Kunashiri, Etorofu and Shikotan Islands, an integral part of Japanese territory, illegally occupied by the Soviet Union'.
- Divided sovereignty on the Korean Peninsula, where some 1.4 million ground forces of the Republic of Korea and North Korea remain deployed against each other across the demilitarised zone (DMZ).
- Competing sovereignty claims of the Chinese regimes on mainland China and Taiwan.
- The unresolved dispute between Japan and China over Senkaku Island in the East China Sea.
- The armed communist and Muslim insurgencies in the Philippines.
- The continuing claim of the Philippines to the Malaysian state of Sabah and its adjacent waters.
- The strong separatist movement in Sabah.
- Competing claims to the Paracel and Spratly Islands in the South China Sea, contested by China, Vietnam, Brunei, Malaysia, Taiwan and the Philippines.
- The Bougainville secessionist movement in Papua New Guinea.
- The Organisasi Papua Merdeka (OPM) resistance movement in West Irian/Irian Jaya.
- The continuing resistance to Indonesian rule in East Timor.
- The Aceh independence movement in northern Sumatra.
- The dispute between Malaysia and Singapore over ownership of the island of Pulau Batu Putih in the Straits of Johore.
- The competing claims of Malaysia and Indonesia to the islands of Sipadan and Ligitan, in the Celebes Sea, some 35 kilometres from Semporna in Sabah.
- Residual conflict in Cambodia.
- Residual communist guerilla operations along the Thai–Lao border in northeast Thailand.
- The Shan, Kachin, Karen secessionist, communist insurgent and pro-democracy rebellions in Burma.
- Insurgency in Bangladesh.
- Hostilities along the Burma–Bangladesh border.
- Territorial disputes between India and Pakistan.
- The Sikh and other insurrectionist movements in India.
- The insurgency in Sri Lanka.

17 International Peacekeeping: Issues for the Region

Hugh Smith

Introduction

The end of the Cold War brought major changes to United Nations peacekeeping, with implications for the Asia-Pacific region. First, it created more favourable political conditions for international peacekeeping. Second, the United States and other major powers could contemplate more active involvement in peacekeeping. China, too, joined the ranks of the peacekeepers, beginning with a small number of observers in UNTSO in 1991 and a major contribution to UNTAC. The major powers have provided not only personnel but also logistics, communications and command capabilities. This infusion of new blood proved fortunate, since the demands of peacekeeping were outstripping the resources available from traditional medium- and small-power contributors.

Japan, hitherto excluded from participation in international peacekeeping by internal political and constitutional constraints, modified long-standing policies of refusing to send military forces overseas even for peacekeeping purposes. Japan sent minesweepers to the Middle East after the Gulf War and subsequently contributed over 600 military engineers plus 75 civilian police to Cambodia. It has also provided military personnel to ONUMOZ and provided support to UNAMIR through a presence in Zaire. Japan has the potential to become a major provider of personnel and equipment, no doubt believing its quest for a permanent seat on the Security Council would be eased by more active peacekeeping.

Third, the end of the Cold War contributed to the greater need for peacekeeping, especially in East Europe, as conflict and disorder erupted in the wake of collapsing communist regimes and crumbling alliances.

What is significant about many of these new peacekeeping operations is their complexity and the ambitious nature of their objectives. The term 'Second Generation' peacekeeping has been coined to describe United Nations operations which go far beyond the traditional form of peacekeeping.[1] Three characteristics of the 'new' peacekeeping stand out. First, the United Nations has taken on the role of actually conducting elections or referendums and ensuring the creation of favourable conditions for voting.

Second, the United Nations has in effect taken over the administration of entire countries in the case of Cambodia and Somalia. The closest precedent for this was the temporary administration of West New Guinea in 1962–63, but that was in the context of an international agreement and the absence of civil war. 'Painting a country blue', as it has been termed, involves far more than simply military personnel. Police, electoral officials, aid specialists, human rights monitors, administrators and many more must now be put on the payroll, while non-governmental organisations also need to be involved in the delivery of aid and in long-term development.

Third, the United Nations has shown itself ready to undertake more forceful operations under Chapter VII of the Charter. Three decades ago the tribulations of the Congo operation convinced many that the United Nations should stay out of internal conflicts unless there was a political settlement and a wish for peace. But the 'lessons' of the past have been put aside in the post-Cold War period. The Gulf War demonstrated that the Security Council could successfully deal with aggression by means of a mandate to its members authorising the use of force. But internal conflicts have also seen the United Nations undertaking more warlike operations. The violent behaviour of factions and the urgent demands of humanitarian relief have encouraged the organisation to entangle itself in complex and often violent conflicts. In Cambodia, the limited violence directed against United Nations personnel saw demands for the use of force against the Khmer Rouge. In this mode the United Nations is coming to resemble more a well-armed policeman than an unarmed or lightly armed mediator.

Since 1988, at least twenty further peacekeeping operations have been mounted by the United Nations and the question has naturally arisen whether the organisation is effectively equipped to carry out all that it has taken on. The Secretary-General's *Agenda for Peace*, published in 1992, represented one attempt to develop an understanding of the changing concepts of peacekeeping and contained suggestions for putting it on a sounder basis.[2] These included the ear-marking by member states of military personnel for United Nations operations, pre-positioned stocks of equipment suitable for United Nations operations, and the establishment of a working fund to allow immediate financing of operations. At the same time, pressure has increased from some of the established contributors for a more professional approach to peacekeeping. Effective planning, a continuously functioning operations centre, standard operating procedures, the establishment of a military staff, rigorous selection of personnel and expanded training are now in train or on the agenda.

These changes in United Nations peacekeeping carry many costs, not least of which is the decline in the 'inviolability' of those wearing the blue beret and the blue helmet. The operations in Somalia and the former Yugoslavia have proved particularly dangerous. The financial burden has also grown rapidly. In 1991 the level of members' contributions to peacekeeping stood at US$420 million. The cost in 1993 was in the order of US$2.8 billion while arrears for peacekeeping contributions amounted to US$1.1 billion.[3]

The political costs to the United Nations must also be considered. The organisation has taken on a range of challenges which in some cases have proven beyond its ability to resolve. The United Nations has become entangled in conflicts of a kind which it largely eschewed for 40 years. The need for support has led the Secretary-General and others to propose a greater role for regional organisations in peacekeeping. In *Agenda for Peace*, Boutros Boutros-Ghali argued that regional action in peacekeeping would 'not only lighten the burden of the Council but also contribute to a deeper sense of participation, consensus and democratisation of international affairs'.[4] The Secretary-General has, perhaps optimistically, suggested that there is a 'new sense' that regional arrangements, whatever their original purposes, have a contribution to make.[5]

In turn, this raises the question as to the prospects for regional arrangements of one kind or another for peacekeeping in the Asia-Pacific area. Four main themes will be examined: (i) the attractions and drawbacks of regional peacekeeping in general; (ii) the experience of peacekeeping among Asia-Pacific states, particularly in the light of the Cambodian operation (UNTAC); (iii) the prospects for peacekeeping within the region, including the concept of a regional peacekeeping force; and (iv) the prospects for an expanded regional role in peacekeeping within the framework of the United Nations.

Regional peacekeeping

Regional organisations have always played a role in the United Nations system. In the drafting of the Charter, it was recognised that they could contribute to international peace though there were some who feared that regional organisations could undermine universal principles and perhaps encourage competitive alliances.[6] At the present time, however, the merits of regional organisations taking on some of the responsibility for the maintenance of international peace and security are clear. The idea is that a regional group of states may be better placed than the United Nations to work for a peaceful settlement of a local dispute. They may share similar goals and dislike the 'general perspective' that the United Nations brings to disputes.[7] Such states may have essential knowledge of the problem in question, be more ready to act quickly and have a strong incentive to do so if a conflict is causing direct problems through, for example, the movement of refugees, pressing humanitarian demands or economic disruption. Such factors may mean that regional organisations have the incentive and endurance to see through a difficult process where the United Nations would be less committed.

There are also practical reasons that could make a regional peacekeeping operation more effective. A force that is drawn from states in the region concerned could be more rapidly deployed, resupplied and reinforced simply by virtue of proximity.

In practice, however, regional organisations do not have a good record in international peacekeeping. First, there is the risk that an operation will be dominated by one power for its own purposes.

Second, there is the inherent political weakness of many regional organisations. None has the power of compulsion which is ultimately enjoyed by the United Nations through resolutions of the Security Council.[8] For example, there is often dispute as to which state or states should take a lead role and, with a 'bewildering variety of purposes and memberships, they often have great difficulty in reaching decisions and taking action'.[9] The differing approaches taken at various times towards the former Yugoslavia by Britain, France and Germany (not to mention the United States) illustrate that, even in Western Europe, strong differences of opinion may emerge.

Third, regional groups may lack the appropriate institutions to develop and manage peacekeeping activities. All have been established for other purposes and there is often a reluctance to compromise original intentions. Certain organisations, indeed, may prefer not to address security issues directly. ASEAN, for example, has proved successful in part because it has for most of its history focused on political security and economic co-operation rather than military security. It is also quite likely that external powers may need to be involved in order to make a settlement possible. This was the case with regard to Cambodia.

Fourth, the theory that regional states are better able to resolve their own disputes tends to fall down under scrutiny. They may have strong interests in a dispute but the interests will not necessarily be identical. Indeed, it is likely that states in the region will take different sides and that support for one side or the other will be all the stronger because of the interests formed by proximity. This is particularly true of internal conflicts where peacekeeping operations are often seen as favouring one side or another. Cambodia is a case in point. Nor are the disputants in such conflicts liable to welcome the presence of neighbouring states on their soil, especially if they believe the neighbour has been intervening in favour of their opponents.[10] Regional forces, in short, tend to lack the impartiality which is normally the mark of United Nations peacekeeping.[11] Australia has experienced this in relation to its role in the Bougainville dispute.

Finally, the actual mounting of a regional peacekeeping operation would also run into the problem of resources. Personnel, equipment, logistics, communications and command functions may not be easily available.

The notion of peacekeeping operations which are purely regional thus faces many difficulties. Such operations have occurred in the past, notably when the Security Council has been deadlocked, but with the end of the Cold War they are likely to be rare. Some kind of United Nations involvement will almost always be sought, even if it is simply the unofficial blessing of the Secretary-General.

Asia-Pacific states and peacekeeping

The prospects for co-operation in peacekeeping in the Asia-Pacific region must remain uncertain for a variety of reasons. One obvious factor is the very diversity of the region. Nonetheless, the record of regional states in international peacekeeping is already reasonably strong. While some — such as Vietnam, Cambodia, Laos and Burma — have not contributed for obvious reasons, most have declared their support for the principles of peacekeeping and demonstrated their readiness to participate (see Table 17.1).

The most significant commitment for many of the regional nations was to UNTAC in Cambodia. Indonesia, Malaysia and Thailand all sent infantry battalions, making it their largest United Nations commitment. Australia, China and Japan also committed relatively significant numbers. Whether the Cambodian government that was established through the elections stands or falls in the longer term, the manner in which UNTAC was established and the participation by regional states has long-term implications for future peacekeeping activities in the region.

The UNTAC operation was based on a settlement among the factions and outside parties which had been brokered in part through Australian efforts.[12] The settlement involved ASEAN and a number of regional countries as well as major external powers in the talks held in Paris that led to the agreement of 23 October 1991.[13] The settlement was made possible by events in Cambodia itself, in the region and in the world at large. Moscow's decision to support a negotiated settlement and to normalise relations with China placed pressure on Vietnam to accept an agreement. For its part China was prepared to exercise leverage over the Khmer Rouge. At the same time, the end of the Cold War made United Nations involvement a thinkable proposition.

The Cambodia settlement was generally welcomed as an example of co-operation among regional states and between them and the major powers at the United Nations. It also provided an opportunity for Asia-Pacific states to work together in the United Nations context. The contributions to UNTAC made by regional nations were unprecedentedly large (see Table 17.2). No other operation has seen so many major contributions from within the region. Particularly important was the opportunity to work with regional countries in a single mission.[14] The involvement of eleven Asia-Pacific states which contributed some 5500 military personnel — about one-third of the Military Component — can be seen as a significant instance of regional security co-operation.

Table 17.1 Contributions by regional states to international peacekeeping (as at 1 June 1994)

Australia	ONUMOZ	16 police
	UNFICYP	20 police
	UNOSOM II	66 military personnel
	UNTSO	13 military observers
	*MFO	[26 military personnel — HQADF]
Brunei		
China	UNTSO	3 military observers
	UNOMIL	15 military observers
	UNIKOM	13 military observers
	ONUMOZ	10 military observers
	MINURSO	20 military observers
Fiji	UNIFIL	643 troops
	UNIKOM	7 military observers
	UNAMIR	1 military observer
	*MFO	350 troops
Indonesia	UNIKOM	6 military observers
	UNOSOM II	4 military observers
Japan	ONUMOZ	56 military personnel
Malaysia	UNIKOM	6 military observers
	MINURSO	6 military observers, 5 police
	ONUMOZ	24 military observers, 35 police
	UNOSOM II	1089 troops, 5 police
	UNOMIL	25 military observers
	UNAVEM II	1 military observer, 3 police
	UNPROFOR	1504 troops, 19 military observers
New Zealand	UNTSO	9 military observers
	UNAVEM II	3 military observers
	UNPROFOR	250 troops (from August 1994), 9 military observers
	UNOSOM II	50 military personnel
	ONUMOZ	2 military observers
	*MFO	25 military personnel
Philippines		
Republic of Korea	UNOSOM II	6 military personnel, 2 police
Singapore	UNIKOM	7 military observers
Thailand	UNIKOM	6 military observers

* Non-United Nations operations
Source: The Military Balance 1994–1995, Brassey's/International Institute for Strategic Studies, London, 1994.

Table 17.2 Contributions by Asia-Pacific states to UNTAC (as at 1 June 1993)

Australia	611 troops, 11 police
Brunei	3 military observers, 12 police
China	402 military engineers, 45 military observers
Fiji	50 police
Indonesia	1795 troops, 17 military observers, 224 police
Japan	602 troops, 8 military observers, 66 police
Malaysia	1063 troops, 29 military observers, 223 police
New Zealand	88 troops
Philippines	127 naval personnel, 224 police
Singapore	75 police
Thailand	720 military engineers

Source: *The Military Balance 1993–1994,* Brassey's/International Institute for Strategic Studies, London, 1993.

Another point of significance for the region was the fact of Japanese involvement. Japan contributed some 600 troops and 75 police to UNTAC, its first venture into international peacekeeping. It also provided the United Nations' Special Representative in Cambodia, Yasushi Akashi.[15] China was also a major contributor to a United Nations operation for the first time, having previously sent only small numbers of observers to UNTSO.

What is particularly remarkable about Japan's first major foray into peacekeeping is that it should have been in Cambodia.[16] The operation was hardly the most promising in terms of the far from negligible level of danger and the uncertain prospects of success. Even more problematic were the memories of Japanese occupation during World War II that are still alive in Southeast Asia. Japan's involvement was a test of Asian reactions to the first use of Japanese ground forces overseas since 1945. ASEAN states publicly supported Japan's presence in UNTAC, but a certain hesitancy could be sensed. President Suharto of Indonesia refrained from using the term Japan Self Defense Force while Thailand stated its concern that the JSDF not be used to promote Japan's economic interests in the region.[17] Malaysia supported Japan's participation in UNTAC but expressed the hope that it would not lead to 'renewed military adventurism'.[18] Singapore was also tentative, stressing need for the JSDF to confine itself to peacekeeping.[19] Nonetheless, no major strains arose.

UNTAC was also significant to the nations of Southeast Asia and Australia, because Cambodia is very much part of their region. Several regional states had direct political and economic interests in Cambodia. Thailand, in particular, was directly affected by the movement of refugees and smugglers across the border with its neighbour. Vietnam's occupation of Cambodia in 1979 had been a barrier to normalisation of its relations with ASEAN. For ASEAN, in general, the Cambodian settlement was the means of removing certain sources of difference and irritation among its members. [20]

UNTAC served to galvanise several regional states into active involvement in peacekeeping. To be sure, this was in part to promote their own interests and to ensure that other states did not take a predominant role. But there was also an element of genuine commitment to the principles of peaceful settlement and regional stability. The smaller states, in particular, may have gained some reassurance from active United Nations interest in the region. In addition, UNTAC contributed to the greater acceptance of a role for Japan and China in the security of the region, albeit under the auspices of the United Nations. And Australia has not only seen the realisation of its ambition for a settlement in Cambodia, but has promoted its policy of 'constructive engagement' with Southeast Asia.[21]

Prospects for Asia-Pacific peacekeeping

Despite the many difficulties, regional peacekeeping activity has proved attractive enough to encourage proposals from time to time for regional peacekeeping forces. Some thought, for example, has been given to a force of this kind among the states of the South Pacific. The idea was first seriously mooted in 1980 by the Prime Minister of Papua New Guinea, Sir Julius Chan, after Papua New Guinea intervened in Vanuatu with Australian logistic support in order to put down a rebellion on the island of Espiritu Santo.[22] The episode demonstrated the effectiveness of co-operation between Australia and Papua New Guinea, concluding with the return of power to an elected government and the withdrawal of the Papua New Guinea force. Nothing came of Chan's proposal at the time, but the idea did not die there.

In the course of the 1980s, island states in the South Pacific became increasingly concerned about threats of one kind or another. Threats from external sources were one problem, but it was internal instability that seemed most dangerous. This perception was reinforced by the coups in Fiji in 1987, the Vila riots in 1988 and the episodic crisis over Bougainville since 1989. Australia and New Zealand were concerned about the prospect of a request for assistance from a South Pacific government in the event of an internal challenge or chronic disorder. They found it difficult to both refuse assistance and grant assistance. Neither wanted to appear as the regional police officer or become entangled in a messy civil war.[23]

In these circumstances, the idea of a multinational force in the South Pacific found some support. Intervention which had the endorsement of the South Pacific Forum, involving forces from more than one country and which could be labelled 'peacekeeping' was likely to prove far more acceptable to all parties than unilateral action.[24] The idea was not without opponents. Some states preferred to rely on existing bilateral relations with Australia or New Zealand while Fiji in particular expressed concern about the possibility of outside interference in domestic politics.[25] Some of the difficulties inherent in regional peacekeeping were clearly evident in Bougainville in its dispute with the PNG government.

Regional co-operation in a United Nations framework

In contrast to regional organisations, the United Nations has many advantages. By and large it is neutral, it can command resources, it possesses the authority of the Charter and it has unparallelled experience. All things considered, the most likely path will be for regional co-operation in peacekeeping within the framework of the United Nations. What UNTAC demonstrated was that a major regional problem was never within the scope of the region itself to resolve; and that only the UN can mount an operation of that scale and complexity. But UNTAC also demonstrated that regional states are able to contribute to the process of settlement and are willing to make substantial contributions to an operation in their region.

Within these constraints, regional co-operation in peacekeeping could develop in a number of ways. First, there is the role which regions can play in preventive diplomacy and in the containment of conflicts. The idea is simply that success in this field will preclude the necessity for peacekeeping operations. It has also been argued that regional organisations such as ASEAN will do best to concentrate on areas where they have a 'comparative advantage', notably activities such as early warning, information and preventive diplomacy.[26] The states of Southeast Asia and the South Pacific have already developed an institutional basis for the peaceful settlement of disputes. Even if the political will is absent, regional organisations can still play a part in containing conflicts by restraining the parties involved and by discouraging precipitate action on the part of their own members or outsiders. The regular series of South China Sea workshops convened by Indonesia and attended by all climants is illustrative.

Second, regional organisations can develop arrangements with the United Nations for the handling of disputes in a co-operative fashion. They could, for example, bring disputes to the attention of the United Nations at an early stage, possibly at a point when a worsening of the situation could be prevented. Involvement of the United Nations could also lend the authority of the organisation to regional actions. The Secretary-General has envisaged a wide variety of arrangements whereby regional organisations and the United Nations could co-ordinate their activities to build international consensus on a dispute and the measures required to address it.[27] This also recognises that the United Nations has certain disadvantages — above all, lack of direct interest and complex decision-making — when trying to mediate a dispute.[28] There is no guarantee that regional organisations will avoid such problems but a combined approach merits consideration. The way in which Asia-Pacific states and the United Nations have jointly managed the problem of North Korea's nuclear weapons potential illustrates some of the possibilities.

As disputes escalate, it will be important for effective arrangements to be worked out between the regional organisation and the United Nations. Much will depend on the existing patterns of co-operation in the region, the availability of resources and the political unity among members. In a changing situation, appropriate responses will vary and the relative roles of the United Nations and the regional organisation concerned will need to be adaptable. In some cases it may be feasible for the United Nations to provide a mandate for action to a regional grouping, in other cases it will be necessary for the United Nations to take a strong lead. Each case will need to be considered on its merits but it is useful for regional organisations to reach framework agreements to govern their relationship with the United Nations.[29]

A third area of common interest among regional states is in reform of United Nations peacekeeping. There is a natural interest among all contributors that peacekeeping operations should become more efficient and more effective.

One area of potential regional co-operation in peacekeeping deserves separate consideration, namely naval peacekeeping. The involvement of navies in peacekeeping has so far been minimal but there are indications that the more ambitious peacekeeping and peace enforcement operations may have a maritime dimension.[30] The flexibility and commonality of naval forces certainly offer prospects for international co-operation.[31] The Asia-Pacific, including as it does vast expanses of ocean but also many potential sources of conflict at sea, could give rise to disputes with a clear maritime dimension. It is possible that any settlement of such conflicts could include a regional naval force with responsibilities such as patrol, surveillance, investigation of incidents and so on — the role which United Nations military observers have played on land for many years.

Conclusion

It is clear that the Asia-Pacific region, or some grouping within it, is unlikely to mount peacekeeping operations of its own volition without some involvement by the United Nations. This is the result partly of the inherent problems in purely regional action, and partly of the nature of the region itself. It can be argued that the region is in fact unlikely to see disputes that lend themselves to peacekeeping operations. Those disputes that are not resolved or contained by regional states may be simply unamenable to any kind of international action. Similarly, a conflict between two or more neighbouring states could create such tension that a regional organisation would be deeply divided and unable to act. To the extent that this is due to the ability to avoid serious conflicts, of course, it is to be welcomed.

Nonetheless, regional groups of states, including Southeast Asia and the South Pacific, may find a significant role to play in international peacekeeping under United Nations auspices. While a combined regional force for participation in United Nations peacekeeping — other than Australia–New Zealand — is several years from fruition, several other avenues for co-operation in the peacekeeping field have been identified. These range from the prevention or containment of disputes to co-operative reform of United Nations peacekeeping and collaboration in the training field. There are some positive signs. The ASEAN states, for example, have since January 1992 formally placed security on the agenda and it is possible that the organisation will over time develop more of a basis for military co-operation.[32] The Five Power Defence Arrangements are also to be used as a forum to discuss peacekeeping and will seek to bring in all members of ASEAN .[33] In other words, 'peacekeeping seems a natural activity for regional co-operation'.[34] Peacekeeping activities, in turn, are clearly conducive to regional security co-operation and confidence-building.

Yet the limits of such co-operation remain apparent. One cannot assume that regional states will take the same view of particular United Nations peacekeeping operations. Malaysia and Indonesia, for example, might be prepared to send forces to a United Nations operation in Bosnia to protect the Muslim population, whereas Australia has unequivocally ruled out such involvement.[35] Again, Fiji has participated in UNIFIL since 1978, an operation to which no other Pacific or Asian nation (apart from Nepal) has contributed. In other words, no necessary commonality of interests and involvement should be expected or demanded outside the region concerned. The situation is in some ways comparable with Australia's participation in the Gulf War, which was welcomed by some Southeast Asian nations such as Singapore, Thailand and the Philippines but viewed with minor irritation by Malaysia and Indonesia.[36] What is necessary — and may have been somewhat deficient in the case of the Gulf War — is for regional states to maintain a dialogue to ensure that each understands the national interests and objectives of the others.

Notes

1 J. Mackinlay, J. Chopra, *A Draft Concept of Second Generation Multinational Operations 1993*, Brown University, 1993. In this chapter, peacekeeping is used generically to refer to First and Second Generation peacekeeping while excluding direct military action of the kind authorised by the United Nations against Iraq.

2 Boutros Boutros-Ghali, *An Agenda for Peace: Preventive Diplomacy, Peacemaking and Peace-Keeping*, United Nations, New York, 1992.

3 S. Ogata, P. Volcker (co-chairmen), *Financing an Effective United Nations*, Ford Foundation, New York, 1993.

4 Boutros-Ghali, *An Agenda for Peace*, p. 64.

5 ibid., p. 65.

6 See the discussion in I.L. Claude, *Swords Into Plowshares*, 3rd edn, University of London Press, London, 1964, especially pp. 105–9.

7 Brigadier General Soedibyo, 'Regional Associations and Peacekeeping in the Asia Pacific Region' in Hugh Smith (ed.), *Peacekeeping: Challenges for the Future*, Australian Defence Studies Centre, Canberra, 1993, p. 163.

[8] Gareth Evans, *Cooperating for Peace: The Global Agenda for the 1990s and Beyond*, Allen & Unwin, Sydney, 1993, p. 78.

[9] Adam Roberts, 'The United Nations and International Security', *Survival*, vol. 35, no. 2, Summer 1993, p. 8.

[10] Paul F. Diehl, 'Institutional Alternatives to Traditional UN Peacekeeping: An Assessment of Regional and Multinational Operations', *Armed Forces and Society*, vol. 19, no. 2, Winter 1993, p. 213.

[11] ibid., pp. 216–17.

[12] Gareth Evans, 'The Comprehensive Political Settlement to the Cambodia Conflict: An Exercise in Cooperating for Peace' in Hugh Smith (ed.), *International Peacekeeping: Building on the Cambodian Experience*, Australian Defence Studies Centre, Canberra, 1994.

[13] Muthiah Alagappa, 'Regionalism and the Quest for Security: ASEAN and the Cambodian Conflict', *Journal of International Affairs*, vol. 46, no. 2, Winter 1993, pp. 439–67. A version of this article is also in the *Australian Journal of International Affairs*, vol. 47, no. 2, October 1993.

[14] Tony Ayers, 'Defence and Change: The Way Ahead for Australia', in D. Horner (ed.), *The Army and the Future*, Directorate of Departmental Publications, Defence Centre, Canberra, 1993, p. 241.

[15] Aurelia George, 'Japan's Participation in UN Peacekeeping Operations: Radical Departure or Predictable Response?', *Asian Survey*, vol. 23, no. 6, June 1993; see also Peter Polomka, *Japan as Peacekeeper: Samurai State, or New Civilian Power?*, Canberra Papers on Strategy and Defence no. 97, Strategic and Defence Studies Centre, Research School of Pacific Studies, The Australian National University, Canberra, 1992.

[16] Japan had sent civilian officials to take part in United Nations supervision of elections in Namibia (1989) and Nicaragua (1990).

[17] Jiji Press, 4 March 1991; Thai ambassador to Japan, Jiji Press, 30 January 1991.

[18] Foreign Minister Abdullah Ahmad Badawi, Reuter, 18 June 1992.

[19] Prime Minister Goh Chok Tong, Jiji Press, 4 March 1991.

[20] For an assessment of Australia's interests see Jenelle Bonnor, *National Interest or Irrational Interest: The Debate on Australian Defence Cooperation with Cambodia*, Working Paper No. 30, Australian Defence Studies Centre, Canberra, November 1994, pp. 21–26.

[21] For the text and extensive discussion of this document, see Greg Fry (ed.), *Australia's Regional Security*, Allen & Unwin, Sydney, 1991.

[22] Greg Fry, 'A South Pacific Peacekeeping Force?' in Hugh Smith (ed.), *Australia and Peacekeeping*, Australian Defence Studies Centre, Canberra, p. 106. The discussion of a South Pacific force relies heavily on this work.

[23] ibid., pp. 112–14.

[24] ibid., p. 115.

[25] ibid., pp. 106–7.

[26] Singapore diplomat, Mark Hong Tat Soon, cited in Evans, *Cooperating for Peace*, p. 78.

[27] Boutros-Ghali, *Agenda for Peace*, p. 65. For a discussion of relations between the OAU and the UN in the peace and security field, see Berhanykun Andemicael, *The OAU and the UN*, UNITAR Regional Study no. 2, Africana Publishing Company, New York, 1976, Ch. 5.

[28] Saadia Touval, 'Why the UN Fails', *Foreign Affairs*, vol. 73, no. 5, September/October 1994.

[29] Evans, *Cooperating for Peace*, p. 79.

[30] See Robert S. Staley II, *The Wave of the Future: The United Nations and Naval Peacekeeping*, International Peace Academy, Occasional Paper, Lynne Rienner, Boulder, 1992.

[31] Mitsuo Kanazaki, 'International Consultative Mechanisms Related to Maritime Security', in Jozef Goldblat (ed.), *Maritime Security: The Building of Confidence*, UNIDIR (Geneva), United Nations, New York, 1992, pp. 154–55.

[32] Muthiah Alagappa, 'Regionalism and the Quest for Security', p. 448.

[33] Department of Defence, Submission to the Defence Sub-Committee, Joint Standing Committee on Foreign Affairs, Defence and Trade, Inquiry into Australia's Participation in Peacekeeping, 20 September 1993, no. 28, p. S 276.

[34] Gil Watters, 'Regional Cooperation for Peacekeeping', in Smith (ed.), *International Peacekeeping*, p. 106.

[35] *Age*, 13 February 1993; *Australian*, 4 May 1993. Note also the criticism by the Malaysian Prime Minister, Dr Mahathir, of the West's failure to protect the Muslim population of Bosnia: *Age*, 2 September 1992.

[36] J. Mohan Malik, 'Asian Reactions to Australia's Role in the Gulf Crisis', *Current Affairs Bulletin*, April 1991, pp. 20–23.

18 The Regional Security Outlook

Stuart Harris

Introduction

The security environment in the Asia-Pacific region, it would appear, is more benign today than it has been for a long time. For many observers, anxiety about the security outlook is limited to uncertainty about how security relationships will look in the region a decade or two ahead. Given the end of the superpower confrontation, and with the United States (and Russia) less important in the regional security environment, major regional powers such as China and Japan (and perhaps India) have become more significant. The question, then, is whether or not the changed great power relationships are potentially threatening rather than stabilising.

Clearly, the regional security environment has changed fundamentally with developments in the late 1980s and early 1990s. Consequently, the basic assumptions of security policies and the bilateral institutional arrangements that reflected those assumptions no longer hold. The changes — the end of the Cold War with the end of the bipolar confrontation of East and West — were global rather than regional, but they affected the region substantially.

Regional tensions had already declined, particularly with a diminished fear of China's interference in the domestic affairs of regional states, although internal insecurities, while diminishing, are far from absent. Nevertheless, the end of the Soviet threat, Russia's substantial withdrawal from the Cam Ranh Bay naval base in Vietnam and improved Soviet and then Russian relations with China all reshaped the regional security environment. Major ideological differences in the region finally ceased when China accepted the Cambodia agreement in 1991.

In examining the regional security outlook, there are several prior considerations. The first concerns what we mean by the region. Here it covers Northeast Asia, Southeast Asia, North America and some aspects of South Asia, notably the Indian Ocean and the Bay of Bengal.

A second concerns how regional issues link up with global issues. Security concerns of countries such as Japan and South Korea are more than just regional. The Gulf War and the potential of Iraq's attack on Kuwait for oil supply interruptions reminded those, and perhaps other countries, of the continued significance of out-of-region factors.

Global developments also affect attitudes to regional players, particularly the United States. This was illustrated by the undisguised concern of Malaysia and Indonesia at the United States' handling of the Gulf crisis, and then its lack of determination over Bosnia. Moreover, economic interdependencies with countries outside the region make inter-regional relations in the security as well as the economic field inevitable.

Nevertheless, the post-Cold War period has refocused attention on regional issues in which the global links are less clear. Moreover, uncertainty about the regional security environment raises questions about the appropriate regional security approach. For some, including those regretting the loss of past certainties, the search seems to be for a candidate to replace the Soviets as the enemy. For others, security threats are limited for at least a decade or more ahead, but there are many longer term strategic uncertainties. For others again, a different concept of security — and perhaps of the nature of the potential threat — is needed.

Specific links between Pacific security and that in the Atlantic are not large, but Pacific security issues attract some global interest beyond that simply of North Korea's nuclear ambitions and its arms exports, and of the South China Sea. Although Russia, China and Japan are players on the world stage in other respects, important global security linkages include the United States' regional presence and its global role; China, as a permanent Security Council member, a nuclear power and an arms exporter; and the global role seen by the United States for Japan (and increasingly, if hesitantly, by Japan itself).

A third consideration concerns what we mean by security. Traditionally, security in the West was understood predominantly in terms of external military aggression or the protection of the frontiers against attack. Security, however, is now widely seen as extending beyond preserving territorial integrity to include threats to a society's core values and to the institutions that underpin those values.

In the region's recent history, security concerns have come less from external sources than from internal political instability linked to ethnic, religious or ideological disputes, even if often aided from outside. In a number of countries, internal concerns remain the priority, as in China, Burma, Vietnam and Indonesia.[1] External involvement on ideological grounds is now a diminished worry, but internal disputes could flow over borders or result in massive population and refugee flows with major impacts on political stability in the receiving country.

More particularly, we now accept the importance of interrelationships among elements of international relations previously largely looked at separately — such as the link between economic and strategic relations.[2] Although economic development was a major means of overcoming internal security threats, rapid economic growth in the region has also facilitated greater military expenditures by regional states, posing challenges to old orders of stability as differential economic growth rates among the major powers lead to shifts in relative power.

Some smaller countries — Australia among them — look to make up for their relatively small size by maintaining a technological edge in their military capabilities. In the future, this will be increasingly difficult to do. In part, this is a question of cost; in part, it is that the United States, in particular, will be more willing to sell advanced weapons systems less selectively in the region.

A fourth consideration arises from how states in the region perceive security issues. There is, moreover, a question of whose perceptions we are concerned with. Those of security and foreign policy communities often differ, and both at times differ from those of the public. There is no necessary consistency in this respect. Public opinion polls in Japan suggest that the official elites are more concerned about the security environment than is the public. Polls in Australia suggest the reverse; the public expresses significant concern,[3] while the security community is less anxious. How the public perceives the security problem can influence defence planning, at least indirectly.

A fifth consideration relates to the time span involved. Major security threats pose few uncertainties in the short term. Major conflicts take time to implement, and preparations can be observed. For small 'partial' conflicts, this is not so. Nevertheless, strategic assessments of the security environment have to respond to what could be the security developments in the region in the longer term future — anything from ten to 30 years down the track. In most regional countries, the uncertainties of the longer term seem more important than those of the shorter term.

Finally, the security environment includes the institutional framework in place for dealing with security issues. This includes alliances, agreements and arrangements of a bilateral or plurilateral kind, various forms of defence co-operation as well as mechanisms for discussion or dialogue on security issues.

The Asia-Pacific region never fitted easily or fully into the bipolar pattern of East–West relations. Nor did the Cold War context override structural change in the region. Nevertheless, bipolarity greatly influenced the region's security framework. For most of the post-World War II years, the United States–Japan security treaty was seen as underpinning the region's security. It was also part of a regional network of alliances, particularly those with South Korea, the Philippines and Australia (and New Zealand until the mid-1980s) that were designed to contain communism. The United States–Japan security treaty remains important, but in the regional security environment now, a bilateral threat symmetry no longer fits the security environment.

The remainder of this chapter considers, first, the political and strategic changes in the region since the end of the Cold War. After discussing relations among the major powers — the United States, China, Japan, India, Korea and Russia — it looks at how the region perceives regional security issues and the response in terms of military buildups.

Asia-Pacific security, post-Cold War

We need to link assessments of the regional security outlook to the new political and geographic realities in the region. In the immediate post-colonial period, threats from within the region, notably from Indonesia under Sukarno, were major issues for Australia and Malaysia. So, too, were nationalist and post-colonial intra-regime conflicts. For the post-World War II period as a whole, however, the global rivalries of the superpowers and their allies and proxies in the region were seen as the overwhelming source of security threat.

Today, although uncertainties in the 'new world order' exist elsewhere, particular uncertainties arise in the Asia-Pacific region. This is because those new circumstances include considerable fluidity in threat perceptions, a multipolar situation with a number of major powers involved — yet one that exists within an almost unipolar, if constrained, United States global framework. This is accentuated by our limited information about internal thinking and indeed about the impacts of leadership changes in some of the major players, notably China and North Korea.

Despite various bilateral security concerns, no common threat exists in the region. There are currently no major security threats on the regional agenda except perhaps North Korea and that may have now been made more manageable by the United States' Framework Agreement. The earlier major threats — Russia and China and in reverse the United States — have diminished, if not gone. Religious and ethnic differences, important sources of dispute in the past, are still potentially significant. Leaving aside South Asia, however, they are largely limited to Southeast Asia. There they have not yet emerged as major new threats, although they remain troublesome in the southern Philippines, Myanmar and parts of Indonesia and China. Yet, without simply getting into worst case forecasting, it is possible to identify many potential security issues.

First, there are many unresolved issues within the region with potential for conflict apart from the Korean peninsula. These include the PRC–Taiwan relationship, the Japan–China (and Taiwan) dispute over the Senkaku (Diaoyutai) Islands, the Kurile (Northern) Islands dispute between Japan and Russia, unresolved border claims in the South China Sea (the Spratly Islands), Indochina (the continuing internal Cambodian discord or Sino-Vietnamese relations), various unresolved border disputes among the members of ASEAN, border disputes and irredentist pressures between China and the central Asian republics, China's periodic claims on Mongolia and even parts of Siberia, sea lanes between the Pacific and

Indian Oceans, the India–China border, Myanmar's potential capacity to involve regional states, the problems of Bougainville (and possibly the Irian Jaya border) for Papua New Guinea, the PNG–Solomon Islands border, and pressure for political development in New Caledonia.

Second, the established relationships between the major powers are changing. The major powers are seen as competing for influence and the possible realignment of alliance relationships in the region could further affect the geopolitical situation. Traditional concerns about strategic alliances are re-emerging; for example, China would be concerned about too close a strategic relationship between the United States and a more militarily oriented Japan, and South Korea and Russia would not want to see a close strategic relationship between Japan and China.

In Southeast Asia, ASEAN has provided an effective organising framework in which individual countries with often sharp bilateral differences take common positions on broad regional issues. It has also encouraged closer regional links with countries nearby — whether through the Treaty of Amity and Co-operation which has been signed, for example, by Papua New Guinea and Vietnam, and the expectation that at some time Laos, Cambodia and Burma will join ASEAN. The potential for large problems in Indochina has not gone away, despite the progress made in Cambodia. Moreover, the membership of ASEAN by Vietnam will complicate ASEAN relations with China. Nevertheless, major realignments of alliance relationships in Southeast Asia are consequently much less likely since, with the presumed end of the Cambodian conflict, ASEAN members can achieve a common position with respect to non-ASEAN states.

By contrast, positions in Northeast Asia in particular have not been firmly established. To some extent, this situation relates to what is happening on the Korean peninsula. More generally, however, it is that the interests of the major powers interact in the North Pacific, with Russia, China, Japan and the United States all having important strategic interests.

Third, a further concern arises from the region's military capacity, discussed in more detail below. Broadly, however, this includes the large military establishments of Japan, Taiwan and India, the possibility of a united, and perhaps nuclear, Korea, and the military modernisation of China. Moreover, both Russia and the United States maintain formidable, if reduced, military capacities.

Fourth, while economic development has diminished, though not removed, the basis for many threats of internal subversion, non-military threats — political, economic, social and cultural — which could affect basic values and the institutions underpinning the maintenance of those values, have grown in relative importance.

For smaller countries in the region, economic growth in the major economies gives rise to mixed perceptions and dilemmas. Growing economic interdependence is likely to limit overt conflicts and is therefore encouraged; but economic growth also facilitates the buildup of military capabilities which, while it can contribute to the concept of 'overlapping plates of armour', could stimulate this perception.

Broader security concerns have emerged, including potential population movements, international drug traffic and environmental developments. Concerns already exist regionally about possible refugee outflows from North Korea or from China should there be adverse internal developments in those countries; or indeed from Hong Kong if British/Chinese relations do not improve before 1997. For Australia, inflows of boat people on a scale somewhat larger than that of the Indochinese in the 1970s would pose major problems. In addition, drugs are now the second most important internationally traded commodity after oil. And a number of regional states would be adversely affected by any rise in sea levels or increased climatic instability as a result of global climate change.

Other threats to core values, at least for governing regimes, could come from the cultural pressures associated with economic growth. Some interests in China argue that the major threat to China's security comes from cultural impacts of the import of international values and that 'peaceful evolution' threatens to undermine domestic political stability.[4]

Fifth, given the potential for instability in the region, the rapidity of political and economic change and our great lack of information, there has been until recently a critical absence of mechanisms for effective regional discussion about regional security. This situation differs substantially from that in Europe and the North Atlantic. It is changing rapidly, however, with a growing level of official and unofficial security debate, notably in the ASEAN Regional Forum (ARF) and CSCAP (the Council on Security Cooperation in Asia Pacific).[5]

Foreign relations among the regional powers

The United States

Despite talk of United States isolationism and potential withdrawal from the region, despite its economic problems, and despite some lowering of the region's strategic interest to the United States, the United States is unlikely to withdraw from the region and the Pentagon has signalled its intention not to do so.[6] This is because the only attack on its national territory in living memory was in the Pacific; because of its long Pacific coastline; because of Honolulu, Guam and its Micronesian interests; because of its rapid trade growth with Japan and other Asian countries, significantly including sales of military hardware; because of its substantial regional investments; because of the relatively low cost of its presence (compared with a predominantly land force presence); and because of its perception of its manifest destiny and of itself as a naval (particularly a Pacific) power with concerns about the openness of sea lines of communication. Domestic United States pressure will, however, maintain the questioning of regional commitments and the extent of burden sharing.

Perceptions in the region may differ on this, and this is an element of the region's uncertainty that the United States has tried to resolve by its undertaking in the latest version of its security strategy for the East Asia-Pacific region.[7] There is a general acceptance that the United States–Japanese security relationship is an important stabilising factor: for some as a way of ensuring the continued United States presence; for many as a means of limiting Japan's military development, particularly with the acceptance that Japan's regional economic and political influence will grow. Most countries in the region want the United States to stay for what is imprecisely termed 'providing a balance' to the regional great powers and to reduce the uncertainty of what they would perceive otherwise as a power vacuum. Moreover, the economic importance of the United States market for most countries remains. A number, however, would wish for that presence without the assertion of United States values, notably human rights, individualism and United States-style democracy, which they see as imposing stresses in matching demands for economic growth and stability with their development of more open societies over a very short time.

Given the continuing dominance globally of the United States, there is some ambivalence among some countries, including China and members of the non-aligned movement such as Malaysia and Indonesia, about the United States presence. There is no unanimity about the need for such a preponderant external influence. Even Thailand, traditionally a close United States ally, is seeking to renegotiate its treaty of amity with the United States, and it declined to allow the United States to station supply ships in its waters because it is sensitive to Chinese opinion on the matter, as well as to regional feelings against foreign bases. For others, uncertainties remain, less about the United States presence itself than its capacity for unilateral and unpredictable action and, more importantly, in regional conflicts, doubts about what United States policy might be in any particular case.

Given the difficulties in United States economic relations with Japan, as well as its economic tensions and human rights pressures with respect to China and to some extent Indonesia, United States influence may decline in the region unless security issues of concern to, or dependent upon, the United States arise again. This could happen were China to threaten the use of force against Taiwan, or if there was a crisis in the Korean peninsula.

China

China has increased its global importance commensurate with its Security Council membership and its rapid economic growth. Chinese leaders are probably correct in saying that, by the end of the century, China will have the resources to be more powerful, with much greater strategic and economic influence. It has so far pursued a generally constructive approach in the United Nations, in APEC and in Korea. It may be less predictable on issues affecting its sovereignty and it will demand a major role in the economic and political development of the region. Moreover, given its longstanding fears of being encircled by hostile powers, China's overall objective, if not to neutralise the influence of the major powers, is at least to ensure some balance in their influence.

A continuing Chinese interest is its relationship with South Korea which has a higher priority for China than North Korea, At the same time, however, China does not want a nuclear North Korea on its border, and would be concerned at the likely reactions of Japan and South Korea in particular, to such a development. It is probably content with North Korea's weakness and its greater dependence on China.

China remains particularly concerned about United States security policies, especially on the Taiwan issue. With its continuing suspicions of both the United States, with whom it still has major ideological and political differences, and with Japan, and while aware of tensions in the United States–Japanese relationship, China is looking to balance its perception of a United States–Japanese aim to dominate the Asia-Pacific region. As well as enhancing links with South Korea and Russia, this includes extending its influence in Southeast Asia, and developing closer relations with the ASEAN countries. This objective is complicated by China's wish to have, on the one hand, a peaceful environment and good relations with ASEAN. On the other, China aims to recover its sovereignty, notably in the South China Sea,[8] and to meet its often articulated concern about access to the natural resources within its ocean claims. So far, China has been careful to limit any overt conflict over the Spratlys to those in the Vietnamese claim area. (Mischief Reef, taken by China in 1995, although in the Philippines claim area, was an unoccupied reef.)

Unlike the West, for the most part, the Asia-Pacific region was not critical of China over the Tiananmen Square killings, and there has been some coming together over issues such as human rights. The region generally has also been supportive of China on issues such as its trade relationship with the United States. All countries in the region recognise that, given its size, geographic position and the consequent implications for political and strategic influence, China's sustained economic growth has great regional as well as global significance, and that China will be an increasingly important participant in regional security issues. Consequently, the Asian approach has been to encourage China's close involvement in bilateral and regional dialogues on a variety of matters, including security.

In the short term, there is no particular concern for most countries about China's intentions in the region, nor about its capabilities, despite its military modernisation program. China's economic modernisation has been driven by an opening up of the Chinese economy to the international system and this has given China a much greater interest in peaceful relations with its neighbours. There is, however, a recognition that by the early part of the next century, a change of policy by those then in charge in Beijing could have serious regional security implications. On the other hand, the question is whether a change is likely and the nature of such a change. On balance we have expressed cautious optimism that China's interest in avoiding conflict with its neighbours will be paramount, although that will depend to a considerable extent on the policy approach towards China taken by neighbours and others, especially the United States.[9]

Japan

Japan has still to adjust its foreign policy to meet the changed circumstances. Debate within Japan about its global role remains complex, but while there remains no consensus, pressure for a shift from the United States security relationship to greater autonomy seems to have diminished. United States–Japan security relations will remain critical to the region's security outlook as will United States attitudes to Japan's regional security role. Much will depend upon the longer term United States approach towards Japan. The previous United States administration's perception of the United States–Japan relationship as part of a partnership spanning the globe (with a united Europe) was obviously unrealistic — and offered problems to others in the region. United States pressure to see Japan play a larger security role in the region seems also to have diminished.

The economic relationship will dominate United States–Japan relations. Apart from what it sees as the difficulties in that relationship, the United States at present has mixed attitudes towards Japan on the security relationship. Pressure will remain on Japan to carry more of the global security burden, but while Japan accepts that it has to accept a greater international burden,[10] it may not easily accept again a commitment to pay, as in the Gulf War, without greater decision-making involvement. Its interest in becoming a permanent member of the Security Council could involve an increased role in overall security issues through a carefully targeted aid program or greater participation in peacekeeping activities. This could have positive benefits, but could also give rise to some concerns regionally as well as domestically.

The region has accepted, with some hesitation, Japan's limited extension of its maritime security role and has not objected to Japan's desire for more political involvement in the region, as in Indochina. However, unless Japan remains sensitive to regional concerns on that score, there could be adverse regional responses with longer term security implications.

Japan has been the region's principal economic partner for many years. Although regional relationships will continue to be based largely on economic linkages, political factors of a regional or global nature are increasingly important subjects of dialogue and consultation. Although the region accepts Japan's need to become a more 'normal' power, it sees this as coming mainly through increased economic relations, including aid. Japan's involvement in international peacekeeping activities is accepted, but only within a United Nations framework. Given Japan's economic pressures, the changed political situation and continued domestic pacifism, Japan's global and regional military security role is likely to remain small in the absence of fundamental and adverse changes in the region.

Despite China's mixed feelings towards Japan, and Japan's similar attitude towards China, Japan shares to some extent China's concern at a unipolar world in which the United States is the sole superpower with no effective offsetting influence. As well as looking to counter the overwhelming influence of the United States, Japan's security interests include a fear of breakdown in governmental authority in China. Consequently, Japan has sought to establish closer links with China, through aid and increased foreign investment.

Long-term relationships between Russia and Japan have remained cool, but it is hard to see differences over the islands north of Japan leading to conflict. Perhaps also significant in recent years, but less likely now to be pursued, was the suggestion that the Japanese should pressure Russia on the northern islands by providing aid to the Central Asian republics. This, however, could lead to difficulties with the Chinese, already sensitive to irredentist activities in these areas.

India

Although India protested the treatment of Indian-Fijians following the 1989 Fijian coup, its response was limited. India's preoccupation with its own subregional problems, and its disposition to look North and West rather than East, tends to marginalise it in discussions of Asia-Pacific security. More recently, however, India has expressed an interest in a 'look East' policy, and closer relations with ASEAN states. The United States has also given more weight to India as a great power than it did in the past. At the same time, India has been in military conflict with China (the border war of 1962), and has demonstrated its military capabilities against Pakistan and in Goa, Sri Lanka and the Maldives. It has a nuclear capacity (a major motive being to match China's capability) and it competes with China for influence in the border states, notably Nepal and Myanmar. India has also shown an interest in Cambodia, giving early recognition to the Hun Sen government, and in security links with Vietnam.

India faces problems through the collapse of the Soviet Union — both an ally and a major supplier of military equipment. It has significant political and economic problems domestically and in its relations with its neighbours, particularly Pakistan. These will remain major preoccupations. The disintegration of the Soviet Union, contrary to some expectations, made China more, rather than less, relaxed about the China–India border, and opened up opportunities for creative diplomacy and pragmatic problem solving.[11]

India is conscious that China's economic growth rate is substantially above its own, but relations between China and India, although not without problems, have improved substantially since 1987. Troop reductions have occurred along the disputed border areas, and sustained attempts made on both sides to negotiate a peaceful solution to a border dispute which in principle should be capable of a negotiated settlement. India's views differ from those of China on some things — such as on Cambodia and Pakistan. On others, however, such as the United States' view of the new world order, human rights or the problems of developing countries, and issues arising in international institutions, they are often in accord.

Although there is scope for misunderstandings between India and China — for example, over India's nuclear and missile development, the future of Tibet, Chinese influence in Myanmar and Nepal, missile sales to Pakistan and Chinese maritime claims in the South China Sea — both countries have considerable interest in maintaining the current relatively good relationship into the future.[12]

Korea

Disputes on the Korean peninsula, including concerns with North Korea's nuclear ambitions, link up with the broader question of Korean reunification. The decline in the North's economy, accentuated by reduced economic aid from Russia and China, is such that, without opening up its economy, fears are held by its neighbours of increased internal disorder. Given the economic burden that a collapse of North Korea would imply for South Korea, as well as a fear of a major refugee flow, the South has some interest in maintaining the present regime in power in North Korea, or at least not seeing its early collapse. On the other hand, increased contact with the South threatens a gradual diminution of the authority of the governing regime in North Korea. Indeed, the slight thawing with respect to the United States, and the North's achievement of its long-held aim for direct negotiations with the United States, has been accompanied by hardening approaches to the South and vice versa.

Were North Korea's nuclear ambitions not to be resolved satisfactorily, despite progress to date, significant shifts in regional power balances could follow. Not only would South Korea, and possibly Japan, respond, but so probably would the rest of the region, with major effects on security perceptions. The effects, however, would not just be regional. A further dimension of a North Korean nuclear capacity would be the reduced credibility of the nuclear non-proliferation regime and of proliferation of weapons of mass destruction generally, with major global implications. For the moment, the region has been reassured by North Korea's commitment to abandon the nuclear option and take its first steps towards a normalised relationship with the rest of the Asia-Pacific community.

Russia

The current Russian regime has been attempting to develop closer relations with the ASEAN countries as well as with its regional neighbours. In general, it has basically withdrawn from any substantial involvement in Southeast Asia, concentrating its limited attention, outside its non-European and central Asian interests, substantially on Northeast Asia. There, concerns do exist at a possible revival of a xenophobic nationalism in Russia. They are likely to have been accentuated by recent developments in Russia, and by the continuing bellicose statements of the leader of Russia's ultra-conservative Liberal-Democratic Party, Mr Zhirinovsky.

Russia has increased economic and political links with China and discussions over common borders are proceeding co-operatively. There is, however, considerable unease in Russia's Maritime Territory at Moscow's border concessions to Beijing[13] and concern at the growing number of illegal Chinese immigrants. Links with Japan remain difficult and President Yeltsin has looked to closer relations with China as a means of putting pressure on Japan and the United States.[14] Russia sees links with South Korea as a valuable offset to continuing difficulties with Japan, balancing the influence of Japan and China in the Koreas.

Threat perceptions and regional military capabilities

The widely held regional perception is that there is no current high-level threat to territory, nor any militarily hostile intentions on the part of regional neighbours. Although intentions can change, in most cases it would be possible to foresee any changes in capabilities sufficient to pose a more direct threat and, presumably, to counter them. Yet arms purchases have risen rapidly in the region. By the early 1990s, the Asia-Pacific region had experienced a sustained buildup of modern conventional weapons systems for the best part of a decade.

In one sense, the expansion of arms purchases in the region need not be a concern. The appropriateness of such unconcern depends upon the motivations involved and motivations are not always clear. Except in Korea and Taiwan, arms purchases appear only partly to be a response to perceived threats. Nevertheless, in Southeast Asia, the South China Sea disputes have already been used, together with India's naval expansion, to justify increased arms purchases. The growth in military expenditures results from various factors, including the region's economic growth, which facilitates increased expenditures; perceived needs to increase military self-reliance, associated with expected reductions in the United States presence; greater need for maritime surveillance and maritime defence capabilities, enhanced by extended maritime boundaries under the United Nations' law of the sea; requirements for defence modernisation involving more sophisticated (and more expensive) equipment; and the needs of prestige.[15] The availability of equipment not now needed elsewhere and pressure from arms suppliers, notably the United States and Russia, have also contributed, as has the influence of corruption.

Threat perceptions in the region have always been more diffuse than in Europe. Although there is now some regional convergence on the characteristics of security concerns, particularly their largely maritime nature, fears of internal disintegration and localised rivalries remain important in various parts of the region.

While military expenditures are likely to grow, they continue to reflect a declining share of national income in most countries in the region.

We concluded earlier that the United States would maintain a significant, if smaller, presence in the region. Given the closing of United States bases in the Philippines, the United States has negotiated new naval access arrangements with Singapore, Malaysia and Indonesia, as well as continued but lower level arrangements with the Philippines. Nevertheless, some states want the assurance of an upgraded security capacity. Malaysia's Prime Minister Mahathir, commenting on plans to double Malaysia's defence spending over the next five years, argued that Southeast Asia should not rely on the United States to act as the region's policeman.[16]

The powerful, if reduced, Russian military capacity in the Far East, and its nuclear capacity, remain potential security concerns. Although no immediate anxiety is evident at present, the possibility of a change in the Russian leadership, or of changed policies within the existing leadership, remains, with implications for Japan, China and Korea in particular.

In addition to the immediate issue of the events on the Korean peninsula and the sense of threat on both sides of the demilitarised zone, the Korean situation is central to many of the regional threat perceptions of the major powers, notably Japan, China and Russia. Korean unification, for example, would put pressure on Korea's immediate neighbours. A united Korea of 70 million people with a large military and economic capacity could contribute to regional stability as a buffer state between the major powers, but there would be negative responses if a reunified Korea inherited the nuclear capabilities of the North. Short of reunification, with a nuclear-capable North, South Korea could still argue its own need for nuclear weapons. Domestic pressure on Japan to take the nuclear path would then grow. It would also involve more basic attitudes about the regional role of the United States, with the United States nuclear umbrella again being seen as a major element of regional security.

Japan is a major military power. Its defence budget is large and, if assessed according to NATO accounting procedures, would be the third largest defence budget in the world. Weapons systems are being systematically upgraded to advanced levels of technology, Japan is extending the range of its air coverage and aerial surveillance capacity, and is planning an enhanced naval capability. Defence expenditure in Japan is being contained and cuts in the numbers of personnel of up to 20 per cent have been foreshadowed.

Japan's threat perceptions gave considerable emphasis to economic security during the Cold War, perhaps more so than military security.[17] In part, this was possible under the protection of the United States–Japan Security Treaty. Now, although watchful of Russian developments and suspicious of China's naval modernisation, Japan is more concerned with developments on the Korean peninsula, not only with North Korea's nuclear developments but with missiles capable of reaching Tokyo.

To Japan, China is not yet a significant military threat, although Japan is wary of increasing Chinese influence in Southeast Asia, Myanmar and Cambodia, in part because of its concerns about its sea lines of communication. Japan is mostly concerned, however, with the threat from China of 'the disruptive effects of disorder, instability, perhaps even Soviet style disintegration in China which would result in thousands, even millions, of boat people heading for Japan'.[18]

Border disputes have existed for a long time in the East, as well as in the South China Sea. China (and Taiwan)'s dispute with Japan over the Senkaku (Diaoyutai) Islands is stirred from time to time — must recently by China's occupation of Mischief Reef in the Spratly Islands. Japan sees this as part of China's incremental recovery of lost territory and, carried to its logical conclusion, it could lead to renewed disputation between Japan and China over the Senkakus.

In the South China Sea, where most Southeast Asian nations have unresolved disputes with China and among themselves, there is occasional sabre rattling or symbolic gestures of some significance from time to time by various of the claimants. The largest power, China, has maintained that it would not use force to resolve the Spratly island issue. Although resources are not the only question at issue over the islands — sea lines of communication and simple sovereignty questions are also important — China has said that it would set aside sovereignty issues and negotiate for joint development of the resources in the sea around the islands.

China remains watchful over the military capability of a nuclear-armed Russia. China's threat perceptions also extend to its southern borders. It has traditionally supported Pakistan, taking Pakistan's side on a number of issues in dispute with India, including Kashmir. It is worried about the Islamic insurgency in Kashmir, given its own problems with Muslim separatists. It opposes independence for Kashmir because of fears that such an independent state would be a potential United States surrogate on China's southern border, adding to what it claims is United States influence in the disturbed situation in Xinjiang and Tibet.[19]

China has a numerically large military. It continues to develop its nuclear capacity and missiles for delivery and probably a chemical weapons capacity. It is modernising its armed forces, but despite that commitment, China's current emphasis remains on the domestic needs of its economic modernisation program.

China's naval capacity is growing, with an increasing, if still small, presence in the South China Sea and beyond. Its quality is also being improved and its capacity increased to sustain operations farther from shore and for longer periods. China has also purchased a small number of modern Russian aircraft. These developments — Chinese arms acquisitions and increases in Chinese defence spending, together with the well-publicised interest of the PLA Navy in an aircraft carrier — have caused some apprehension in the region. However, China has sought to reassure its neighbours that its emphasis on peaceful relations and the peaceful resolution of disputes will continue.

It is hard to see much reason for such concern at present. China has reduced its military forces from a peak of 4.7 million to a little over 3 million; its military strategy has shifted to coping with short-duration conflicts on its borders and to protecting its maritime interests; when adjusted for inflation, the increases in its budget are much smaller, even 'very meagre';[20] most of its aircraft and its submarine fleet is old and substantially obsolete; and military modernisation is still not receiving a high priority in Chinese budgetary allocations. Consequently, China's power projection capacity, presently small, is likely to remain so for some considerable time.[21] In addition, China has some 21 borders to protect (fifteen land and six ocean borders), most disputed in some degree. It needs a capacity to defend those borders that makes comparisons with the defence capacities of other countries in a more secure position — such as Australia — somewhat problematic.

Nevertheless, apart from its capacity for political (and policy) instability, China's military capacity is seen by many as posing the major long-term security threat to the region. China's efforts to expand and modernise, although still limited, reflect its desire to be able to defend its position in the Spratly Islands, to protect its sea lanes in the South and East China seas, to provide a credible threat to Taiwan if judged necessary, to project power in other adjoining maritime areas in which potential disputes exist, to match Japan's substantial maritime capacities, and presumably, to back political coercion elsewhere if necessary.

For China, United States influence in Taiwan, including the provision of arms, is seen as threatening China's sovereignty. No Chinese leader wants to be the one that 'lost' Taiwan, especially as in post-Deng Xiaoping China, the Taiwan issue could become a source of competition and rivalry in China, in Taiwan and between China, Japan and the United States.

Taiwan's security perceptions are dominated by the repeated threat by China to use force should the island declare independence. Again, pessimists see this as a real threat, with concerns at conflict escalation involving the United States (and possibly Japan). Firm moves towards independence would cause a major upset. Hong Kong's experience will be very relevant, less as an example than as a stimulus to Taiwan's independence supporters if things go wrong. An optimistic view, however, is that the Chinese threats are a necessary bluff, without which Taiwan may well move towards formal independence. China's naval buildup, although still not very substantial, does reflect an underlying aim on the part of China's military to be prepared for such a contingency. At present, however, China has a limited capacity to blockade Taiwan, but cannot take threats of military action much further.

India is a large military power. For example, in the region — apart from the United States — only China and Russia have more military aircraft. India's planned naval expansion has been limited by financial constraints but the intention remains to expand, including the upgrading of naval and air facilities in the Bay of Bengal. Some Southeast Asian nations have expressed concern at India's potential for expanded influence.[22] Regional attention has been directed particularly to the upgrading of India's naval and air facilities on its island territories (the Andaman and Nicobar Islands) in the Indian Ocean close to Sumatra. In the longer term, India and China are potential regional rivals and developments in Indian policies and military buildups will be watched cautiously by Southeast Asian states, and by others to whom the sea lanes through the Indian Ocean and the Malacca Straits are important.

Conclusion

Despite these regional developments, it is possible to foresee a continuation of the remarkable degree of peace and stability currently in place in the Asia-Pacific region. There is less insecurity and more opportunities for co-operation and confidence-building than at any time in the recent past. This reflects a continued United States presence because of continued American interests in the region, 'Japan's non-military strategy, China's huge domestic preoccupations, relative restraint in defence expenditure by China, Japan and India and the mosaic of interlocking economic interests and military capabilities that have developed in ASEAN and East Asia over the last two decades'.[23]

Nevertheless, in view of the continued growth in arms expenditures and the potential for escalating arms buildups and conflict from misperception and inadvertence, multilateral mechanisms for security dialogue in the region will grow in importance. Hence the importance of increased development of confidence-building, mutual trust and exchanges of different perspectives. For this reason, regional security forums, both of a first track and second track diplomacy nature, such as the ARF and, potentially, CSCAP have a major contribution to make to maintaining the region's peace and stability.

In developing new security arrangements, the growth in self-confidence of the nations in the region that economic development has engendered and their need for more equitable treatment by major powers will need to be accommodated. Given the concern at the unilateral nature of United States policy development during the Cold War years, multilateralising the debate on regional security policy might help deal with the new situation and respond to those new needs in a positive fashion.

Notes

[1]   Dewi Anwar Fortuna, 'Indonesia's Regional Outlook', in Chandran Jeshuran (ed.), *China, India and Japan and the Security of Southeast Asia*, Institute of Southeast Asian Studies, Singapore, 1993, p. 226.

2   Stuart Harris, 'The Economic Aspects of Security in the Asia-Pacific Region', *Journal of Strategic Studies*, vol. 17, no. 3, September 1995.

3   Pauline Kerr and Andrew Mack, 'The Future of Asia Pacific Security Studies: Australia', paper to a conference on The Future of Asia Pacific Security Studies and Exchange Activities, Bali, 12–15 December 1993.

4   Stuart Harris, 'Reading the Chinese Tea Leaves', in Stuart Harris and Gary Klintworth (eds), *China as a Great Power: Myths, Realities and Challenges in the Asia-Pacific Region*, Longman Cheshire and St Martins Press, Melbourne and New York, 1995.

5   Jusuf Wanandi, 'The Future of ARF and CSCAP in the Regional Security Architecture', paper to the 8th Pacific Roundtable, ASEAN-ISIS, Kuala Lumpur, 8 June 1994.

6   United States Department of Defense, 'United States Security Strategy for the East Asia Region', US Wireless File, 27 February 1995.

7   Joseph Nye, Assistant Secretary of Defense, comments, USIS Worldnet Interview, 7 March 1995.

8   Chen Jie, 'Major Concerns in China's ASEAN Policy', in Chandran Jeshuran (ed.), *China, India and Japan and the Security of Southeast Asia*, p. 161.

9   Stuart Harris and Gary Klintworth, 'China and the Region After Deng' in Stuart Harris and Gary Klintworth (eds), *China as a Great Power*.

10 Ichiro Ozawa, *Blueprint for a New Japan*, Kodansha International, Tokyo, 1994.

11 Gary Klintworth, *The Practice of Common Security: China's Border with Russia and India*, CAPs Paper No 4, Chinese Council of Advanced Policy, Tapei, October 1993.

12 Mohan Malik, 'Conflict Patterns and Security Environment in the Asia Pacific Region — The Post-Cold War Era', in Kevin Clements (ed.), *Peace and Security in the Asia-Pacific Region: Post-Cold War Problems and Prospects*, Dunmore Press, Napier, 1993, pp. 31–57.

13 Interfax, Moscow/BBC Monitoring Service, 15 February 1995.

14 G. Christofferson, 'The Greater Vladivostok Project: Transitional Linkages in Regional Economic Planning', East-West Center, Hawaii (unpublished).

15 Desmond Ball, *Trends in Military Acquisitions in the Region: Implications for Security and Prospects for Constraints and Controls*, Working Paper No. 273, Strategic and Defence Studies Centre, Research School of Pacific Studies, The Australian National University, Canberra, July 1993.

16 *Age* (Melbourne), 22 December 1993, p. 6.

17 Nobutoshi Akao (ed.), *Japan's Economic Security*, Gower, London, 1983.

18 Brian Bridges, 'Japan: Hesitant Superpower', *Conflict Studies 264*, Research Institute for the Study of Conflict and Terrorism, London, September 1993.

[19]   *Far Eastern Economic Review*, 13 January 1994.

[20]   Harlan Jenks, cited in Gary Klintworth and Desmond Ball, 'China's Arms Buildup and Regional Security' in Stuart Harris and Gary Klintworth (eds), *China as a Great Power*.

[21]   John Caldwell, *China's Conventional Military Capabilities, 1994–2004*, Center for Strategic and International Studies, Washington, 1994.

[22]   Klintworth, 'The Practice of Common Security', p. 21.

[23]   Klintworth and Ball, 'China's Arms Buildup and Regional Security', p. 2.

19 Conclusions

Gary Klintworth

S o where do the preceding eighteen chapters leave us? James Richardson finds the case for pessimism about the security outlook for the Asia-Pacific region to be wanting. Despite uncertainties, he concludes that there are grounds for cautious optimism. These include the continued engagement of the United States in the Western Pacific, the likelihood of continued strong economic growth and the development of multilateralism and regional economic, diplomatic and infrastructural co-operation.

There is an absence of perceptions of threat — in the orthodox sense — in the Asia-Pacific region, whether imminent or in the next seven or eight years. Of course, as Leszek Buszynski and Bob Lowry point out in their respective chapters on Southeast Asia and Indonesia, security for developing societies is a broader concept than military security, and embraces ethnic, economic, social and religious considerations. There are uncertainties about Indonesia, as the chapters by Buszynki and Lowry both point out. Indonesia's future looks as opaque, certainly to outsiders, as does post-Deng China. In terms of geography, moreover, the ASEAN states inevitably worry about China and its future role in the region. Nonetheless, as Buszynski observes, for most of the ASEAN states, the region security outlook has never been more favourable. According to Lowry, Indonesia perceives no threat of a major conflict with any other state.

The indigenous economic and military capabilities that the ASEAN states, Japan, South Korea and Taiwan have developed over the last two decades have helped stabilise the region. In particular, the rapid economic growth of the ASEAN states and the accompanying buildup of their defence capabilities — described in the chapter by Graeme Cheeseman and Richard Leaver — has created what the United States Defence Department describes as a layer of 'overlapping plates of armour'.[1] In effect, while non-communist countries in the region are more self-reliant and better able to resist overt or other forms of pressure from larger powers, none of them possesses significant military power. Indonesia, for example — the largest of the ASEAN states — does not possess power projection capabilities while Taiwan's security relies on deterrence based on strong, defensive (rather than offensive) capabilities. These capabilities are conducive to regional peace and stability and, in turn, Australia's northern approaches are more secure.

The South Pacific, concludes Stephen Henningham, is essentially pacific, apart from small peacekeeping mediation issues. There is no foreseeable external threat to the South Pacific region, mainly because it has been and remains effectively part of the United States and Australian sphere of influence.

Forecasts of great power rivalry in the wake of a United States withdrawal overlook important and continuing American interests in the Western Pacific. Coral Bell concludes that the United States remains the necessary 'balancer' in the region and that alarmist theses about some kind of United States withdrawal or 'disinvolvement' are contradicted by the facts of geography and demography: the United States is pre-eminently the Pacific power. Stuart Harris draws the same conclusion.

There is no foreseeable challenge to American naval dominance of the Asia-Pacific. The former Soviet military presence at Cam Ranh Bay and Danang and in the Indian Ocean, once an obsessive preoccupation for regional defence analysts, is no more.[2] America has unmatched military power and influence throughout the Western Pacific, a dominance that it is likely to retain until well into the next century. Indeed, as Leaver and Cheeseman suggest, the military technology gap is likely to continue to widen in favour of the United States. In any event, the United States' role of balancing other powers in the region is one that most countries support, including China and Japan. China is reassured by the United States' containment of Japan, while Japan is reassured by the United States' role in balancing China, Russia and the Koreas.

Japan's defensive strategy has not changed, according to Richard Leaver. What has changed in the last few years is the acceptance, certainly by Australia, of the need for Japan to play a larger role in the region. In 1984, in contrast, Australia's position was that any expansion of Japanese defence activity in the Asia-Pacific region was not to be encouraged. Leszek Buszynski notes a similarly relaxed attitude about Japan amongst most of the ASEAN states.

Several of the ASEAN states, however, are acquiring advanced weapons systems. China is buying modern aircraft and submarines from Russia. Taiwan has contracts for modern fighter aircraft from the United States and France. Is there an arms race underway? Leaver and Cheeseman conclude that, while there has been an upgrading of regional arms inventories, and force modernisation for a variety of reasons, the suggestion that there is an arms race is misleading. They concede that the growing economic potential of the region could sustain an arms race but, for the moment, their view is that such a judgment is premature. This view is supported by trends in defence expenditure as a percentage of GNP. In nearly all cases, including China, the ratio has either declined or remained steady whereas an arms race should be accompanied by rising shares of national product devoted to the military. This is not the case in the Asia-Pacific region at present.

Elsewhere, Japan feels much less threatened from the north.[3] It is cutting its defence forces by 20 per cent. If Russia does solve the Northern Territories issue, the door to Russian–Japanese rapprochement and co-operation could open. Meanwhile, Japan is promoting a new version of its old vision of a sphere of co-prosperity in the Asia-Pacific based on Japan's wealth and vigour, more aid programs, and continued close co-operation with the United States. This would facilitate implementation of the Japanese vision of an Asia-Pacific region built on co-operation, peace and stability — or what Jimmy Carter and Yasuhiro Nakasone called 'structural coordination and harmonisation' of the Japanese and American economies'.[4] This is not impossible to attain given the common global economic, political and security interests of the two countries.[5] With 40 per cent of the world's GNP between them, both declared in the Tokyo Global Joint Action Plan that they had forged a global partnership with special responsibility for shaping the new world era.[6]

In the Korean peninsula, inter-Korean talks have reached their most promising phase since the early 1970s. South Korea worries more about how it will digest the North rather than how it might deal with a surprise attack. Ian Wilson, however, adds a note of caution about North Korea, not least because the North Korean political system is particularly 'opaque' and because of complex political changes both there and in Washington, South Korea and Japan. Nonetheless, he concludes that there is a reformist wing in Pyongyang that, given time, is likely to shift North Korea away from its current status as a troublemaking regional 'flashpoint'.

China is free from external threats for the first time in perhaps two centuries — good reason, perhaps, why smaller states might feel threatened by their large neighbour. But China has improved relations with all its neighbours in the Asia-Pacific, including Indonesia, Singapore, Taiwan and Vietnam. Relations with India, once threatened by a renewed border war in 1987, have markedly improved. Issues that could lead to tension involving China and its neighbours revolve around disputed claims to islands and maritime resources in the East and South China Sea but, as Jim Richardson points out, these are not matters which tend to generate great wars. China has offered to put aside the sovereignty issue in the interests of joint economic development. However, China will need to review its hard-nosed approach in disputes over island territories with smaller neighbours such as Vietnam and the Philippines if it wants to avoid fuelling easily aroused perceptions of an expansionist great power China. There are some signs that China is sensitive to these fears — for example, its willingness to ratify the UN Convention on the Law of the Sea, and clarify the extent of its ocean claims in the South China Sea.

Gary Klintworth suggests that much of the instability and conflict in the Asia-Pacific region over the last century stemmed from China's poverty, its insecurity and weak defences. A relatively confident China, secure internally and externally — a China that can feed a quarter of the world's population and provide an economic stimulus for the dynamism of the Asia-Pacific community, including Taiwan — ought to be conducive to regional stability. China's rapprochement with Japan and the United States in the 1970s has been matched by a normalised Sino–Russian relationship. This has contributed directly to tension reduction in the Korean peninsula and conflict resolution in Indochina, notably Cambodia. The end of the Cold War and China's open door policy have also provided new opportunities for Taiwan. As China and Taiwan draw together economically, military tension in the Taiwan Strait has eased, notwithstanding sabre-rattling reminders from Beijing of its claim to a right to use force if Taiwan tries to secede.[7]

Russia has halved troop levels on the border near China and is preoccupied with its internal affairs. Currently it perceives 'no potential foe in the area'.[8] It has played a positive role in the Korean peninsula and seeks to join the mainstream of the Asia-Pacific community. As Greg Austin and Tim Callan conclude in their chapter, Russia is in the position of supplicant and there is therefore little likelihood that it will be able or would desire to play a destabilising role in the region in the foreseeable future.

India is likely to remain preoccupied with its internal affairs. Its nuclear program and relations with Pakistan will persist as ongoing issues. So too will the extent to which India's interest in neutralising China coalesces with that of the United States and the countries of Southeast Asia. According to Sandy Gordon, however, New Delhi does not want to lose the benefits that have accrued from its current rapprochement with China. India, moreover, is unlikely to emerge as an Indian Ocean power, let alone a great power, for at least another decade or more. It lacks force projection capabilities — indeed, the Indian navy is shrinking while the Indian air force consists mainly of tactical fighters with no long-range strike or air-to-air refuelling capabilities.

Vietnam has significantly reduced its armed forces. It retains its instinctive fear of China and, while it disputes Chinese claims to islands in the South China Sea, it has come to terms with China, secured its borders with Cambodia and in 1995 it normalised relations with the United States and Japan. Indochina is in transition, as Carl Thayer observes, from being a zone of contention to becoming three discrete states moving towards market economies, with doors open to foreign investment and membership of ASEAN.

The chapters by Andrew Elek and Peter Rimmer suggest that spreading transport and communications networks and market forces are beginning to overwhelm old political divides. Thus the opportunities for, and the demands of regional economic co-operation are growing stronger and stronger. This will not prevent war, but it makes conflict less likely. Co-operation and preservation of regional peace and stability are becoming a preferred option for most states in the Asia-Pacific region. The APEC mechanism, in particular, helps to reinforce good neighbour policies of pragmatism, mutual benefit, regular dialogue, transparency, consensus building and the peaceful settlement of disputes. Countries with economic credentials like Japan, South Korea and Taiwan are gaining increased influence, a trend that other states — including China, Vietnam and in due course perhaps North Korea — will seek and are seeking to emulate.

As Trevor Findlay concludes, the Asia-Pacific region is entering a fascinating era in which genuine attempts are being made to establish a co-operative security regime. The recently signed Australia–Indonesia Agreement on Maintaining Security is the latest example of this positive regional trend. As Singapore's deputy prime minister and defence minister, Tony Tan, observed, the Agreement was another 'building block in a web of measures to ensure peace in the region'.[9] Desmond Ball agrees with this judgment in his chapter on the institutionalisation of what has been a proliferation of security and confidence-building proposals in the Asia-Pacific region in the last few years. However, Ball questions whether the new co-operative institutions will be strong enough to manage the extraordinary changes and the increasing complexities that he claims characterise the regional security environment.

One of the problems in analysing security in the Asia-Pacific region might be that many analysts lack an understanding of Asian culture and history, Asian concepts of 'face' and consensus (mentioned by Bob Lowry), as well as the Asian sense of nuance. Too often, analysts resort to Eurocentric realist perspectives on international relations and conflict resolution when the reality is that the countries of the Asia-Pacific region are, for the first time in over a century, defining their security priorities and policies free from the pressures and the conflicts imposed on them by external, mainly European, great powers.

Of course, not all the indicators are positive and reassuring, and ten, let alone twenty, years is a long long way down the track. Reassurances will be need to be given — most of all, perhaps, both to China and by China. There will be also need to be adjustments and realignments as small states in the Western Pacific adjust to the rise of a greater China. In many ways, much of that adjustment and realignment has already occurred. Challenges posed by existing disputes and uncertainties, such as how Japan, China and the United States adjust to their new post-Cold War roles and the future of China and its defence and foreign policies — if and when it comes a superpower — will no doubt weigh heavily on the minds of regional security analysts. These dilemmas are flagged by Stuart Harris.

But, as Harris points out, the positive trends and the opportunities, not least the growing habit of dialogue on co-operation and security in the Asia-Pacific, should not be overlooked. In Korea and Cambodia, the major powers amply demonstrated a capacity to move regional co-operation beyond mere dialogue and consultations. In the United Nations-spon-sored Cambodian peace settlement, as discussed in the chapter by Hugh Smith, regional states demonstrated their ability to work together in a practical co-operative manner. In particular, there was a substantial con-tribution of personnel and a commitment to co-operation from countries as diverse as Japan, China, Australia and several of the ASEAN countries. If the Asia-Pacific region is ready to co-operate and if the time is ripe for a regional forum on co-operative security, it is precisely because the insti-tutional building blocks and the attitudinal ones are already well estab-lished. As the latest version of United States Strategy for the East Asia-Pacific Region concluded:

> the increased economic integration and interdependence of the Asia-Pacific region has given nations a shared interest in preserving the peace that underpins their prosperity. Because relations among the major powers in Asia are more constructive than at any time in the past century, the post Cold War period provides an excellent and unique opportunity to shape a positive and cooperative security environment in the Asia-Pacific region.[10]

It is a case of "seize the moment, seize the hour", something that regional leaders have shown they have grasped at the APEC meeting in Osaka in November 1995, and at the ASEAN Leaders' Summit in Bangkok in December 1995.

Notes

[1] US Department of Defense, *United States Security Strategy for the East Asia-Pacific Region*, Washington, February 1995, p. 14.

[2] Admiral James Lyons, Commander-in-Chief of the US Pacific Fleet said whilst in Sydney in February 1987 that the former Soviet base at Cam Ranh Bay had 'resulted in the most dramatic change in the world strategic out-look since the Soviet invasion of Afghanistan', *Australian*, 10 February 1987.

[3] *Age*, 16 October 1991. This report refers only to a peace treaty. Sources in the Japanese Foreign Ministry mentioned the possibility of a non-aggression pact once the Northern Territories are returned to Japan.

[4] ibid. See also the *Japan–US Alliance and Security Regimes in East Asia*, A Workshop Report prepared by Ralph Cossa, Institute for International Policy Studies, Tokyo Centre for Naval Analysis, Virginia, 1995.

[5] Masashi Nishihara, 'Japan–US Security Cooperation: A Japanese Per-spective', *Symposium*, Tokyo, 9–10 May 1991.

[6] *Australian*, 10 January 1992. See also Ichiro Ozawa, *Blueprint for a New Japan: The Rethinking of a Nation*, Kodansha International, Tokyo, 1994.

7   *A Study of a Possible Communist Attack on Taiwan*, GIO, Taipei, 1991, p. 12. Chinese President Yang Shangkun's warning to Taiwan that 'those who play with fire will perish by fire' (*Australian*, 15 October 1991) matches Taiwanese Premier Hau Pei-tsun's view, expressed when he was Defence Minister, that 'if Chinese communist forces invaded Taiwan to stop it becoming independent, his armed forces would not fight them': *Free China Journal*, 25 December 1989. Both have a common interest in maintaining the credibility of a threat from the mainland.

8   Colonel Timofei Leshchov, a Russian Far East military spokesman, cited in *China Post*, Taipei, 27 May 1992.

9   Quoted in the *Australian Financial* Review, 21 December 1995.

10 US Department of Defense, *United States Security Strategy for the East Asia-Pacific Region*, p. 13.

Index

ABRI, 95, 96, 97, 99, 100, 107
ACDA, 198, 201, 204
Aceh, 95, 96, 130, 261
advanced weapons systems, 294
Agreed Framework, 113, 115, 116, 117
Agreement on Advance Notification of Strategic Exercises, 229
Agreement on Dangerous Military Activities, 229
Agreement on Notification of Ballistic Missile Tests, 229
air forces, regional, 211
air safety standards, 171
air transport, 188–192
  air routes, 188–90
  airports, 190–92
  in China, 189
Ali Alitas, 120, 121, 122
alliance relationships, changes in, 1
American Micronesia, 148
Anti-Ballistic Missile Treaty, 222
ANZUS alliance, 29, 55, 150
APEC, 1, 15, 16, 36, 38, 44, 58, 73, 86, 102, 125, 177, 238
  Bogor Declaration, 162, 175
  emergence of, 160–61
  Framework for Trade and Investment Co-operation, 162
  heads of government meeting, 234
  Indian membership of, 75
  Indonesian commitment to, 100

influence of ASEAN, 169
initiatives, 168
involvement in security issues, 234–35
Japanese support for, 53
objectives of, 161–62
policy-oriented consultations, 174
product standards, 168
and regional stability, 160–76
role of, 172
sectoral working groups, 173
Seoul Declaration, 161, 162, 165
structure, 166
APEC IV, 162
ARF, 1, 36, 76, 254, 255
armies, regional, 211
arms buildup, 7, 13
  regional, 14–15
arms control agreements
  bilateral, 231
  multilateral, 231
arms control, measures, 30, 211, 219–44
  multilateral, 220
  nuclear, 221–26
arms exports, 212–14
arms imports, 203–10
  conventional weapons, 204
  increased sophistication of, 210
  major weapons imports, 203
  value, 203
arms market, 212
arms production, 212–14

in ASEAN countries, 213
    domestic, 211
arms race, 294–95
    regional, 1, 43
    social indicators of, 198–201
arms sales, by China, 41–42
arms spending, 286
    trends in, 198–218
arms trade, conventional, 198–218
arms transfer agreements, 41
ASEAN, 2, 7, 10, 15, 16, 24, 40, 55, 72, 73,
    102, 120, 161, 165, 172, 175, 231, 232, 235,
    236–40, 238, 272
ASEAN-PMC, 236, 237, 250, 251, 252, 254
ASEAN ISIS, 250, 251, 252, 255
    countries, 33
    and India, 74
    and Indochina, 144
    and Indonesia, 102–3
    influence on APEC, 169
    Institutes of Strategic and International
        Studies, 235
    and Japan, 56, 123, 125
    Leaders' Summit, 298
    multilateralism, 125; as regional organi-
        sation, 127; Foreign Ministers Meeting,
        86, 237
    Post-Ministerial Conferences, 16, 86, 248
    Regional Forum, 16, 37, 38, 43, 44, 73, 86,
        215, 237–40, 248, 249, 280
    and regional security dialogue, 236–38
    Senior Officials Meeting, 237, 249, 253, 255
    Vietnam's membership of, 279
ASEAN Declaration, 104
Asia Development Bank, 179, 184
Asia Pacific Economic Cooperation
    (APEC), see APEC
Asia-Pacific community, 17
Asia-Pacific Investment Code, 170, 174
Asia-Pacific Roundtable, 15, 250
Asian Arms Transfer Register, 238
Asian identity, 19
Asian tigers, 66
Association of Southeast Asian Nations
    (ASEAN), see ASEAN
Association of Southeast Asian Nations
    Regional Forum (ARF), see ARF
Australia's Strategic Planning in the 1990s,
    52–54, 57, 58
Australia
    as aid donor, 149
    as part of Asia, 150
    as regional player, 149–50
    economic relationships, 149
    international trade, 166
    role in region, 157
    security, 28–29

Australia–Indonesia Agreement on Main-
    taining
    Security, 297
Australia–Japan Business Cooperation
    Committee, 15
Australia–Japan relations, 50–64
    economic relations, 57, 58–61
Australia–US relations, 24, 51
American alliance, 51
    nuclear bases in Australia, 30
    special relationship, 51, 56–57
    trade and, 30–31

Baht Zone, 162
ballistic missiles, support of, 227
Berlin Wall, collapse of, 52, 57
bilateralism, 31
bilateral relations, 36
Biological Weapons Convention (BWC), 228
    Review Conference, 228
biological weapons, 221
biological disarmament, 227–28
bipolarity, 277
Bogor Declaration, 162, 175
border disputes, 7, 278, 288
    agreements with China, 36
    Indian–Chinese, 278
    in Indochina, 140–41
    Russo-Japanese, 7
    Sabah–Kalimantan, 102, 261
    Sino-Russian, 7, 85
    Sino-Indian, 7
Bougainville, 151–52, 154, 155, 157–57, 261,
    265, 269
British Commonwealth Micronesia, 148
Burma, 261
Bush, George, 24, 27, 29, 30, 31, 222, 233

Cam Ranh Bay, 275, 294
Cambodia, 16, 73, 132, 261, 278
    border disputes, 140–41
    ethnic Vietnamese in, 141
    external threats, 139–40
    internal threats, 138
    military, 142
    national security policies in, 133, 134,
        136–38
    peacekeeping in, 36, 105, 129, 263, 264
    settlement in, 266, 268, 275, 297
Cambodian People's Party, 134
Chemical Weaopons Regional Initiative
    (CWRI), 227
Chemical Weapons Convention, 221
chemical weapons, 221
chemical disarmament, 227–28
Chernomyrdin, Prime Minister, 84
China threat, 35

China, 35–49
  air transport, 189–90
  arms expenditure, 14
  arms production, 212
  defence capabilities, 42–43, 288–89
  defence modernisation, 42
  economic growth, 38, 165, 182
  economic reform, 38
  as economic superpower, 192
  economic uncertainty in, 12
  effect of geography and infrastructure, 182–83
  as export market for Hong Kong, 39
  foreign relations, 281–83
  future role in region, 121–23
  as good citizen, 36
  inflation rates, 41
  military expenditure, 37, 40–41, 201–2
  military role, 2
  navy, 122
  open door policy, 35
  potential breakup of, 39
  problems, 39
  as regional power, 2, 36, 37–38
  regional role, 296
  role in peacekeeping, 262
  security from external threats, 37
  as source of regional instability, 2
  strategic circumstances, 37
  as target of West, 44
  see also Greater China
China–India relations, 43, 74–75, 123, 285
China–Japan relations, 7
China–Russia relations, 43, 83
China–South Korea relations, 282
China–Vietnam relations, 43
Chinese Economic Area, 192
Christopher, Warren, 26, 30
Clinton, Bill, 22, 23, 24, 26, 27, 28, 30, 32, 33, 113, 116, 117, 223
Cold War, 23, 29
  impact of end, 1, 7, 9, 10, 14, 22, 30, 52, 113, 177, 215
  security following, 120–31, 278–80
collective security, 34
communications, 184–88
Comprehensive Test Ban Treaty, 221, 224
Conference on Disarmament, 219
Conference on Security and Co-operation in Asia (CSCA), see CSCA
Conference on Security and Cooperation in Europe (CSCE), see CSCE
confidence and security building measures (CSBMs), see CSBMs
confidence and security, process, 245–62
  proposals for, 246–47, 260

consensus building, 171
containerisation, 182
containment in Pacific, 56
conventional military hardware, acquisition by ASEAN states, 2
conventional weapons, sources, 208–9
  imports of, 204
  control of, 230
  disarmament, 230
Council for Security Cooperation in the Asia-Pacific (CSCAP), see CSCAP
Crawford, Sir John, 160
CSBMs, 103, 219, 225, 228–230, 238, 245–62
CSCA, 36, 233, 237, 246
CSCAP, 16, 17, 76, 102, 211, 215, 235, 250–51, 254, 280, 290
  future activities, 252–53
  Working Groups, 252
CSCE, 229, 233, 234
  Forum for Security Co-operation, 229
Cultural Revolution, 121
cultural differences, 19

Datuk Seri Mohammed Najib bin Tun Abdul Razak, 247
De Gaulle, Charles, 17
decolonisation, in Pacific, 153–55
Delors, Jacques, 17
Democratic People's Republic of Korea, see North Korea
democratic government, 8
Deng Xiaoping, 12, 38, see also post-Deng era
dialogue channels, 16
Dibb Report, 57
disarmament, measures, 211, 219–44
  global disarmament, 219
  impact of, 241
dispute resolution, 174–75
drug traffic, 280

East Asian ascendancy, 164–65
East Asian bloc, 165
East Asian Economic Caucus, 15, 102, 124, 165–66
East Asian Economic Grouping, 124
East Asian tigers, 165
East Timor, 95–96, 130, 261
  Australian Timorese community, 96
economic associations, within region, 162
economic co-operation, 4, 170
economic growth, 11–13
  in developing economies, 1
economic integration, regional, 163, 167
economic interdependence, 3–4, 8
Electronic Data Interchange, 185
environmental concerns, 12, 280

European Union, 72
Evans, Gareth, 36, 233, 246
external powers, role in regional security, 121–25
external security concerns, 125–28

Fiji, 148, 151
    coups in, 156, 157, 269
fishing disputes, 127, 152
    drift net fishing, 152
fissionable material, cutoff of production, 224
Five Power Defence Arrangements, 272
flashpoints in region, 7, 13
foreign relations, 280–86
free trade, 12
    areas, 162–64
freight, 179–84
FUNCINPEC, 137

Galbraith, J.K., 27
Galluci, Robert, 114
Gandhi, Rajiv, 78–79
GATT, 59, 102, 160, 166, 235
General Agreement on Tariffs and Trade (GATT), see GATT
global arms control, 219, 221
    agreements, 232
    impact of, 241
global interdependence, 192
global markets, 12
globalisation, 12, 65
Goh Chock Tong, 124
Gong Ro-myong, 115
Gorbachev, Mikhail, 81, 111, 133, 134, 222, 233, 236
Gration, General Peter, 43
great power rivalry, end of, 3
Greater China, 38–49
    definition of, 38
    economy of, 43
    see also Hong Kong, Macao, Taiwan
    Greater East Asia Co-Prosperity Sphere, 177
Greenhouse Effect, 153
Group of Seven Most Industrialised Nations (G-7), 105
    internal security, 107
growth miracles, 60
growth triangles, 4, 162, 163–64, 178
Gulf War, 15, 29, 43, 262, 272, 276

Habibie, Dr, 99, 100
Han Seung-joo, 115
Hawke, Bob, 29, 31
Helms, Jesse, 33
historical legacies in region, 9–10

Hong Kong, 26, 38, 39
    Chinese sovereignty over, 175
    reunification with mainland, 122
    Sino-British agreement on, 178
    Taiwan–China trade through, 181
Hubbard, Tom, 116, 117, 118, 225
human rights issues, 18, 25, 44, 45
    links with trade, 26, 36
    Western focus on, 3
Hun Sen, 137, 284

IMF, 102
Incidents at Sea Agreements (INCSEA), 229
India
    arms control in, 241
    defence capabilities, 67–69
    economic reform, 66, 67
    foreign relations, 284–85
    GDP, 68
    globalisation, 67–69
    look East strategy, 75
    as major player, 2
    military role, 2
    modernisation, 70
    naval buildup, 75
    naval expansion, 286
    as nuclear power, 76, 225
    as part of Asia-Pacific, 11, 75–765
    peacekeeping contribution, 75
    political instability, 69–71
    regional role, 65–78
    security, 67–69
    Sikh movement, 261
    and Southeast Asia, 72–74
    US investment in, 72
Indian Ocean Zone of Peace (IOZP), 231
India–Bangladesh relations, 69
India–Malaysia relations, 73
India–Pakistan relations, 69, 70, 71, 71, 261, 296
India–Russia relations, 67
India–Singapore relations, 73
India–Sri Lanka relations, 73
India–Thailand relations, 73
India–US relations, 71–72
Indochina, 132–48
    border disputes, 133
    co-operation with ASEAN, 144
    dissolution, 132, 133
    foreign investment in, 132
    Indochina bloc, 144
    maritime boundaries, 133
    national security policies in, 133–34
    peaceful evolution in, 138
    Soviet Union in, 133
    telecommunications, 187

see also Cambodia, Laos, Vietnam
Indonesia, 94–107
  alliances, 105
  authoritarian rule, 98;
  communist insurgencies in, 128, 261
  defence capabilities, 106
  defence policy, 101–3
  defence spending, 101–2
  democratisation, 129;
  domestic politics, 98–99
  economy, 100–101
  GDP, 95
  GNP, 100
  infrastructure, 183
  internal security, 95–96, 129
  military strategy, 105–6
  peacekeeping contribution, 105
  relations with India, 104
  relations with Malaysia, 104
  relations with the Philippines, 104
  relations with Vietnam, 104
  role of Islam, 96–98
  security concerns, 94–95
  security outlook, 103–5
  self-reliance, 105–6
  social reform, 98–99
  suppression of political activity, 95
Indonesian Armed Forces, *see* ABRI
Indonesian Straits, 94
Indonesia–Papua New Guinea relations, 150
information networks, 184–88
  technologies, 185
inhumane weapons, 221
Institute of Strategic and International Studies (ISIS) Malaysia, 15–16
institutions
  multilateral,
  regional, 15–17
Intermediate Nuclear Forces Agreement (INF), 222–23
internal security concerns, 128–30
International Atomic Energy Agency (IAEA), 36, 112, 113, 225
International Maritime Bureau, 126
International Maritime Organisation, 103
International Monetary Fund (IMF), *see* IMF
International Red Cross, 72
international economic transactions, 167
  impediments to, 168–69
international investment, 163
international order, new, 21
international society, 8–9
investment, 4
Iranian revolution, 98
Irian Jaya, 95, 96, 130, 151, 261, 279
Islam, role in Indonesia, 96–98

Islamic Conference Organisation (ICO), 105

Japan Institute of International Affairs, 250
Japan Self Defense Force, 268
Japan
  anti-Japanese feeling in Australia, 55–56
  anti-militarist attitudes, 7
  arms imports, 204
  arms sales, 212
  defence activity, 54
  economic contribution, 123
  expansion of arms production, 212
  foreign policy, 53
  foreign relations, 283–84
  as major player, 2
  military role, 2, 287
  regional sensitivity to defence spending, 54
  strategic orientation, 54
  trade and investment links, 8
  trade surpluses, 59
  US occupation of, 55
Japanese Economic Co-operation Bank, 179
Japanese Self-Defence Forces, 23
Japan–China relations, 7, 43
Japan–Russia relations, *see* Russia–Japan relations
Japan–US relations, 1, 2, 26
  economic, 58
  special relationship in, 51, 56–57
Jiang Zemin, 83, 84

Kashmir, 71, 72, 74, 288
Kazakhstan, 226
Keating, Paul, 31, 59
Khmer Rouge, 129, 132, 133, 136–37, 139, 141, 263, 266
Kiichi Miyazawa, 124, 236
Kim Il-sung, 32, 109, 110, 111, 116
Kim Jong–il, 109, 111
Kim Young-sam, 82, 236
Korea, 7, 109–19
  American policy on, 32
  demilitarised zone, 110, 287
  division of, 10, 177, 261
  juche socialism, 111
  North–South relations, 110–12, 113
  reunification, 110–12
  see also Korean Peninsula, North Korea, South Korea
Korean Peninsula, 109–19, 279, 287
  nuclear issue on, 4
Korean People's Army, 113, 116
Korean War, 23, 233
  Soviet involvement in, 81
  US involvement in, 23, 33
Korean Workers Party, 2

Koreas, disputes between two, 7, 14
   relationship with Russia, 82–83
Kurile Islands, 80, 86, 261, 278
Kuwait crisis, 2, 58, 276

land transport, 182–84
Lao People's Revolutionary Party, 135
Laos, 132
   border security, 139
   external threats, 139–40
   internal threats, 138
   military, 142
   national security policies in, 133, 134, 135
   political system, 134
   smuggling from Thailand, 139
   territorial disputes, 139
Law of the Sea Convention, 103, 152, 210, 286, 295
Lee Kuan Yew, 17, 24, 126, 165
legitimacy conflicts in Asia-Pacific, 261
liberalisation, unilateral, 164
Libya, 96
Ligatan, 127, 261
Lisbon protocol, 223

Macao, 38
Mahathir, 124, 234, 254, 287
Malaysia, communist insurgencies in, 128
Malaysia–Philippines relationship, 127
Malaysia–Singapore relationship, see Singapore–Malaysia relationship
Malaysia–Thailand relationship, 127–28
Manchuria, Russian occupation of, 80
Mao Zedong, 38
market access barriers, 168–69
market forces, role in trade, 59
market liberalisation, 16
market socialism, in China, 36
market-driven economic integration, 162–64, 166
Marshall Islands, 149
Matignon Accords, 154
Melanesia, 148
middle power internationalism, 57
militarisation, 231
military assistance programs, foreign, 211
military balance, 7
military capabilities, regional, 286–90
military expenditure, 199, 200, 201–3, 287
   by NIEs, 209
   China, 201–2
   expansionary pattern of, 209
   regional, 201
   Taiwan, 201–2
   see also arms sales
military technology gap, 294

Mischief Reef, 37, 123; see also Spratly Islands
Missile Technology Control Regime (MTCR), 226
missile proliferation control, 226–27
MITI, 124
most favoured nation status, for China, 18, 25
multilateralism, 31, 32
Mururoa, 153
Myanmar, 123, 129, 130, 238–39, 279

NAFTA, 72, 124
nationalism, 9
NATO, 23, 31
Natuna Islands, 104
navies, regional, 211, 247
New Caledonia, 148, 153, 154
New Zealand
   opposition to nuclear weapons, 30–31, 223
   relations with Australia, 150, 157
   relations with US, 223
new world order, 22, 278
Newly Industrialising Economies (NIEs), see NIEs
newly industrialising countries, see NICs
NICs, 9, 11, 60, 124
NIEs, 185
   arms expenditure, 209
Nixon, Richard, 27
Nixon Doctrine, 57
Non-Proliferation Treaty, 249
Norodom Ranariddh, 136, 137, 141
North American Free Trade Agreement (NAFTA), see NAFTA
North Atlantic Treaty Organisation (NATO), see NATO
North Korea, 2, 10, 24, 109–19, 238–39
   air transport, 190
   airports, 192
   arms control, 241
   arms production, 212
   economic downturn, 112
   economy, 110
   foreign policy, 110, 112
   Framework Agreement on nuclear weapons, 225, 278
   infrastructure, 184
   as nuclear power, 2, 3, 4, 13, 26, 112, 113–14, 287, 270
   potential economic collapse, 115
   telecommunications, 187
   UN involvement in, 36
North Korean–Russian relations, 82
North Pacific Co-operative Security Dialogue (NPCSD), 235
northern territories, 10, 233, 238

Nuclear Non-Proliferation Treaty, 112, 222, 224–26
nuclear arms control, 221–26
  global arms limitation agreements, 221
nuclear proliferation, 6, 15
nuclear testing in Pacific, 31, 153, 222, 223
nuclear weapons, 7, 221
  cuts in, 221

Ona, Francis, 156–57
one China, two governments, 14
ONUMOZ, 262
Open Skies Agreement, 229
open regionalism, 178
open trade policies, 164
opening to the outside world, 164
Operation Team Spirit, 117
Organisation for the Prohibition of Chemical Weapons (OPCW), 228
overcrowding, 6
overseas Chinese, influence of, 8

Pacific Basin Economic Council (PBEC), see PBEC
Pacific community, 17
Pacific Economic Cooperation Conference, 15
Pacific Economic Cooperation Council (PECC), see PECC
Pacific Forum, 250
Pacific islands
  Australian aid to, 149
  Australian policy towards, 150
  economic issues, 152–53
  indigenous communities, 154
  influence in region, 148–60
  peacekeeping and, 269
Pacific Trade and Development (PAFTAD), see PAFTAD
Pacific War
  US involvement in, 33
  effect on Australia–Japan relations, 55–58
PAFTAD, 15, 177, 251
Pakistan
  arms control in, 241
  as nuclear power, 225
Pancasila, 97, 101
Papua New Guinea, 148, 150, 151–52, 155, 158, 269
  aid to, 149, 152–53
  and Bougainville, 156–57
  see also Bougainville
Paracels, 37, 44, 45, 141, 179, 261
Partial Test Ban Treaty, 219, 222
particularism, 62
  in Australian foreign policy, 51
  in Japanese foreign policy, 51

PBEC, 15, 177
peace through strength, 215
peaceful evolution, strategy of, 138
peacekeeping, 36, 105
  and Asia-Pacific States, 266–69
  Indian contribution to, 75
  international, 262–74
  Japanese involvement in, 283
  naval peacekeeping, 271
  prospects in Asia-Pacific, 269
  reform of, 271
  regional organisations and, 265
  regional role, 271
  regional, 264–66
  resources for, 265
  second generation, 263
  UN mandates for, 53
  UN members' contributions to, 264, 267
PECC, 36, 59, 86, 161, 175, 177, 251
Perry, William, 30, 72
Philippines
  communist insurgencies in, 128
  US bases in, 23, 236, 287
Philippines–Malaysia relationship, see Malaysia–Philippines relationship
piracy, 126, 253
PLA, 40, 41, 42, 123
Plaza Agreement, 124
policy networks, 16
political democracy, 18
pollution, marine, 253
Polynesia, 148
population movements, 280
ports, 179–80
  container, 180, 181
post-Deng era, 12, 39, 75, 123
production networks, 163
public goods, regional, 167

Qian Qichen, 83, 122

Ramos, Fidel, 127, 128
Rangoon bombing, 110
Rao, P.V. Narasimha, 27, 71
Reagan, Ronald, 29, 222, 233
Red Cross, see International Red Cross
refugee movements, 253, 276
Regional Arms Register, 246
Regional Maritime Surveillance and Safety Regime (REMARSSAR), 246
regional co-operation, basis for, 161
regional community, 6–21
regional hegemon, role of, 13
regional instability, 12
regional institutional co-operation, 16
regional policy making, 174

regional security community, 19
regional security dialogue, 232–34
  institutionalisation of, 246
  multilateral, 233
regional security environment, 275
regional security forum, multilateral, 44
regional security outlook, 275–92
regionalism, 31
open, 167–68
Republic of Korea, *see* South Korea
rivalries between states, 7
Royal Cambodian Armed Forces, 136
Russia
  Asia-Pacific trade, 86
  foreign policy, 88
  foreign relations, 285–86
  history in Asia-Pacific, 80–81
  impact on regional security, 87–88
  investment in, 86
  military capabilities, 87, 296
  role in region, 79–89
  see also Soviet Union
Russian civil war, 80
Russia–Japan relations, 10, 85–86, 88

Saburo Okita, 160
SEANWFZ, 103, 120, 237, 249
SEATO, 31, 56
second track diplomacy, 235, 249–50, 255
Security Co-operation in the Asia-Pacific
  (SCAP), 250
security structure of region, 32
security
  dialogue, 15
  economic aspects of, 8
  threats to, 13–15
Senkakus, 38, 261, 278, 288
Seoul Forum for International Affairs, 250
shared economic interests, 169–70
shipping routes, 180–82
Siberia, Russian forces in, 2
Sihanouk, King, 137
Singapore, arms expenditure, 209
Singapore–Malaysia relationship, 126–27
Sipadan, 127, 261
SIPRI, 198, 201, 203, 204, 207
Solomon Islands, 148, 151–52
South China Sea Workshops, 44, 246
South China Sea, 7, 36, 38, 40, 44, 45, 261,
  278, 282, 286, 288, 295
  4th Conference on, 122
  crisis in, 130
  Vietnamese claims over, 141
South Korea, 110, 114
  arms production, 212, 213
  defence expenditure, 113, 115

democratisation, 111
  nuclear weapons, 113
South Korea–Russia relations, 83, 88
South Pacific Forum, 155, 232, 269
South Pacific Nuclear Free Zone, 219, 224, 231
South Pacific Nuclear Free Zone Treaty, *see*
  Treaty of Rarotonga
Southeast Asian Nuclear Weapons Free
  Zone (SEANWFZ), *see* SEANWFZ
sovereignty conflicts in Asia-Pacific, 261
Soviet Union, 24
  as arms supplier, 207
  collapse of, 37, 44
  conflict in, 2
  foreign policy, 133
  trade relations with Asia, 81
Soviet–Chinese relations, 80–81, *see also*
  China–Russia relations
Soviet–Korean relations, 81
special economic zones, 163, 178
Spratly Islands, 14, 37, 104, 123, 141, 179,
  238, 246, 261, 278, 288
Sri Lanka, insurgency in, 261
START I and II, 222
state sovereignty, concept of, 3
Stockholm International Peace Research
  Institute (SIPRI), *see* SIPRI
Straits of Malacca, 103
Strategic Arms Limitation Treaties (SALT I
  and II), 222
Strategic Review 1993, 52–54
Strategic Studies USA, 16
strategic alliances, 279
strategy, study of, 50
Suharto, President, 97, 99, 100, 107, 268
Sun Yat-sen, 177

Taiwan, 7, 10, 14, 35, 38, 39, 177, 294
  arms expenditure, 14, 201–2
  arms production, 213
  Chinese claims on, 38, 44, 45, 234, 261, 278,
    282
  defence capabilities, 289
  investment in China, 8, 14
  lifting of trade restrictions with China, 178
  reunification with mainland, 122
telecommunications, 185, 186–88; boom, 185
telephones, *see* telecommunications
territorial conflicts in Asia-Pacific, 10, 261
Thailand
  communist insurgencies in, 128
  constructive engagement policy, 129
Thailand–Malaysia relationship, *see*
  Malaysia–Thailand relationship
Third Indochina War, 133
threat perceptions, 286–90

Tiananmen massacre, 44
Tibet, 288
independence, 44
Timor Gap Treaty, 122
Tokyo Global Joint Action Plan, 295
track two diplomacy, 15
trade barriers, 178
trade blocs, 166
trade liberalisation, 170
trade, 4
regional, 160
transport and communications networks,
  177–97, 296
  integrative role of, 178
Treaty of Amity and Co-operation, 279
Treaty of Rarotonga, 153, 231
Tumen River economic development zone,
  4, 112, 162

UNAMIR, 262
United Nations Transitional Authority in
  Cambodia (UNTAC), see UNTAC
United Nations, 85, 264, 270
  Asian Arms Transfer Register, 238
  changing role of, 263–64
  China's membership of, 36
  Conventional Arms Transfers Register,
    237
  Department for Disarmament Affairs, 235
  Development Program, 38
  involvement in North Korea, 36
  peacekeeping role, 36, 53, 105, 237, 263
  regional co-operation and, 270–71
  Security Council, 36, 38, 105, 129, 262, 263,
    266, 276
  see also peacekeeping
United States Arms Control and Disarmament Agency, 41
United States
  as arms supplier, 207
  changing role in region, 32–34, 121
  commitment to regional stability, 2
  economic interests in region, 22
  foreign relations, 280–81
  interventionism, 33
  as military force, 39
  Pacific alliance system, 56
  policy in region, 22–34
  as regional balancer, 294
  regional presence, 276
United States–India defence agreement, 72
UNTAC, 138, 262, 264, 266, 269, 270

contributions to, 268
UNTSO, 262, 268
Uruguay Round, 53, 59
US Arms Control and Disarmament
  Agency (ACDA), see ACDA
US–Australia relations, see Australia–US
  relations
US–China relations, 18, 25, 26; trade, 26
US–Indian relations, 27
US–Japan relations, see Japan–US relations
US–Japan Security Treaty, 22, 23, 277, 287
US–North Korea relations, 116
US–Vietnam relations, normalisation of, 178

Vanuatu, 148, 154, 269
Vienna Accord on CSBMs, 229
Vietnam, 132
  air transport, 190
  airports, 192
  arms production, 212
  army, 135
  defence capabilities, 143–44
  defence doctrine, 142
  defence industries, 143
  external threats, 139–40
  internal threats, 138
  maritime concerns, 141–42
  military, 142
  national security policies in, 133, 134–35
  political system, 134
  special defence zones, 135
Vietnam War
  Australian involvement in, 29, 50, 233
  US involvement in, 33

Wanandi, Jusuf, 252
weapons, 221
Western
  culture, 28
  ethnocentrism, 6
  values, 17–19
Western Samoa, 149
World Bank, 13, 179
World Trade Organisation (WTO), see WTO
WTO, 72, 166, 174, 175

Yeltsin, Boris, 82, 83, 84

Zone of Peace, Freedom and Neutrality
  (ZOPFAN), see ZOPFAN
zones of production, 162–64
ZOPFAN, 102, 103, 120, 231, 237, 249